Courts, Law, and Politics in Comparative Perspective

Courts, Law, and Politics

in Comparative Perspective

HERBERT JACOB

ERHARD BLANKENBURG

HERBERT M. KRITZER

DORIS MARIE PROVINE

JOSEPH SANDERS

Yale University Press   New Haven and London

To our children

Published with assistance from the Louis Stern
Memorial Fund.

Designed by Sonia L. Scanlon.

Set in Times Roman type by The Clarinda
Company, Clarinda, Iowa.
Printed in the United States of America by
BookCrafters, Inc., Chelsea, Michigan.

Library of Congress Cataloging-in-Publication Data

Courts, law, and politics in comparative
perspective / Herbert Jacob . . . [et al.].
     p.   cm.
     Includes bibliographical references and index.
     ISBN 0-300-06378-4 (cloth : alk. paper).
—ISBN 0-300-06379-2   (pbk. : alk. paper)
     1. Courts.   2. Judicial process.   3. Law
and politics.   I. Jacob, Herbert, 1933–
K2100.C68   1996
347'.01—dc20   95-44020
[342.71]   CIP

A catalogue record for this book is available from
the British Library.

The paper in this book meets the guidelines for
permanence and durability of the Committee on
Production Guidelines for Book Longevity of the
Council on Library Resources.

10 9 8 7 6 5 4 3 2 1

Contents

Preface

My coauthors and I have long been curious about how law and the courts intersect with politics in countries other than those in which we have a special interest, and have chafed at the absence of a substantial body of comparative sociolegal studies. This book is intended to help fill that gap.

Our book is intended for two audiences. On the one hand, it is intended for our peers, to open their eyes and to stimulate their research. Rich opportunities await comparative researchers in the politics of courts and law. Such research must overcome the usual obstacles of comparative scholarship in addition to those that the obscurities of legal systems impose. Laws and courts are firmly embedded in social structures and practices that often lie beneath the surface of everyday life. They are not easily uncovered. Yet, as we show, much is to be learned from at least beginning that task.

Our second audience is students. Courses in the United States on the judicial process and introductions to legal systems focus heavily on familiar American materials. Many students remain unaware that the American legal system is an exception to what prevails in most of the rest of the world. Even European students have few means to learn about legal practices and the impact of political forces in countries other than their own.

We chose England, Germany, France, Japan, and the United States for this book partly because they are our areas of expertise and partly because they constitute a significant portion of the variability of politics and legal structure that exists in the world. However, large gaps remain. Muslim legal systems and the politics of Muslim countries are quite different from those which we describe. Further variations on our themes will be found in China. The countries of South and Southeast Asia as well as those in sub-Saharan Africa combine elements of the legal systems of their prior colonial rulers with indigenous traditions. Still other variations are likely to be found among the countries of Latin America. Finally, a whole new world of law and politics is unfolding in Eastern Europe and the former Soviet Union. However, one has to begin somewhere; we hope our readers find this volume a useful and stimulating point of departure.

In writing this book, the authors met several times over the course of more that two years and repeatedly exchanged manuscripts. We began with a common outline but have not rigidly adhered to it, preferring to follow the logic of analysis as it unfolded for each country. Nevertheless, each chapter emphasizes important common elements: the role of law and legal institutions in maintaining social order both in criminal matters and in ordinary disputes; the ways in which legal professionals stand as gatekeepers to legal institutions; the links that judges have with politics and with other governmental institutions; and the manner in which courts are policymakers and become entangled in political disputes. Unlike books in comparative law, this volume does not focus on doctrinal elements of the law or the role of supreme courts, although both are elements of our analysis.

Unlike many projects of this sort, this book is not the product of a large grant. I invited my collaborators in early 1992 to join in writing a comparative analysis that would "place the legal system in its larger social and political context." Without the promise of research funds or travel grants, they agreed to undertake the task. Each of us benefited from research support from our home institutions, from the advice of colleagues, and from encouragement by colleagues eager to see the final product. We are grateful for that support.

We also wish to thank the discussants of early versions of portions of this book, which were presented at the June 1993 meetings of the Law and Society Association and the September 1993 meetings of the American Political Science Association. We have also benefited from careful readings by anonymous reviewers who alerted us to inconsistencies and errors. We hope none remain, but if they do, they are our responsibility.

Herbert Jacob

1

Introduction

HERBERT JACOB

The legalization of political disputes has typically been viewed by American scholars as unique to the United States and the policymaking role of the Supreme Court as rooted in the distinctively American practice of judicial review. Many scholars proceed in their analyses as if courts intersected with politics only in the United States, and their analyses focus principally on the policymaking role of American courts because that is where all the political action appears to take place. Because courts rarely play as visible a policymaking role in other countries, an unspoken premise is that legal systems provide little explanatory power for understanding politics outside the United States and, conversely, that politics is insignificant in helping to explain the operation of the legal system elsewhere. Even in the United States, many political scientists marginalize the study of law and courts: while studies of the Supreme Court's policymaking role persist and a vigorous sociolegal analysis of legal institutions continues, they do so outside the mainstream of American political science.[1]

In this book we seek to demonstrate that the intersection of law, courts, and politics is not a uniquely American phenomenon. It is ubiquitous. However, the paths by which law, courts, and politics come together vary dramatically from country to country, sometimes intersecting in ways far more subtle and less visible than in the United States. While many American political activists view litigation as another form of politics, their peers in other countries do not routinely consider going to court to achieve policy objectives. Nor do politicians outside the United States frequently appoint their allies to the bench. Nevertheless, when legal institutions promote personal safety, allocate burdens and benefits, define standards of fairness, and oth-

---

1. Martin Shapiro, *Public Law and Judicial Politics,* in Ada W. Finifter (ed.), *Political Science: The State of the Discipline II* (Washington, D.C.: American Political Science Association, 1993), p. 365.

erwise influence political agendas, they engage in a continuous dialogue with the political arena.

Courts, Law, and Politics

No widely accepted paradigms exist which model the relationship between law, courts, and politics in a cross-national context. Shapiro focuses on courts and compares their activities on selected dimensions in England, in civil law systems on the European continent, in imperial China, and in Islamic countries.[2] However, the link with political institutions and political events remains undeveloped. Becker develops an elaborate definition of courts and focuses principally on judges' perceptions of their roles in decision making, an enterprise that leads him to concentrate principally on high appellate courts and judges.[3] As is evident in Tate's review of extant theories, most focus on the role of constitutional courts; none try to account for how courts fit into the dispute-processing routines of a society, how they handle common disputes, the ways in which they are affected by the structure of the legal profession and the dialogue that exists among law, courts, and politics.[4] There is a tension between studies that focus on the rich context in which legal and political practices occur in different nations and studies that seize upon apparently similar cross-national indicators of such common variables as the ideological direction of supreme court decisions or the social backgrounds of judges while neglecting the surrounding context of national politics and national legal systems.[5] In this book we attempt to take a middle road. We pay

2. Martin Shapiro, *Courts: A Comparative and Political Analysis* (Chicago: University of Chicago Press, 1981).

3. Theodore L. Becker, *Comparative Judicial Politics: The Political Functionings of Courts* (Chicago: Rand McNally, 1970).

4. C. Neal Tate, ''Judicial Institutions in Cross-National Perspective: Toward Integrating Courts into the Comparative Study of Politics,'' in John R. Schmidhauser (ed.), *Comparative Judicial Systems: Challenging Frontiers in Conceptual and Empirical Analysis* (London: Butterworths, 1987), pp. 7–33. Note that the recent special issue of *Comparative Political Studies,* 26, no. 4 (1994), which was devoted to comparative judicial politics, examined only constitutional courts and the quasi-constitutional European Court of Justice.

5. Examples of studies focusing on context include Donald Kommers, *The Constitutional Jurisprudence of the Federal Republic of Germany* (Durham, N.C.: Duke University Press, 1989), and Alec Stone, *The Birth of Judicial Politics in France* (New York: Oxford University Press, 1992). Examples of studies focusing on cross-national indicators include Theodore L. Becker, *Comparative Judicial Politics* (Chicago: Rand McNally, 1970); Glendon A. Schubert, *Political Culture and Judicial Behavior* (Lanham, Md.: University Press of America, 1985); and Donald W. Jackson and C. Neal Tate, *Comparative Judicial Review and Public Policy* (Westport, Conn.: Greenwood Press, 1992).

close attention to peculiarities of national legal and political practices, but we also identify commonalities. Moreover, we examine not only how law and courts affect the high and mighty but also how they touch the common person and how politics, courts, and law consequently interact.

Widespread consensus exists that law, courts, and politics are important for three sets of activities that are central to every modern state: policymaking, social control, and regime legitimation. Policymaking, which lies at the core of government activity, encompasses not only the development of new policies but also the alteration of existing practice. For many observers it includes even the implementation of programs because critical decisions about the scope of the policy are made during the implementation process. Social control is a central task of every modern state. People demand safety; economies require stable expectations about market behaviors and the enforcement of promises when they are not voluntarily kept. Finally, regimes need the loyalty of their citizens. The demands made in the name of social control and the policies the state implements must at least meet with acquiescence from the populace if a regime is to survive. Each of these activities has legal, judicial, and political elements: the legal often overlaps with the judicial; the political affects both the legal and judicial; the judicial interprets the legal and impacts the political. Disentangling these relationships in the varied contexts of five nations is the task of this book. We turn first to law.

LAW

Law in the contemporary Western world is almost universally perceived in positivist terms. It is recognized as the product of social and political forces rather than as edicts of a divine power or as a mysterious leftover from a dim past. Legislatures explicitly create new laws and revise old ones; executive officials issue decrees. In democratic polities, everyone presumes that law reflects the values of dominant political coalitions. Indeed, a desire to control the formulation of law and its implementation informs the entire political enterprise.

Beyond this almost universal perception, however, one encounters many variations in the form and structure of law. Western law has conventionally been divided into two distinct categories: a civil code tradition and a common-law tradition. The civil code finds its ancient roots in Roman law but is also the product of the French revolution.[6] Where French armies conquered they imposed the Napoleonic civil code. Thus the legal systems of almost the entire continent of Europe can be traced to this common ancestor. In the intervening years, each country has added or subtracted details, but the com-

6. John Henry Merryman, *The Civil Law Tradition* (Stanford, Calif.: Stanford University Press, 1969).

mon parentage remains apparent. A distinctive feature of the civil code was its design as a seamless body of legal prescriptions, based on simple principles that could be understood by lay people. Scholars were its principal drafters, and they considered law as a science rather than as a political art. In keeping with the contempt with which French revolutionaries held judges of the old regime and the revolutionaries' commitment to popular sovereignty, the drafters of the civil code granted little authority to the judiciary. Judges were to apply the law, but their decisions were not given authority as precedents. At the same time, lawyers remained overshadowed by magistrates and judges in the conduct of trials. Courts were *state* institutions rather than a battleground for attorneys sponsored by private interests.

The second category of Western legal systems is those based on what is described as the common law.[7] Its origins lie in England with the gradual development of legal authority as interpreted by the monarchy's judges. In the English version, however, parliamentary authority became supreme; no written constitution provided opportunities to declare Acts of Parliament unconstitutional. However, Parliament did not begin to write comprehensive legal codes until the twentieth century, and many gaps existed in the law. Courts filled that vacuum by decisions in disputes brought to them. By citing their earlier decisions as precedent, courts built up a large body of case law without challenging the authority of Parliament. English settlers brought this common law to the American colonies. However, the adoption of a written constitution in the United States quickly allowed judges to exercise judicial review in a manner unknown to nineteenth-century England. In addition, both in England and in the United States the principal drafters of law have been judges, lawyers, and politicians rather than academic scholars. Law is not considered a science, but rather a pragmatic endeavor. Moreover, lawyers play a central role in litigation. Courts (and judges) sit passively until activated by private interests as represented by lawyers.

These two types of law, however, no longer are as distinct as they were during the nineteenth and early twentieth centuries. In the 1970s judges began to cite their own decisions as precedent in many civil code countries and even dispute the authority of legislatures. Over time the seamless structure of the civil code showed ruptures as new laws addressed novel social and economic problems. At the same time, common law countries—particularly the United States—codified segments of their law, though not with the same single-minded attentiveness to basic principles as the civil code. Common

7. Henry J. Abraham, *The Judicial Process*, 6th ed. (New York: Oxford University Press, 1993), pp. 7–16. The term *common law* apparently originally referred to the law common to the country as a whole as opposed to local law. See Penny Darbyshire, *Eddey on the English Legal System*, 5th ed. (London: Sweet & Maxwell, 1992), p. 186.

law judges have become somewhat more active although not yet equalling their civil code peers; civil code lawyers have become more aggressive although not yet matching their common law counterparts.

While common law and civil code legal systems demarcate significant variations in national legal practices, one must also take into account national differences in the willingness of people to employ the law to resolve their disputes and in the perceived acceptability of litigation as an alternative to other modes of dispute processing. Some American researchers find that when people in the United States seek to resolve disputes they act ''in the shadow of the law.'' Mnookin and Kornhauser suggest that remedies that might be obtained by litigation lurk in the background during many negotiations and that court action is often viewed as a viable strategic alternative.[8] It is not true, however, that Americans think about law in all their disputes, and abundant evidence exists in other countries that multiple normative orders exist which sometimes push litigation to the periphery of dispute processing.[9] Some scholars argue that social norms and habitual behaviors lead some people away from thinking about legal rights when they confront a dispute; the Japanese are sometimes identified as reflecting such preferences.[10] However, current scholarship has challenged this interpretation and points instead to legal institutions that restrict access to courts and to legal remedies in addition to attitudes toward the law.[11]

The combination of circumstances that lead people to invoke the law, therefore, vary not only with public attitudes toward law but also with insti-

8. Robert H. Mnookin and Lewis Kornhauser, "Bargaining in the Shadow of the Law: The Case of Divorce," *Yale Law Journal* 88 (1979), pp. 950–997.

9. Stewart Macaulay, "Elegant Models, Empirical Pictures, and the Complexities of Contract," *Law & Society Review* 11 (1977), pp. 507–528; Sally Merry, *Getting Justice and Getting Even: Legal Consciousness among Working-Class Americans* (Chicago: University of Chicago Press, 1990); Herbert Jacob, "The Elusive Shadow of the Law," *Law & Society Review* 26 (1992), pp. 565–590. On societies with multiple normative orders see Jane F. Collier, *Law and Social Change in Zinacantan* (Stanford, Calif.: Stanford University Press, 1973); John J. Griffiths, "What Is Legal Pluralism?" *Journal of Legal Pluralism & Unofficial Law* 24 (1986), p. 1.

10. Takeyoshi Kawashima, "Dispute Resolution in Contemporary Japan," in A. von Mehren (ed.), *Law in Japan* (Cambridge: Cambridge University Press, 1963). Cited in Setsuo Miyazawa, "Taking Kawashima Seriously: A Review on Japanese Legal Consciousness and Disputing Behavior," *Law & Society Review* 21, No. 2 (1987).

11. John Owen Haley, "The Myth of the Reluctant Litigant," *Journal of Japanese Studies* 4 (1978), p. 359; John Owen Haley, "The Politics of Informal Justice," in Richard Abel (ed.), *The Politics of Informal Justice,* Vol. 2 (New York: Academic Press, 1982); Frank K. Upham, *Law and Social Change in Post-War Japan* (Cambridge: Harvard University Press, 1987); V. Lee Hamilton and Joseph Sanders, *Everyday Justice: Responsibility and the Individual in Japan and the United States* (New Haven: Yale University Press, 1992).

tutional arrangements. A willingness to mobilize the law to challenge the actions of government agencies depends not only on the perceived legitimacy of such a challenge but also on such particulars as the availability of legal assistance, the willingness of courts to accept jurisdiction, the presence of alternative forums for hearing such complaints, the costs and risks associated with making complaints, and the benefits that may be gained by proceeding one way or another.[12] Resort to law for more personal remedies—such as compensation for injuries resulting from auto accidents or damages arising from contractual disputes—also varies with such circumstances, which are the product of government policy as well as social customs.

Although the use of law *by* government to impose social control appears to be universal, the procedures used to do so vary considerably. Every modern state has an organized police force that intervenes when common crimes occur, but their organization and practices are diverse. Many of the behaviors made punishable by the law are quite similar among modern states. At the margins, however, criminal law tells an acute observer much about what kinds of liberties are valued in a nation. Court procedures vary considerably from country to country and reveal the degree to which people tolerate intrusion into their private lives and the categories of residents who are privileged or disadvantaged in the application of the criminal process.

Thus law has two potential effects. One empowers people in disputing among themselves and with government agencies; the other empowers the government to punish deviant behavior. However, the circumstances under which the government or citizens mobilize law are complex; they include both structural elements that make courts accessible and perceptual elements that lead people to consider legal remedies when processing their disputes.

COURTS

The second dimension of this inquiry is the judiciary. Courts are not simple to define. Shapiro has suggested that their essence is to be found in the triad consisting of two disputants and an authoritative third party decision maker, often incorporating efforts to negotiate or mediate in order to avoid all-or-nothing solutions to disputes.[13] The forms these characteristics take have important implications for the power of the judiciary.

Many countries possess a single, centralized judiciary. Like many other agencies of government, such a court system has branches throughout the

12. The widespread use of the term *legal mobilization* stems from Frances Kahn Zemans, "Legal Mobilization: The Neglected Role of the Law in the Political System," *American Political Science Review* 77 (1983), pp. 690–703. For an exposition of a highly contingent view of legal mobilization, see Michael W. McCann, *Rights at Work: Pay Equity Reform and the Politics of Legal Mobilization* (Chicago: University of Chicago Press, 1992), pp. 6–12.

13. Supra note 1.

country. Such courts are likely to be staffed by judges and other personnel appointed, rewarded, and disciplined by the central government. Courts often reflect the degree of centralization of the governments of which they are a part. In countries whose government is decentralized, courts are also likely to be decentralized, with each regional government possessing its own court system staffed by judges and other personnel responsive to its distinctive circumstances. The more that regional governments enjoy political autonomy, the more likely it is that their courts will be independent of national authorities. Particularly significant for understanding the intersection of courts with politics is the degree to which a single final court of appeals exercises the power to reconcile conflicting lower court decisions. The greater the power of such high courts to render final judgments, the more likely it is that their judgments take on the color of public policy pronouncements.

Another important dimension of courts is their degree of specialization. In some countries almost all courts have general jurisdiction to hear most kinds of disputes. In other countries courts and courtlike tribunals have very specialized jurisdiction, with some courts hearing criminal cases, others judging civil disputes between citizens, still others deciding labor disputes, and additional tribunals processing disputes between citizens and particular agencies such as those providing social services or collecting taxes. They constitute another form of fragmentation of judicial power.

A third characteristic of judiciaries is their accessibility. Some are designed to be readily available to ordinary citizens without their hiring lawyers or other intermediaries. The forms that must be filled out have been kept simple; procedures have remained informal; and legal jargon is minimized. Other judicial systems restrict access by establishing a host of technical hurdles; a faulty answer on a form or an incorrectly formulated claim may defeat the case. To understand the accessibility of courts, one must examine both the range of options available to those with grievances and the organization of legal advice and assistance. One needs, however, to look beyond the number of lawyers in a country or the particular structure of their work settings. Lawyers do not possess a monopoly over legal advice in many countries; they do not necessarily enjoy the central role in disputing that they do in the United States. Moreover, access to legal advice and information about courts intersects with the attitude toward law and litigation that exists in a country.

Finally, the roles of judges and lawyers within courts varies considerably. In addition to the tendency of judges in civil code systems to be more active than those in common law courts, judges vary in their background and recruitment. In many countries, judges are civil servants who begin their careers after specialized university and postgraduate education and serve as judges the remainder of their working lives. Promotions as well as disciplinary actions occur within the context of a quasi-bureaucratic organization. In other countries, judges ascend to the bench after careers in private practice or as politicians; no bureaucratic promotion ladder exists and disciplinary action may come from outside the judiciary rather than from judicial superiors.

Thus courts are institutions with traits that vary from country to country. Some characteristics—such as career judgeships—may insulate them from ordinary politics, whereas others—such as the existence of powerful final appellate courts—may propel them into political controversy. Some courts open their doors to all cases, including political disputes; others carefully restrict access and keep cases with political overtones at arm's length.

POLITICS

The third dimension of concern is politics. David Easton's now widely accepted generic definition describes it as the process that produces an authoritative allocation of values.[14] Such a definition of politics applied to the law and courts sensitizes observers to the myriad ways in which they allocate freedom, privilege, status, advantage, and money. Law as the symbol of legitimate power and courts as authoritative instruments of states cannot escape making such distributions. Both the law and courts tend to be conservative social institutions because they usually reflect established interests and groups. In this broad sense, law and courts inevitably intersect with politics.

However, politics is often perceived to denote a narrower set of phenomena; it is often understood in the sense of *partisan* or *electoral* activities or the advocacy of particular solutions to public problems. Judges and lawyers often deny their association with those narrower elements of the political arena. The degree of association is an open empirical question, but important links indisputably exist. Take, for instance, the degree to which politicians become involved in selecting, promoting, and disciplining judges. In every country some ties exist between politicians and judges. At the very least, judges, as government officials, have connections with politically responsible officers. Some governments expend considerable effort to keep such connections remote; in others, they strive to maintain close control over judgeships. The link between politicians and judges is particularly visible for those who sit on high courts that may decide on the validity of government programs.

The intersection among politics and law and the courts may also be shaped by the breadth of state capacity.[15] The larger the reach of the state, the more law and courts become agents of state power. Damaska suggests that courts in highly interventionist states become instruments of state policy in ways

14. David Easton, *The Political System* (New York: Knopf, 1953).

15. Theda Skocpol, "Bringing the State Back In: Current Research," in Peter B. Evans, Dietrich Rueschemeyer, and Theda Skocpol, *Bringing the State Back In* (Cambridge: Cambridge University Press, 1985), pp. 3–43.

that courts in less interventionist states do not.[16] The broader the range of governmental intervention, the more numerous the occasions in which disputes between citizens and government arise; the narrower the range, the more often disputes are simply between citizens. The more disputes involve government agencies, the greater the potential involvement of courts or court-like tribunals in the political arena. Thus, for example, a dispute over the results of medical care in a country where medical care is provided largely by private doctors is likely to take the form of a tort suit between two private parties. However, if a government agency provides the care, the dispute is between the patient and a government agency, and it may more readily escalate into a challenge of the policy underlying the alleged shortcoming rather than the performance of the individual physician.

A final characteristic of the political arena to which we must be attentive is the degree of state centralization. Decentralized regimes may be more likely to have decentralized judiciaries. This is especially true for those federal regimes where tribunals are part of local (or regional) governments and apply local and regional laws. In addition, the degree of centralization may affect the involvement of courts in overtly political controversies. Centralization concentrates power in either the legislative or executive branch, leaving the judiciary overshadowed by the other core institutions. The more centralized a state, the more likely it is that its legislative and executive institutions will attract activists who seek to influence policy, for those two branches are where policy decisions are made. Conversely, in less centralized states, controversies may gravitate toward litigation because policymaking is diffused through many institutions.

Thus, like the law and courts, political contexts vary enormously, affecting the ways in which law and courts intersect with politics, but they do not exclude politics from law or the courts. If one is looking only for constitutional review or political appointment of judges as signposts of the intersection, one may miss it. If one also looks for court decisions about social programs or the impact of regime characteristics on the shape of judicial institutions, the intersection will be more apparent.

DYNAMICS OF CHANGE

The overlapping of law, courts, and politics do not remain constant over time. Not only do each of these dimensions continually respond to changing social and economic circumstances, but they also bear the marks of formative events in national histories. In France, as in all of Europe, the defining event was the French Revolution with the destruction of ancient privileges and the es-

16. Mirjan R. Damaska, *The Faces of Justice and State Authority* (New Haven: Yale University Press, 1986).

tablishment of the civil code. In Germany, a series of national cataclysms has repeatedly buffeted the law, courts, and political arena: the unification of Germany under the leadership of Prussia in the last third of the nineteenth century, Germany's defeat in World War I and the end of the Second Reich, the emergence of the Weimar Republic, the Nazi dictatorship and its defeat in World War II, the subsequent division of Germany into a democratic republic in the West and a communist state in the East, and finally the re-unification of Germany under the aegis of the West German Federal Republic in 1990. In Japan, the Meiji Restoration in the nineteenth century led to the importation of Western legal norms and practices, while the defeat of Japan in World War II brought strong American influence upon legal institutions. England, by contrast, has been relatively unmarked by such events. Although English legal and political development is not an entirely smooth curve, it shows none of the sharp bumps of France and Germany, or even of Japan. English law, courts, and political practices reflect a long and almost uninter-rupted tradition displayed in peculiar practices (like wigged judges) and quaint titles (like Lord Chancellor). In the United States, the legacy of English colonialism and the nation's autonomy from Europe led to an idiosyncratic development of its law, legal institutions, and politics. The nation's isolation, which lasted until World War I, effectively insulated it from most of the major trends in European politics—both from the immediate effect of the French Revolution and later from the wave of socialist politics that washed over Europe in the late nineteenth century and the first two-thirds of the twentieth.

The last years of the twentieth century have also been full of change. In addition to the impact of reunification on Germany, the development of Eu-rope as a single trade zone has generated powerful centripetal forces affecting national law and judicial practices in each of the countries participating in the European Union. The United States is also no longer isolated from such changes, as it exports not only goods and services but also legal expectations; at the same time, it must adapt some of its legal practices to those its ex-porters face in markets around the world. The North American Free Trade Agreement (NAFTA) and the General Agreement on Tariffs and Trade (GATT) contain numerous provisions that may draw legal practice in the United States closer to those of other nations.

Thus, how politics affects law and courts and the impact of law and courts on politics can be fully comprehended only with an understanding of national histories and contemporary dynamics. For instance, the distrust of courts is deep-seated in France; the nation's memory extends back beyond the French Revolution. But French statesmen have been instrumental in building trans-national European institutions. Likewise, Japanese courts may look like West-ern courts and the legal code they employ may resemble Western law, but

Japanese legal institutions stand in the shadow of a long national history which promotes consultative practices that are distinctly non-Western. Nevertheless, Japan, like all nations, must accommodate the legal practices of the nations with which it trades.

Policymaking, Social Control, and Legitimation

The discussion of law, courts, and politics suggests three separate perspectives through which one may view the public and private life of a nation. The particular activities on which we shall focus are policymaking, social control, and regime legitimation. Each of these activities may operate in the law, in the courts, or in politics, and each looks different depending on the perspective which one adopts. Policymaking seen as a political process differs from policymaking viewed as a judicial process; social control by the law and in the courts appears distinct from social control imposed by such political activities as mass rallies. Legitimation through politics may have different dimensions than legitimation through the law. However, each perspective adds to our understanding of what at first appears to belong entirely to one dimension or another.

POLICYMAKING

Policymaking lies at the core of the political process; it is one of the prizes of winning elections or seizing power. Courts also make policy when they apply the law to new situations and interpret it in novel ways. Their decisions become policy statements because they and other courts cite their previous interpretations or the interpretations of more authoritative courts when making later decisions. American scholars routinely speak of the policymaking function of the U.S. Supreme Court, and its interpretations are watched with great care not only by lawyers but also by political activists, who understand the weight of those decisions in the policymaking and policy implementation process. Other U.S. courts, particularly the state supreme courts and U.S. Courts of Appeal, also participate in the policymaking function, although to a lesser degree. Some scholars even speak of occasional policymaking by trial courts in the United States.[17]

Three ingredients to this process exist to a greater or lesser extent in other countries. The first is the interpretive activity of courts; courts everywhere interpret the law as they apply it to concrete situations. The second is the habit of courts to cite their previous decisions or those of higher courts to

17. Lynn Mather, "Policy Making in State Trial Courts," in John B. Gates and Charles A. Johnson, *The American Courts: A Critical Assessment* (Washington, D.C.: Congressional Quarterly Press, 1991), pp. 119–157.

justify their interpretation. This principle of *stare decisis* or precedent has a particularly strong hold in common law countries, although it sometimes guides courts elsewhere as well. The third is the existence of higher courts with broad authority to review lower court decisions and to impose a uniform rule of interpretation. Such an institutional design is also not universal, but it exists to some degree in many countries.[18] Viewed in this broader way, judicial policymaking occurs in many settings outside the United States, particularly in the form of judicial review of administrative actions.

Public perception of the policymaking function of courts also varies widely. It is more widely accepted in the United States than elsewhere. The degree to which the public and political activists recognize and approve of this function has important implications for the involvement of courts in the political arena. As the succeeding chapters demonstrate, policymaking decisions of appellate courts have had a substantial impact on the political arena of the five countries we analyze. However, the relationships established by this judicial function vary in subtle but significant ways. In some circumstances it may pull the law and courts into a political maelstrom that may threaten to leave permanent scars on those institutions. The obstructionist rulings of the U.S. Supreme Court between 1933 and 1937, for example, provoked President Franklin Delano Roosevelt's court-packing plan, which was averted only by a change in court rulings.

SOCIAL CONTROL

A second kind of activity perceptible along the three dimensions of law, courts, and politics is their role in implementing social control. Every country has criminal laws and uses them to maintain what the authors of the U.S. Constitution termed "domestic tranquility" and what contemporary Americans more colloquially call "law and order." Roughly the same set of common crimes are outlawed in every country, in addition to unique provisions their criminal codes possess. Every country uses the law to legitimize the imposition of harsh sanctions on lawbreakers. Criminal law and criminal courts thus engage in a dual function. On the one hand, they punish criminals and seek to incapacitate them by sending them to prison or to rehabilitate them by enrolling them in special medical, educational, and social programs. On the other hand, the provisions of the criminal code and the ritual of criminal courts dramatize the dominant norms of the society and inculcate them in the citizenry. The lessons taught by criminal justice are intended to reinforce the many private social control mechanisms which exist in a society to make it a safe place for the law-abiding.

18. Mauro Cappelletti, "The Expanding Role of Judicial Review in Modern Societies," in Shimon Shetreet (ed.), *The Role of Courts in Society* (Boston: Martinus Nijhoff, 1988), pp. 79–96.

In addition, social control is a central ingredient of the dispute-processing role of courts. Courts everywhere are one instrument that may be used to obtain authoritative verdicts in private disputes. However, their accessibility and the range of disputes that come to them varies widely. Consequently, courts play diverse roles in enforcing the norms of social and commercial behavior that are essential for the smooth functioning of the economy and for tranquil relationships between individuals. In some countries, courts play a very large role in disputes over injuries and damages arising from automobile accidents; in others, administrative agencies or mediation and conciliation services are more prominent in handling such disputes. In some countries, landlords and tenants resort primarily to courts to settle arguments; in others, such disputes go to specialized tribunals. In almost all countries, however, disputants look to courts for authoritative judgments in a wide range of circumstances. In doing so they ensure that officially approved norms are employed in processing disputes and that private individuals do not enforce their will through violent means.

Social control is also an important focus of political activity. Control requires norms to distinguish permitted behavior from the forbidden; social control privileges some segments of the community over others. Not only must norms be chosen, but procedures and alternative disputing processes must be selected; such choices empower some categories of disputants while handicapping others. Each forum produces a distinctive flow of remedies and redistribution of funds from the party adjudged at fault to the party whose damage claim is affirmed. In each country, the determination of whose interests shall be privileged and what procedures shall be used is one that repeatedly surfaces in the political arena and evokes fundamental political conflicts over the distribution of private and public goods.

LEGITIMATION

The third activity affected by law, courts, and politics is regime legitimation. Few regimes can govern long by brute force alone. They require consent and acquiescence because they rely in large part on voluntary compliance resulting from a widespread consensus that it is right to obey the law. Recent research by social psychologists suggests that obedience to the law depends not only on a feeling that the substantive injunctions of the law are fair but also that courts impose them fairly.[19] Procedure is important. Law, courts, and politics constantly reinforce regime legitimation or diminish it. When government disappoints people's expectations, either in the substance of pol-

19. E. Allan Lind and Tom R. Tyler, *The Social Psychology of Procedural Justice* (New York: Plenum Press, 1988); Tom R. Tyler, *Why People Obey the Law* (New Haven: Yale University Press, 1990).

icies or in the manner in which people are being treated, their faith in government diminishes. Such effects are not only products of politics; the courts and the law may also increase or decrease regime legitimacy. Verdicts that appear injust produce political repercussions—whether in France over the complicity of government officials in spreading the AIDS virus to hemophiliacs, in Japan over the poisoning of villagers living near plastics factories, or in the United States over the acquittal of Los Angeles police officers pictured on videotapes beating an African American named Rodney King. In the political arena, such effects are beginning to be measured; a recent study of negative advertisements in U.S. election campaigns suggests that they increase voter apathy and voter cynicism about public officials.[20] The effects of court actions have not been studied but are the subject of considerable speculation.[21]

Plan of the Book

The following chapters examine the characteristics of the intersection of law, courts, and politics I have discussed. We describe the structure of law and of courts as well as some of the most pertinent features of the political arena. In doing so, we pay particular attention to the ways in which law is perceived and the consequences which flow from those differences. We focus particularly upon:

- the structure of courts and access to them;
- the manner in which politics and law are differentiated or amalgamated;
- the ways in which politics affects the selection of judges;
- the ways in which courts are perceived as legitimate forms for addressing political conflicts;
- legal consciousness among citizens;
- the ways in which the legal profession is organized and the kinds of work lawyers do; and
- the manner in which law and courts are used as social control mechanisms.

20. Stephen Ansolabehere, Shanto Iyengar, Adam Simon, and Nicholas Valentino, "Does Attack Advertising Demobilize the Electorate," *American Political Science Review* 88 (1994), pp. 829–838.

21. F. L. Morton, "Judicial Activism in France," in Kenneth M. Holland (ed.), *Judicial Activism in Comparative Perspective* (New York: St. Martin's Press, 1991), pp. 144–145; Upendra Baxi, "Taking Suffering Seriously: Social Action Litigation in the Supreme Court of India," in Neelan Tiruchelvam and Radhika Coomaraswamy (eds.), *The Role of the Judiciary in Plural Societies* (New York: St. Martin's Press, 1987), pp. 32–60; Radhika Coomaraswamy, "Toward an Engaged Judiciary," Ibid., p. 16; Shapiro, supra note 2, pp. 23–24.

We examine these issues in five countries chosen to represent much of the industrialized world but also because their legal systems have been studied sufficiently by sociolegal scholars to allow the kind of analyses that follow. The United States and England represent common law legal systems; France and Germany are the dominant models for civil code systems. Japan is an example of a country in which civil code and common law features have been added to a traditional indigenous legal tradition.

In each country we examine some common settings chosen to represent a variety of contexts in which law and courts intersect with politics. One of these is the manner in which criminal justice is pursued; we focus on criminal justice because in every country courts are a major participant in that process and the principal agent of the regime in enforcing its version of social order. A second setting we examine involves the manner in which law and courts address ordinary disputes of ordinary people because they reveal how law and courts maintain social order in economic and social affairs. Third, we examine the manner in which law and courts are used by major economic interests; here the principal players in the economy cash in their political chips to police the economic arena and provide a reliable setting for doing business. Fourth, we look at how legal institutions affect the processing of constitutional issues and participate in policymaking.

Each of these types of disputes and conflicts will be discussed in the following chapters, but not in the same sequence or with the same emphasis because each country's legal system is to some extent unique. In-depth examinations of the peculiarities of each country's political and legal practices allows one to understand similarities and discern significant differences.

Let me close with the caveat that this book examines only a narrow segment of world legal and political systems. Each of the nations (except Japan) that we examine is rooted in Western traditions, and even Japan has been heavily influenced by them. None represent the Muslim legal tradition and the political and legal processes that exist in such places as Indonesia, Pakistan, most of the Middle East, and portions of Africa. We examine law, courts, and politics only in countries that enjoy high standards of living with abundant resources with which to pursue disputes. None of the countries we examine are handicapped by primitive levels of technology or inadequate channels of communication among the mass public and public officials as well as between them. The cultural and legal traditions of such countries, their social structures, their available resources, and the range of disputes that exist all differ in substantial ways from those we describe. They must remain the subject of other books.

2

Courts and Politics in

the United States

HERBERT JACOB

Law and courts in the United States have direct and powerful links to the political arena. The habit of bringing social conflict into the legal arena is deeply embedded in American political culture. Law's roots extend into the political arena, where political coalitions in legislative bodies and partisan adherents in the executive branch formulate much of the law that governs the United States. Thus norms favored by governing coalitions become embedded in law and govern the disposition of the innumerable ordinary disputes that come to courts. In addition, disputants in the United States frequently invoke the law in political disputes in order to obtain court rulings that will have widespread political consequences. Moreover, judges in the United States often have strong ties to political activists. These links are not peculiar to the United States, but their strength derives from distinctively American conditions and structures.

This chapter highlights those links in the context of the conditions and structures that nurture them. The United States possesses a highly decentralized and fragmented governmental structure. Although it is the premier world power, its reach in domestic affairs is decidedly limited. In addition, many people view going to court as a respectable and viable way to engage in disputes. These characteristics have important consequences for the operation of courts and their relationship to the political arena. We shall examine them first in the abstract and then in the specific contexts of criminal justice, civil justice, and constitutional litigation.

Links with the Political Arena
WHAT COURTS DO

One set of links between courts and politics arises from what courts do; their actions and functions in the United States are not different from those in many other countries. Their manifest task is to process disputes and impose solutions on the disputants. In doing so, courts are not neutral arbiters who resolve disputes while blindfolded. Quite to the contrary, courts impose the socially approved values embedded in the laws of the land. Thus, they act as one of the instruments of control available to a society and as a conspicuous agent of *governmental* social control, even though court decisions are rarely perceived as political acts. Few people think that imposing a ten-year sentence on a rapist has political consequences, yet it sends a signal to women that their safety is taken seriously and it signals the general population that the state is seeking to assure tranquility. On the other hand, when in October 1994, a Maryland judge sentenced a husband to eighteen months in jail with work release for killing his wife after finding her in bed with another man, advocates for women and many others were outraged by the signal that sentence seemed to send. As one commentator put it, "the prosecution sold his wife out."[1] The punishment given rapists, murderers, and other offenders may enhance or erode people's trust in courts and in justice.

In other cases the courts precipitate massive redistributions of resources whose scope is not unlike government taxation and expenditure. Thus litigation over health problems caused by asbestos have amounted to many hundreds of millions of dollars; 150,000 claims had been filed in 1990, and plaintiffs who had settled received an average of $42,000.[2] In the same year, auto accidents cost an estimated $137 billion, much of which was covered by insurance payments to the victims.[3]

If the courts did not perform these functions, other government or private institutions would be called upon to do so. The fact that the United States relies on courts to a larger extent than many other countries affects the costs of government and the efficiency of policies. It also privileges policy advocates who have good lawyers as compared to those who possess influence only in governmental institutions other than courts.

Another strong link between politics and courts in the United States stems from the courts' exercise of judicial review. American courts review the constitutionality of statutes enacted by legislatures and also routinely examine the legality of actions by executive officials. The courts' receptiveness to suits challenging the actions of other branches of government invites those who lose in the legislative or administrative arenas to seek success in the

---

1. Ann G. Sjoerdsma, "Justice: 18 Months for a Wife's Life," *Chicago Tribune,* Nov. 14, 1994, Sec. 1, p. 21.

2. Barnaby J. Feder, "Appeals Court Blocks Plan for Asbestos Compensation," *New York Times,* Dec. 5, 1992, p. C1.

3. Lawrence Blincoe and Barbara M. Faigin, *Economic Cost of Motor Vehicle Crashes, 1990.* Washington, D.C.: U.S. Department of Transportation, National Highway Traffic Safety Administration, NHTSA Technical Report, Sept. 1992. Report No. DOT HS 807–876, p. 11.

judicial arena. Thus many issues that have been processed by Congress, state legislatures, or administrative agencies come to the courts. In 1993, for instance, as the North American Free Trade Agreement (NAFTA) was being considered in Congress, opponents went to the federal courts to stop Congressional action until an environmental impact statement had been filed. Although the courts eventually decided that they did not have jurisdiction over the matter, the court action posed a serious threat to the treaty. It was politics played on judicial turf.[4] Likewise, the abortion issue has bounced back and forth among legislatures, executive agencies, and the courts.[5] The inclination of political activists to resort to the courts makes litigation in some instances simply an extension of politics.

Courts also play a central role in the policymaking process even when they do not exercise the power of judicial review. Litigants routinely ask courts to grant them the rights and privileges that legislation has bestowed on them but that they have been unable to exercise. Many of these cases result from private actions, and the court forces private parties to comply with the law. However, sometimes the villains are government officials, and the court directs its judgment against them. Implementation, however, is rarely a simple matter of applying the law; it often involves interpretation because it is not clear whether the law as written applies to the exact circumstances of the case before the court. Most interpretations involve only small elaborations of the statute, and they may not be perceived as an alteration of the original policy. However, in the aggregate, some see even this as policymaking.[6] In a few instances, the departure of the court from established policy is so great that its decision is widely perceived as constituting a new policy crafted by judges, not by legislators or administrators.

Because courts are so often drawn into the policymaking process in the United States, they cannot escape having an impact on politics. Their actions are never simply mechanical applications of rules to fact. If they were, judges would easily be replaced by computerized robots. The essence of their task is to exercise judgment, and in doing so they smooth out rough edges of existing policy as well as sculpt new policy.

CAREER LINKS

The careers of judges and other judicial personnel create other kinds of links to the political arena. In most countries, judges are career civil servants; their life-

---

4. *Wall Street Journal*, Sept. 27, 1993, p. A3.

5. Barbara Hinkson Craig and David M. O'Brien, *Abortion and American Politics* (Chatham, N.J.: Chatham House, 1993).

6. Lynn Mather, "Policy Making in State Trial Courts," in John B. Gates and Charles A. Johnson (eds.), *The American Courts: A Critical Assessment* (Washington, D.C.: Congressional Quarterly Press, 1991), pp. 119–158.

long commitment to service within the judiciary endows them with the same career perspective as other civil servants. In the United States, judging is not a lifelong career and is not entered through competitive examinations. Rather, it is a political position to which most incumbents bring a background of political activity and interest. Judges come to the bench in mid-career after significant political activity brings them to the attention of voters or appointing authorities.

For instance, between 1963 and 1992, between 58 and 73 percent of federal appeals judges had a record of party activism before their appointments; among federal district judges, between 49 and 61 percent had such a background.[7] A typical example of such a judge was Paul J. Kelley, who had served in the New Mexico House of Representatives for four years, was a member of the New Mexico Republican State Central Committee, worked for the Reagan-Bush Re-Election Committee in 1984 and the Bush-Quayle election in 1988. When he was appointed by President George Bush to the Tenth Circuit Court of Appeals in 1992, he was a member of a large Santa Fe law firm.[8] State judges, who far outnumber their federal counterparts, are even more frequently schooled in politics.[9] A majority are themselves elected, often in partisan elections where they run as Democrats or as Republicans. But even when they do not obtain (or retain) office through elections, they must win the attention of key political officials in order to be appointed by them.[10] In addition, most prosecutors win their office by election or political appointment.

Such political backgrounds are quite unusual for judges and prosecutors in other countries. Most follow a nonpolitical career in the judiciary which begins after completing law school. Even where judges are selected at mid-career from the bar, as in England, they come from relatively nonpartisan backgrounds. Thus there is a different kind of sensitivity to the political arena in the United States judiciary than elsewhere.

However, judges everywhere are agents of the state and are committed to uphold the norms of the regime. In the United States, that is signified by their oath to uphold the Constitution (and in the case of state judges, to uphold the constitution of their state). Commitment to regime norms, of

7. Sheldon Goldman, "Bush's Judicial Legacy: The Final Imprint," *Judicature* 76, 6 (1993), pp. 282–297.

8. Ibid., p. 289.

9. Mary Cornelia Porter and G. Alan Tarr (eds.), *State Supreme Courts: Policymakers in the Federal System* (Westport, Conn.: Greenwood Press, 1982); G. Alan Tarr and Mary Cornelia Aldis Porter, *State Supreme Courts in State and Nation* (New Haven: Yale University Press, 1988).

10. For characteristics of state appellate judges see Henry R. Glick and Craig F. Emmert, "Selection Systems and Judicial Characteristics: The Recruitment of State Supreme Court Judges," *Judicature* 70 (1987), pp. 228–235.

course, begins much earlier and is perhaps most marked in the judges' training as lawyers during which they receive prolonged, concentrated inculcation
in the values of the regime. In the United States that includes a commitment
to such values as the rule of law and individual rights as enumerated in the
Bill of Rights. The entire political process of judicial recruitment makes it
unlikely that someone who rejects those values will become a judge.

POLITICAL ROOTS OF LAW

Finally, the political roots of law bring political considerations to the work
of the judiciary. Political links between legislative enactments and judicial
interpretations are particularly strong in the United States. American law develops almost entirely in response to particular problems and crises as presented to legislatures and courts. In legislatures, these occasions activate interest groups and electoral constituencies who pursue solutions beneficial to
themselves. The statutory language that legislatures eventually adopt does not
flow from the pens of legal experts but results from political compromises,
a process that often favors ambiguity in order to gain the votes needed for a
winning coalition in the legislature. Thus the legal prescriptions that judges
must follow are the direct product of political conflicts. In civil code countries
like Germany, France, and Japan, legal experts have far more influence, and
much of the law derives from its purported logic and structure rather than
from momentary political coalitions. Moreover, those countries are also parliamentary democracies where the ruling coalition usually can guarantee the
votes needed to adopt legislative proposals of the government. Consequently,
there is less need for compromise and the resultant ambiguity.

Thus there are numerous links between the legal and political arenas in
the United States. While many official spokespersons such as leaders of the
bar and chief justices deny the intrusion of politics into the work of American
courts, that denial has been decisively rejected by scholarly examinations of
the American judiciary.

Institutional Peculiarities of American Courts

The distinctiveness of the judicial process in the United States stems from a
combination of singular characteristics of American law, politics, and government: the fact that the government is a federal rather centralized regime
and the principles of separation of powers and checks and balances. Joined
with these structural traits of government are two characteristics of the legal
system: its common-law tradition and foundation on an adversarial process
vigorously pursued by a large number of lawyers. The distinctive American
legal and political tradition privileges key myths about American life. Let us
examine each of these traits and their consequences.

FEDERALISM, SEPARATION OF POWERS, AND CHECKS AND BALANCES

Government in the United States is divided between national and regional entities. The national government centered in Washington, D.C., grew enormously in power during the twentieth century, but it continues to share many functions with the governments of the fifty states. The states not only enjoy a considerable degree of fiscal autonomy by raising much of their own revenue but also control the delivery of many government services to their citizens. In addition, they boast of considerable popular attachment; people think of themselves as Texans, New Yorkers, or Hoosiers (Indianans). Each state has its own popularly elected legislature, which enacts its own laws involving most ordinary disputes and defining most crimes and their punishments. Thus there are fifty separate state statutes on almost every subject regulated by law; those laws share many common features but are full of idiosyncratic elements reflecting the politics of individual states. Disputes invoking those laws usually go to state courts staffed by judges and other personnel recruited through the state political process.

The national government has its own laws and its own courts—the federal district courts, courts of appeal, and the Supreme Court, as well as administrative tribunals attached to executive or quasi-executive agencies. They hear disputes centering on national laws and cases involving citizens of several states (the so-called diversity jurisdiction). Many cases can go to either set of courts, but most come to state courts, which are more numerous and are often located closer to litigants than federal courts.

The national government has no control over the fifty state courts. Federal courts are not hierarchical superiors to the state tribunals; they do not provide the staff for state courts; they are not generally part of the same career path for judges; they provide none of the funds state courts need to operate. State courts are obligated to follow the interpretation of the U.S. Constitution by federal courts, but if they evade that duty, the federal courts have no disciplinary powers over them. Moreover, the final judicial word about the interpretation of state laws usually rests with state, not federal courts.

Thus American law is an unparalleled maze of jurisdictions and substantive provisions. Often the general outline of various state legal provisions are quite similar, but the details differ. At other times, states differ sharply on policy issues and dissent from federal policies. This is true even for such mundane regulations as those involving an application for a driver's license, the payment of taxes, and the liability of persons involved in auto accidents. Such diversity presents opportunities for those litigants with sufficient resources to choose between different sets of statutes as well as different courts in which to pursue their claims.

In addition to federalism, implementation of the principles of separation of powers and checks and balances also creates complexity in the U.S. legal system. In the United States, the executive, legislature, and judiciary constitute coequal branches of government. The constitutions governing the national government and the states specify that each branch enjoys autonomy from the others. Neither the legislature nor the executive may order courts to undertake a particular course of action or decide cases in a specified way. Constitutional provisions also prohibit reducing the salaries of judges or removing them except by specified procedures. Thus, legislatures and the executive possess limited leverage over the courts.

However, courts are not entirely autonomous. The judiciary does not control its own sources of revenue and must rely on appropriations from legislatures; the jurisdiction of the courts is also specified by statute in many cases. Unlike in many other countries, courts in the United States have little influence over who fills their positions, nor do they regulate their tenure. Moreover, the political process by which judges and other court officials attain their positions makes the courts dependent on other elements of the governmental structure. For the national courts, for example, the President appoints judges with the consent of the Senate; they serve for life and can only be removed by impeachment, a very difficult process requiring collaboration by the Congress.[11] United States Attorneys, who prosecute federal crimes, are also presidential appointees. Every president seeks to place an imprint on the judiciary through the appointment of judges. Every national administration uses its control over federal prosecutors to influence the course of criminal justice. The states vary considerably in the manner by which judges reach office; in some they are appointed by governors for fixed terms; in others they are independently elected for fixed terms.[12] Most prosecutors are elected. Thus routes to office sensitize courts in the United States to their external environments rather than to the preferences of other courts and judges. They also promote cautious decision making that normally remains within the bounds of the current political consensus.

Finally, the power of courts to interpret legislation constitutes an important element of the system of checks and balances of American government. The dominant tradition of judicial interpretation is that judges must respect the language of legislation, but that does not foreclose their interpreting it when the occasion arises.[13] Normally judges take the words lawmakers provide and interpret them as best they can with little ensuing conflict with the legislature.

11. Sheldon Goldman, "Federal Judicial Recruitment," in Gates and Johnson, supra note 6, pp. 189–210.

12. Herbert Jacob, "State Courts," in Virginia Gray and Herbert Jacob (eds.), Politics in the American States, 6th ed. (Washington, D.C.: Congressional Quarterly Press, 1996).

13. Benjamin N. Cardozo, The Nature of the Judicial Process (New Haven: Yale University Press, 1921, rpt. 1960).

Sometimes, however, clear policy differences separate judges from legislatures with the result that judicial interpretations lead to legislative amendment, further judicial interpretation, and sometimes further legislative amendment. That is part of the system of checks and balances between the two branches of government.

THE COMMON-LAW TRADITION

The power of courts to refer to their own previous decisions and regard them as binding grows out of the common-law tradition the United States inherited from England at the time of the American Revolution. In the ensuing years, many other characteristics of the common-law tradition have fallen into disuse—most particularly the penchant of judges to find the law in prevailing norms of behavior where no statutory law existed. Since the beginning of the twentieth century, legislatures have enacted specific statutes in most areas of the law, so that few gaps remain to be filled in by common-law interpretation.

Nevertheless, the common-law tradition has left an indelible imprint on American law. One consequence lies in the training of lawyers. The principal materials that introduce fledgling attorneys to the law are appellate court cases rather than statutes or underlying legal principles. Thus the legal profession is inculcated with a court-centered view of the law which considerably enhances the power of courts. This contrasts sharply with a code-centered view of law typical among jurists in France and Germany. In addition, the common-law tradition of making decisions case by case and letting policy gradually emerge from this flow of decisions is consonant with an American penchant for tackling even the biggest problems incrementally. While the French, for instance, are reputed to prefer grand solutions based on principle, Americans are wary of large-scale schemes. The common-law tradition of case-by-case adjudication fits the American preference well.

THE ADVERSARIAL PROCESS

Closely associated with the common-law tradition is the adversarial process by which the two parties to a case present their evidence to the court, and the court (the judge and sometimes a jury) decides the outcome. Two features of the adversarial process are particularly important: the passivity of the judge (and court) and the activity of the adversaries.

American courts are largely passive; they wait for cases to come to them, and, when the cases arrive, they wait for the adversaries to proceed. This is especially true for civil cases, but it also governs many of the events in criminal courts. For instance, after an arrest a person must be arraigned before a judge, usually within twenty-four or forty-eight hours; the charges themselves, however, are defined by a prosecutor whom the court does not control. Judges set bail but almost always rely on the recommendation of the prosecutor and on whatever information the defense presents. Subsequent decisions depend entirely on the information presented by prosecutors and defense counsel rather than on independent investigation by the judge. In civil matters, the law specifies fewer deadlines, and therefore the court is even more passive.

The obverse side of judicial passivity is activity by lawyers, who control the judicial process in the United States. They have sole responsibility for investigating the circumstances leading to a court case and for presenting information they deem relevant. Information they decide to withhold simply does not become available to judges and juries. Lawyers also control the pace of litigation; they may proceed swiftly if their clients' and their own interests demand rapid action; conversely, they may move at a snail's pace if they so desire. Almost every element of court proceedings reflects the preferences of attorneys. While judges wear the robes of state authority, in fact, they are often hostage to attorneys' tactics in American courts.

THE LEGAL PROFESSION

Lawyers dominate the legal arena in the United States. They enjoy a monopoly on representation of clients before courts and are the most common representatives before other tribunals as well. They have a stranglehold on almost all activities surrounding legal documents such as the drafting of contracts and wills, the closing of real estate transactions, the handling of bankruptcies, and the negotiation of personal injury settlements. They are prominent in legislatures and executive departments and often hold key positions in business enterprises. In other countries, other professionals perform many of these activities; thus it is not surprising that there are more lawyers in the United States than elsewhere (see table 2.1). The sheer number of lawyers and their domination of the legal process gives the legal arena in the United States a distinctive cast.

The process of becoming a lawyer is also different in the United States than elsewhere in that it requires more university training but no apprenticeship. To become a lawyer in the United States normally requires seven years of postsecondary education that is very costly. In 1993 dollars, the cost in tuition and lost wages amount to at least $175,000 and is often more.[14] Despite that cost, however, 125,000 students were enrolled in law schools in 1985 (80 percent attended full-time) and 37,000 graduated that year.[15]

14. For the details of this calculation, see Herbert Jacob, *Law and Politics in the United States*, 2d ed. (New York: HarperCollins, 1995), p. 120.

15. On pass rate, see Richard L. Abel, *American Lawyer* (New York: Oxford University Press, 1989), pp. 254–256; on admissions, Barbara A. Curran and Clara N. Carson, *The Lawyer Statistical Report: The U.S. Legal Profession in the 1990s* (Chicago: American Bar Foundation, 1994), p. 2.

Table 2.1 Lawyers in Selected Countries (Estimated)

	Reported number	Date	Source
Belgium	24,000	1984	A
Canada	42,710	1986	B
China	47,461	1986	C
England and Wales[a]	58,857	1985	D
	45,500	1985	E
France[b]	27,700	1990	F
	27,215	1983	G
	26,029	1983	H
West Germany[c]	116,000	1985	I
Italy[d]	46,401	1985	F
Netherlands	5,124	1986	J
Spain	34,234	1985	K
United States	655,191	1985	L
World total, based on best available data = 1,908,844			

Notes
[a]Includes both solicitors and barristers.
[b]Source G includes lawyers in private practice only.
[c]All practice settings.
[d]Private practice only.

Sources
A. Luc Huyse, "Legal Experts in Belgium," in Richard L. Abel and Philip S. C. Lewis, eds., *Lawyers in Society,* vol. 2, *The Civil Law World* (Berkeley: University of California Press, 1988), table 6.7.
B. David A. Stager and Harry W. Arthurs, *Lawyers in Canada* (Toronto: University of Toronto Press, 1990), tables 6.1 and 6.2.
C. Hao Pan, "Lawyers and Law Firms in Contemporary China—Toward a Framework of Interpretation," paper presented at the 1992 annual meeting of the Law and Society Association, Philadelphia.
D. Richard L. Abel, *The Legal Profession in England and Wales* (Oxford: Blackwell, 1990), tables 1.16 and 2.14.
E. David S. Clark, "The Organization and Status of Lawyers," in *General Reports, Ninth World Conference of Procedural Law: Role and Organization of Judges and Lawyers in Contemporary Societies,* 1991, table 1.
F. Richard L. Abel, "Comparative Sociology of Legal Professions," in *Lawyers in Society,* vol. 3, *Comparative Theories.* (Berkeley: University of California Press, 1989), table 3.2.
G. Stephen P. Magee and William A. Brock, *Black Hole Tariffs and Endogenous Policy Theory: Political Economy in General Equilibrium* (New York: Cambridge University Press, 1989), table 8.1.
H. Anne Boigeol, "The French Bar: The Difficulties of Unifying a Divided Profession," in Abel and Lewis, eds., *Lawyers in Society—The Civil Law World.*
I. David S. Clark, "The Selection and Accountability of Judges in West Germany: Implementation of a Rechsstaat," *Southern California Law Review* 61 (1988), p. 1807.
J. Kees Schuyt, "The Rise of Lawyers in the Dutch Welfare State," in Abel and Lewis, eds., *Lawyers in Society—The Civil Law World.*
K. Richard L. Abel, "Lawyers in the Civil Law World," in Abel and Lewis, eds., *Lawyers in Society—The Civil Law World.*
L. Barbara Curran et al., *Supplement to the Lawyer Statistical Report: The U.S. Legal Profession in 1985.* Chicago: American Bar Foundation, 1986, p. 3.
Table adapted from Marc Galanter, "News from Nowhere: The Debased Debate on Civil Justice," *Denver University Law Review,* 71 (1993), pp. 104–109.

After graduation, aspiring lawyers must usually pass a bar examination in the state in which they wish to practice. The examination has two parts: the first contains questions about the law and the second requires that the budding lawyer be free of such character blemishes as a criminal record. Even lawyers who do not plan to appear before a court must pass this examination, for giving legal advice without a license is a criminal offense in every state. About two-thirds of those who take the examinations pass, and between 1977 and 1990 approximately 30,000 new lawyers were admitted to the bar each year.[16] Not all who graduate from law school and pass the bar examination work as lawyers; some go into business or other occupations.

Those who practice law do so in a number of different settings, most of which are entirely free of government control. In 1991 approximately 42 percent of lawyers worked in law firms, although many of those firms were relatively small; these attorneys principally service businesses. About 9 percent worked in law departments of large corporations, handling most of the routine legal affairs of those enterprises. Another 34 percent had their own law office and worked alone; these attorneys handle the affairs of individual clients including criminal matters, family affairs, personal injury incidents, home purchases, wills, and the like. Finally, approximately 15 percent worked in government positions, staffing prosecutor's offices, legal departments of government agencies, public defender's offices, and the like.[17]

All of these work settings except government offices are part of the private economic sector. The government has little influence over the fees that attorneys charge, the services they offer, the conditions they attach to serving clients, or the tactics they employ.

The attraction of law to young people in part reflects the sizable economic rewards that some lawyers obtain. Beginning salaries in 1993 for associates in the largest law firms immediately after finishing law school were in the $80,000 range; partners earned several times as much.[18] However, a large number of attorneys earn quite modest incomes; for instance solo practitioners in Arizona had a median income of only $22,000 in 1976 while the median income of law firm partners in that state was $40,000; since then the income of top lawyers has risen sharply but that of the lowest quartile has

16. Ibid., p. 269. Note this is a larger number than those who graduated from law school in 1985 because those who take the examination are not necessarily those who graduated in that year.

17. These estimates are based on data on *active* lawyers: Curran and Carson, supra note 15, p. 7.

18. Edward Frost and Margaret Cronin Fisk, "The Profession After 15 Years," *National Law Journal,* Aug. 9, 1993, p. 1.

not fared as well.[19] Indeed, more than half of all 1992 law graduates had not found a law position six months after graduation.[20]

In addition to very visible high incomes, legal education leads to a large number of influential positions in American society. Many legislators are lawyers (although fewer during the 1990s than earlier in the century). Many high-level administrative positions in federal and state governments go to attorneys who often shuttle between government positions and their law firms. In the Clinton administration, two-thirds of the cabinet-level positions were initially filled with lawyers, although many of these appointees spent more time in government and politics than in active legal careers.[21] A sizable number of top management positions in private enterprises also go to lawyers. Finally, all judgeships, except mostly rural justices of the peace, are open only to lawyers.[22]

Consequently, the lawyer's view of policy and politics is widely diffused in American society. Not all lawyers think alike about policy issues, but their influence exerts itself in concerns about procedure and rights which pervade large portions of the American political process. In addition, the lawyer's adversarial pose permeates many nonjudicial arenas such as academic disciplinary hearings, divorce settlement negotiations, and complaints to medical insurers. With the pervasiveness of lawyers in American society, it is not surprising that many Americans consider suing when faced with a dispute—what Robert Kagan calls "adversarial legalism."[23]

POPULISM IN THE JUDICIARY

Juries add an element of populism to the otherwise lawyer-dominated judicial process in the United States.[24] Defendants in criminal trials may request a jury; juries are also available in many civil trials. Because there is a strong perception that conviction after jury trials draws more severe penalties, not many defendants demand a jury.

Both the composition and powers of juries in U.S. courts are quite distinctive. Although the details vary from place to place, the men and women who serve on juries are conscripted by the courts to serve normally for a

19. Abel, supra note 15, p. 302.

20. *National Law Journal,* Aug. 9, 1993, p. 1.

21. Thomas R. Dye, "The Friends of Bill and Hillary," *PS* 26 (1993), p. 693.

22. Doris Marie Provine, *Judging Credentials: Nonlawyer Judges and the Politics of Professionalism* (Chicago: University of Chicago Press, 1986).

23. Robert A. Kagan, "Do Lawyers Cause Adversarial Legalism? A Preliminary Inquiry" *Law & Social Inquiry* 19, 1 (Winter 1994), pp. 1–62.

24. Harry Kalven, Jr., and Hans Zeisel, *The American Jury* (Boston: Little, Brown, 1966); Robert E. Litan (ed.), *Verdict: Assessing the Civil Jury System* (Washington, D.C.: Brookings Institution, 1993).

single trial or for a period of about two weeks. The jurors are drawn from a pool of voters, licensed drivers, and other listings. The goal in using such lists is to have a representative cross section of the community serving on juries. Jurors receive no special training. Nevertheless, they have sole responsibility for rendering verdicts. After hearing a trial they deliberate outside the presence of the judge or any other legal advisor. If a jury acquits in a criminal case, no appeal is possible. Although studies comparing jury decisions with rulings that judges might have made indicate some differences between them, most decisions are the same.[25]

DISTINCTIVE FEATURES OF LEGAL AND POLITICAL TRADITION

Three sets of widely held beliefs affect the American legal system. The first is the propensity to privilege individual rights over community concerns. Americans appear more oriented toward self-interest and less toward community well-being than many other peoples in the world. That belief is buttressed by a conviction that through pursuit of self-interest, overall welfare will be enhanced. In legal affairs, the concern for self-interest has manifested itself with an insistence on individual rights in many spheres of life. Patients assert that they have a right to expect error-free treatment by doctors; consumers contend that they have the right to purchase defect-free goods from manufacturers; those fearful of crime argue that they have a right to own guns; large segments of the population clamor for freedom from governmental interference in what they do with their property, how they finance their health care, or where they send their children to school. Concern for the common good does not inhibit litigation asserting individual rights and privileges. More emphasis is placed on rights than obligations both in political discourse and in legal affairs.

Support for this stance comes from the national Constitution, which for many Americans is a quasi-religious icon of their vision of the United States. The assertion that a government action violates constitutional rights is a powerful political argument that leads many political controversies to be debated not simply on the basis of the merits of the substantive proposals under consideration but also on their "constitutionality." Moreover, it readily channels political conflict to the courts.

The Constitution specifies rights, in addition to reinforcing the widespread belief in the United States that government ought to be limited. The Constitution itself appears to grant limited powers to the government, reserving, in the words of the Tenth Amendment, "The powers not delegated to the United States by the Constitution, nor prohibited by it to the States . . . to the States respectively, or to the people." While not a source of voluminous jurispru-

---

25. Kalven and Zeisel, supra note 24, report that only 22% differ.

dence in the twentieth century, this provision captures a sentiment that is perhaps as widespread in contemporary times as it was in the eighteenth century.[26] As a consequence, government in the United States has been weaker and less intrusive than those of most other advanced industrial societies. Public law has played a smaller role and private law a larger one than in many other countries.

Finally, an important—if incompletely realized—strand of the social and political tradition surrounding the legal process is a commitment to egalitarianism. Status has little formal role in American law. Even the president can be subject to the law; it is not uncommon for highly placed officials to run afoul of criminal statutes and see their careers end abruptly with a conviction for a crime. However, the courts are not completely blind to status. As in the society as a whole, racism persists in the legal process and in the courts. Many African Americans and other racial minorities struggle against bias born of their social standing, their income level, and stereotypes of unproductive behavior, which affect their ability to use courts and their treatment in them.[27]

SUMMARY

The legal system of the United States has many distinctive features that reflect the nation's political structure and traditions. Its institutions are highly fragmented in a manner corresponding to the federal, decentralized character of American political institutions. Those institutions produce a highly variegated body of substantive law which reflects the diversity of the country. American law also reflects the common-law tradition in which it is rooted and the adversarial process which governs many formal proceedings. The extraordinarily large legal profession exerts considerable influence in promoting adversarial proceedings not only in courts but in many other venues. At the same time, a populist element persists in the occasional adjudication by citizen juries.

Finally, the legal system in the United States reflects core values of the nation's political and legal tradition, particularly an emphasis on individual rights, a focus on the constitutionalism of proposed actions, limited government, and aspirations of egalitarianism. With these general characteristics in mind, we examine in some detail how the United States implements criminal justice and civil proceedings and how it handles issues which raise the constitutional issues to which we have alluded.

26. Forrest McDonald, "Tenth Amendment," in Kermit Hall (ed.), *Oxford Companion to the Supreme Court* (New York: Oxford University Press, 1993), pp. 861–863.

27. Coramae Richey Mann, *Unequal Justice: A Question of Color* (Bloomington: Indiana University Press, 1993).

Criminal Justice in the United States

Criminality is legendary in the United States. It does not surprise Americans that a youngster garbed in a Halloween costume who does not respond to the command, "Freeze," is shot dead by a nervous homeowner who thinks his house is about to be invaded by a robber.[28] That tragic incident in a New Orleans suburb on Halloween night 1992 symbolizes many Americans' fear of crime, the availability of hand guns, and the banality of violence.

It is a task of government to control lawlessness. The writers of the U.S. Constitution expressed this mandate by proclaiming that government should secure "domestic tranquility"; Americans frequently speak of the need for "law and order." Most countries employ a criminal justice system for this function, but in the United States there is a widespread feeling that the criminal justice system has failed. Americans expect it to suppress crime, and it has not done so. That failure has thrust criminal justice into the middle of the political arena.

APPARENT DIMENSIONS OF FAILURE

We may compare crime in the United States to two standards: the experience of other countries and its own past experience. Compared to other countries, rates for violent crimes are extraordinary. For homicides, rapes, and robberies, for instance, they are 2.7 times as high as those in France, 4.5 times that of Germany, and 61.5 times that of Japan.[29] Even granting difficulties in cross-national comparisons and the fragility of the statistics, the United States ranks very high in the incidence of violent crime.

Historical data do not clearly show a substantial rise in crime in the United States since 1975. Two series of data that measure crime report somewhat different trends. The Uniform Crime Reports, which depends upon the police to record crimes they know about, shows a 50 percent rise in crime between 1975 and 1990. The National Crime Survey, which depends upon a survey of the population for reports of victimization, indicates that the rate of violent crimes declined by 10 percent between 1975 and 1990, household burglary rates, 42 percent, and household larceny, 30 percent, although automobile thefts rose by 5 percent. Thus evidence about the rise of crime between 1975 and 1990 is quite ambiguous. However, between 1960 and 1975, before the crime surveys had begun, offenses known to the police almost tripled. If any credence is to be given to those numbers, crime had already risen to a very high level when the crime surveys began.

28. *New York Times,* Oct. 21, 1992, p. A10.
29. See Chapter 6; A. Didrick Castberg, *Japanese Criminal Justice* (Westport, Conn.: Praeger, 1990), p. 12. Castberg reports higher property crime rates for Britain, West Germany, and France than for the United States. However, American property crime is so vastly underreported that the comparison is not very reliable.

In addition, drug trafficking and abuse have been major problems. Although no reliable measures of drug offenses exist, there seems to be a wide consensus that the incidence of drug abuse has not abated and the violence associated with drug trafficking has not diminished. This despite the fact that 869,000 arrests were made for drug violations in 1990, for a rate of 449 per 100,000 inhabitants.[30]

Public perception of crime follows the rising trend line of the police statistics more closely than the decline of the victimization surveys. That may be because police statistics get more play in the media, particularly on local television; local numbers are available, whereas the crime survey produces only national estimates. However, national media coverage is also important. The Gallup Poll and others periodically ask respondents to identify what they think is the most important problem facing the country. Crime had never been mentioned more frequently than other problems until the end of 1993 when it jumped to the top of the list by a wide margin just after there was intense media coverage of the problem. The same relationship between media coverage and mass opinion occurred in 1988 and 1989 when there was much reporting about drug abuse and drugs became the most frequently mentioned national problem in the polls.[31]

Large portions of the public also consider public safety to be a real problem in their cities and neighborhoods. Every Gallup Poll between 1972 and 1992 shows a large plurality of people perceiving more crime in their neighborhood than in the previous year; in no year did more than 20 percent think that crime in their neighborhood had decreased. In 1990, a majority of those polled considered New York, Miami, Washington, Detroit, Chicago, and Los Angeles unsafe. A majority considered the smaller cities of Boston, San Diego, Dallas, Houston, Seattle, and Minneapolis safe, but each of those cities except Seattle and Minneapolis were considered unsafe by at least 25 percent of the respondents.[32] Thus very large numbers of Americans think some aspects of crime are a serious national problem, perceive crime to have increased in their neighborhood, and feel that large portions of urban America are unsafe.

Another indicator of the continuing nature of the crime problem has been the attention devoted to it in election campaigns. Crime has been an important issue (as defined by its use by candidates) in every presidential election between 1964 and 1988 and was very prominent in the Congressional elections

30. Timothy J. Flanagan and Kathleen Maguire, *Sourcebook of Criminal Justice Statistics—1991* (Washington, D.C.: U.S. Department of Justice, Bureau of Justice Statistics, 1992), pp. 372, 257, 433.

31. Jeffrey D. Alderman, "Leading the Public: The Media's Focus on Crime Shaped Sentiment," *The Public Perspective* (March–April 1994), pp. 26–27.

32. Flanagan and Maguire, supra note 30, pp. 185, 192–193.

of 1994. It is often the premier issue in mayoral elections and a significant one in many gubernatorial contests.[33] Typically every candidate for these offices promises to do more about crime—enact tougher laws, hire more police officers, or build more prisons. By their statements, these highly placed public officials reinforce popular perceptions that criminal justice is ineffective.

A final indicator of apparent failure of the criminal justice system comes from data about the disposition of cases. Data from thirty-five prosecutor's offices across the country shows that only 56 percent of all arrests for serious crimes lead to a conviction, and that only about three-fifths of the convictions lead to incarceration, most for a short jail sentence.[34] Two alternative conclusions may be drawn from these data, and neither flatters the performance of the criminal justice system. One plausible conclusion is that criminal courts are terribly inefficient, letting almost half of all those accused of serious crimes go free; moreover, a majority of those convicted receive a light sentence. Reflecting this view, Senator Phil Gramm, a conservative Republican from Texas, wrote: "[Criminals] commit crimes because they think it pays. Unfortunately, in most cases they are right: in America today, crime *does* pay. . . . Analysts point to the breakdown of the family, the effects of television violence and the failure to teach moral values in our schools. While these factors have an impact, they overlook the main culprit: a criminal justice system in which the cost of committing crimes is so shamelessly cheap that it fails to deter potential criminals."[35] A second interpretation of the data might lead us to conclude that the criminal courts are winnowing the innocent from the guilty; however, we must then ask why the police are so inefficient that almost half of all those they arrest should not have been accused of a crime?

Gramm's sentiments are widely shared, despite that fact that the United States incarcerates a higher percentage of its citizens than other industrialized countries. In the case of homicides, for instance, the United States had 7.5 more convicts in prison per 1,000 population than England and 5.3 times more than West Germany in the early 1980s; it imprisoned 9 times more

33. On mayoral races: Herbert Jacob, *The Frustration of Policy: Responses to Crime by American Cities* (Boston: Little, Brown, 1984), pp. 35–39; Anne M. Heinz, Herbert Jacob, and Robert L. Lineberry (eds.), *Crime in City Politics* (New York: Longman, 1983); *New York Times,* Oct. 18, 1993, p. A1. On gubernatorial issues: *New York Times,* Oct. 1, 1993, Sec. B, p. 5; Oct. 24, 1993, Sec. 4, p. 1.

34. Barbara Boland, Catherine H. Conly, Paul Mahanna, Lynn Warner, and Ronald Sones, *The Prosecution of Felony Arrests, 1987* (Washington, D.C.: U.S. Department of Justice, Bureau of Justice Statistics, 1990).

35. *New York Times,* July 8, 1993, p. A11.

robbers than England and 4.7 times more than West Germany.[36] This appears to be the consequence of both a higher crime rate in the United States and a greater propensity to send convicted offenders to prison. By 1993, the United States had put more than one million offenders in prisons and held almost another half million in local jails.[37]

THE DISTINCTIVE CONTEXT OF AMERICAN CRIMINAL JUSTICE

The widespread perception of failure by criminal justice is embedded in a political setting that is distinctive to the United States. Three characteristics are central: its fragmentation, its politicization, and its embedded ideology of individualism.

Fragmentation

The American legal system reflects the fragmentation of government and politics. For criminal justice this means that, unlike most other advanced industrial societies, the United States scatters authority and responsibility for criminal justice across the entire landscape of governmental institutions. Each level of government—national, state, and local—shares important criminal justice duties. State legislatures enact most laws outlawing criminal behavior and setting punishments, but Congress has in recent years increasingly made criminal behavior subject to federal law with its own enactments.[38] Thus many offenses may violate both state and federal laws. Moreover, the exact description of each criminal offense and the penalty attached to it vary from one jurisdiction to another.

City police departments perform most policing functions. More than 9,700 cities each had their own police departments employing a total of 348,000 officers in 1991. In addition, the national government employed 65,000 officers divided among the Federal Bureau of Investigation (FBI), the Drug Enforcement Agency (DEA), the Immigration and Naturalization Service (INS), and the Bureau of Alcohol, Tobacco, and Firearms (ATF) to enforce federal criminal statutes. In addition, state governments use state patrols as well as specialized agencies, totaling 109,000 officers, and county sheriffs' departments use another 140,000 officers to police rural areas. Thus a total

36. James P. Lynch, "A Comparison of Prison Use in England, Canada, West Germany, and the United States: A Limited Test of the Punitive Hypothesis," *Journal of Criminal Law and Criminology* 1 (1988), pp. 180–217, esp. 193.

37. Darrell K. Gilliard and Allen J. Beck, "Prisoners in 1993," *Bulletin* (Washington, D.C.: U.S. Department of Justice, Bureau of Justice Statistics, June 1994).

38. See particularly the contents of the Crime Bill of 1994. *New York Times*, Sept. 14, 1994, p. 1.

of 1.6 million police officers are available to combat crime.[39] In many places city police, county officers, state patrols, and federal agents operate on the same turf.

In addition, as noted, the national and state governments employ separate court systems to adjudicate allegations of criminality. Because many courts handle both civil and criminal cases, it is impossible to estimate exactly how many courtrooms or judges work in the criminal justice process.

Finally, each level of government possesses its own set of prisons, as well as alternative programs for punishing convicted offenders. City and county jails house prisoners while they await trials or serve brief sentences (generally less than a year). Each state has its own penal system consisting of separate prisons for young offenders, male and female convicts, and for convicts deemed to require varying degrees of security. The federal government has yet another set of penal institutions. In 1990, the states spent $15.3 billion for their prisons, while counties and cities spent another $8.1 billion for their jails; the federal government spent an additional $1.5 billion on its prison system.[40]

No central direction of these institutions exists. In the federal government, the Department of Justice controls the FBI, DEA, and INS, but not ATF agents or forest and park rangers. Federal prosecutors and prisons are part of the Justice Department, but the federal courts are entirely autonomous. Even more fragmentation exists at the state level, with almost every county having its own elected prosecutor and sheriff and every city and county employing its own police in addition to small state police organizations. Completely autonomous courts are organized geographically by county. Most counties also have their own jail but send their most serious offenders to state penal institutions. Each state, of course, possesses its own legislature which enacts criminal statutes for that state alone.

Each of these autonomous institutions responds to its own organizational and political imperatives. Legislators pass harsh criminal laws to show that they care about public safety, although they often know that these laws cannot be fully enforced. Police make arrests to display their vigor in combatting crime, aware that many of those whom they apprehend will not be prosecuted. Prosecutors accommodate their overwhelming caseloads by quietly dismissing some cases while noisily convicting other defendants whom they know will not be imprisoned. Judges show their concern for public safety by sentencing convicts to prison for terms they know cannot be completed. Prisons

39. Kathleen Maguire, Ann L. Pastore, and Timothy Flanagan, *Sourcebook of Criminal Justice Statistics—1992* (Washington, D.C.: U.S. Department of Justice, Bureau of Justice Statistics, 1993), pp. 61, 23.

40. Ibid., p. 7.

had become so overcrowded in 1990 that one of every five state penal institutions in the United States was under court order to limit its population because of overcrowding; the prison systems respond by releasing inmates they know are not rehabilitated.[41]

Consequently, no single crime control policy exists in the United States. Each component of the criminal justice system responds to its own imperatives and its own constituencies. Sometimes they compete with each other to show their commitment to law and order; at other times, they try to hand off difficult cases or problems to another component of the system. Almost always the several institutions of the criminal justice system are out of synch with each other, concerned to protect their own reputation and turf.

The impact of this fragmentation can be illustrated by an analysis of prison overcrowding in California.[42] During the 1980s, the jail and prison population more than tripled in California. Zimring and Hawkins show that the growth in prison populations was not directly related to changes in California's crime rate. Rather, local variations in the propensity to incarcerate those convicted of crimes were partly responsible. In Los Angeles the incarceration rate tripled between 1980 and 1990, whereas it doubled in the rest of the state. The incarceration rate itself is the product tens of thousands of decisions by police to make an arrest, of thousands of plea agreements between prosecutors and defense counsel, and of subsequent decisions by hundreds of judges. All of these occurred without supervision by a central authority.

Moreover, various categories of criminals contributed to different degrees to the rise in the prison population. Half of all prison admissions were men and women who were released before the end of their terms but reincarcerated because of a violation of their parole conditions. In many instances, parole violators are charged with a crime that by itself might not qualify for a prison term. Decisions to send parole violators back to prison, however, are made by prosecutors and judges without input from the prisons. They are a quick and easy way to dispose of cases and get rid of the offenders. In addition, one-quarter of all inmates in California were drug offenders, but drug arrests are very much the product of police priorities that change over time independent of the situation of the prisons. Finally, a large portion of the increased inmate population in California came from very sharp rise in the predisposition to send nonviolent thieves to prison. Zimring and Hawkins conclude: "Decentralized decisions on the part of prosecutors and judges were the most important explanation of increased imprisonment in the 1980s."[43]

41. Ibid., p. 113.

42. Franklin E. Zimring and Gordon Hawkins, *Prison Population and Criminal Justice Policy in California* (Berkeley, Calif.: Institute of Governmental Studies Press, 1992).

43. Ibid., p. 40.

As in California, decentralized decisions dominate crime control policy across the United States. City officials control only the police, and policing by itself cannot control the incidence of crime. State legislators control only the language of the criminal code, but its implementation rests with the police, prosecutors, judges, and prison officials. Federal officials control only a tiny portion of the criminal justice establishment, and that control is divided among many competing players. Consequently, public officials in the United States are generous with rhetoric but can devise only fragmentary or symbolic responses to the problem of crime with such actions as increasing statutory penalties, increasing the police forces, or building new prison facilities.

Politicization

A second key characteristic of criminal justice in the United States is how deeply it is embedded in electoral politics.[44] Many of the key posts in the criminal justice system are elective offices: mayors (who are responsible for policing), sheriffs (who run county jails), most prosecutors, and many judges. Electioneering provides opportunities for challengers to highlight poor performance by incumbents and generates unrealistic promises for improvement from incumbents and challengers alike. After the election of a new mayor, it is almost routine to replace the police chief.[45] When a new prosecutor is elected, most supervising prosecutors and many assistants are replaced. Even candidates for positions with little authority over criminal justice, such as presidential and gubernatorial candidates, find crime an attractive issue. Candidates know that taking a strong stand against crime will win points with voters.

One reason that crime is so much on voters' minds is that crime dominates the presentation of local news on television. Every night brings a new edition of murder and mayhem in large cities. Crime is the lead story of many broadcasts and occupies as much time as the longest segments of those newscasts—the weather forecast and the sports report. Even though people may not experience crime directly, they experience it vicariously through these broadcasts and may perceive it as a threat to themselves.[46] Addressing that threat is an attractive electoral gambit.

44. Stuart A. Scheingold, *The Politics of Street Crime: Criminal Process and Cultural Obsession* (Philadelphia: Temple University Press, 1991).

45. Jacob, supra note 33, pp. 97–98.

46. George E. Antunes and Patricia A. Hurley, "The Representation of Criminal Events in Houston's Two Daily Newspapers," *Journalism Quarterly* 54 (1977), pp. 756–760; Sanford Sherizen, "Social Creation of Crime News: All the News Fitted to Print," in Charles Winick (ed.), *Deviance and Mass Media* (Beverly Hills, Calif.: Sage Publications, 1978), pp. 203–224; Duane H. Swank, Herbert Jacob, and Jack Moran, "Newspaper Attentiveness to Crime," in Herbert Jacob and Robert L. Lineberry (eds.), *Government Responses to Crime: Crime on Urban*

A consequence of this politicization is that responsible officials seek short-run, limited solutions to a long-term problem requiring comprehensive approaches. Elected officials need almost instant results, before the next election, two or four years hence. They also need policies whose execution they can directly control so they are not at the mercy of some remote bureaucrat or electoral rival. Consequently, the most common responses to crime in the United States have been quick fixes. One has been to change statutory penalties, which often has little consequence in practice. Another is to increase the number of police officers, which immediately shows a greater police presence but has little impact on the crime rate other than seeming to increase it through improved reporting procedures. A third popular quick fix is to build more prison facilities, which has the added advantage of providing employment both to those who build them and those who staff them but which may do little more than attract still larger numbers of inmates from a seemingly infinite pool of potential offenders.[47]

The concern for the next election also has the consequence of fostering incompatible goals. Thus the California legislature established in 1987 a Blue Ribbon Commission on Inmate Population Management with the instruction: "It is the intent of the Legislature that public safety shall be the overriding concern in examining methods of . . . heading off runaway inmate population levels. . . . Public safety shall be the primary consideration in all conclusions and recommendations."[48] Of course, prison populations cannot be decreased without some risk to public safety. But given this set of instructions, the Blue Ribbon Commission could formulate only banal recommendations.

Individualism

Individualism, the dominant creed in the United States, is reflected in many ways in the criminal justice system. Perhaps the most evident is the insistence of many to the "right" to own handguns, even if they never go hunting and even though the guns are not used as part of an organized militia to which the Second Amendment refers. In 1991, 40 percent of those polled in a national survey reported having a gun in their home or garage.[49] For many

---

Agendas (Washington, D.C.: U.S. Department of Justice, National Institute of Justice, 1982), pp. 77–118; Janice A. Beecher and Robert L. Lineberry, "Attentiveness to Crime in Political Arenas," Ibid., pp. 15–76.

47. Peter F. Nardulli, *Prison Capacity and Sentencing Severity: A Look at Illinois, Michigan, and Pennsylvania* (Champaign: University of Illinois Institute of Government and Public Affairs, 1983).

48. Franklin E. Zimring and Gordon Hawkins, *Prison Population and Criminal Justice Policy in California* (Berkeley, Calif.: Institute of Governmental Studies Press, 1992), p. 18.

49. Flanagan and Maguire, supra note 30, p. 215.

people, gun ownership has become symbolic of control over their private space. While the majority of Americans favor regulation of gun ownership, an insistent minority has been able to block its adoption on a national scale.

Individualism is also reflected in a deep distrust of governmental authority. In the criminal justice process that distrust is engraved in the Fourth, Fifth, Sixth, and Eighth Amendments to the Constitution, which provide an array of safeguards against prosecutorial abuse of people accused of crimes. They require informing accused persons of the exact charges against them, permitting accused persons to confront witnesses against them, and allowing the accused to have counsel to assist in their defense. They prohibit forcing defendants to testify against themselves or imposing excessive bail or cruel or unusual punishment. They guarantee all defendants "due process of law." These constitutional provisions also prohibit trying someone twice for the same offense. The Supreme Court has extended these protections to the states, where the vast majority of criminal prosecutions occur.

The consequence is that all participants in the criminal justice process pay a great deal of attention to procedure. Police must inform those whom they arrest of their rights; prosecutors must move according to court guidelines; defendants may invoke their rights throughout the process. No credible evidence exists that the invocation of these rights hinders criminal prosecutions to any substantial degree, but they make the process highly legalistic, difficult for victims to comprehend, and frustrating to many a police officer and prosecutor.[50] Until the 1960s, many of these rights were routinely violated in many state courts; they were vigorously extended by the U.S. Supreme Court during the tenure of Chief Justice Earl Warren, but at the cost of politicizing criminal procedure as never before. Opponents of extending these rights to all accused persons have made concerted efforts in Congress to repeal the exclusionary rule, by which evidence obtained in a procedurally faulty manner cannot be used against a defendant. Free lawyers for indigent defendants never became a popular program. Court actions and large appropriations have been required to keep prison conditions humane enough to avoid violation of the "cruel and unusual punishment" clause of the Eighth Amendment to the Constitution.

50. Thomas Y. Davies, "A Hard Look at What We Know (and Still Need to Learn) About the 'Costs' of the Exclusionary Rule: The NIJ Study and Other Studies of 'Lost' Arrests," *American Bar Foundation Research Journal 1983* (1983), pp. 611–690; Peter F. Nardulli, "The Societal Cost of the Exclusionary Rule: An Empirical Assessment," *American Bar Foundation Research Journal 1983* (1983), pp. 585–610; Craig D. Uchida and Timothy S. Bynum, "Search Warrants, Motions to Suppress, and 'Lost Cases': The Effects of the Exclusionary Rule in Seven Jurisdictions," *Journal of Criminal Law & Criminology* 81 (1991), pp. 1034–1066.

An Example of the Criminal Justice Process in Action

I shall illustrate the ways in which these characteristics affect the processing of alleged offenders with the example of an armed robber in Chicago, a metropolitan area where the criminal justice system has been studied extensively.[51]

Most robbers who intimidate their victims by displaying their weapon are eventually caught, although they may make several heists before the police arrest them.[52] Because they confront their victims, they are more easily identified than burglars. They often make mistakes and are not good calculators of their odds of success. As criminologist Bruce Jackson has observed: "Most criminals I know are people who screw up a lot; they figure the odds badly. They find themselves in positions they would rather not be in, they deal with people they don't like or trust very much, and they measure life not so much by success as by avoidance of failure."[53] Thus ordinary robbers are caught as they try to sell their loot, use the stolen money, or brag about their feats to someone who then turns them in.

Which police force pursues the robber depends on the site of the robbery. If the robbery occurs in the city of Chicago, Chicago police will respond to the call; they are professional, experienced, and possess many high-tech devices to assist them in apprehending robbers. If, however, the robbery occurs in a low-income suburb like Ford Heights, a small, poorly trained, and poorly equipped police department will handle the case. If the victim is a bank, the Federal Bureau of Investigation will be called, because bank robbery is a federal crime. If, however, the target is a liquor store, a grocery, or just an ordinary citizen, the offense is a state crime and only city police are involved.

How vigorously police pursue a robber depends on the demands being made on their resources. If robberies are attracting much attention because of media reports, police will make greater efforts. If, however, they are being called upon to crack down on gang violence or drug dealing, it is likely that they will devote less time to a robbery. At any given time, police in one

51. James Eisenstein and Herbert Jacob, *Felony Justice: An Organizational Analysis of Criminal Courts* (Boston: Little, Brown, 1977); Peter F. Nardulli, *The Courtroom Elite: An Organizational Perspective on Criminal Justice* (Cambridge, Mass.: Ballinger, 1978); Peter M. Manikas, Mindy S. Trossman, and Jack C. Doppelt, *Crime and Criminal Justice in Cook County: A Report of the Criminal Justice Project* (Chicago: Criminal Justice Project of Cook County, 1989). I am using the masculine form to refer generally to robbers, who can, of course, be male or female.

52. John E. Conklin, *Robbery and the Criminal Justice System* (Philadelphia: J. B. Lippincott, 1972).

53. Bruce Jackson, *Law and Disorder: Criminal Justice in America* (Urbana: University of Illinois Press, 1984), p. 19.

community may be targeting armed robbers while those in a neighboring community may be focusing their efforts on garage break-ins.

Chicago is immense, with an area of 228 square miles in the central city alone and more than six million inhabitants in the metropolitan area. While most people stay in their own or nearby neighborhoods, it is easy for criminals to travel to distant communities to commit their crimes. The police have little contact with most of the inhabitants, as they patrol their beats mostly by car. They have no way of keeping track of the comings and goings of outsiders. Thus solving any particular robbery depends as much on mistakes made by the offender as skilled detective work by the police; many arrests come from the police being in the right place at the right time or taking advantage of the miscues most robbers make, such as coming back to the same place to rob another victim. Sometimes local residents also provide tips, but in many neighborhoods police do not routinely get cooperation from residents.

When the police make an arrest, their next steps depend upon the age of their prisoner. If he is under the age of 16, he may be handled as a juvenile, although if in his early teens and facing an armed robbery charge in Chicago, he would be handled as an adult despite his youth. If the prisoner is an adult, the police take the suspect to their station house. At the time of his arrest, they read him his Miranda rights which inform him of his right to call an attorney, to have a public defender if he cannot hire his own lawyer, and to refuse to answer the police officer's questions (the name Miranda stemming from the Supreme Court case establishing these rights). Most defendants, however, cooperate with the police to some extent, and many confess to their crimes. If the police feel they have enough evidence to charge their prisoner, they contact the prosecutor who works at the police station and who supervises arrests in that area. Then, within twenty-four hours of the arrest, the police take the prisoner to a courtroom where a judge informs him of the charges and sets conditions for release while the case is pending.

If the defendant cannot afford his own attorney—and most cannot—the judge assigns a public defender to the case in Chicago. The public defender works for a large government office specializing in criminal defense. In many other cities, the judge assigns a private attorney to defend the accused and the county pays the bill.

Which prosecutors handle the case and before which court again depends on the offense that is charged. If it is a bank robbery, the U.S. Attorney handles the case before the Federal District Court of Northern Illinois. If the robber held up a liquor store, he will be prosecuted by the Cook County State's Attorney before the Circuit Court of Cook County (a state court despite its name). If the robber held up both a bank and a liquor store (on successive nights), police may send him either to the federal prosecutor and the Federal District Court or to the state prosecutor and the Circuit Court of Cook County. The potential penalties facing the robber are substantially different in the two courts.

Whatever the court, the case will be on hiatus for several weeks. Prosecutors and defense attorneys use some of that time to prepare the case by interviewing witnesses, reviewing the physical evidence (for example, the loot that was in the possession of the defendant), and pursuing preliminary legal actions. One of the most important of these for the defendant is an attempt to discredit whatever evidence the prosecutors possess by claiming that it was seized through an illegal search or obtained through illegal interrogation. If the police, for instance, happened upon the stolen property while looking in the trunk of the defendant's car without his permission as he was being given a speeding ticket, the defendant's attorney may petition to keep this evidence out of court because it was seized in violation of the Fourth Amendment's prohibition of unreasonable searches and seizures. In fact, however, such motions are relatively uncommon in robbery cases, which rely more on witness testimony than on physical evidence, and they rarely succeed. A study in seven U.S. cities in the mid-1980s showed that only 1.5 percent of all defendants were freed as the result of such a motion.[54]

During the interval between arrest and trial, preliminary proceedings also occur. In the Cook County Circuit Court defendants like this one are brought to court for a preliminary hearing at which a judge must decide whether there is sufficient evidence to meet the "probable cause" standard for holding a defendant. Then a grand jury of twenty-five or so citizens selected from voting lists hears evidence presented by prosecutors and votes whether or not to issue a felony indictment. The grand jury usually does the prosecutor's bidding, but it gives a veneer of public participation to the process of deciding which offenders to charge and with which offenses. The indictment leads to another arraignment at which a judge informs the defendant of the new charges against him and again sets bail. This procedure is more streamlined in the federal courts.

As the trial date draws near, the prosecutor and defense attorneys (sometimes in the presence of the judge to whom the case is assigned) meet to discuss the case and a possible guilty plea.[55] The meeting may occur at the initiative of the defense attorney, who asks the prosecutor what penalty the

54. Uchida and Bynum, supra note 50.

55. Eisenstein and Jacob, supra note 51; James Eisenstein, Roy B. Flemming, and Peter Nardulli, *The Contours of Justice: Communities and Their Courts* (Boston: Little, Brown, 1987); Lief H. Carter, *The Limits of Order* (Lexington, Mass.: Lexington Books, 1974); Milton Heumann, *Plea Bargaining: The Experiences of Prosecutors, Judges, and Defense Attorneys* (Chicago: University of Chicago Press, 1977, 1978).

prosecutor will recommend if his client pleads guilty. At other times, the prosecutor initiates the meeting with a specific offer: if the defendant pleads guilty to a specified offense, the prosecutor will recommend a particular sentence. The sentence that the prosecutor offers depends on such matters as the amount of leeway permitted by the criminal code for the offenses charged, the number of different charges facing the defendant, his prior criminal record, the amount of harm incurred during the crime, and the office's plea bargaining policy. Almost every charged offense may be replaced by a slightly less serious "included" offense. For instance, an armed robbery may be replaced by a simple robbery or by an *attempted* armed robbery. However, in many cases, the robber has also been accused of committing other crimes for which the penalty is lighter. The many potential deals which the prosecutor may offer the defendant include sentencing on one of the less serious offenses, allowing the defendant to serve his prison time on all offenses concurrently rather than consecutively, overlooking a prior criminal record so that the defendant does not receive the enhanced penalty given to habitual criminals, recommending a sentence at the low end of the scale of usual penalties, endorsing probation rather than incarceration, and suspending the sentence entirely.

Approximately 90 percent of all defendants plead guilty before a trial begins.[56] However, the court receives the guilty plea in an open session at which the defendant affirms that he is making the plea voluntarily and the prosecutor stipulates the evidence that would have been presented at trial to justify a conviction. The judge may reject the change in the charges that the prosecutor recommends but rarely does so. However, sentencing usually is delayed until further information about the defendant is collected. The judge may impose a harsher or more lenient sentence than the one recommended by the prosecutor, but most of the time the sentence is close to the one agreed upon.

Only about 10 percent of charges like the one we have been considering go to a full trial in most jurisdictions in the United States. About half of those are heard by a jury while the remainder (at the option of the defendant) are heard by a judge alone. Once begun, such trials run without interruption until completed. Trials consider both documentary and oral testimony, but most of the testimony is oral, with witnesses describing what they saw and heard during the robbery and the apprehension of the defendant. The prosecutor must prove the defendant's guilt beyond a reasonable doubt. If a jury hears the case, conviction in Chicago requires a unanimous vote of the twelve jurors (in some places it is fewer) who deliberate outside the presence of the

56. Barbara Boland, Catherine H. Conly, Paul Mahanna, Lynn Warner, and Ronald Sones, *The Prosecution of Felony Arrests, 1987* (Washington, D.C.: U.S. Department of Justice, Bureau of Justice Statistics, August 1990).

judge. Upon conviction, the judge pronounces a sentence after gaining additional information on the defendant.

Defendants convicted after a trial usually receive somewhat harsher sentences than those who pleaded guilty because the court takes the view that the defendant showed no remorse or responsibility for his acts.[57] On the other hand, about one-third of those who go to trial win an acquittal.[58] These outcomes reflect that fact that defendants who face weak evidence of their guilt are more likely to choose a trial if the charges are not dismissed through pretrial negotiations with the prosecutor.

If the defendant is sentenced to a prison term, the convicted criminal goes to a facility run by the level of government in whose court he was convicted. Those convicted in a federal court go to a federal prison operated by the Bureau of Prisons in the Department of Justice. Those convicted in state courts go to a state penitentiary if their sentence exceeds one year. How long an armed robber serves in prison depends not only on the sentence he was given but also on the rules of the particular prison system which he enters and the subsequent crowding of its facilities. Most prisons award time for good behavior such as staying out of trouble, volunteering for unpleasant work, and the like. The more "good" time a prisoner accumulates, the earlier his release. Increasingly, however, states and the federal government have enacted mandatory sentence laws which require that the time imposed by the judge be served fully before the prisoner is released. Most armed robbers like the one we have considered are likely to spend considerably more than four years in prison.[59]

What happens to persons while serving prison terms depends upon the programs available for their prisons. Where the public and legislature feel particularly punitive, prisons have few educational or therapy programs to modify the behavior of their inmates; doing time is just that. Where the public and legislatures feel less punitive and where public funds are available, a large array of rehabilitative programs may be available to prepare inmates for their return to the streets. However, past experience has shown that such programs do not reduce recidivism substantially.[60] Many first-time inmates

57. Eisenstein and Jacob, supra note 51, pp. 269–271; Eisenstein, Flemming, and Nardulli, supra note 55, p. 252.

58. Boland et al., supra note 56.

59. Patrick A. Langan, Craig A. Perkins, and Jan M. Chaiken, "Felony Sentences in the United States, 1990," *Bulletin* (Washington, D.C.: U.S. Department of Justice, Bureau of Justice Statistics), Sept. 1994, p. 8.

60. Robert Martinson, "What Works—Questions and Answers About Prison Reform," *The Public Interest* (Spring 1974), pp. 22–54. A slightly more conservative conclusion is that we do not know whether anything works. See Susan E. Martin, Lee B. Sechrest, and Robin Redner (eds.), *New Directions in the Rehabilitation of Criminal Offenders* (Washington, D.C.: National Academy Press, 1981).

return to prison for another offense after their release because they go back to the same neighborhood and the same family situation, but with fewer legitimate employment opportunities than before because many employers will not hire ex-convicts. Until they become too old to commit most crimes, many repeat their trip through the criminal justice process.

Structure, Process, and Results

The robbery case illustrates some of the consequences of the peculiar structure of the criminal justice system in the United States. The fragmentation of the process, its politicization, and its roots in individualism leave clear footprints at each stage of the process. They easily lead to perceptions of failure.

At each stage, a defendant faces different sets of officials who have no structural relation to those encountered before. The city police turn him over to a county or federal prosecutor. They, in turn, place his fate in the hands of a judge who is organizationally autonomous from both the police and prosecutor. If convicted and sentenced to prison, a new set of officials is encountered. What makes the process function at all is that these separate officials become dependent upon one another as they work together; they therefore learn to accommodate one another to at least some degree. Prosecutors, for instance, depend upon the police for most of the evidence they use to convict defendants. Police depend upon prosecutors to make their arrests stick. Consequently, although police and prosecutors often spar with one another, they also signal each other about their mutual needs. Police let prosecutors know what evidence they are likely to present and in what categories of crime they need to make frequent arrests. Prosecutors in turn signal to the police what kinds of evidence they need to charge the suspect rather than release him and which charges they will take seriously and which they will dismiss as frivolous. Many of these understandings escape written protocols; they remain oral understandings that are conveyed among these officials through their daily contact with each other.

The same kind of accommodation occurs among prosecutors, defense counsel, and judges, who in many jurisdictions form an informal work group in which these participants work collaboratively rather than adversarially.[61] Prosecutors rely upon defense counsel to convince their clients to accept guilty pleas; defense counsel depend upon prosecutors to obtain relatively favorable outcomes for their clients. Judges count on plea agreements between prosecutors and defense counsel to help them dispose of their burgeoning dockets. Each of these three participants leans upon the others to

---

61. Eisenstein and Jacob, supra note 51; Eisenstein, Flemming, and Nardulli, supra note 55.

help reduce the uncertainty of outcomes and to expedite the processing of cases. The resulting accommodations may be thought of as "going rates," which are informal understandings about the severity of punishment that will be assigned to particular degrees of criminal conduct.[62] Individual cases may occasionally veer off these benchmarks because of idiosyncratic facts, but on the whole they provide a guideline that coordinates action between officials who work with one another on a daily basis.

The mutual accommodation that occurs in criminal courtrooms takes place in an adversarial stage setting. Prosecutor and defense counsel pose as adversaries and sometimes that posture reflects reality. However, perhaps as often the pose disguises collaboration between the two. Moreover, the judge is not the completely disinterested party that formal legal theory in the United States demands, for the judge *is* interested in moving cases off the docket and guilty pleas are the most expeditious process for doing so.

Another striking feature of the process is the influence exercised by the defense over the process, in part owing to the individualistic ideology so widespread in the United States. The criminal justice process is characterized by the rights accruing to defendants; however, they must be asserted by the defendant or his counsel to become operative. It is the defendant who chooses whether to forego a trial and plead guilty, and it is the defendant who, if he chooses a trial, opts for a jury or bench trial.

The defendant's influence is in part the consequence of the adversarial pose of the proceedings. Once a defendant has reached court, most decisions about the conduct of the case are made by the defense attorney and the prosecutor rather than the judge. It is they who determine the depth of the investigation into the crime and often the outcome of the case. Judges may veto a plea agreement, but they normally feel bound by it because it accommodates understandings that maintain a smooth flow of business in their courtroom.

Because defense attorneys and prosecutors control the process, the extent of resources available to them is very important. Most defendants do not have money to hire their own lawyer; as we have already noted, their attorney is hired by the state to represent indigents. In some jurisdictions such attorneys are paid approximately the same as prosecutors, but they cannot draw on police investigative resources in the same way that prosecutors do.[63] Both public defenders and prosecutors typically have very heavy caseloads, with the result that they invest little time in preparing individual cases. Defendants

62. Eisenstein, Flemming, and Nardulli, supra note 55.

63. Roger A. Hanson, Brian J. Ostrom, William E. Hewitt, and Christopher Lombardias, *Indigent Defenders Get the Job Done and Done Well* (Williamsburg, Va.: National Center for State Courts, 1992).

with greater resources—such as stockbrokers accused of security fraud, individuals accused of organized crime, or wealthy persons accused of ordinary crimes—can obtain more thorough investigations and mount a more aggressive defense strategy which may match or exceed those of the prosecutor.[64] The greater resources of such defendants may be employed at a trial, but they may also be deployed in informal negotiations with prosecutors in order to negotiate a milder punishment than other defendants would receive.

There is little accommodation of this sort between courts and prisons because their officials experience little interdependence and have very little contact with one another. Judges occasionally tour prisons, and prisons sometimes send judges information on the amount of space that is available for additional prisoners. In individual cases, prison (or parole) authorities may consult the judge or court that sentenced a particular prisoner before releasing him on parole, but that is unusual since court officials are unlikely to have a vivid recollection of a particular felon several years after he was sentenced. Thus, the organizational distance between courts and prisons is usually a real chasm that remains unbridged by informal arrangements.

The decentralization, fragmentation, and furtive collaboration of this process have real effects on outcomes. Unofficial accommodations sometimes conflict with publicly proclaimed policy and are rarely openly acknowledged. Outsiders, such as victims, are excluded because they might block the accommodations that prosecutors, defense counsel, and judges find useful. Hence, substantial suspicion of the process and misunderstanding arises among the general public and crime victims who often do not understand what has happened. However, those officials in separate segments of the criminal justice process who do not collaborate informally often experience frustration and antagonism precisely because they lack procedures to overcome conflicting intentions and goals.

In addition, the potential for conflict between autonomous prosecutors, police, and prison officials may be exacerbated by electoral and partisan rivalries. In Chicago during a portion of the 1980s, for instance, the city police were under the control of Democratic mayors, the state's attorney was a Republican who wanted to become mayor, and the governor (who was responsible for state prisons) was a Republican who often wanted the mayor's legislative support for his projects. At the same time, the U.S. Attorney was a Republican who was quite happy to embarrass the city's Democrats with charges of judicial corruption. Under such circumstances, the politics of crime control become very complicated.

---

64. The most notorious example of that advantage occurred in the trial of O. J. Simpson for the murder of his ex-wife and an acquaintance of hers.

The example of the Chicago robber also highlights the ways in which the several segments of the criminal justice process respond to their own constituency pressures. Senior police officials examine their crime statistics and allocate their officers and investigative staffs according to where crimes are being reported and where citizens and politicians are pressuring them for more coverage. In Chicago and other cities, aldermen often relay citizen concerns about crime to the police, and police officials may find it necessary to respond to such concerns, even if the problem is not as serious in the alderman's ward as in other parts of the city. Prosecutors respond to different pressures. They must meet statutory deadlines in processing cases or dismiss them; such dismissals look bad in the media, and prosecutors therefore are under continuing pressure to move cases to disposition. Most of the work of the prosecutor's office occurs in obscurity; so many crimes occur in cities like Chicago that they are not even listed in the newspaper, and no one outside the prosecutor's office, the defense counsel, and the accused and their relatives and friends keeps track of individual cases. However, when especially brutal crimes come to the prosecutor, the media gives those cases special attention. Any other case publicized by the media also receives special treatment. Thus the prosecutor's priority list does not necessarily reflect the concerns of the police.

When judges sentence convicted offenders, they respond to the concerns of legislatures (which specify the range of permissible punishments), to the agreements reached between prosecutors and defense counsel in plea bargains, to the recommendations of prosecutors, and to their own perceptions of community standards of the severity of crimes. One result is that the informal going rates vary from place to place. Crimes which appear routine in Chicago may be considered horrendous in a small town where prosecutor, defense counsel, and judge may agree that a much harsher sentence is justified. Even in a single state no one supervises all the autonomous agencies to produce uniformity or to establish similar priorities.

The very obscurity of the processing of such routine crimes contributes to the politicization of the criminal justice process in the United States. Although few normal crimes and their punishment are in the news, the crimes themselves become part of the background of urban life that people experience. Small clusters of people in the neighborhood of a crime know about them through the victim's relatives, friends, and neighbors. Not many of these people, however, learn about the apprehension of suspects or their punishment. Thus the criminal event is known to the victim and relatives, friends, and neighbors, but the police arrest of a suspect or the punishment a court gives to the convicted offender often is not publicized. Consequently, large numbers of citizens perceive a low level of public safety, and they think the crime problem has become more severe in their neighborhood with each passing year. Given the lack of publicity that attends most work of police and courts, it is understandable that about two-thirds of all respondents in national surveys believe that too little money is spent to "halt the rising crime rate."[65] Such opinions are fodder for the campaigns of elected officials who wish to appear to be tough on crime.

Yet the strong streak of individualism also displays itself here. While most people want something done about crime, many remain fearful of big government. Thus a majority as large as that which endorsed tough measures against crime at the same time opposed permitting police to search a home without a warrant. Moreover, most Americans disapprove of wiretapping.[66] Such responses reflect the concern of respondents about crime, on the one hand, but the widespread distrust of intrusive government, on the other. Constitutional rights remain dear to Americans even in the face of a perceived inability to control crime. When faced with the specter of both big government and personal crime, Americans are uncertain which they should fear more.

Civil Disputes: Ordinary People, Big Business, and Government

Courts and law not only impose social control in criminal incidents; they also intervene in a vast number of disputes that characterize everyday social life. Disagreements about obligations, differences between expected and achieved results, relationships which sour, and accidents may happen to anyone. It is a fundamental obligation of government to keep these disputes from boiling over into violence and to establish conditions under which social and economic endeavors may flourish. One of the functions of law is to maintain or bring order to these situations.

THE EXTENT OF LITIGATION IN THE UNITED STATES

A model of disputing that has gained wide acceptance in sociolegal scholarship suggests that disputes follow a trajectory from harm to confrontation.[67] When an event causes an injury or harm, the victims may feel aggrieved and blame someone else. They may then make a claim against that other party

---

65. Flanagan and Maguire, supra note 30, p. 187. Note that fear of crime is lower in rural areas even though rural areas have fewer and less well trained police forces. However, crime rates are lower and people can keep track of local happenings in small rural communities. Thus it is likely that they know about arrests and convictions as well as about crime.

66. Ibid., pp. 200–201, 208–209.

67. William L. F. Felstiner, Richard L. Abel, and Austin Sarat, "The Emergence and Transformation of Disputes: Naming, Blaming, Claiming . . .," Law & Society Review 15 (1980–81), pp. 631–654.

for restitution or compensation. If the claim is denied, the dispute is then processed in one of several ways: it may be negotiated, mediated, submitted to arbitration, or sent to court for adjudication. During any of these processes, however, the claimant may decide to withdraw the claim. None of these processes necessarily resolve the dispute; disputes often survive long after a decision has been made in favor of one party or the other. The dispute may erupt many months later in a slightly different context, or it may be carried to a different forum for further processing. It requires satisfaction or exhaustion to end disputes.

Considerable disagreement exists over whether people in the United States are particularly disputatious. A large body of opinion holds that Americans are much more likely to dispute than in earlier eras and that they are more likely to engage in disputes than many people who live elsewhere. The evidence for this assertion comes partly from the huge sums of money which are sometimes sought in product liability and medical malpractice suits, from suits in which children seek a divorce from their parents, and from statistics which suggest that the number of lawsuits has grown swiftly over the past several decades.[68]

Closer examination of this evidence, however, casts considerable doubt on this picture of contemporary Americans. First, none of the evidence directly counts the disputes; it enumerates only lawsuits in courts. No comprehensive statistics covering all disputes exist for the past or the present. The number of lawsuits on a per capita basis may not be higher now than it was a century ago, although the character of claims has changed.[69]

Moreover, the amounts of money involved in ordinary suits are not particularly large. Using lawyers' perceptions of the monetary stakes in suits they were handling, Kritzer found the median stake in 1978 to be $4,500 in state court cases and $15,000 for those in federal courts.[70] When we look at actual damages obtained rather than those claimed, we find that the median settlement or judgment in state courts was only $3,500 in state courts and $6,500 in federal courts.[71] The larger amount sought at the time that lawsuits are filed is an attention-drawing device, not an indication of what is expected. Some litigants file suits for millions of dollars, but these reflect extraordinary situations. Other cases, such as those of children seeking a divorce from

---

68. Cf. Marc Galanter, ''Reading the Landscape of Disputes: What We Know and Don't Know (and Think We Know) About Our Allegedly Contentious and Litigious Society,'' *UCLA Law Review* 31 (1983), pp. 4–71.

69. Wayne V. McIntosh, *The Appeal of Civil Law: A Political-Social Analysis of Litigation* (Urbana: University of Illinois Press, 1990).

70. Herbert M. Kritzer, *The Justice Broker: Lawyers and Ordinary Litigation* (New York: Oxford University Press, 1990), p. 31. These data exclude cases in small claims courts.

71. Ibid., p. 136.

parents, push the outer boundaries of law, but they also involve quite special circumstances, such as where a child has been raised for many years by foster parents or where the fact that a child was mistaken for another at birth became known only many years later.[72]

Thus, we do not know with any certainty that disputing or litigating is more frequent or intense now in the United States than in the past. As we shall see in the following chapters, the same difficulties also make it impossible to judge whether Americans dispute more frequently than the English, the French, the Germans, or the Japanese. It may be, however, that Americans use their courts more often or in different ways than do disputants in other countries.

CULTURAL AND STRUCTURAL CORRELATES OF DISPUTES AND LITIGATION

Many scholars have pointed to widespread beliefs as well as structural characteristics in a society as correlates of disputing. Four may be of particular importance in the United States: widely held theories of causality, rights consciousness, the availability of disputing forums, and patterns of relationships.

If there is a difference in disputing between Americans in the 1990s and those in the 1850s, it may be partly due to differences in ideas about causality. Fate was more often blamed for misfortunes then. If a physician failed to heal a patient, the physician was not sued, because the practice of medicine at best had a high rate of failure. Deaths from pneumonia were not ascribed to smoking or working with hazardous materials. Workplace accidents were not attributed to the faulty design of equipment. Injuries caused in such situations became compensable as the understanding of their causes improved and as it became evident that prohibiting compensation often simply shifted their cost upon the poor. Workplace accidents became the object of safety legislation and many compensation schemes at the end of the nineteenth century. Medical malpractice, however, did not reach its heyday until the 1970s, by which time the presumption was that doctors had a responsibility to heal the ill, and, if they did not, something may have gone wrong.[73]

Another set of factors leading to disputes and litigation is rights consciousness. Assessing blame does not depend only on causal theories; it also hinges on the belief that one has a right to be free of harm and that others may not impose harm with legal impunity.[74] These ideas appear to have a

72. *New York Times*, Aug. 19, 1993, Sec. 4, p. E1.

73. Lawrence M. Friedman, *A History of American Law* (New York: Simon and Schuster, 1973), pp. 475–487, 685.

74. Lawrence M. Friedman, *The Republic of Choice* (Cambridge: Harvard University Press, 1990), p. 96.

wide currency in the United States. One often hears about "rights" associated with such concepts as property, privacy, parenthood, and procedure. When people believe that their legal rights have been violated, they seek vindication in private forums or in the courts. Such legal consciousness is widely thought to encourage litigation in the United States; particularly in the domain of tort liability, such as auto accidents, medical malpractice, and faulty products, Americans appear to expect those who do harm to accept responsibility whether it be on the road or in the medicine cabinet.[75] However, in some instances legal consciousness in the United States leads to less litigation than elsewhere. This is perhaps most apparent in grievances about job terminations. Terminations in the United States routinely occur with cruel swiftness—the employee is fired without warning and immediately escorted from the work place. However, until recently jobs were not associated with rights and almost none of the grievances aroused by such incidents went to court. Neither law nor custom routinely provided employees in the United States rights to their positions unless they were working under a union contract or other special arrangement. They could be fired at the employer's whim without recourse. However, the Age Discrimination in Employment Act of 1967, which made it illegal to discriminate on the basis of age, has been slowly recognized as a potential weapon by employees to recover damages, if not the job itself. Especially during the recession of 1989–92, when a large number of people were let go, an increasing number of employment termination grievances went to court.[76]

The relative absence of litigation over job security in the United States illustrates another correlate of disputing and litigation: the role of institutional structures in providing an arena to process conflicts. Not only does the substantive law in the United States not protect job tenure in most instances; there also are no special tribunals to handle work place disputes. Even when workers wish to make a claim against their employer, they must use the general jurisdiction courts or initiate an administrative appeal within one of several agencies that might have jurisdiction such as the Equal Employment Opportunity Commission (EEOC) or the National Labor Relations Board (NLRB). Workers in Germany are protected by an elaborate set of rules, and a set of tribunals routinely handles the many disputes that arise from job terminations. Those tribunals have a distinctive tripartite structure and are especially hospitable to such disputes.[77] In general, the United States has a

75. Lawrence W. Friedman, "The Six Million Dollar Man: Litigation and Rights Consciousness in Modern America," *Maryland Law Review* 39 (1980), pp. 661–677.

76. *New York Times*, Dec. 12, 1993, p. 1.

77. Erhard Blankenburg, "Task Contingencies and National Administrative Culture as Determinants for Labour Market Administration," typescript, March 1978.

relatively meager set of alternative forums for processing routine disputes; if many go to court, it is partly because no attractive alternatives exist.

Another institutional factor which we have already described is the very large size of the legal profession and its monopoly over court services. Lawyers are easy to find although it may be difficult to locate one with appropriate skills and an affordable rate schedule. Lawyers also play a prominent role in many of the alternative dispute processing arenas that have in recent years developed such as divorce mediation, commercial arbitration, and labor mediation. The ubiquitous presence of lawyers tends to push alternative processes into formalistic and legalistic procedures which resemble courts.

Finally, the patterns of relationship in the United States affect disputing. The closer the relationship, the more likely it is that claims either are not made or are resolved informally.[78] Americans, however, are much more dependent on people whom they scarcely know than they were in the past. In such mundane activities as grocery shopping, corporate entities now operate a supermarket rather than a neighborhood grocer, butcher, baker, or general store merchant who supplied earlier generations and who was personally known to his customers. At the work place, most people are now employed by large corporations rather than by bosses with whom they could build a relationship, if not a friendship. Total strangers cause many injuries in the context of automobile accidents. Even many family relationships are strained by high geographic mobility which leads adult children, parents, uncles, aunts, and cousins to live many miles from each other, and by a high divorce rate which isolates many family members. While it is difficult to estimate how different people in the United States are from those of other advanced industrial societies, many observers believe that these relationships are more distant in the United States than elsewhere where the market place remains dominated by small enterprises or by large enterprises which emphasize close, long-term relationships with workers or customers.

OUT-OF-COURT NEGOTIATIONS

In response to what is perceived as a rising tide of litigation stemming from unresolved claims, a concerted effort has been made since the 1970s to establish more alternatives to litigation.[79] While the United States has fewer institutionalized settings for nonjudicial proceedings than many other countries, a great deal of negotiating activity occurs in most disputes before they

78. William L. F. Felstiner, "Influences of Social Organization on Dispute Processing," *Law & Society Review* 9 (1974), pp. 63–94.

79. Robert T. Roper, "The Propensity to Litigate in State Trial Courts, 1981–1984, 1984–1985," *Justice System Journal* 11 (1986), pp. 262–281.

proceed to trial. Indeed, the vast majority of cases filed in court are settled by negotiation and never come to trial.

Negotiations that resolve disputes take place in private and thus are never counted. However, the number of settled suits suggests that negotiations thrive in the United States. This is true for situations involving closely related parties and those involving strangers; fewer than 10 percent of all cases filed in court go to trial.[80] The percentage of settled cases in which disputants know each other (as in divorce) and in which the disputants are strangers (as in automobile accidents) appear to be quite similar. Thus, negotiations are the dominant mode of decision making for disputes in the United States.

Negotiations occur in many settings. Probably the largest number of negotiations occur between principals of the dispute with no outsider present. Much of the negotiating in divorces takes place around kitchen tables between the spouses; most complaints between consumers and stores are straightened out at customer service counters or over the telephone; even in automobile accident cases, many claims are negotiated directly between the injured party and an insurance company.[81]

When principals to a dispute seek assistance in the United States, they typically turn to attorneys, both for negotiations that take place out of court and for those occurring in court settings. In addition to negotiations, other kinds of third-party interventions have become more common in the United States. One of these is mediation, where a neutral third party is chosen by the disputants to facilitate negotiations. Mediation has a long history in union-management disputes in the United States. Since the 1970s, it has also spread to domestic disputes and such everyday issues as landlord-tenant disputes, disagreements between neighbors, and unresolved disputes between customer and merchants.[82] One indicator of the rise of mediation is the growth of organizations like the Academy of Family Mediators, which in the early 1990s was growing at a rate of more than 20 percent per year and by 1993 had more than 2,000 members, and the Society for Professionals in Dispute Resolution, which in 1993 had a membership of 3,000.[83] Many members of

80. Kritzer, supra note 70, p. 73.

81. Herbert Jacob, "The Elusive Shadow of the Law," *Law & Society Review* 26 (1992), pp. 565–590. Jack Ladinsky and Charles Susmilch, "Community Factors in the Brokerage of Consumer Product and Service Problems, 1983," Madison, Wisc., University of Wisconsin Disputes Processing Research Program, Working Paper 1983–14. H. Laurence Ross, *Settled Out of Court: The Social Process of Insurance Claims Adjustment* (Chicago: Aldine, 1970).

82. Peter S. Adler, "The Future of Alternative Dispute Resolution: Reflections on ADR as a Social Movement," in Sally Engle Merry and Neal Milner (eds.), *The Possibility of Popular Justice: A Case Study of Community Mediation in the United States* (Ann Arbor: University of Michigan Press, 1993), pp. 67–88.

83. Private communication, Executive Office, Academy of Family Mediators and Executive Office, Society for Professionals in Dispute Resolution.

these organizations are attorneys. A large number of community mediation services has also appeared which in both small and large cities process thousands of disputes every year.[84] In some places, use of such mediation services is required before a dispute can be brought to trial.[85] Some mediation services involve volunteers lacking any particular professional training; others utilize social workers or lawyers.

Arbitration services also involve neutral third parties selected by the disputants.[86] Whereas in mediation, the third party simply facilitates negotiations, in arbitration the third party decides the outcome of the dispute. The findings of arbitrators are usually enforceable in a further court proceeding. Arbitration is very common in the United States in work place disputes where workers have a collective bargaining contract. Arbitration is also common in disputes between commercial buyers and sellers; it is routinely specified in agreements that customers sign when they agree to have a brokerage firm buy or sell stocks and bonds for them and when they sign insurance contracts. No register of arbitration proceedings exists and therefore no count is available. However, like court-mandated mediation, court-annexed arbitration is used more frequently to divert cases away from adjudication by a court trial. Attorneys often serve as arbitrators.

COURT PROCEEDINGS IN CIVIL CASES

As with the criminal justice process, federalism complicates civil proceedings. Civil cases may be brought to state or federal courts, depending on the character and size of the claims, but state courts handle the majority.

Exactly what may be claimed depends upon the statutes and their interpretation by courts in previous cases. Each state's laws specify what remedies may be claimed, the kind of proof required, and the procedures that must be followed. The laws of the fifty states and those of the federal government have many similarities, but sometimes the differences are crucial to potential litigants. The harmonization of procedural and substantive law among the states has been promoted by private associations of lawyers such as the National Conference of Commissioners on Uniform State Laws, which drafts model codes that form the basis of much state legislation, and the American Law Institute, which issues "restatements" of law that attempt to provide authoritative interpretations of the law. However, many details of the law and of legal procedure vary from state to state and from state courts to federal courts.

84. Adler, supra note 82.

85. Craig A. McEwen, Lynn Mather, and Richard J. Maiman, "Lawyers, Mediation, and the Management of Divorce Practice," *Law & Society Review* 28 (1994), p. 153, note 6.

86. Raymond Broderick, "Court-annexed Compulsory Arbitration: It Works," *Judicature* 72 (1989), pp. 217–225.

People may file lawsuits without legal representation (so-called pro se suits), but usually only in simple divorce cases or in cases involving very small amounts of money. Except in small claims courts, which are designed to be used without attorney assistance, it is difficult for nonlawyers to master the necessary forms and navigate the deadlines and procedural requirements. Courts generally give little assistance to the unrepresented litigants. Therefore, attorneys usually represent plaintiff and defendant. For legal assistance with personal problems, clients go to lawyers working in small firms or by themselves. Such lawyers often are generalists, with minimal resources for researching the client's case.

However, the lawyers helping corporations work in quite different settings than those serving individual clients.[87] They work for the corporation itself as employees in a corporate legal department or work in large law firms retained by a corporation. In either case, the lawyer is likely to be highly specialized, have substantial resources to research the issue, and often is quite familiar with the client's problem because she has worked for the client before. The large law firms that service corporations rarely work for individuals.

In most instances litigants pay their own attorneys. Attorneys taking civil cases may be paid on a contingent fee, flat fee, or hourly rate.[88] Under a contingent fee arrangement, client makes no payment to the attorney unless the claim succeeds; if the attorney wins a settlement or judgment, she normally charges between one-quarter and one-third of the settlement. Contingent fees are most common in tort cases where an injury has been alleged. Other cases are more likely to be financed by a flat fee for which the attorney agrees to do whatever is necessary to obtain a satisfactory outcome or by an hourly fee for the attorney's time. Individual litigants are most likely to retain an attorney on a contingent fee (except in divorce cases); corporations generally pay their attorneys on an hourly basis. Each party to a dispute usually pays for his or her own attorney whether they win or lose the case. Thus, except when the fee is contingent, parties to a dispute risk considerable amounts of money when they retain an attorney; even if they win, the attorney's fee reduces their net gain.

Those too poor to hire an attorney must turn to privately financed legal aid clinics, use the services of a government-supported legal assistance office, or depend on the pro bono free assistance of a private attorney. The coverage of these programs has been spotty at best.[89] Most offices have resources

87. John P. Heinz and Edward O. Laumann, *Chicago Lawyers: The Social Structure of the Bar* (New York: Russell Sage Foundation, 1982).

88. Kritzer, supra note 70, p. 59.

89. Richard L. Abel, *American Lawyers* (New York: Oxford University Press, 1989), pp. 132–34.

sufficient to negotiate cases only for their clients; they generally do not take pro bono cases to trial. Many needs of low-income clients remain unmet because the offices are too distant from clients or because they have insufficient funds to handle the cases that come to them.

Attorneys seek to control every phase of civil litigation. They provide the client with guidance about whether to file a suit, where to file it, how much to demand, and how to proceed with it. Attorneys try to make it difficult to go against their advice. However, in some kinds of personal plight cases, such as divorces, it is not unusual for clients to abandon their attorney and hire another, even though such a move often costs an additional retainer fee.

Many attorneys routinely file complaints in civil courts without intending to take the case to trial. The filing of the case is simply a statement that the claim is to be taken seriously. Once a complaint has been filed, the defendant must respond to it or risk a default judgment. In cases like debt collection and eviction suits, defaults commonly occur; in personal injury cases, they are very rare. After the defendant has answered the complaint, each side collects evidence to be used in a trial or in negotiations. Each side gathers its own documents and witnesses; they also may demand documents from the other side (discovery) and interrogate witnesses from the other side (depositions). In cases involving very large sums of money, thousands of documents may be requested and hundreds of depositions taken. In ordinary cases, however, lawyers spend little time on these or other efforts; Kritzer reports that attorneys spent only a median of nineteen hours on cases in state courts and forty-five hours on cases in federal courts (where the cases are generally more complex); 23 percent of this time was spent on discovery (where it was used), but more than one-third of the cases involved no discovery.[90]

Negotiations may occur during any portion of this process. In many instances private efforts at negotiating the dispute occur before the claimant goes to an attorney. The attorney conducts further negotiations before a trial is scheduled, which may be a date many weeks or months after the original filing. Galanter has called the process "litigotiation."[91] Most negotiations between court filing and trial occur outside the judge's presence. Typically, only those cases which are approaching trial come within the ambit of the court's settlement conference, where intense negotiations, often in the presence of a judge, occur during a one- or two-hour time slot. If the settlement conference fails to produce an agreement, negotiations may continue during the trial. When they succeed, they cut short the formal proceedings.

90. Kritzer, supra note 70, pp. 83, 86, and 92.
91. Marc Galanter, "The Regulatory Function of the Civil Jury," in Robert E. Litan (ed.), *Verdict: Assessing the Civil Jury System* (Washington, D.C.: Brookings Institution, 1993) pp. 61–102.

While this description makes it appear as if attorneys exert considerable effort in negotiating cases, that is generally not true. The majority of cases before state courts (where attorneys file most cases) consume fewer than twenty hours of total effort; this time is spread over many months and includes conferences with the client, telephone calls, correspondence, as well as negotiations with the other party's attorney. Kritzer reports that in 40 percent of cases, attorneys devote fewer than three and a half hours to negotiations; another 20 percent consume between three and a half and five and a half hours. In most cases, there were at most only two rounds of negotiation: an initial offer and counteroffer and a final settlement. Kritzer identified three patterns of negotiations.[92] In some cases, attorneys seek maximum results for their client requiring serious concessions from their adversary; these rarely occur in ordinary cases as indicated by the infrequency of prolonged negotiations. A second type is "appropriate-result, consensus oriented," in which attorneys agree fairly readily on liability issues and then seek an appropriate settlement on damages based on a consensus of what the situation warrants. Such negotiations may take longer since more information needs to be communicated in order to reach a consensus. A third type of negotiation by attorneys is pro forma, in which attorneys go through the ritual of negotiations but without really bargaining; typically, a demand is made and an acceptable offer follows. Pro forma negotiations occur in categories for which there is a "going rate" of compensation that is widely recognized, such as many personal injury cases where the claims are relatively small.

Attorney control of clients simplifies negotiations. Attorneys speak the same language (often an informal shorthand) and rarely have an emotional stake in their cases. Clients, on the other hand, often speak past each other; they have an emotional as well as a financial stake in the dispute. They also lack much of the information that guides attorneys, especially expectations about what is a "good" settlement. Consequently, clients often make demands which attorneys find unreasonable, and attorneys expend considerable effort in informing such clients about the complexity of the process. Indeed, lawyers may mystify it in order to persuade the client to leave matters in their hands.[93]

The interest of attorneys in settlement is often quite simple: they seek an optimal balance between their fee and the effort they invest. Unlike their clients, they do not want the highest possible settlement because that may involve a high risk of no settlement and may require such a large investment

92. Herbert M. Kritzer, *Let's Make a Deal: Understanding the Negotiation Process in Ordinary Litigation* (Madison: University of Wisconsin Press, 1991), pp. 32, 37, 118–127.

93. Austin Sarat and William L. F. Felstiner, "Law and Strategy in the Divorce Lawyer's Office," *Law & Society Review* 20 (1986), pp. 79–92.

of resources that the net gain for the attorney is not increased. Moreover, the timing of a settlement may be of less concern to attorneys than to their clients, since lawyers are more interested in maintaining a steady cash flow of fees than they are in closing any particular case. Clients, on the other hand, often need the proceeds of a settlement or judgment in order to pay their medical bills or other expenses.

Much conflict between attorneys and their clients has been documented with respect to personal injury cases arising from automobile accidents as well as in other situations.[94] It is not unusual for tension to exist between clients and attorneys over the efforts made by the attorney and his or her success in obtaining a settlement. The more the attorney controls the negotiations, the less the client's sometimes uninformed demands get in the way of settlement.

The few cases that cannot be settled eventually reach the courtroom for trial. Jury trials are available in many civil matters, and in most jurisdictions the majority of tort cases that go to trial are decided by juries.[95] The exception is cases where plaintiffs are corporations rather than individuals; in such cases many attorneys and clients prefer bench trials because they apparently have more confidence in the expertise of the judge and prefer not to worry about the uncertainty of a jury verdict.[96] When juries are used, they decide not only factual issues but also often determine the amount of the judgment. When juries are not used, the judge rules on factual issues and the size of the judgment. Single judges preside over the trials. No reliable count exists of the use of juries in civil cases.

Exactly which court will hear a particular dispute depends on the procedural rules in the jurisdiction. In most states at least two levels of trial courts hear civil cases; one is for minor cases and another for those involving larger amounts of money. The first kind of cases are often heard in a small-claims court, which uses less formal procedures and encourages disputants to appear without an attorney. Trials in such courts generally take little time. Cases involving larger sums of money go to state courts which are generally located in county seats; they employ the full panoply of civil procedure and require considerable investment on the part of the litigants. The jurisdiction of federal trial courts (district courts) has been so constructed that they handle only matters involving relatively large sums of money. Like the higher state courts, procedure in federal courts is formal and prolonged.

94. Douglas E. Rosenthal, *Lawyer and Client: Who's in Charge* (New York: Russell Sage Foundation, 1974); Kritzer, supra note 92, pp. 99–111.

95. Brian Ostrom, David Rottman, and Roger Hanson, "What are Tort Awards Really Like: The Untold Story from the State Courts" *Law & Policy* 14 (1992), pp. 81–82; Galanter, supra note 91, p. 67.

96. Ibid.

Although relatively few trials occur, they have a considerable impact on the out-of-court processing of other cases. Trials often are an option, albeit a remote one, and attorneys conduct their negotiations with that possibility in mind. The high cost of trials, the amount of work required to prepare for them, the uncertainty of their outcome, and the delay involved in scheduling them are factors that promote settlements before a trial date is reached. However, the results of trials have an impact on settlements, for they help establish a going rate which negotiators use to reach settlements. Many trial outcomes are reported in special publications so that attorneys negotiating a similar case may know what the trial alternative might yield.[97] Yet negotiated settlements are not widely disseminated, and knowledge of them is generally limited to the attorneys involved. This gives a special advantage to attorneys who are repeat players in one or another type of dispute. Those attorneys who process many claims of one sort (for example, claims agents for insurance companies use their knowledge of past settlement outcomes). Attorneys who have a less specialized practice and who therefore know less about the normal outcomes of negotiations guess the going rate or depend on trial outcomes for their information about what constitutes a reasonable settlement.

Disputants with varying resources have different opportunities in the civil justice process. These differences may be illustrated by two examples: one involving ordinary litigation of the sort examined by Kritzer and his associates, and the other involving substantial claims between large corporations.

DISPUTES ARISING FROM AUTOMOBILE ACCIDENTS

Disputes arising from automobile accidents constitute the most common litigation in the United States.[98] They generally involve individual plaintiffs who have been injured or whose property was damaged and another individual who allegedly caused the harm and who usually is insured in whole or in part. In some states, the defendant's insurance company may be sued; in most, however, the insurance company is a shadow defendant unrevealed to the judge or jury if the case goes to trial but who manages the defendant's case since its stake in the outcome is large.

Police play an important role in auto accident cases because they are usually called to the scene and often make an on-the-spot determination of who is at fault by issuing a traffic citation to one of the drivers. Thus, issues of liability may be settled almost immediately, although in some cases no ticket is issued or both parties are given tickets and liability must be settled by negotiations or decided at trial.

---

97. Galanter, supra note 91, pp. 84–86, discusses the difficulties in using this kind of information.

98. The following is based on Ross, supra note 81.

The offending driver or the insurance company often gets in touch with the injured party soon after the accident with an offer to settle the damage claim. The smaller the claim, the more likely it is that it will be settled informally in this way without involvement by attorneys. Indeed, many people settle small claims against them without involving their insurance company because they believe it will be cheaper to pay the claim directly rather than have the insurance company pay it. If the insurance company pays, it may subsequently charge them a higher premium. However, if the claim is large or if the injured party finds the offer made by the other driver insufficient, both parties are likely to go to an attorney. In many instances, the attorney chosen was used by a friend or relative or is an acquaintance through their church, club, or neighborhood. Most attorneys do not specialize in personal injury law, and although many advertise an expertise in such cases, large numbers of clients go to attorneys who handle them only occasionally in the midst of a general practice of law which includes many other matters.[99]

Attorneys accept such cases almost always on a contingent fee basis, but only if it seems likely that they can obtain a favorable result. Cases that seem risky are rejected or taken only on an hourly fee basis or retainer (sometimes in addition to a contingent fee). As Kritzer concludes, "the presumption of most lawyers in ordinary litigation may well be that all of the cases that come in the door will be accepted, assuming that there is a reasonable chance of success and that time and other resources for handling the case are available."[100]

Thus three gatekeepers screen accident cases. Police do so by their reports and decisions on giving a traffic citation. The offending driver and/or his insurance company do so by making an initial offer that may forestall a dispute. Attorneys do so by accepting or rejecting clients.

Attorneys who accept personal injury disputes first collect information from their clients. They need to learn about the details of the accident and specifics about the injury and damage as well as information about the other party. Some attorneys then contact the other party or the insurance company, in particular when the damages are relatively small and a swift settlement is likely. However, many immediately file a suit in the state or federal court (depending on the circumstances of the accident). Only then do they begin negotiations. Often several months pass between the client's initial contact with an attorney and the beginning of negotiations (which often involve only a single phone call). That time lapse is the product of the time that it takes to collect relevant information and the attorney's work style. In many cases, the negotiations are pro forma, with both attorneys quickly recognizing the going rate for the injury. However, it remains the task of the plaintiff's at-

99. Heinz and Laumann, supra note 87.
100. On fees, see Kritzer, supra note 92, pp. 56–60.

torney to convince her client that the settlement should be accepted.[101] That is often accomplished by emphasizing the costs, time, and risks involved in pursuing the matter further.

In cases of serious injury, the process extends over a much longer period of time. It takes more time to estimate what the final costs are likely to be. The insurance company has less incentive to agree to a settlement because large amounts of money are involved. In some instances, the company's internal operating policies may require a court judgment before a claims agent is authorized to pay the claim. Thus some claims, mostly relatively large ones, go toward trial. However, many judges are likely to seek a negotiated settlement before trial.[102]

One forum judges use to push parties toward settling their disputes is a settlement conference, which brings them together in an effort to agree on those matters which are not disputed and to narrow the differences on the remaining issues. When judges participate in such conferences, they may indicate the amount of damages likely to be awarded based on their experience. Such estimates produce a powerful incentive to compromise, and many cases are settled at this stage. A few are settled as a jury is being selected because the disputants, upon seeing the jurors, prefer accepting the offered settlement over risking a jury verdict.

When disputants reach a settlement out of court, they ask the court to dismiss the case or they simply let it lie fallow until it is eventually removed from the court docket for want of prosecution. Most settlements do not need approval from a judge and are never entered in public records. They surface only if a further dispute occurs about carrying out the settlement, such as when promised payments are not made. Because the courts make no formal decision in these cases, no appeals occur.

Yet some automobile injury cases do go to trial; the best estimate is that only 2 percent of cases filed in court reach the trial stage.[103] Most of these are decided by juries, with a verdict in favor of the plaintiff occurring in about two-thirds of the cases and yielding a median judgment of $19,000.[104]

The cost of processing automobile injury claims is high. It often takes much time, involves expensive legal assistance, and clogs court dockets even though relatively few cases actually go to trial. The process has not been routinized as it has in many other countries. The costs are borne partly by

101. Rosenthal, supra note 94.

102. Kritzer, supra note 92, p. 82.

103. Data are for 1992. Steven K. Smith, Carol J. DeFrancis, and Patrick A. Langan, "Tort Cases in Large Countries," *Special Report* (Washington, D.C.: U.S. Department of Justice, Bureau of Justice Statistics, 1995).

104. Data are for 1989 from Ostrom, Rottman, and Hanson, supra note 95, pp. 82–85.

claimants, who net less than they might otherwise, and by purchasers of insurance, who pay higher premiums.

BUSINESS LITIGATION: APPLE v. FRANKLIN

In cases involving corporations, jury trials occur less frequently. For instance, many more than half of all contract trials are before a judge alone without a jury.[105] Such cases often involve complex situations that disputants would rather entrust to a judge than a jury.

When corporations fight, stakes may seem higher and the resources that can be invested are much greater than in personal litigation. Like individuals, most business firms avoid litigation because of its expense and disruptive consequences for the relationships, in this instance, with suppliers and customers.[106] However, sometimes no close business relationships are involved and the long-term stakes seem so high that all-out warfare in the courts results. One of those battles, with lasting results for the computer industry, occurred in the 1980s between two computer companies, Apple and Franklin.[107]

It is important to note the context in which this dispute occurred. Personal computers were just beginning to appear on the market. One of the largest sellers of those computers, Apple Computer Corporation, decided to stake its claim on a closed design, which made it difficult for competitors to create compatible machines. The sale of personal computers depends largely on the availability of software programs for them, and software publishers do not risk large development costs to design software for computers which have a small user base. Therefore, Franklin, a small company, had to emulate the Apple computer if it were to market its product successfully since software would probably not become available for a Franklin machine that was different from the Apple II—a leader in the market. IBM was about to enter the market with a still different machine, and given IBM's dominance in large computers, it was certain that the IBM machine would command a large market share and attract much software support.

The dispute arose when Franklin copied parts of the copyrighted operating instructions that Apple had encoded on a computer chip and which were essential for the machine to operate Apple software programs. Franklin sold their machines at a lower price than Apple and threatened to take a substantial share of Apple's market. Therefore, Apple sued Franklin for violation of its

105. Galanter, supra note 91, p. 65.

106. Stewart Macaulay, "Elegant Models, Empirical Pictures, and the Complexities of Contract," *Law & Society* 11 (1977), pp. 507–528.

107. The description of the Apple versus Franklin dispute is based on the *Wall Street Journal,* Jan. 5, 1984, p. 10; *Infoworld,* Jan. 30, 1984; Andrew J. Rodau, "Protecting Computer Software," *Temple Law Quarterly* 57 (Fall 1981), pp. 527–552.

copyright of the computer instructions embedded on its chip. There was no dispute about what Franklin had done; the dispute centered on whether Apple could protect its product by copyrighting the instructions that were encoded on a computer chip. Copyright law had not been written with computers in mind; the issue had never been decided by a court.

Thus began one of the most important cases in the development of the personal computer business. It was not initially settled out of court because Apple wanted a definitive statement of its legal rights, which would determine its strategy for developing new computers. Franklin was fighting for its life; if it lost, it could no longer market its principal product and would owe large amounts of money to Apple for damages. Given the legal and technical complexities of the case, both parties agreed to its being heard by a judge rather than jury. The case was brought before a federal district court because copyright law is federal law. The judge decided that Apple's claims were valid, and the U.S. Court of Appeals upheld the trial judge's decision.

The parties negotiated an out-of-court settlement on damages because Apple, having won on the principal issue, the copyright decision, had little to fear from potential manufacturers of compatible machines. Therefore it could agree to damages from Franklin that were less than the maximum it might have obtained through a court judgment. Apple proceeded to market a new generation of computers known as the Macintosh. Again, Apple opted for a design which could not be emulated by competitors, in contrast to IBM's open architecture, which invited dozens of manufacturers to produce compatible machines. Franklin left the personal computer business.

Apple's use of the courts illustrates a quite different dimension of civil litigation than is displayed in most litigation by ordinary citizens. Apple used the courts to solidify a privilege it claimed under the law but that had not previously been affirmed—the right to copyright software embedded in computer chips. It did not wait for Congress to enact such a provision into copyright law, although Congress did so a few years later. Rather, Apple used the courts to expand its rights under existing law. It could do so because it commanded considerable resources: expert legal assistance, the money to pursue the discovery procedures necessary to establish the facts of this case, and the time needed to see the litigation wend its way through trial and appellate courts. Moreover, because this was not the only controversy that Apple had with competitors, Apple was able to choose this particular case to pursue its goal; it was not the prisoner of circumstances as most individual clients are with only a single grievance to pursue.

SUMMARY

The courts assist in settling or themselves decide a vast number of disputes in the United States. Rarely do these court processes involve issues that immediately spill over to other political arenas. The very fact that the courts produce a solution acceptable to disputants keeps many potential conflicts out of the political arena. However, that is not always the case, even in disputes involving ordinary citizens that might be handled routinely in other countries. During the 1980s, some large medical malpractice judgments led insurance companies to increase premiums sharply for doctors and hospitals; in turn, doctors complained vigorously and some specialists such as obstetricians withdrew from practice entirely in some locations. This spurred many state legislatures to consider setting an upper limit on malpractice awards, which provoked bitter conflicts between lobbyists for the medical profession and those for trial lawyers.[108] For several years, this was one of the chief issues for state legislatures.[109] Similarly, the occasional award of very large punitive damages has made the authorization of such damages a prominent political issue; it was included as an item in the Republican platform on which many Republican Congressional candidates campaigned in 1994.[110]

The routine settlement or judging of civil cases also has less conspicuous political consequences. As we have noted, the conditions under which disputants seek relief for their grievances systematically favors some and disadvantages others. The most disadvantaged in the United States are the poor or near-poor who face obstacles obtaining adequate legal services, who have difficulty weathering the delays inherent in processing civil disputes, and who are unable to use the courts strategically in the same ways that repeat-players do. As long as the disadvantaged expect and accept such treatment, it has no immediate political effects, although it does lead to skewed outcomes. When those expectations and consent to such outcomes disappear, political trouble brews. Biased court outcomes have rarely in themselves sparked powerful political protests in the United States, but they have been a contributing factor in several instances, including the intrusion of injunctions in labor strikes in the early part of the twentieth century and segregationist decisions by local southern judges during the civil rights movement during the 1950s.

Finally, the civil courts provide an alternative governmental arena for implementing and sometimes developing public policies which have broad consequences but are crafted with relatively little public input. The litigation

108. See, for instance, testimony of James S. Todd, acting executive vice-president of the American Medical Association before the Subcommittee on Health, U.S. House Committee on Ways and Means at Hearings on Issues Relating to Medical Malpractice, Apr. 26, 1990, p. 35. 101st Congress, 2d Session Serial 101–96, Cat. No. Y4.W 36:101–196.

109. *The Book of the States 1976–77* (Lexington, Ky.: Council of State Governments, 1976), p. 426.

110. This platform, the Contract with America, promised passage of a "Common Sense Legal Reform Act," which would include "reasonable limits on punitive damages and reform of product liability laws to stem the endless tide of litigation." James W. Robinson with Ross Colliau, *After the Revolution* (Rocklin, Calif.: Prima Publishing, 1995), p. 22.

between Apple and Franklin was more than a private dispute because the law that the courts developed in that case had a broad impact on the consumption of a growing number of goods and services as the American economy became more computerized. Such outcomes from "private" civil litigation are not uncommon. Sometimes they cause interests who had no voice in the court case to carry their disagreement with the outcome to legislatures; sometimes they lead to continued litigation as an increasing number of interests find the emerging law inimical to their welfare. Although this activity begins in trial courts, it usually ends in appellate tribunals because those who wish to change law and policy usually seek forums with broader jurisdiction than trial courts. It is to those tribunals that we now turn.

Policy, Politics, and Appellate Courts

Appellate courts in the United States are quite different from those in many other countries. That is particularly notable in terms of their structure, personnel, and jurisdiction.

Federalism affects the structure of appellate courts just as it does the remainder of the legal system but its consequences are even more striking. As with the rest of the judiciary, different sets of appellate courts handle appeals from state courts and from federal courts. Each state's appellate courts have little contact with those of the other states. Decisions bind courts only in the states where the decision was made. Other state appellate courts may defer to them, but there is no systematic process by which this occurs. Courts that lead in developing precedent tend to be in large states, but much depends on the personnel of those courts at any particular time, and different courts are leaders in different eras and even over particular issues.[111] Thus, case law is different in each of the fifty states. Sometimes the differences are trivial, but sometimes they are quite dramatic. Unless the issue involves a federal question (usually when one of the parties alleges that the state court decision violates some provision of the U.S. Constitution), the U.S. Supreme Court does not impose a uniform rule on the state courts.

The structure of appellate courts differs from state to state. In 1992, thirty-eight of the fifty states had intermediate courts of appeal which hear most appeals; in all but small states, these intermediate courts operate within a region of the state.[112] All states also have a supreme court (although not all use that name), which is the final arbiter of cases arising within state courts

111. Gregory A. Caldeira, "On the Reputation of State Supreme Courts," *Political Behavior* 5 (1983), pp. 83–108; Henry R. Glick, "Judicial Innovation and Policy Re-Invention: The State Supreme Courts and the Right To Die," *Western Political Quarterly* 44 (1991), pp. 71–92.

112. Maguire, Pastore, and Flanagan, supra note 39, p. 86.

involving state law. Oklahoma and Texas, however, have separate supreme courts for civil and criminal matters.

Cases first heard by federal trial courts (the federal district courts) or heard by a federal administrative tribunal go to an entirely different set of appellate courts: the U.S. Courts of Appeal. Twelve such courts each operate in a region of the country and receive appeals originating there; there is also a federal Court of Appeals which hears customs and patent appeals. One of the courts hears only cases originating in the District of Columbia and is therefore important because many disputes involving the national government originate in the nation's capital. Appeals from decisions by the Courts of Appeal go to the U.S. Supreme Court, which also receives appeals from decisions by state supreme courts, but only when the lower court decision involves a federal question.

Thus fifty-one separate structures of appellate courts exist in the United States. They are loosely connected by their common subordination to the U.S. Supreme Court in a limited set of cases. For the most part, however, they operate with almost complete autonomy.

A second major structural characteristic of appellate courts in the United States is that they are all relatively small. The largest rarely have more than fifteen judges; most have far fewer.[113] Appellate courts thus operate as small groups, and the judges know each other much better than in the trial courts of large urban areas, where dozens of judges work within the same court structure. Consequently, there is less formal administrative structure governing the internal operation of appellate courts. On intermediate courts, subsets of judges hear most cases, so that different decisions may emerge from a single court, depending on the judges who hear the cases. However, in most of the supreme courts (including the U.S. Supreme Court), all the judges participate in every case.

Appellate courts in the United States differ from those of other countries in that judges are not required to have experience as trial judges and an appellate position is not part of a formal career hierarchy. As in trial courts, judges reach their positions by various routes.[114] In some states they are elected; in others they are appointed by governors; in a substantial number, they are chosen by a "merit" system, which involves preliminary screening by a committee of judges, lawyers, and sometimes lay people, which proposes a list of potential appointees to the governor. The governor then appoints from this list, and the nominee serves one year before facing the electorate

---

113. For state appellate courts, see Maguire, Pastore, and Flanagan, supra note 39, pp. 80–81; for federal Courts of Appeals, see *U.S. Government Manual* (Washington, D.C.: Office of the Federal Register, National Archives and Records Administration, 1993).

114. They are summarized in Maguire, Pastore, and Flanagan, supra note 39, p. 86.

in an uncontested retention election in which the judge must win a majority of votes in order to stay in office. In all but four states, appellate judges serve for specific terms; in the median state the term is eight years, which is longer than any other elected official in the United States.[115]

Federal appellate judges, like federal trial judges, serve life terms. They are nominated by the president and confirmed by the Senate. Presidents have more control over appellate appointments than over trial judgeships because individual senators have a weaker claim to particular appointments, as those judges serve a region rather than in a single state. These appointments are important politically because presidents can leave the stamp of their administration on the courts for a long period after they have left office. For instance, twelve years after Jimmy Carter left the presidency, three-quarters of his appointees to the appellate bench remained active on the bench and constituted one-quarter of all federal appellate judges.[116]

The men and women appointed to federal appellate courts almost always have served in political positions, possess close ties to the president's team or his party, or share the general ideological position of the president and his advisors. Thus, for instance, President Ronald Reagan appointed Morris S. Arnold, a former chairman of the Arkansas Republican Party, to the U.S. District Court in 1985, and President George Bush elevated him to the Court of Appeals in 1992. Bush also appointed Jane Roth, wife of Republican Senator William Roth, to the Court of Appeals. Reagan used a special office in the White House as well as the Office of Legal Policy in the Department of Justice to screen judicial appointments, with the consequence that his appointments reflected more ideological consistency with the administration than ever before.[117] That was significant for Reagan's conservative cause, because he was the only president to serve two full terms since Franklin Roosevelt and was able to make many more appointments than his immediate predecessors (see figure 2.1).

Several consequences flow from the ways in which appellate judges reach their positions. Many judges are in close touch with political trends. While they enjoy more autonomy than most high officials because of their long term of office and because of a widely held view that courts should not be subjected to ordinary political pressures, their earlier experiences have usually sensitized them to political affairs. Few are naive about politics, and a handful remain active behind the scenes, most notably Supreme Court Justices Felix Frankfurter and Abe Fortas. Frankfurter gave advice to President Franklin

115. Ibid.
116. Sheldon Goldman, "Bush's Judicial Legacy: The Final Imprint," *Judicature* 76 (1993), p. 285.
117. Ibid.

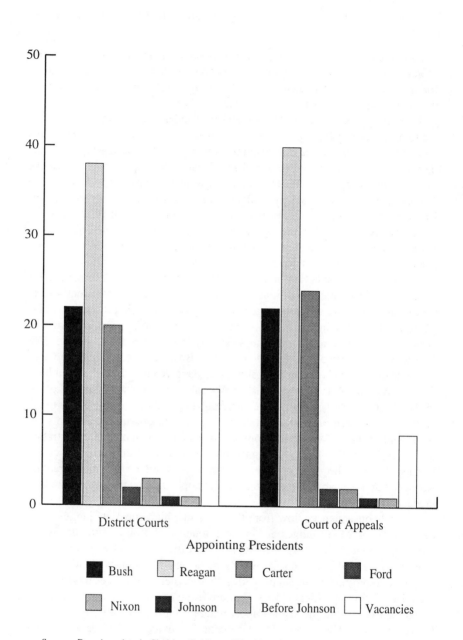

Source: Based on data in Sheldon Goldman, "Bush's Judicial Legacy: The Final Imprint," *Judicature* 76 (1993), p. 295.

Figure 2.1. Presidents Who Appointed Judges of U.S. District Courts and Courts of Appeal (as of November 3, 1992)

Delano Roosevelt about New Deal policy initiatives and presidential appointments long after he went on the Supreme Court; Fortas continued his close relationship with Lyndon B. Johnson.[118]

The lack of a career judicial corps also means that, in some ways, American appellate judges lead more insular professional lives than do appellate judges elsewhere, for they are almost never transferred from one appellate court to another. Judges on state and federal appellate courts work in entirely separate institutions; not even an outstanding state appeals judge may work temporarily on the federal bench. The only possible move is a permanent appointment to a federal court, and some state supreme court justices do become judges of the U.S. Courts of Appeal. However, it is almost as likely that a person ambitious for higher office will seek an elective office or appointment to an executive position in the federal government. Thus in 1993, the newly elected mayor of the city of Detroit was a former Michigan Supreme Court justice.[119] Howell Heflin served as chief justice of the Alabama Supreme Court before his election to the Senate in 1978. Moreover, careers in each state's judiciary are completely isolated from that of the other states; there is no possibility of moving from the supreme court of a small state to that of a larger and more influential state. While state judges win federal judgeships on rare occasions, even at the highest levels federal judges do not move from their position in the federal judiciary to state courts.

A third distinctive set of features of appellate courts in the United States is their jurisdiction. With very few exceptions (for example, the separate criminal and civil appellate courts of Oklahoma and Texas), appellate courts have a general jurisdiction and hear all kinds of cases. No special courts exist for such sensitive political issues as the apportionment of legislatures or the extent of legislative or executive powers. The ordinary appellate courts hear such cases, in addition to most appeals from administrative tribunals.

This lack of specialization means that appellate courts hear an enormous array of issues. About 20 percent of all appeals in the federal Courts of Appeals are criminal convictions;[120] that proportion is higher in intermediate state appellate courts because most criminal trials originate in state courts

118. Bruce Allen Murphy, *The Brandeis—Frankfurter Connection* (New York: Oxford University Press, 1982); Laura Kalman, *Abe Fortas: A Biography* (New Haven: Yale University Press, 1990).

119. *New York Times*, Nov. 4, 1993, Sec. A, p. 24.

120. Donald R. Songer, "The Circuit Court of Appeals," in Gates and Johnson, supra note 6, p. 37; J. Woodford Howard, Jr., *Courts of Appeals in the Federal Judicial System: A Study of the Second, Fifth, and District of Columbia Circuits* (Princeton, N.J.: Princeton University Press, 1981), p. 26.

and appeals must go to the state appellate courts. The remainder are appeals from civil cases and administrative tribunals. The specific mix of such cases varies considerably from one court to another.[121] For instance, the federal Court of Appeals for the District of Columbia hears a very large proportion of all appeals from federal administrative proceedings because of its location in the nation's capital. Other federal Courts of Appeals hear many fewer of such cases. When the civil rights movement was most active in the 1960s and 1970s, the Fifth Circuit was the most important court for deciding desegregation and voting rights cases. The Second Circuit court, which sits in New York and covers cases arising in the New England states, hears an unusual proportion of appeals in large commercial litigation because of its location in the hub of the nation's financial community.

Some appellate courts have discretion over which cases they hear while others do not. The right in the United States of every litigant to appeal once from a trial verdict produces a very large number of routine cases that involve no novel issues of law. A major task facing appellate courts is to separate the momentous from the routine. Many use staff attorneys to screen the cases and recommend a decision in routine cases to the judges, who often adopt the staff's decisions without further consideration.[122] Such cases are decided entirely on the record of the trial and on the briefs that each side presents the court. More significant cases, on the other hand, often receive much more extended treatment by the appellate judges themselves.

Courts which enjoy discretion over which cases they hear have lighter case loads and fill their dockets with cases that appear to raise significant issues of law and policy. Most state supreme courts and the United States Supreme Court are in that position. The discretionary powers of these courts creates a narrow funnel which permits only a few cases to reach the highest courts. The United States Supreme Court hears oral argument in as few as 100 cases per year, selected from approximately 5,000 in which lawyers ask for review. In a study of three U.S. Courts of Appeal in 1986, only .4 percent of all cases decided by them were later given full review by the Supreme Court.[123]

The U.S. Supreme Court exercises its discretion to hear cases based on many factors, among which the stance of the Solicitor General is quite important, but so are the identity of the lower appellate court, the voting split in the lower court, the presence or absence of conflict between courts on the issue, the outcome in the lower court, and the significance of the issues in

121. Howard, supra note 120.

122. Thomas Y. Davies, "Affirmed: A Study of Criminal Appeals and Decision-Making Norms in a California Court of Appeals," *American Bar Foundation Research Journal 1982* (1982), pp. 543–648.

123. Songer, supra note 120, p. 48.

the case (which are reflected in the other indicators as well).[124] Because only four votes from the nine justices bring a case onto the Supreme Court's docket, a minority on the Court may force consideration of issues which at the outset do not command majority support.

THE POLITICAL ROLE OF APPELLATE COURTS

Many characteristics of appellate courts in the United States bring them into the political arena. I have already described the political backgrounds of many of their judges, their lack of specialization, the breadth of their jurisdiction, and their discretion to choose cases. To these must be added the manner in which they announce their decisions, the participation of politically involved groups and officials in the decision-making process, the recognition of the courts' political role by the mass media, and the courts' exercise of judicial review.

Appellate courts do not simply announce most of their decisions; rather, they accompany them with opinions that explain the legal reasoning behind the decision. This "opinion by the court" is usually signed by all members of the court who agree with it. On the U.S. Supreme Court (as well as some other appellate courts) a strong tradition of dissent exists. Many decisions include dissenting opinions; there are also often concurring opinions in which justices indicate that they agree with the decision of the court but do not agree with the underlying reasoning expressed in the court's opinion. During the Supreme Court's 1989 term, for instance, when it decided 134 cases, 64 percent of the decisions were accompanied by one or more dissents and 42 percent had one or more concurring opinions.[125] Other appellate courts have much lower dissent rates, but dissents and concurrences occur. The custom of writing opinions and the habit of dissenting invite appellate courts to address the policy issues underlying the cases they choose to decide. American appellate courts do not disguise the fact that their decisions frequently have policy consequences.

They would have difficulty denying the policy impact of their decisions because of another characteristic of the appellate process—the involvement of interest groups. It has become quite common for interest groups to intervene in appellate cases by submitting amicus curiae (friend of the court) briefs in which they not only suggest legal strategies the court might follow

124. The solicitor general is a political appointee of the president who works in the Department of Justice and handles all U.S. government litigation before the Supreme Court. See the fuller discussion of the significance of this office below. H. W. Perry, Jr., *Deciding to Decide: Agenda Setting in the United States Supreme Court* (Cambridge: Harvard University Press, 1992).

125. Lawrence Baum, *The Supreme Court*. 4th ed. (Washington, D.C.: Congressional Quarterly Press, 1993), p. 127.

but also draw attention to the political implications of the case. For instance, such briefs often note the size of the group submitting the brief and the impact a decision would have on the group's membership, on the national economy, or for social conditions and political activities in the nation. The parties directly involved in the case are no less shy in pressing their policy concerns on the court. Few appeal to the U.S. Supreme Court with the argument that their case involves only narrow, technical legal issues.

Moreover, a political official of the federal government, the solicitor general, plays a key role in the work of the U.S. Supreme Court; indeed, the position has been called "the tenth Justice."[126] The solicitor general provides an important link to the political arena as the federal government's attorney in the Supreme Court. The office screens all federal litigation; no agency can appeal a case without the solicitor general's approval. The solicitor general is a political appointee of the president and is almost always a distinguished lawyer (often a law professor) whose policy views are consonant with the president's. The solicitor general has no formal veto power over what cases the Court hears, but, in practice, the Court pays close attention to the solicitor general's recommendations. In the past, the Supreme Court has agreed to hear a case 75 to 90 percent of the time when the solicitor general recommended it; no other group or attorney approaches that record of influence.[127]

Adding to the political role of U.S. appellate courts is the fact that media coverage of the U.S. Supreme Court decisions (and, less frequently, of other appellate courts) has become a standard element of the news operations of American television, radio, and newspapers.[128] Television networks have "legal correspondents" who specialize in analyzing court decisions. When a vacancy occurs on the Supreme Court, speculation in the media—reflecting the concerns of leading politicians—focuses on the ways in which the political direction of the Court may be altered or reinforced by a new appointment. A similar recognition of the political character of courts occurs with lower appellate courts. For instance, the 1993 decision by the Circuit Court of Appeals for the District of Columbia holding that military regulations prohibiting gays from serving were unconstitutional was noted

126. Lincoln Caplan, *The Tenth Justice: The Solicitor General and the Rule of Law* (New York: Knopf, 1987); Rebecca Mae Salokar, *The Solicitor General: The Politics of Law* (Philadelphia: Temple University Press, 1992).

127. Perry, supra note 124, pp. 112–139.

128. Robert E. Drechsel, "Uncertain Dancers: Judges and the News Media," *Judicature* 70 (1987), p. 271; Ethan Katsh, "The Supreme Court Beat: How Television Covers the U.S. Supreme Court," *Judicature* 67 (1983), pp. 6–11; Elliot Slotnick, "Media Coverage of Supreme Court Decision Making: Problems and Prospects," *Judicature* 75 (October–November 1991), pp. 128–142.

by the media as emanating from a panel consisting of that court's most liberal members.[129] When Governor Mario Cuomo of New York appointed a new member of that state's highest court, the *New York Times* reporter not only noted her gender (female) and ethnicity (Hispanic) but also wrote, "Justice Ciparick, a Democrat who lives on the Upper East Side of Manhattan, is considered a liberal jurist who will be replacing one of the court's more conservative members. But court watchers said they do not expect her to shift the court significantly from its centrist position on most issues."[130]

Finally, the doctrine that courts may (and, in the eyes of many, should) review the constitutionality of executive and legislative actions has had broad implications for appellate courts. Judicial review motivates disgruntled litigants and frustrated interest groups to turn to the appellate courts for relief, and almost any political issue may reach the courts. For instance, those who desire more vigorous protection of wildlife as well as those who wish to preserve the jobs of lumber workers may go to court to challenge actions of the U.S. Forest Service.[131] Those who want more protection of the civil rights of homosexuals have gone to court. Opponents of the North American Free Trade Agreement sought a court injunction against Congress's consideration of the treaty before an environmental impact statement had been prepared.[132] Close elections are sometimes contested in courts on grounds of irregularities in their conduct; the apportionment of legislative bodies, the power of executive officials to issue regulations, and many other political issues regularly reach the courts for adjudication.

All these disputes begin in trial courts, where judges often make significant decisions. Because of their political importance, however, such cases often reach appellate courts, whose decisions are both more authoritative and have broader jurisdictional reach. Once again, the federal structure of the courts has great consequence because state and federal courts may reach quite different decisions. For instance, the U.S. Supreme Court became more conservative as the result of twenty uninterrupted years of appointments by Republican presidents from Richard Nixon through Ronald Reagan.[133] Advocates for the expansion of civil liberties consequently turned to state supreme courts and appealed their cases on the basis of state constitutional provisions which

129. *New York Times*, Nov. 17, 1993, pp. A1 and A24; a similar case was decided in a like fashion in 1994: Stephen Labaton, "Appeals Court Upholds Academy's Removal of Gay Midshipman," *New York Times*, Nov. 23, 1994, p. A11.

130. *New York Times*, Dec. 2, 1993, p. B8.

131. Natalie Angier, "Appellate Ruling Called a Threat to Endangered Species Act," *New York Times*, Nov. 22, 1994, p. B12.

132. *Wall Street Journal*, Sept. 27, 1993, p. A3.

133. Note that Jimmy Carter did not make a single appointment to the Supreme Court.

in many instances are more explicit than the vague protections offered under the U.S. Constitution.[134]

The list of issues on which appellate courts in the United States have issued controversial opinions since 1960 is long. The Supreme Court ruled on such issues as the ability of the media to publish secret government documents known as the Pentagon Papers (*New York Times v. United States*); the degree of protection enjoyed by political, commercial, and pornographic expression;[135] the circumstances under which schools, transportation, and other public facilities must be free of racial discrimination;[136] the scope of prohibited sexual harassment (*Harris v. Forklift Systems*); the conditions under which capital punishment is acceptable (*Furman v. Georgia*); allowable religious practices in governmental settings;[137] the patentability of computer software (*Diamond v. Diehr*) and of manufactured micro-organisms (*Diamond v. Chakrabarty*); and numerous issues raised by environmental protection laws.[138] In each of these areas, the Supreme Court, as well as other appellate courts, have interpreted statutes and reviewed their constitutionality.

Thus numerous forces impel high appellate courts into the political arena in the United States. However, their political style is quite distinctive for American politics. While the party affiliation of judges is often noted when they are appointed or elected, they do not typically vote according to partisan blocs when making decisions. Appellate courts are much less affected by electoral cycles than other organs of government. Only a fraction of the elected judges face the electorate in any given year and often they do not face opposition. Thus, the work cycle of courts does not revolve around the proximity of elections as much as legislatures and executives. Moreover, the courts are almost impervious to the annual (or biennial) budgetary cycles that govern the agenda of legislatures and executives, because courts have no role in the process of examining every governmental activity in the process of passing appropriations to fund them. Finally, the President and state governors have no device like the State of the Union address to tell high appellate

---

134. Kenneth C. Haas, "The 'New Federalism' and Prisoners' Rights: State Supreme Courts in Comparative Perspective," *Western Political Quarterly* 34 (1981), pp. 552–571; Peter J. Galie, "The Other Supreme Courts: Judicial Activism Among State Supreme Courts," *Syracuse Law Review* 33 (1982), pp. 731–1023; Craig F. Emmert, "Issues in State Supreme Court Judicial Review Cases," paper presented at the Southern Political Science Association Meeting, Atlanta, Georgia, November 1988, typescript.

135. For a brief review of these cases see Bill F. Chamberlin, "Speech and the Press," in Hall (ed.), supra note 26, pp. 808–816; and Patrick M. Garry, "Commercial Speech," Ibid., pp. 169–170.

136. Earl M. Maltz, "Race & Racism," Ibid., pp. 698–705.

137. Frederick M. Gedicks, "Religion," in Hall, supra note 26, pp. 717–726.

138. *National Law Journal*, Nov. 29, 1993, p. S24.

courts which issues they would like to see addressed. That is done indirectly by the solicitor general for the federal courts on a case by case basis; there is no parallel communication route for most state high courts.

All of these factors lead to the emergence of policy agendas for the courts which do not coincide with the agendas of presidents, legislatures, or other high officials. However, decisions by appellate courts sometimes have dramatic consequences for the agendas of legislatures and high executive officials.

The highly visible political character of American appellate courts has also affected the way in which they have been described and studied. This is particularly true for the U.S. Supreme Court where, since C. Herman Pritchett's 1948 study, *The Roosevelt Court*, scholars have tracked the ways in which justices coalesce in voting blocs along a liberal-conservative dimension on human rights (civil rights and civil liberties) and economic issues.[139] This has led to the observation that U.S. Supreme Court justices vote in fairly predictable patterns that appear to reflect their underlying attitudes on these issues.[140]

THE IMPACT OF APPELLATE COURT DECISIONS

All the characteristics which impel appellate courts into the political arena make it probable that court decisions substantially affect other political institutions and political processes. Understanding the extent of that effect and the ways in which it becomes manifest has been the object of much research by political scientists as well as other court observers, focusing on two questions.

The first explores whether appellate courts have any kind of impact; the second inquires whether judicial decisions produce social change. The second question requires far more demanding evidence, as one must link particular outcomes to specific court decisions. Thus, if one wishes to discern whether the Supreme Court's 1954 decision in *Brown v. Board of Education* led to desegregation of the nation's schools, one needs to examine the course of school desegregation before and after the *Brown* decision. If one finds that desegregation increased after *Brown,* one then needs to determine whether other social, economic, or political forces operating at the same time might be equally or more responsible for the results than the *Brown* decision. The most careful analysis of that kind, by Gerald Rosenberg, concludes that the courts played only a small role in school desegregation in comparison to

139. C. Herman Pritchett, *The Roosevelt Court: A Study in Judicial Politics and Values, 1937–1947* (New York: Macmillan, 1948).

140. Jeffrey A. Segal and Harold J. Spaeth, *The Supreme Court and the Attitudinal Model* (New York: Cambridge University Press, 1993).

Congressional passage of the Civil Rights Act of 1964; nor does Rosenberg assign much responsibility to the Court's *Brown* decision for the civil rights movement that stirred the United States beginning with the Montgomery, Alabama, bus boycott in 1955–56.[141] Examining other issues such as availability of abortion, Rosenberg finds that institutional constraints on the courts prevent it from having as large an effect as the plaintiffs in these cases wished. However, where the courts enjoyed substantial political support, as in decisions involving the environment and the reapportionment of legislatures, court decisions had a substantial effect.

Rosenberg concludes that courts are constrained from "producing significant social reform" by the limited nature of constitutional rights, their lack of judicial independence (and hence dependence to some degree on the good graces of other governmental institutions), and their inability to control implementation.[142] Rosenberg's conclusions are misleading, however, because they provide no standard against which to measure judicial impact. Several such metrics may be suggested which lead to somewhat different conclusions.

One measure of impact is the degree to which court decisions affect the agendas and actions of other governmental institutions and political actors. By that metric, courts have a frequent and substantial impact on the political process. While large portions of the mass public may not have been aware of *Brown*, as is true for most Supreme Court decisions, school boards were put on notice by local chapters of the NAACP. School boards and other public education officials had to deal with segregation in a new legal context. The dramatic confrontation between President Dwight D. Eisenhower and Arkansas Governor Orville Faubus in Little Rock in 1957 was a direct consequence of *Brown* and subsequent judicial decisions and proved to be a landmark in the mobilization of public debate over school desegregation.

There are many examples of court decisions ringing the door bell at other institutions and causing them to respond to issues raised by them. Thus, the Supreme Court decision requiring provision of legal counsel to indigent defendants charged with serious offenses (*Gideon v. Wainright*) created an explosive growth of legal organizations responsible for providing such lawyers. Likewise, almost all criminal suspects arrested by the police are given Miranda warnings, which the Court required to alert such individuals that their statements may be used against them and that they have a right to an attorney. Although police misconduct has not been eliminated by these warnings, as

141. Gerald N. Rosenberg, *The Hollow Hope: Can Courts Bring About Social Change* (Chicago: University of Chicago Press, 1991); see somewhat critical reviews by Michael W. McCann and Malcolm M. Feeley in *Law and Social Inquiry* 17 (1992), pp. 715–760.

142. Ibid., p. 35.

Rosenberg suggests, the police have been required to respond to the Court's decision.[143]

Many other examples of the power of court decisions to alter legislative and administrative agendas exist. Sometimes the courts mobilize strong support from otherwise quiescent sectors of society; at other times they trigger strong opposition. One example of the power of the courts to unleash opposition in ways that define the political agenda occurred during the Bush administration over the issue of civil rights.[144] As the Supreme Court became more conservative with Reagan's appointments of associate justices Sandra Day O'Connor, Antonin Scalia, and Anthony M. Kennedy, and of William H. Rehnquist as chief justice, the Supreme Court issued a series of rulings narrowing the scope of Title VII of the Civil Rights Act of 1964.[145] These made it more difficult for plaintiffs to obtain relief from alleged racial or sex discrimination in employment practices. Those decisions aroused a storm of protest from civil rights groups and their supporters in Congress. Although President Bush had won a resounding electoral victory in 1988, he failed to win a Congressional majority; his Democratic opposition seized upon these rulings as a lever to strengthen its support from minorities and women and vigorously pursued legislation to overturn these rulings. The Democratic majority passed a bill in 1990 to overturn these decisions but Bush vetoed it on the ground that it required hiring quotas, a stand that many observers interpreted as an appeal to blue-collar voters who had supported him and President Reagan. The Democrats had insufficient votes to override the veto but returned to the fray in 1991. In the meantime, the Supreme Court issued two additional rulings which made bringing complaints of employment discrimination to the federal courts increasingly difficult.[146] In 1991, however, Bush's position weakened, for two additional events heightened emotions further. One was a strong showing in a Republican primary election by a former Ku Klux Klan member, which tarred the party with charges of racism; the second were the allegations of sexual harassment aimed at Bush's Supreme Court nominee Clarence Thomas. The result was an agreement by Bush to sign the bill which became the Civil Rights Act of 1991. Thus, for

143. Ibid., p. 326.

144. The following is based on an account in *1991 CQ Almanac* (Washington, D.C.: Congressional Quarterly Press, 1992), pp. 251–261.

145. See particularly *Wards Cove v. Atonio* 490 US 642 (1989); *Patterson v. McLean Credit Union*, 491 US 164 (1989); *Price Waterhouse v. Hopkins* (1989); *Martin v. Wilks* 490 US 755 (1989); *Lorance v. AT&T Technologies* (1989); *Independent Federation of Flight Attendants v. Zipes* (1989). Also involved were *Library of Congress v. Shaw* (1986); *Crawford Fitting Co. v. J. T. Gibbons* (1987).

146. *West Virginia University Hospitals v. Casey* (1991) and *Equal Employment Opportunity Commission v. Arabia American Oil Co.* (1991).

a two-year period, Supreme Court decisions dominated a large portion of the President Bush's domestic agenda. These were not issues that the president or the Republican party wished to highlight, but in the face of Democratic opposition stirred by the Court's rulings, they had no choice.

The courts' political impact can be better understood in a framework suggested by Johnson and Canon, who propose that the process by which courts affect the political arena involves the manner in which various audiences or targets of court decisions react to them.[147] Court decisions are subject to interpretation by various private parties and public officials. Most prominent among them are other judges (often in lower tier courts) who interpret appellate rulings in the course of processing litigation, as well as lawyers and law academics who interpret court rulings in their briefs and publications. Second, there is an implementing population consisting of institutions and individuals who have the responsibility of applying the law, such as the police when they issue Miranda warnings or school administrators when they establish school attendance boundaries. Third, Johnson and Canon describe a secondary population consisting particularly of the media which publicize and frame court rulings in ways that attract political attention or obscure them. Finally, the presumed beneficiaries and targets of court decisions are supposed to feel the ultimate brunt of court decisions; whether they do so depends on the factors I have discussed earlier about the conditions under which people bring litigation, as well as on the actions of the interpreting and implementing audiences.

Keeping these four audiences in mind allows one to appreciate the complexity of court impact. It does not come about as the direct result of some explosive force. Rather, court decisions ripple through layers of social structure and independent political forces, producing easily discernible consequences for politicians and government officials in the United States.

Conclusion

Many elements combine to create interactions between law, courts, and politics in the United States. When we review the characteristics we noted in the previous chapter, we can easily recognize the degree to which justice and politics influence each other in the United States.

The radical decentralization of many dimensions of social, political, and legal affairs in the United States leaves a mark on the design of the intersection of law, courts, and politics. It creates multiple opportunities to make law, to access the courts, and to utilize the political arena. Decentralization

147. Charles A. Johnson and Bradley C. Canon, *Judicial Policies: Implementation and Impact* (Washington, D.C.: Congressional Quarterly Press, 1984).

gives influence and power to groups that have only local or regional strength and debilitates the power of national majorities. It also establishes a system of competition and conflict among governmental institutions in state and national governments that Americans call the separation of powers. All of these characteristics combine to endow courts in the United States with extraordinary opportunities to meddle in the political arena. Court decisions often alter agendas of other governmental institutions. By dint of both statutory interpretation and judicial review based on constitutional interpretation, the courts have become a major player in the policy process. The other side of the coin, however, is that executive officials and legislatures do not hesitate to appoint judges who reflect current political coalitions. Although most judges vigorously assert their independence, judicial independence in the United States is subtle and sometimes appears fragile.

However, the active role of American courts in the political arena is not simply the product of government structure. It also may be the result of a widespread view in the United States that it is legitimate to sue the government when things are not going well; Americans appear to be quite conscious of their rights and think about disputes in terms of their rights. Thus, disputants bring political objections about old and new programs to the courts and assert their rights in civil disputes with other individuals as well. Access to the courts in cases involving political issues is eased by the existence of interest groups who specialize in supporting such cases both at trial and during appellate proceedings. Moreover, the large number of lawyers scrambling for business sometimes allows disputes to go to court which might otherwise be settled or which might simply fade away.

Access to courts is far from universal in the United States. Disputants who can obtain backing from interest groups are advantaged but such cases constitute only a tiny portion of the caseload of American courts. In disputes which evoke civil remedies, high-income individuals have a substantial advantage over those with low incomes; repeat players have an advantage over occasional litigants; corporations have an advantage over most individuals. However, several practices mitigate these results. In criminal cases, all defendants facing serious charges receive free legal assistance if they cannot afford to hire their own attorney; in addition, the very poor receive free legal aid in some civil cases. Finally, contingent fees makes it possible for many low-income claimants to hire attorneys when such a fee arrangement is appropriate.

The relatively free access to courts is counterbalanced, however, by the paucity of quasi-judicial institutions in the United States. Few administrative tribunals exist; access to them is not always easy. Consequently, those affected by a government decision such as denial of social security or welfare benefits or those whom the law directs to an administrative procedure such as people who suffer racial or gender discrimination on a private job have in recent years had considerable difficulty obtaining a hearing.[148] As later chapters show, that stands in stark contrast to the rich structure of administrative tribunals open to French and German disputants.

Finally, the social control functions of the courts visibly intersect with politics. Crime control has been a premier issue of elections at every level of government in the United States in the last third of the twentieth century. Various courts ranging from the U.S. Supreme Court to lowly trial courts have been accused of coddling criminals; judges at every level are routinely evaluated in the media according to the toughness of their treatment of criminals. At the same time, civil disputes also reflect social control functions of the courts but they attract far less consistent political controversy. A few high profile cases, such as asbestos damages, medical malpractice, and a handful of product liability cases involving conspicuous products such as automobiles or medical devices, attract occasional attention in the political arena. Underneath that surface calm, however, the legal arena is constantly buttressing or eroding public confidence in the quality of justice that government in the United States brings to its people.

148. B. Dan Wood, "Does Politics Make a Difference at the EEOC?" *American Journal of Political Science* 34 (1990), pp. 503–530; Peter T. Kilborn, "Backlog of Cases Is Overwhelming Jobs-Bias Agency," *New York Times,* Nov. 26, 1994, Section 1, p. 1; Cornell W. Clayton, *The Politics of Justice: The Attorney General and the Making of Legal Policy* (New York: M. E. Sharpe, 1992).

3

Courts, Justice, and Politics in England

HERBERT M. KRITZER

As the previous chapter made clear, the prominent role of courts in the United States arises from close and direct links between law and politics, in no small part because the image of "a government of laws, and not of men" marks the American polity.[1] Not so in England,[2] where researchers and teachers treat law and courts as clearly distinct from politics. This has important implications, as two English scholars observed that "generations of belief in the apolitical tradition of law . . . necessarily condition the legal

The preparation of this chapter was assisted by funds provided as part of the Glenn B. and Cleone Orr Hawkins Professorship. Sections of the chapter were presented at the 1993 meetings of the Law & Society Association and the American Political Science Association. I should like to thank Heather A. Quinn for her excellent assistance during the early stages of the research that went into this chapter; I should also like to thank Nancy Paul of the University of Wisconsin Law Library for her extensive assistance, and Ruth Sanderson, the government documents librarian at the University of Wisconsin Memorial Library. Graham Wilson, Phillip Thomas, Alan Paterson, Hazel Genn, Anthony Barker, and Ross Cranston read and commented on various sections, or provided input at key points as the manuscript developed. Their help was greatly appreciated, but the responsibility for what appears here is mine.

1. This oft-quoted phrase originally appeared in the constitution of the Commonwealth of Massachusetts drafted in 1776 by John Adams; see Page Smith, *John Adams* (Garden City, N.Y.: Doubleday, 1962), p. 441.

2. The United Kingdom, which consists of England, Wales, Scotland, and Northern Ireland (plus a number of islands in the English Channel and the Irish Sea), have several distinct court systems, including three primary systems: the English system (which is used in England and Wales), the Scottish system (which combines elements of the common law and civil law), and the Northern Ireland system (which is reasonably similar to the English system). These three systems intersect in two ways: they share a court of last resort (the Judicial Committee of the House of Lords) and they share a chief judicial officer, the Lord Chancellor, who effectively selects judges of major courts in all three. In this chapter, I discuss the English system, albeit in some sections I will by necessity refer to "Britain" because the information available covers England, Wales, and Scotland (which together constitute Great Britain). I should also note that

profession."[3] Many key legal actors believe that their actions are devoid of political content and act differently than they would if they recognized their actions as embedded in politics. Nonetheless, law and courts are crucial elements in the English system, reflecting the centralized nature of the political process. As in all developed countries, law and courts are key mechanisms of social control in England, and through both decisions and ritual they serve important legitimation functions. And, in contrast to the historical image of English courts as creatures of Parliament and consistent with developments in other countries, English courts have become more directly involved in policymaking over the past two decades, reflecting a combination of changing roles of the state and influences of such supranational entities as the European Commission on Human Rights.[4]

A part of the supposed nonpolitical role of law and courts in England has to do with the concept of politics. If politics refers only to action oriented around parties, elections, or Parliament, then it may be reasonable to conclude, at least for most of the twentieth century, that law and courts are less enmeshed in politics in England than in the United States. Written constitutions at the state and national levels constrain the actions of legislative institutions in the United States; legislatures (and executives) must defer to these basic laws, which can be modified only by extraordinary, extralegislative action. Thus, in the United States, the actions of the explicitly political branches of government are constrained by laws which are subject to judicial interpretation and enforcement. In contrast, England lacks a written "basic law," and the traditional governing principle is parliamentary supremacy:[5] Parliament has the final say on what it can do, and it can change any law that it so chooses. That has changed somewhat as a result of England's grow-

---

several minor areas of the United Kingdom—the Channel Islands and the Isle of Man—have their own court systems; see Elizabeth M. Moys, *Manual of Law Librarianship: The Use and Organization of Legal Literature*, 2nd ed. (Boston: G. K. Hall, 1987), pp. 48–51; or J. H. C. Morris (ed.), *Dicey and Morris on the Conflict of Law*, 9th ed. (London, Stevens, 1973), p. 15.

3. Carol Harlow and Richard Rawlings, *Pressure Through Law* (London: Routledge, 1992), p. 6.

4. See Mauro Cappelletti, *The Judicial Process in Comparative Perspective* (Oxford: Clarendon Press, 1989), pp. 11–24.

5. This does not mean that England lacks a "constitution," only that the constitution takes a different form and plays a different role. There is extensive writing on the British constitution, both from the viewpoint of how it structures government and as a body of case law. See, for example, D. C. M. Yardley, *Introduction to British Constitutional Law*, 7th ed. (London: Butterworths, 1990); or T. C. Hartley and J. A. G. Griffith, *Government and Law: An Introduction to the Working of the Constitution in Britain*, 2nd ed. (London: Weidenfeld and Nicolson, 1981); or T. R. S. Allan, *Law, Liberty and Justice: The Legal Foundations of British Constitutionalism* (Oxford: Clarendon Press, 1993).

ing ties to Europe and as judges are more willing to enter into areas previously deemed to be off-limits to the courts.

Until the twentieth century, courts (and lawyers) in England dealt almost exclusively with issues arising under judge-made common law.[6] For example, most criminal law in England originated as common law, not as acts of a legislative body. It was only in the past hundred years or so that courts in England began to interpret and apply substantial bodies of statutory law. In the United States, legislative institutions began creating and courts began applying statutes from the founding of the country.

This does not mean that issues decided by the courts rather than by the Parliament lack political significance: crime and property lie at the center of much political discourse. Furthermore, the decisions of the courts on questions that are ostensibly narrow can have broad ramifications. This is true in the United States and in England. For example, in the United States the effective endorsement of the property rights of slave owners by the Supreme Court (in the Dred Scott decision of 1857) was a major catalyst leading to the Civil War. In England, almost one hundred years earlier, a court decision virtually ended the institution of slavery.[7]

Subtle differences in the meaning of the word *law* may also be at work. In the United States, *law* has long had an expansive meaning, flowing from the "government of laws and not of men" ideology. To implement this ideology, representative bodies create law, and courts act to enforce them. In contrast, *law* in England took on a more restrictive meaning, referring largely to the common law created through decisions of judges. For much of English history this referred primarily to the sanctioning of behavior deemed to be criminal and to the ownership (including inheritance and transfer) of property.[8] The result is that people in England may view *law* more narrowly than do people in the United States.

In this essay I shall use broad interpretations of the meanings of both *law* and *politics*, which make clear the interconnection of politics and the judicial system. At the same time, as I shall demonstrate, the political process in England has been used to make choices about what should and

6. The term *common law* evolved to refer to law that was common to the entire country of England, in contrast to local customary law that applied only to a particular region; Penny Darbyshire, *Eddey on the English Legal System*, 5th ed. (London: Sweet and Maxwell, 1922).

7. In this case, *Somerset v. Stewart* (1772), the court ruled that slave owners in England could not use the law of property to enforce their ownership and that slaves could use judicial procedures such as habeas corpus to prevent owners from holding them against their will; see Harlow and Rawlings, supra note 3.

8. This interpretation comes from my reading of Brian Abel-Smith and Robert Stevens, *Lawyers and the Courts: A Sociological Study of the English Legal System, 1750–1965* (London: Heinemann, 1967).

should not be in the courts. These choices do not eliminate the need for adjudication but do lead to alternative venues that lack the connotations of courts.

In the sections that follow, I shall consider the following topics:

- the structure and staffing of legal institutions (that is, the courts and the legal professions);
- social control and how it is distributed between the criminal and civil justice systems;
- maintenance of the legitimacy of the English administrative state through the use of quasi-judicial institutions to resolve conflicts that arise between the state and those seeking services and benefits from the state, and the increasing role of the courts in overseeing those institutions;
- policymaking functions of the courts, vis-à-vis both the commercial life of the country and mediation between citizens and the state with regard to individual rights.

Legal Institutions in England

The many ways of organizing and staffing legal institutions can make explicit or downplay the connections between law and politics, in terms of the direct and indirect linkages among central institutions, in terms of who key players are and how they come to occupy the roles that they do, and in terms of the allocation of functions among various players and institutions. After this section, a brief overview of legal institutions in England, I shall discuss in more detail the interrelationships that are relevant to understanding the operation of the judicial institutions and their influences on other aspects of the governmental and political system.

LEGAL PROFESSIONS AND LEGAL SERVICES

As in the United States, the courts are the realm of lawyers, both as advocates and as adjudicators. Unlike the United States, France, Germany, and Japan, nonlawyers play a prominent role in the criminal justice system in England, at least at the lower levels. Like the United States, but unlike the other countries, persons with the title "judge" began their careers as practicing lawyers; there are not separate career ladders for lawyers and judges. Unlike the United States, but like the other countries, there is not a single legal profession; until 1994, the formal division of the legal profession in England into solicitors and barristers controlled who may appear as advocates in the higher courts and who may sit as a judge in those courts.

The current structure has been in place since the nineteenth century; before that time, there were a variety of other legal professions (attorneys, conveyancers, serjeants-at-law, King's Counsel).[9] In the late 1980s, about 50,000 solicitors were in practice, compared to about 6,000 barristers.[10] Although it is usual to describe the division of labor between the two professions as barristers serving as courtroom advocates (traditionally appearing in wigs and gowns) and solicitors being the office lawyers, this is an oversimplification.

Barristers, known collectively as "the Bar," have the right to appear as an advocate in any type of court in England[11] and possess a near monopoly on advocacy in the higher trial courts and in appellate courts (called "right of audience"). However, in order to represent someone in court, a barrister must be hired ("briefed") by a solicitor; a potential client may not go directly to a barrister. Solicitors may initiate court actions, but they normally limit their advocacy to appearances in Magistrates' Courts and County Courts, in addition to the administrative tribunals that handle many of the disputes that arise between the bureaucracy and citizens (for example, over social security benefits).[12] Changes during the mid-1990s allowed solicitors to obtain broad rights of audience in higher courts, but this has yet to make a significant impact.

In addition to serving as courtroom advocates, barristers function as legal consultants on highly technical or specialized legal issues. These include matters such as estimating the amount of damages in personal injury cases and advising on technical points of law. In addition to initiating court actions and appearing as advocates in lower courts, solicitors provide a range of legal services (drafting wills, writing contracts, and so on), and until recently possessed a monopoly on handling the transfer of real property ("conveyancing"). Neither solicitors nor barristers possess a monopoly on providing legal services, other than specific rights of audience in court and, until the mid-1980s, conveyancing.

This latter point is important because it means that there are legal service providers who do not possess formal legal credentials. Thus, accountants in England provide many services related to corporate financial matters that

9. Ibid.

10. See *A Time for Change: Report of the Committee on the Future of the Legal Profession,* Chairman: Lady Marre (London: General Council of the Bar and the Law Society, 1988), p. 36; the figure for barristers is for 1987 and the figure for solicitors is for 1985–86.

11. See David Pannick, *Advocates* (Oxford: Oxford University Press, 1992).

12. For a recent overview of the role of tribunals in the English system, see Hazel Genn, "Tribunals and Informal Justice," *Modern Law Review* 56 (1993), pp. 393–411. The name *County Courts* has a different connotation from that term in the United States, where it usually refers to courts that have as their jurisdiction a specific county. In Britain, County Courts simply refer to courts out in the counties as opposed to the High Court, which was historically based in London; there is no relationship between county boundaries and the catchment areas for specific county courts.

lawyers provide in the United States. The largest providers of legal advice in England are the local Citizens' Advice Bureaux (CABs), which provide walk-in advice to citizens on a broad range of matters (legal and otherwise). CABs are locally funded, with salaried managers but largely volunteer advice givers. There are also a variety of more specialized advice services (for example, consumer, immigrant) that typically use nonlawyer providers.

One last distinction between the work of solicitors and that of barristers is important for understanding the intersection of law, courts, and politics in England. In the United States, we frequently identify individual lawyers and law firms with the clients they regularly represent. Thus, "plaintiffs' " lawyers in the United States regularly represent injured individuals in personal injury cases (and these lawyers have their own organization, the Association of Trial Lawyers of America). The "defense bar" consists of those lawyers who usually represent insurance companies in such litigation. This is also true for labor disputes and especially in criminal cases. Thus, lawyers in the United States tend to be partisans, not just in a single case, but in their overall practices.

In England much the same is true for solicitors, but not for barristers. Barristers tend to specialize substantively (for example, in criminal law or matrimonial law), but do not become partisans. A barrister might appear for a plaintiff in one case and for the defendant in the next.[13] The fact that a barrister appears for an insurance company in a case does not in any way preclude that same barrister appearing for a plaintiff involved in an action defended by that same insurance company in the next case. Traditionally, the rule for barristers is that a barrister who has time available must, except under special circumstances, take any client ("accept any brief") who comes along who is willing to pay the barrister's fee, regardless of which side the client is on and regardless of the barrister's feeling about the client's case.[14] As a result, barristers typically tend to align more with the court and its processes than with any particular type of client.

Not only are barristers and solicitors distinguished by the kinds of work they do, but historically the two groups of practitioners have been drawn from different segments of society. Barristers came from the upper middle class and the aristocracy; solicitors came from the lower middle class and the working class. Barristers obtained their education at "public" (private) schools and the elite universities of Oxford and Cambridge; solicitors went

---

13. This may be changing; see John Morison and Philip Leith, *The Barrister's World and the Nature of Law* (Milton Keynes: Open University Press, 1992), p. 61.

14. J. R. Spencer, *Jackson's Machinery of Justice* (Cambridge: Cambridge University Press, 1989), p. 339. One way a barrister can avoid a case is to request a fee higher than the client is willing to pay; see Richard L. Abel, *The Legal Profession in England and Wales* (Oxford: Basil Blackwell, 1989), p. 92.

to state-supported secondary schools and to regional universities, if they had university education. Barristers attended dinners at the Inns of Court to listen to barristers and learn the art of advocacy from them; solicitors worked at apprenticeships in the offices of small firms of solicitors to learn what they needed to qualify to practice.[15]

These differences in practice style, training, and background are important because, as I shall discuss in more detail below, most trial judges are drawn from the ranks of barristers, and all appellate judges have been barristers. Furthermore, the Bar has a long-standing association with government and politics. This may be in part because at one time holding a parliamentary seat often served as a stepping stone for barristers who desired to become judges,[16] although this does not seem to be the case today. Still, certain key governmental offices—Lord Chancellor, Attorney-General, and Solicitor-General—can be held only by barristers.[17] Furthermore, because most barristers are based in London and most solicitors work in cities, towns, and villages outside London, it is fairly easy for barristers to combine their legal work with parliamentary office. Two additional factors facilitate this: there is no requirement in the English political system that members of Parliament (MP's) be residents of the districts (constituencies) that they represent, and Parliament traditionally meets in the afternoon and evening (with major business conducted after supper), which allows barristers to make their court appearances in the morning and early afternoon.

COURTS AND OTHER ADJUDICATORY FORMS

Trial courts in England are divided according to civil versus criminal matters and less serious/complex versus more serious/complex cases.[18] The two levels of criminal courts are the Magistrates' Court and the Crown Court; the two levels of civil courts are the County Court and the High Court (see figure 3.1). The lines between the various courts are not always straightforward, because the "lower" courts often handle preliminary matters for the "higher" courts, and certain issues involving civil or administrative matters, such as some matrimonial issues, paternity cases, and granting of licenses to sell alcoholic beverages, appear in the Magistrates' Court, which otherwise handles less serious criminal cases. In addition, there are two levels of appellate courts: the Court of Appeal, which is the first level appellate court,

15. See Abel, supra note 14.

16. David Sugarman, "Blurred Boundaries: The Overlapping Worlds of Law, Business and Politics," in Maureen Cain and Christine B. Harrington (eds.), *Lawyers in a Postmodern World: Translation and Transgression* (New York: New York University Press, 1994), p. 114.

17. See R. J. Jackson, *The Machinery of Justice in England*, 7th ed. (Cambridge: Cambridge University Press, 1977), p. 431.

18. See Spencer, supra note 14, pp. 3–10.

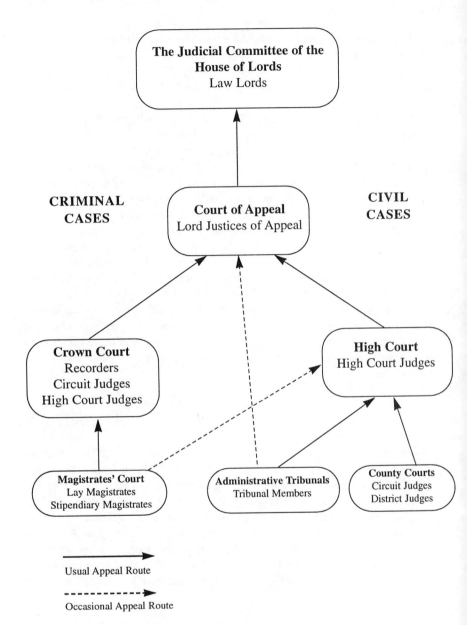

CRIMINAL CASES

CIVIL CASES

The Judicial Committee of the
House of Lords
Law Lords

Court of Appeal
Lord Justices of Appeal

Crown Court
Recorders
Circuit Judges
High Court Judges

High Court
High Court Judges

Magistrates' Court
Lay Magistrates
Stipendiary Magistrates

Administrative Tribunals
Tribunal Members

County Courts
Circuit Judges
District Judges

Usual Appeal Route

- - - - - - - - - - ▶
Occasional Appeal Route

Figure 3.1. The Structure and Staffing of the English Court System

and the Judicial Committee of the House of Lords (or, more simply, the House of Lords), which is the court of last resort. Last, a host of administrative tribunals, including appellate bodies, handle mainly routine disputes between the government and citizens over issues such as disputes between landlords and tenants over the amount of rent, and between employers and employees over charges of discriminatory treatment.[19] The Lord Chancellor—a cabinet member who is also the chief judicial officer (as well as the presiding officer of the House of Lords)—and the Lord Chancellor's Department administer the English court system.[20] Figure 3.1 shows the structure of the court system, along with the types of judges who regularly staff each court.

Most of the persons with the title "judge" or "recorder" are experienced barristers.[21] Most of the solicitors who have been appointed to judicial office have been at the lowest level (assistant recorder); the first solicitor was appointed a High Court judge in 1993. The dominance of barristers on the bench (other than Magistrates' Court) is important because barristers are less likely to come to the bench with an orientation toward one side than would be the case for solicitors.[22] It is also an important contrast to the United States, where lawyers come to the bench with a predominant experience as prosecution or defense attorneys or as advocates for plaintiffs or defendants.

In contrast to the apparent demand that judges come primarily from the ranks of experienced courtroom advocates, most magistrates are not even lawyers. With the exception of a small number of paid, full-time stipendiary magistrates in major urban centers, magistrates are unpaid laypersons. New magistrates must participate in a program of training before sitting to hear cases. Most magistrates hear cases for at least twenty-six half-day sessions per year. Lay magistrates sit in panels (usually of three), with assistance and advice from the Magistrates' Clerk (who is a solicitor); stipendiary magistrates normally hear cases sitting alone.

The staffing of administrative tribunals is in a state of flux. Originally, tribunals were to be informal, nonlegalistic forums that would deal with routine problems efficiently. Increasingly, tribunals operate like formal courts,

19. Appeals from some tribunals may go directly to the Court of Appeal; Spencer, supra note 14, p. 93. However, for most tribunals, the appeal route is to the High Court; ibid., p. 152.

20. See Robert Stevens, *The Independence of the Judiciary: The View from the Lord Chancellor's Office* (New York: Oxford University Press, 1993).

21. Circuit court judges must either have ten years' experience as a barrister or five years' experience as a recorder; recorders must have ten years' experience as either a barrister or a solicitor.

22. Compare this to the situation in the United States, where lawyers who become judges often have followed careers in which they represented a particular perspective such as plaintiffs' personal injury lawyers (see chapter 2).

as evidenced by the increasing requirement that the chairperson of a tribunal panel be trained in the law. Most panels now have at least one lawyer who presides, and there is some evidence that when lawyers are on panels, they tend to dominate.[23]

While in the United States the selection of judicial personnel is explicitly political (through the electoral process or directly involving the elected executive), the English selection system suppresses politics as we commonly speak of it. At the lowest level, the Magistrates' Courts, local advisory committees recommend candidates to the Lord Chancellor's Department, and the Lord Chancellor formally appoints individuals to serve as magistrates.[24] Above this level, the appointment of judges is technically by the Crown, but in practice the Lord Chancellor selects judges for the trial courts. For much of the twentieth century, the Lord Chancellor's Permanent Secretary (a civil servant) had substantial effective power over appointment of judges because that individual personally handled the screening and consultation.[25] The Lord Chancellor now relies upon a separate office within the department, the Judicial Appointments Group, for assistance in identifying and screening potential judicial appointees.[26] There has been increasing pressure to make the selection process less secretive, and in 1994, for the first time, judicial vacancies were publicly advertised, and persons other than sitting judges and officials from the Judicial Appointments Group participated in the screening process.[27] At the appellate level, formally the Prime Minister selects the members of the Court of Appeal and the Judicial Committee of the House of Lords, in consultation with the Lord Chancellor (which usually means the Lord Chancellor handles it);[28] however, the Lord Chancellor, with the assistance of the Judicial Appointments Group, plays the key role.

Despite the more explicit political element in judicial selection in the United States, there tends to be more emphasis on professional qualifications in the United States than in England. The lower reaches of the judicial system in England utilize substantial numbers of lay decision makers, often in highly visible roles (as magistrates and as members of administrative tribunals).

23. See John Baldwin, Nicholas Wikeley, and Richard Young, *Judging Social Security: The Adjudication of Claims for Benefit in Britain* (Oxford: Clarendon Press, 1992).

24. Spencer, supra note 14, pp. 404–408.

25. See Brian Abel-Smith and Robert Stevens, *In Search of Justice: Law, Society and the Legal System* (London: Allen Lane, 1968), p. 175.

26. See Spencer, supra note 14, p. 364.

27. See *Guardian Weekly*, July 18, 1993. "Jobs for Judges Advertised for the First Time," *Independent*, Sept. 28, 1994, p. 6.

28. See J. A. G. Griffith, *The Politics of the Judiciary*, 4th ed. (London: Fontana, 1991), p. 17.

While lay judges in the United States still staff some of the lowest courts (justice of the peace, town courts), these courts have little visibility (many, if not most, are not "courts of record") and play a minor role in the larger judicial system.[29]

Among legal professionals selected to judgeships, the backgrounds of the persons selected in England and the United States differ sharply. In England, the emphasis is on professional experience and qualifications; high court judges are selected from the elite of the Bar. Few judges selected to the English higher courts in recent years (13 percent) have had experience as members of Parliament.[30] In the United States, the emphasis is on a combination of legal professionalism and political experience (see chapter 2).

In earlier periods in English history, there was much more emphasis on political experience in selecting higher court judges. Between 1832 and 1906, 58 percent of the judicial appointments to appellate courts went to members of Parliament, and until the 1920s party patronage was an important consideration in the Lord Chancellor's selection of judges.[31] One man, Lord Halsbury, served as Lord Chancellor during most of the last twenty years of this period; one writer described Lord Halsbury's selections as "men of little or no legal learning whose previous career in public life had been largely in the service of the Conservative Party or else were relations of [Lord Hals-

29. While these courts are not particularly visible, there are on the order of 13,000 lay judges serving in these courts; D. Marie Provine, *Judging Credentials: Nonlawyer Judges and the Politics of Professionalism* (Chicago: University of Chicago Press, 1986), p. xi. These nonlawyer judges constitute 40–45% of the judicial personnel of the state and federal judiciaries— about 29,100 state judges according to *State Court Caseload Statistics: Annual Report 1992* (Williamsburg, Va.: National Center for State Courts, 1994), p. 259, plus about 1,825 federal judges, including magistrates, according to Timothy J. Flanagan and Kathleen Maguire (eds.), *Sourcebook of Criminal Justice Statistics 1991* (Washington, D.C.: U.S. Department of Justice, Bureau of Justice Statistics, 1992), p. 69. In England, as of 1994, there are about 30,000 lay magistrates but only about 3,000 law-trained judges (including judges from Law Lords down to stipendiary magistrates); see "Lord Chancellor Seeks More Women and Ethnic Minority Judges," Lord Chancellor's Department Press Release, Reuter Textline, May 23, 1994, for the number of law-trained judges, and *Judicial Statistics Annual Report 1993* (London: HMSO, 1994), henceforth cited as *JSAR*, p. 92 for the number of lay magistrates.

30. See Burton M. Atkins, "Judicial Selection in Context: The American and English Experience," *Kentucky Law Journal* 77 (1988–89), p. 598. This figure appears to be for the period around 1970, and represents a decrease for 23% only 14 years earlier; see Griffith, supra note 28, p. 33.

31. H. J. Laski, *Studies in Law and Politics* (New Haven: Yale University Press, 1932), pp. 164–180. Gavin Drewry, "Judicial Politics in Britain: Patrolling the Boundaries," *West European Politics* 15 (1992), p. 15.

bury]."[32] Today, active involvement in party politics does not seem to be a major factor in selection to the higher courts.

While political involvement is relatively unimportant in the judicial selection process, social standing remains important, reflecting the dominance of barristers on the bench and the fact that barristers are much more likely to come from upper status groups, although this may be less true in the latter years of the twentieth century than it was at mid-century and before.[33] Moreover, only successful and well-regarded barristers, and similarly situated solicitors, receive appointments. Although persons from humble backgrounds can achieve significant success in legal practice and become candidates for judicial appointments, persons from upper status backgrounds continue to dominate in these professions. About three-quarters of the judges of the High Court and Court of Appeal sitting in 1969 had attended "public" schools, with an equal number having graduated from Oxford or Cambridge; although this may have changed some in the past twenty-five years, an observer writing in 1987 noted that, "English judges tend to be elderly gentlemen most of whom have had a public school education."[34] Moreover, given the requirements of success, those from less privileged backgrounds who achieve it "are not likely to be very critical of the legal order."[35] Of the total of almost three thousand judges (other than magistrates) sitting as of May 1, 1994, less than 10 percent were women and only about 1 percent were nonwhite.[36]

Judges normally serve until reaching retirement age.[37] Technically, superior judges hold office "during good behavior subject to a power of removal by Her Majesty on an address presented to Her Majesty by both Houses of Parliament," although only one judge has ever been removed under the pro-

32. R. F. V. Heuston, *The Lives of the Lord Chancellors, 1885–1940* (Oxford: Clarendon Press, 1964), p. 36.

33. See Abel, supra note 14, pp. 74–76, 348–349.

34. Henry Cecil, *The English Judge* (London: Stevens & Sons, 1970), p. 27; see also C. Neal Tate, "Paths to the Bench in Britain: A Quasi-Experimental Study of the Recruitment of a Judicial Elite," *Western Political Quarterly* 28 (1975), pp. 118–119. David Pannick, *Judges* (Oxford: Oxford University Press, 1987), p. 57.

35. Spencer, supra note 14, pp. 376–377.

36. "Lord Chancellor Seeks More Women and Ethnic Minority Judges," UK Government Press Release, Reuter Textline, May 23, 1994.

37. As of 1993 retirement age for judges is 70, although the Lord Chancellor may grant permission for judges to continue on the bench until age 75 (Judicial Pensions and Retirement Act 1993. §23); until 1993, the retirement age had been 75 for "superior" judges (those who sit on the High Court, the Court of Appeal, and in the House of Lords), and 72 for other judges. Spencer, supra note 14, p. 371.

cedure. The Lord Chancellor can remove lower judges on such grounds as incapacity or misbehavior (or, in some cases, malfeasance).[38]

THE POLITICAL IMPLICATIONS OF THE STRUCTURE OF LEGAL INSTITUTIONS

Of the countries considered in this volume, the legal institutions of England most closely resemble those of the United States. Yet, even with this resemblance, there are major differences. Diversity and lack of hierarchy mark the judicial system in the United States, whereas the English system is unified and hierarchical, with control of the courts concentrated under the Lord Chancellor. This centralization extends to the selection of judges other than at the lowest (Magistrates' Court) level. Another striking difference is the absence of partisan (party-related) and political patronage considerations in the selection of judges, which proceeds not from any aspects of formal structure but from informal norms. Note that I do not describe the selection as "nonpolitical," because the Lord Chancellor is highly sensitive to the kinds of decisions that his choices will make when they come onto the bench; the Lord Chancellor is unlikely to appoint someone who has a reputation as a radical, on the left or the right, or someone whose views do not conform to the Lord Chancellor's regarding the appropriate role of the judiciary. The norms that exclude explicit partisan considerations also preclude the removal of judges whose decisions depart from the Lord Chancellor's expectations.

The structure of the legal professions in England creates substantially greater access barriers than is the case in the United States. For example, the divided profession will confront the potential English litigant with the possibility of having to pay for two different lawyers, the solicitor to initiate the action and the barrister to present the case to a judge. As I will detail later, access to the courts is further hampered by rules relating to paying for legal actions. Whereas in the United States, economic incentives arising from fee structures and lay juries have led to readily available legal services for actions involving monetary compensation, similar incentives do not exist in England, with the result that the barriers to legal action at least appear to be greater.

Law and Order in England: Crime, Justice, and Politics

As in most of the industrialized world, England has experienced a substantial increase in reported crime over the past quarter century, which has led to political debate and to changes in the criminal justice system. While at times the debate has been loud, I shall argue that crime and justice has remained as a second-tier issue behind the cluster of economic issues that Margaret Thatcher made the central focus during her eleven and a half years as prime

38. Ibid., pp. 368–369.

minister (1979–1990). Partly, this is because the English system insulates the state actors in the criminal justice system—judges, prosecutors, and police—from direct contact with the day-to-day democratic process.

However, law and order, crime, and criminal violence have come to symbolize social and economic change that political leaders do address in a direct fashion. Conservative leaders express concerns about traditional values, hierarchy and deference, and norms of order (perhaps symbolized by Britons' willingness to stand in orderly queues under all sorts of conditions). Part of this concern is a reaction to the increasing heterogeneity of English society, particularly in urban settings where there are large Asian, African, and Afro-Caribbean communities.[39] Although there is some perception in England that these nontraditional components of English society account for a decrease in the orderly nature of life, mainline political leaders have not used race as a symbol of crime and violence (or crime and violence as a symbol of racial distinctions).

Contrast this to the United States, where politicians have frequently equated crime with race (see chapter 2). The centrality of race in American politics, combined with the difficulty in using race as an explicit campaign issue, has made crime, criminals, law and order, and other variants a first-tier political issue in the United States.

In Britain, while politicians have raised the crime issue, and while citizens will describe crime as a serious problem when asked specifically in a close-ended fashion, citizens typically do not identify crime as one of the two most urgent problems facing the country. Of much more concern is the decades of economic crisis Britain has struggled with, and the sharp economic turns produced by Thatcher's economic policies. The resulting response to crime in England has been primarily a technocratic and bureaucratic one. The focus has been largely on making the criminal justice system more efficient in the hope that it will more effectively deter and otherwise suppress crime; there has been almost no social or economic response to the perceived crime problem. Critics of criminal justice policy make connections between economic and social dislocation and increasing crime,[40] but this has not been a concern of the Conservative government that controlled Britain for more than fifteen years, starting in 1979.

CRIME

As in the United States, there are two general ways of assessing levels of crime. The first involves official statistics, normally in the form of crimes

---

39. See "Racial Prejudice Alive in UK," *Guardian Weekly*, Mar. 26, 1995, p. 13.

40. Michael Brake and Chris Hale, *Public Order and Private Lives: The Politics of Law and Order* (London: Routledge, 1990); Barry Loveday, "Right Agendas: Law and Order in England and Wales." *International Journal of the Sociology of Law* 20 (1992), pp. 297–319.

reported to the police. The second involves surveying potential crime victims about their experiences over a specified time period. Both kinds of information indicate an increase in crime and crime rates in England.

Official figures show a steady increase in crime, starting in about 1955.[41] At that time, the number of offenses per 100,000 population recorded by the police (in England and Wales) was around 1,000; by 1962 this doubled, and it doubled again by 1974, and yet again by 1987, when it stood at almost 8,000 offenses per 100,000 population.[42] By 1992, this figure had risen to almost 11,000.[43] This rate of increase is greater than for the equivalent indicators in the United States, but it dropped about 5 percent in 1993 and again in 1994.[44] As is true of all official crime statistics of this type, the increases may reflect changes in factors other than the number of crimes committed: people may become more willing to report crimes to the police, police may change how and what they record, and the definition of specific categories may change either by statute or through inflation (which results in petty offenses becoming reportable categories).

While the kinds of gross statistics discussed above can hide many interesting variations, in England the increase in crime rates has been across the board. Still, some offenses have seen faster increases than have others. For example, during the period 1981–91, all crimes increased 6 percent per year, while robbery and violence against persons (excluding sexual offenses) increased at 8 percent and 7 percent per year, respectively; burglary and the category of fraud and forgery each increased at a rate of 5 percent per year. The slowest growing category of cases is sexual offenses, which increased at a rate of only 4 percent per year; the fastest growing category, at 10 percent, is "other offenses," although this category constitutes less than 1 percent of all "notifiable" offenses recorded by the police.[45] Crimes of violence are a very small percentage of crimes reported to the police, however,

41. All figures discussed in this section are based on figures reported in the annual *Criminal Statistics: England and Wales* (London: HMSO), henceforth cited as *CSEW*; Spencer, supra note 14, p. 174, summarizes many of the figures through 1985.

42. *CSEW 1990,* pp. 20, 24.

43. *CSEW 1992,* p. 20.

44. "Property Crime Shows Fall but Violence is Growing," *Guardian,* Sept. 28, 1994, p. 4; "Crime Figures Creeping Upward," *Guardian Weekly,* Apr. 23, 1995, p. 10. In chapter 2, Jacob reported that between 1975 and 1990, the U.S. Uniform Crime Reports showed an increase of about 50%, about half the increase for roughly the corresponding period in Britain.

45. *CSEW 1991,* pp. 29, 55. About half of the cases in this category are "indecent assault on a female"; another 15% are "rape"; and 10% are "unlawful sexual intercourse with a girl under 16"; ibid., p. 47. About one third of these cases are "trafficking in controlled drugs"; about 30% are "going equipped for stealing"; the balance include kidnapping, riot, blackmail, perverting the course of justice, and absconding from lawful custody (ibid, p. 54).

making up around 5 percent of the total, as compared to the United States, where violent crimes constituted 10 percent of the offenses in 1990.[46]

The method of measuring the incidence of crime by surveying potential victims ("victimization" surveys) began in the mid-1960s in the United States. In England the Home Office (which is responsible for police, prisons, criminal procedure, and the organization and finance of the lower criminal courts) has conducted a series of such surveys starting in the early 1980s.[47] As is generally the case with victimization surveys, interviewers hear about many more offenses than do the police. Strict comparisons are difficult due to the nature of categories that are used, but the Home Office researchers sought to make such comparisons by carefully matching their categories to those used by the police.[48] Best estimates of the percentage reported to the police vary sharply by offense category, from a high of more than 90 percent for theft of a motor vehicle to a low of 13 percent for robbery and theft from a person.[49] The mix of offenses found in the crime surveys also differs from those reported to the police. While only 5 percent of the offenses reported to the police involve interpersonal violence, around 17 percent of those detected through the crime surveys involve violence.[50]

The data available leave little doubt that the incidence of crime has been growing in England. How does the incidence of crime compare to the United States? The answer is mixed. Violent crimes, particularly violent crimes involving firearms, appear to be more frequent in the United States. In contrast, property crimes may be as frequent, and some types more frequent, in England. The best comparison is for auto theft, because of the high likelihood that the victims of such thefts will report the loss to the police. The rate of auto theft in England is almost twice that of the United States (1,215 per 100,000 residents in England compared to 650 per 100,000 in the United

---

46. Ibid. See Uniform Crime Report figures in *Statistical Abstract of the United States* (Washington, D.C.: GPO, 1992), p. 80, henceforth cited as *SAUS*.

47. Each survey involved interviews with about 10,000 persons. The methodology and primary findings of the surveys are reported in Pat Mayhew, David Elliott, and Lizanne Dowds, *The 1988 British Crime Survey*, Home Office Research Study No. 111 (London: HMSO, 1989); Mike Hough and Pat Mayhew, *The British Crime Survey: First Report*, Home Office Research Study No. 76 (London: HMSO, 1983); and Mike Hough and Pat Mayhew, *Taking Account of Crime: Key Findings from the Second British Crime Survey*, Home Office Research Study No. 85 (London: HMSO, 1985).

48. See Mayhew, Elliott, and Dowds, supra note 47, pp. 100–103.

49. *CSEW 1991*, p. 22.

50. Calculated from Mayhew, Elliott, and Dowds, supra note 47, p. 13. The rate of increase in crime found in the crime surveys is roughly comparable to that in the offenses reported to the police (ibid.).

States).[51] This contrast would be even sharper if it were based on the total number of automobiles because there are fewer cars per capita in England than in the United States; proportionally fewer people own cars in England, and many fewer own more than one car. While armed robberies may be less common in England, burglaries may be more common; comparing greater Manchester to New York City, the robbery rate in New York is many times that of Manchester, but the burglary rate in Manchester is about double that of New York City.[52]

CRIMINAL JUSTICE SYSTEM

The Police

While England has a centralized structure of government and administration, the police force has remained relatively decentralized. The political organization of England involves three levels: national, county, and local. As noted previously, the primary national ministry with responsibility for criminal justice is the Home Office, headed by the Home Secretary. While the police force for the Greater London area, known as the Metropolitan Police,[53] falls directly under the control of the Home Secretary, each of the forty-one police forces outside the Greater London area is under the control of its chief constable. The local police authority appoints the chief constable, subject to the approval of the Home Office,[54] but can remove the chief constable only for corruption or misconduct. The local police authority has budgetary and financial control over the police, but a chief constable who believes he is not receiving the requisite support can turn to the Home Office for additional resources. This structure thus gives broad powers to the chief constables and frees them from most political control and from political accountability.[55] At

51. William Schmidt, "Britons Try All Contraptions to Halt Rampant Car Theft," *New York Times*, Mar. 28, 1994, p. 1. An International Crime Survey, covering 20 countries, found that England had the highest rate of car theft of any of the countries in the study; see *Guardian*, Apr. 21, 1994, p. 8.

52. Peter Hetherington, "City Life Too Tough, Say Kids from USA," *Guardian Weekly*, Feb. 20, 1994, p. 10.

53. There are actually two police forces in the London area, the Metropolitan Police and the City of London Police; the latter, the existence of which recognizes the unique historical position of the City (an area approximately one-mile square—London's financial district), is primarily under the control of the authorities of the City of London.

54. The police authority is distinctly local, and is composed two-thirds of members of county and local councils and one-third of local magistrates. Not only must the final choice be approved by the Home Office, but the short list from which the choice is made must be approved by the Home Office as well; Brake and Hale, supra note 40, p. 46.

55. Spencer, supra note 14, pp. 225–227.

the same time, chief constables have increasingly looked to national institutions, including the Inspectorate of Constabulary, the Association of Chief Police Officers, and the Home Office to establish expectations and norms for the conduct of their leadership of their individual police forces.[56]

As in the United States, the police have responsibility for investigation and interrogation. The Police and Criminal Evidence Act of 1984 (PACE)[57] sets out their powers to collect criminal evidence through such activities as stop and search on the street, entry and seizure of property, and arrest and detention of suspects.[58] While English criminal law maintains the principle that the police cannot require a suspect to answer questions, the police have the power to take into custody persons who refuse to give their name and address when stopped. Suspects in police custody have a right to have a solicitor present during interrogation, and while there is in many communities a "duty solicitor" to provide coverage at the police station for suspects who request representation, the program is not fully effective because of lack of funding.[59]

In the United States the exclusionary rule is the most visible (and controversial) method for deterring police misconduct vis-à-vis the collection of evidence and the questioning of suspects. While there is no rule in England for excluding evidence obtained through illegal searches, the English courts do exclude confessions and statements obtained by the police through inappropriate means. For example, a jury acquitted a man accused of murdering a seven-year-old boy after the judge excluded from evidence the defendant's confession that the judge described as having been extracted by "oppressive methods."[60] With regard to illegally obtained evidence, aggrieved persons can (and regularly do) bring a civil suit for damages. In the United States one seldom hears of a successful private lawsuit seeking damages from the police for violation of a citizen's rights (the Rodney King case in Los Angeles being a prominent exception); this in large part reflects the reluctance of lay juries to reach verdicts against the police. In England, successful lawsuits against the police are a fairly regular occurrence, largely because professional

---

56. Robert Reiner, *Chief Constables: Bobbies, Bosses, or Bureaucrats?* (New York: Oxford University Press, 1991), p. 285.

57. In England, acts of Parliament are referred to by name and date, such as the Criminal Justice Act 1990, whereas in the U.S. the reference would be the Criminal Justice Act *of* 1990.

58. Historically, police also had significant responsibility prosecution. The Prosecution of Offences Act 1985 removed the prosecution function from the police and established the Crown Prosecution Service as an independent body.

59. Spencer, supra note 14, pp. 218–221.

60. *Guardian Weekly,* Nov. 28, 1993, p. 11.

judges, not lay juries, decide civil cases, and the judges do not feel as compelled as juries to support the police.[61]

In summary, police in England operate in a sharply different context than do their counterparts in the United States. American police departments enforce fifty-one different sets of state criminal laws (plus countless local ordinances), whereas in England there is a single set of criminal laws. Constitutional protections afforded citizens restrict police in the United States, where police are very responsive to local political pressures; in England they are more isolated. English police officers rely primarily upon acts of Parliament (PACE is an example) to define their powers and the limits of their actions. While most of the English criminal justice system is national (law, courts, corrections, prosecution), police forces are local in structure with a modicum of local control.[62]

Lawyers in the Criminal Process

As in the United States, lawyers handle prosecution in court. However, the two branches of the English legal professions share prosecutorial activities. Solicitors handle most out-of-court preparation of cases and court appearances in the Magistrates' Court; under some circumstances, defense solicitors can appear in the Crown Court, but this court is largely the province of barristers (who have "rights of audience" in all courts that consider criminal cases, from the Magistrates' Court to the House of Lords).[63]

Historically, prosecution was largely a private affair, even when public funds paid for it. Until the year 1985, the primary public bodies that pursued prosecutions were the local police forces. Before that time private prosecutions were common, particularly for offenses such as shoplifting, where some police forces left it to shop owners to bear the cost of prosecution rather than draw upon their own limited resources to prosecute cases.[64] When the police did prosecute, local authorities hired a solicitor to handle the prosecution on

61. In 1993, a judge found against six officers of the Metropolitan Police who had arrested, assaulted, and prosecuted three trade unionists who had come to London to picket at a newspaper involved in a labor dispute; the three plaintiffs received £87,550 in damages (*Guardian Weekly*, July 4, 1993, p. 3).

62. For more on policing in England, see Malcolm Young, *An Inside Job: Policing and Police Culture in Britain* (Oxford: Oxford University Press, 1991).

63. Spencer, supra note 14, p. 179. As of summer 1995, a small number of solicitors had obtained general rights of audience in the Crown Court; see "Solicitor Advocates Aim to Compete," *Solicitor's Journal*, July 7, 1995, p. 645.

64. Spencer, supra note 14, p. 214. Private prosecution opens the door to all sorts of actions; Spencer notes the successful prosecution of the *Gay News* for blasphemy during the 1970s for attributing homosexuality to Jesus.

their behalf, but it was the police officer who formally instituted the proceedings.

Since 1985, the Crown Prosecution Service (CPS), a national organization under the direct control of the director of public prosecutions, who in turn is responsible to a member of the cabinet (the Attorney-General), handles the prosecutions previously handled by police solicitors.[65] The CPS has four regions, within which are thirty-one areas; except for Greater London, each area is covered by one or more police forces. While the CPS handles the prosecution, the police normally institute the criminal proceedings. The CPS has no power to compel the police to continue an investigation if the CPS believes that the case warrants prosecution but the police have chosen not to institute proceedings; the CPS can discontinue the prosecution of a case instituted by the police, but this does not appear to be a common occurrence.[66] This continued dominant role of the police vis-à-vis prosecution contrasts sharply to the police-prosecutor relationship in the United States, where the prosecutor is the dominant actor.

Members of the Crown Prosecution Service present cases in the Magistrates' Court. For Crown Court cases, the CPS handles the out-of-court work but must retain private barristers to appear in court on its behalf. The Bar fought hard to maintain its monopoly on Crown Court advocacy and succeeded in blocking advocacy by CPS staff, even those who are themselves barristers. The Crown Prosecutor and the barrister may not agree in their evaluations of a case; even though the CPS retains ("briefs," in English parlance) the barrister, once the trial is about to start (or is under way), the barrister is in charge if a disagreement arises. Thus, if the barrister believes that it is advantageous to accept a plea to a lesser charge at the door of the courtroom, but the police and the prosecutor want to stand firm on the original charge, the barrister prevails.

This formal authority may be offset by a barrister's dependence on receiving criminal briefs from the Crown Prosecutor for a significant share of their income. A sizable number receive a majority of their income from this work (most of which involves appearing as advocates in the Crown Court). One study reports that, excluding the elite of the Bar, between 40 and 50 percent of the income of barristers is from criminal work.[67] This does not

65. While the CPS primarily conducts criminal proceedings on behalf of the police, it may, but is not required to take over private prosecutions and prosecutions instituted by other governmental bodies (e.g., offices dealing with consumer protection, taxation, etc.). About one-fifth of all prosecutions are started by governmental agencies other than the police; Spencer, supra note 14, p. 228.

66. Ibid., p. 230.

67. Abel, supra note 14, p. 366.

mean that each barrister obtains that proportion of his or her income from criminal work, but that barristers who do criminal work tend to specialize in that area, at least in part because they need a high volume of work to generate an adequate income from the fairly low fees.[68]

From this description it should be clear how differently prosecution operates in England compared to the United States. Most chief prosecutors in the U.S. obtain office through a political process: by political appointment (U.S. Attorneys who prosecute most federal offenses) or by direct election to office (most "district attorneys"). Most staff attorneys in prosecution offices are political appointees; very few such offices rely upon a civil service selection system. The Crown Prosecution Service is a national bureaucracy, with staff hired through civil service processes. In addition, independent barristers play a major role in the prosecution of criminal defendants in serious cases, while private lawyers play almost no role in prosecution in the United States. The dependence of large numbers of English barristers on criminal work for their livelihood creates a vested interest in maintaining a major role for nongovernment actors in the prosecution process, and the requirement that the Crown Prosecution Service retain outside counsel to appear for it in the Crown Court reflects this interest.

Persons accused of criminal acts in England are entitled to legal counsel, both in the courts that handle minor cases (the Magistrates' Courts) and in the courts that hear more serious cases (the Crown Court). The structure of representation for the prosecution—solicitors handling work in the Magistrates' Court and preparation of cases for the Crown Court with barristers providing trial advocacy in the Crown Court—is the same for the defendant.[69] One key difference between the prosecution and defense is that after guilty pleas in Magistrates' Court, solicitors who represented defendants sent to Crown Court for sentencing may appear in Crown Court, while the Crown Prosecution Service must brief a barrister to speak for it at the Crown Court.[70] Although a defendant who can afford it must pay for his or her solicitor and barrister, if one is used, legal aid pays for representation of the vast majority of represented criminal defendants.

For many years there were problems with providing indigent representation in the Magistrates' Courts at initial appearances. Now, legal aid pays a solicitor (the "duty solicitor") to be present in Magistrates' Court to provide assistance to defendants. The duty solicitor is not there to defend in a con-

---

68. See ibid, p. 115.

69. See Mike McConville, Jacqueline Hodgson, Lee Bridges, and Anita Pavlovic, *Standing Accused: The Organisation and Practices of Criminal Defence Lawyers in Britain* (Oxford: Clarendon Press, 1994).

70. See Marre, supra note 10, pp. 149–150.

tested case or to assist a defendant in proceedings that are preliminary to transferring the case to the Crown Court ("committal proceedings")[71] but to assist in applying for legal aid, applying for bail, and making a plea of mitigation (if a defendant wishes to plead guilty).

A defendant who needs criminal legal aid beyond what the duty solicitor can provide applies to the Magistrates' Court for a grant of aid, which one or more magistrates or the magistrates' clerk grants or denies. Once granted aid, the defendant may hire a lawyer whom legal aid will pay. For cases that go to Crown Court, if the magistrates refuse a grant of aid, the defendant may reapply to the Crown Court.[72] More than 90 percent of defendants tried in the Crown Courts rely on legal aid; eligibility for legal aid in criminal matters depends not just on the applicant's ability to pay for representation, but also the "interests of justice."[73] The heavy reliance on legal aid results in the government paying virtually all of the lawyers involved in the criminal justice system, whether on the prosecution side or on the defense side.

In addition to rights of audience, there is one other important difference between solicitors and barristers in the criminal process. Although individual solicitors tend to represent only one side—the prosecution through solicitors directly employed by the government and the defense through solicitors in private practice[74]—barristers may appear for the prosecution in one case and the defense in the next. In practice, only about one-third of barristers doing criminal work regularly appear for both the prosecution and for the defense; another one-third appear exclusively for one side or the other.[75] There is a pattern of younger barristers relying more on the defense side and then shifting over to the prosecution as they gain experience.[76] Moreover, because of the relatively low fees paid for criminal work, barristers tend to move to other areas of practice as they gain experience.[77]

Criminal Courts

The jurisdictions of the two criminal courts, Magistrates' Courts and the Crown Court, overlap in significant ways. Magistrates' Court handles less

---

71. The Criminal Justice and Public Order Act 1994, §44, replaced the committal hearing with an administrative procedure for transferring cases from the Magistrates' Court to the Crown Court; the role of the duty solicitor under the new system is not clear.

72. Almost all applications for legal aid are granted; *JSAR 1993*, pp. 98–99.

73. See *JSAR 1992*, p. 93. Marre, supra note 10, p. 74.

74. See Mike McConville, Jacqueline Hodgson, Legg Bridges, and Anita Pavlovic, *Standing Accused: The Organisation and Practices of Criminal Defence Lawyers in Britain* (Oxford: Clarendon Press, 1994).

75. Abel, supra note 14, p. 115.

76. I infer this from variations in source of income depending on years of experience; see ibid., p. 366.

77. Marre, supra note 10, p. 80.

serious offenses (summary offenses) and preliminary proceedings in serious offenses; Crown Courts handle trials and sentencing in more serious offenses (''indictable offenses''). The Magistrates' Court deals with those offenses that are purely summary offenses (having an unlicensed television, most traffic offenses, assaulting the police, driving under the influence, criminal damage below a specified value). However, magistrates must refer the most serious offenses (''purely indictable'') such as homicide, rape, kidnapping, robbery, and spying, to the Crown Court for trial and sentencing. Four intermediate categories of offenses are triable in Magistrates' or Crown Court and are called ''either-way offences'': theft, fraud, burglary, reckless driving, and drug offenses.

For the most serious offenses, the Magistrates' Court provides what amounts to a preliminary hearing (''committal proceedings''), which only determines that the prosecution has evidence relevant to the offense charged.[78] In either-way offenses, the magistrates can refer the case to Crown Court if the magistrates, the prosecutor, or the defendant so chooses, and about 20 percent are thus reassigned.[79] The magistrates send the case to Crown Court if they do not wish to impose sentence, usually because they believe the offense merits harsher sanctions than they can mete out. The Crown Prosecutor will also request ''committal'' to have available the more severe sanctions that Crown Court can impose. The defendant will request referral to Crown Court in order to have a right to a jury trial; typically this is done in hopes of securing an acquittal, although most of the defendants who request committal eventually decide to plead guilty.[80]

Magistrates' Courts

Magistrates' Courts are locally based. Outside large urban areas, a panel of two or three unpaid lay magistrates, assisted by a professional, law-trained clerk, hear cases; the clerk manages the proceedings and advises the magistrates on points of law and procedure.[81] In large urban areas, particularly metropolitan London, one also finds law-trained, ''stipendiary'' magistrates; in fact, in a busy urban Magistrates' Court a stipendiary magistrate can be sitting in one courtroom while a panel of lay magistrates sits in the courtroom

78. The magistrates also make an initial determination concerning bail; see Spencer, supra note 14, p. 249.

79. *CSEW 1992*, p. 124.

80. See Carol Hedderman, and David Moxon, *Magistrates' Court or Crown Court? Mode of Trial Decisions and Sentencing*, Home Office Research Study No. 125 (London: HMSO, 1992), p. vi. *Times* (London), July 7, 1993, p. 4, reports that 83% of those ''defendants who elect a Crown Court trial change their plea to guilty.''

81. Spencer, supra note 14, pp. 186–188, 415–419.

next door.[82] For summary offenses, the Magistrates' Court tries and sentences. It is the duty of the magistrates to both determine guilt or innocence (if the plea is other than guilty) and impose a sentence; there are no juries. Magistrates' Court deals with approximately 70 percent of the summary offenses at the defendant's first appearance.[83] Sentences usually consist of fines; almost none involve imprisonment.[84]

Magistrates may deal with the intermediate either-way offenses in a variety of ways. They may accept a plea of guilty and sentence, try the case without a jury and (sentence if they convict), accept a plea of guilty and commit to Crown Court for sentencing, or commit to Crown Court for trial and possible sentencing. Magistrates commit about 20 percent of those accused of either-way offenses for trial to Crown Court; they refer another 2 percent or so of either-way offenses to Crown Court for sentencing after a determination of guilt in Magistrates' Court (either by a guilty plea or a summary trial).[85] The overwhelming proportion of such cases dealt with in the Magistrates' Court involve a plea of guilty; and most contested cases—77 percent in 1987–88—end in guilty verdicts.[86] Magistrates acquit only about 2 percent of those charged with indictable offenses.[87] Very few of those sentenced for indictable offenses by magistrates go to prison, 40 to 50 percent receive fines, and about one-third receive what amounts to probation.[88]

Crown Court

Crown Court, created in 1971 by combining two older courts (Assizes and Quarter Sessions), tries and sentences the most serious offenses.[89] Unlike

82. See Shari Seidman Diamond, "Revising Images of Public Punitiveness: Sentencing by Lay and Professional English Magistrates," *Law & Social Inquiry* 15 (1990), p. 198.

83. *CSEW 1992*, p. 130.

84. *CSEW 1992*, p. 149.

85. *CSEW 1992*, p. 131. Only something less than 6% of indictable offenses must be referred to Crown Court—about 25,400 out of 452,900 indictable offenses in 1990 (computed from pp. 131–132). Calculated from *CSEW 1992*, p. 133.

86. See Michael McConville and John Baldwin, *Courts, Prosecution, and Conviction* (Oxford: Clarendon Press, 1981), pp. 6, 212. *Guardian Weekly* reports more recent research by the Home Office showing that only 30% of contested cases in Magistrates' Court end in acquittals (July 18, 1993, p. 11).

87. Ibid.

88. *CSEW 1992*, p. 149. One might speculate on whether lay and stipendiary magistrates differed in their sentencing practices; Diamond, supra note 82, studied magistrates in London and found that lay magistrates tended to be less severe than stipendiaries for burglary cases but little difference for theft cases. Using hypotheticals, she found a consistent tendency for stipendiaries to prefer more severe sentences than lay magistrates.

89. For an interesting portrait of one Crown Court, see Paul Rock, *The Social World of an English Crown Court: Witness and Professionals in the Crown Court Centre in Wood Green* (Oxford: Clarendon Press, 1993).

Magistrates' Court, a jury can determine guilt and innocence. Also unlike Magistrates' Court, which is local, the Crown Court is a national court; judges from anywhere in England can sit at any of the ninety Crown Court Centres around the country, including the Old Bailey, now known officially as the Central Criminal Court. The judges hearing cases in the Crown Court may be High Court judges, circuit court judges, or recorders.[90] In practice, circuit judges handle the majority of cases in Crown Court, with recorders and assistant recorders hearing most of the rest; High Court judges hear only 2–3 percent of cases.[91]

About 18 percent of the cases in the Crown Court are there by requirement. A majority end in up the Crown Court by the decision of the magistrates, with 30 percent coming by the choice of the defendant.[92] Most defendants committed to Crown Court plead guilty. One study found that 60 percent pleaded guilty in 1978; by 1985, this had risen to 70 percent, and it has remained at this level.[93] Of those who plead not guilty, an increasing proportion obtain acquittals. In 1993, the acquittal rate stood at 58 percent, compared to 50 percent in 1978.[94] The majority of the acquittals come through the direction of the judge, either by discharge (called "dismissal" in the United States) or by directed verdicts of acquittal; in 1993 only about 42 percent of acquittals were actually decided by a jury.[95] However, juries appear to be increasingly likely to acquit; the acquittal rate in 1985 was about 33 percent, but this had risen to 37 percent in 1990 and 1991.[96] In 1987–1988, acquittals after trial overall stood at about 50 percent.[97]

Jury Trials

Trials in Crown Court are usually before juries, which typically consist of twelve persons. Historically, conviction required unanimity, but the Criminal Justice Act of 1967 allowed ten jurors to convict.[98] The jury trial process is

90. The title "recorder" comes from the title of the person who presided at sittings of Quarter Sessions, one of the courts that preceded the Crown Court; Spencer, supra note 14, p. 366n1.

91. *JSAR 1993*, p. 64.

92. *Times* (London), July 7, 1993, p. 4.

93. McConville and Baldwin, supra note 86, p. 6. *JSAR 1985*, p. 73. *JSAR 1990*, p. 63; *JSAR 1992*, p. 61; *JSAR 1993*, p. 64.

94. McConville and Baldwin, supra note 86, p. 6. *JSAR 1993*, p. 65.

95. *JSAR 1993*, p. 65. Eight years earlier, juries accounted for 52% of acquittals.

96. Computed from *JSAR 1985*, p. 72, *JSAR 1990*, p. 61, and *JSAR 1991*, p. 63.

97. McConville et al., supra note 74, p. 212.

98. Spencer, supra note 14, p. 259. Strictly speaking, ten jurors can convict if the jury consists of eleven or more persons; nine jurors can convict if the jury consists of ten persons. Only about 15% of those convicted had a jury that was nonunanimous in its verdict (see *JSAR 1993*, p. 66).

similar to that in the United States, with two noteworthy exceptions in addition to nonunanimous verdicts. First, the barristers representing the prosecution and defense appear gowned and wigged, as does the judge, who, if he is a High Court judge, is addressed as "my lord" (or "my lady" if the judge is one of the few women on the High Court bench), rather than "your honor."[99] Second, the judge provides a "summing up" which can include, in addition to a summary of the evidence and legal instructions, comments on the relevance of pieces of evidence and on the credibility of witnesses. The summing up is not supposed to lead the jury in a particular direction, and one study that included interviews with defendants found a general view that "the summing-up by the judge had as a rule been balanced and fair."[100] However, it is not "unknown for judges, while emphasising that matters of fact are for the jury and not the judge, to comment on the facts in such a way as to attempt to influence the jury in one direction or the other."[101] In a survey conducted for a Royal Commission on criminal justice, judges acknowledged that their summing up often "point[ed]" the jury "towards acquittal or towards conviction"; in a sample of cases from around England, 11 percent of the judges said that they had pointed toward acquittal and 21 percent toward conviction (although most said they had pointed "somewhat" rather than "strongly" in that direction).[102]

What difference does trial by jury versus trial by judge make? As in the United States, judges seem to be more inclined to convict when juries acquit than inclined to acquit when juries convict.[103] While there is some evidence of a convergence in recent years of the decisions of American judges and juries, there is no such convergence in England.[104]

The English criminal justice system avoids a major issue that confronts jury trials in the United States: the problem of pretrial publicity. The Criminal

99. Judges of both levels of appellate courts are also addressed as "My Lord" or "My Lady"; circuit judges and recorders are addressed as "Your Honour"; see Cecil, supra note 34, p. 44.

100. John Baldwin and Michael McConville, *Jury Trials* (Oxford: Clarendon Press, 1979), p. 85. Of course, there are exceptions. This study quotes one defense solicitor (p. 72), "in legal terms the summing-up was wholly wrong. It was such that the judge said: 'Well, the prosecution witness did not identify the defendant but nevertheless he was the man who took the money.' "

101. *Royal Commission on Criminal Justice: Report* (London: HMSO, 1993), p. 123, henceforth cited as *RCCJ*.

102. Michael Zander and Paul Henderson, *The Royal Commission on Criminal Justice: Crown Court Study* (London: HMSO, 1993), p. 130.

103. See Baldwin and McConville, supra note 100, p. 46; compare to Harry Kalven and Hans Zeisel, *The American Jury* (Chicago: University of Chicago Press, 1966).

104. See Zander and Henderson, supra note 102, pp. 163–164; James Levine, *Juries and Politics* (Pacific Grove, Calif.: Brooks/Cole, 1992), pp. 121–127.

Justice Act of 1967 severely limited reporting of committal proceedings in Magistrates' Courts unless the magistrates choose not to commit to Crown Court. Ordinarily the press can report only matters of the formal record (charges, names of parties, and so on). However, the limitations on reporting can go well beyond committal proceedings if the judge determines it is in the interest of justice. A prominent example involved Winston Silcott, who was convicted of killing a police constable during a riot in the Tottenham section of London in October 1985. At the conclusion of the murder trial in March 1987, the news media reported that while he had been in jail awaiting trial for the killing of the constable, Silcott had been tried and convicted of killing a man at a party in December 1984 (he was out on bail awaiting trial on that charge at the time of the Tottenham riots). Prior to his conviction on the riot-connected murder, there were no newspaper reports of the 1984 charge or the trial in connection with that charge (or of Silcott's three prior murder charges and trials). All these reporting restrictions had the goal of avoiding the prejudicing of potential jurors.[105]

Criminal Appeals

The structure of the appellate process for criminal cases varies depending upon whether the Magistrates' Court had dealt with the matter as a summary offense or the Crown Court had dealt with it as an indictable offense. A disgruntled defendant whom the magistrates had convicted can appeal points of fact or law to Crown Court, or, if the issue is only one of a point of law, to the High Court. In the former case when the issue involves a matter of fact, a panel consisting of a circuit judge or a recorder sitting with at least two (but not more than four) magistrates provides what amounts to a new trial, rehearing previous witnesses, hearing new witnesses, and considering any other new evidence that may be available. The Crown Court can send the matter back to Magistrates' Court or do anything the magistrates could have done, including modifying the sentence upward or downward.[106]

In raw numbers, the volume of such appeals is fairly large—almost 25,000 in 1994.[107] However, this is only about 2 percent of the approximately one million criminal cases (nonmotoring) dealt with each year in the Magistrates' Courts.[108] Recall, however, that defendants contested only about 8 percent of cases in the Magistrates' Courts, three-quarters of which ended in convic-

105. See *Times* (London), Mar. 20, 1987, p. 1, 3. Silcott's conviction in the Tottenham riot case was thrown out by the Court of Appeal in 1991 after it was revealed that police documents had been tampered with and that the police had fabricated evidence (*Times* [London] *Index 1991*, p. 275).

106. Spencer, supra note 14, p. 198.

107. *JSAR 1993*, p. 62.

108. *CSEW 1991*, p. 18.

tion after a summary (nonjury) trial.[109] If one presumes that appeals come mostly from contested cases, then roughly one-third of the magistrates' convictions in contested cases lead to appeals to the Crown Court. Furthermore, the appeals do represent a genuine review. In 1992, the Crown Court disposed of 19,691 appeals from Magistrates' Court: "allowing" 32 percent (reversing the magistrates) and "modifying" the magistrates' decision in 15 percent.[110]

Although both sides can appeal matters involving only points of law to the Crown Court, the more productive route is to appeal such decisions to the Divisional Court under a procedure called "judicial review."[111] This asks a court to ensure that a governmental body is correctly applying the law.[112] In practice the number of cases is quite small, only about five hundred per year.[113]

Appeals from decisions of the Crown Court go to the criminal division of the Court of Appeal.[114] Appeals can address a conviction or the sentence imposed.[115] While anyone convicted in Crown Court may file an appeal, there is not an automatic right to have that appeal fully heard. A defendant must first secure "leave to appeal." A single judge reviews the appeal request, and only if this judge grants leave does the appeal go forward to a full hearing.[116] In recent years, about one-third of those seeking leave to appeal obtain it.[117]

In 1993, the Court of Appeal heard a total of about 2,800 criminal appeals (this figure excludes cases in which leave to appeal was denied): one-third against conviction and two-thirds against sentence. The success rate in appeals against conviction was 45 percent, compared to 69 percent against

109. Strictly speaking, these figures are only for indictable offenses; however, for purposes of discussion, I will assume that roughly the same proportions apply to purely summary offenses.

110. Computed from *CSEW 1992*, p. 63.

111. The Divisional Court is a part of the Queen's Bench Division of the High Court. There are two different procedures; one called judicial review and one called "case stated"; see Spencer, supra note 14, pp. 198–200. For counting purposes, I have not distinguished between the two. While only the defendant may appeal on a factual issue (i.e., the prosecution cannot appeal an acquittal), either the prosecution or defendant can appeal on a point of law.

112. Judicial review is dealt with in more detail below.

113. *CSEW 1992*, p. 14; only 30–40% of these appeals succeed.

114. The panel of judges hearing criminal appeals is typically composed of a combination of one Lord Justice of Appeal (a judge of the Court of Appeal) and two High Court judges from the Queen's Bench Division; Spencer, supra note 14, p. 201.

115. If the sentence is appealed, the Court of Appeal can reduce the sentence, let the original sentence stand, or increase the sentence.

116. If the single judge denies leave to appeal, the defendant may renew the application to the "full court" (i.e., a panel of judges). In 1992 there were 677 such applications, but only 145 were successful; *CSEW 1992*, p. 12.

117. *JSAR 1993*, p. 11.

sentence;[118] these high success rates should not be surprising given the initial screening of the applications for leave to appeal. The absolute number of successful appeals (about 400 against conviction and about 1,300 against sentence) is tiny when compared to the volume of cases in the Crown Court: about 16,500 convictions after trial (a successful appeal rate of about 2.5 percent), and close to 80,000 defendants sentenced, 40–45 percent of whom are imprisoned (a successful appeal rate of less than 2 percent).[119]

Parties can appeal decisions of the Court of Appeal in criminal cases to the House of Lords. Leave to appeal to the Lords must be granted either by the Court of Appeal or by the Lords themselves. In 1992, parties filed twenty-three applications for "referral to [the] House of Lords" with the Court of Appeal; the Court granted only seven.[120] That year the House of Lords dealt with exactly the same number of petitions for leave to appeal in criminal cases and granted only six.[121] Thus, few criminal cases get to the House of Lords, and criminal matters make up only about a quarter of the cases considered by the Lords.[122]

The Guilty Plea Process in England

The figures discussed previously make it clear that most defendants in England plead guilty, whether in Magistrates' Court or in Crown Court. This pattern is similar to that in most jurisdictions in the United States. To what degree does the dominance of guilty pleas involve plea bargaining—pleading guilty in return for a reduction in charges and/or sentence?

When a pair of criminal justice researchers first suggested that plea bargaining might be going on in England, that suggestion ignited a firestorm of protest from participants in the criminal justice system. In 1974, John Baldwin and Michael McConville (from the Institute of Judicial Administration in Birmingham) undertook a major study of Crown Court dispositions in Birmingham Crown Court. In the course of the research, which involved 2,406 defendants, the researchers interviewed the small number of defendants who pleaded guilty late in the process to find out what accounted for the last-minute change of plea. In the course of the interviews, they heard numerous reports of what they labeled plea bargaining. Only 29 percent of the 121 defendants interviewed reported no deal or pressure and that they pleaded guilty simply because they were in fact guilty.[123] The nature of the bargaining

---

118. Computed from *JSAR 1993*, p. 12.

119. *JSAR 1993*, pp. 62, 65. This combines "imprisonment" and "young offender institution" as reported in *CSEW 1991*, p. 138.

120. *JSAR 1992*, p. 12.

121. *JSAR 1992*, p. 10.

122. Based on data in *JSAR 1992*, pp. 10–11.

123. John Baldwin and Michael McConville, *Negotiated Justice: Pressures to Plead Guilty* (London: Martin Robertson, 1977), p. 28.

ranged from an explicit offer and acceptance (18 percent) to pressure from the barrister to plead guilty without any specific offer (40 percent).

As word of this research began to circulate within the legal community, several prominent figures mounted an effort to suppress reports of the findings. As described by one writer, the "legal profession was furious at the suggestion that lawyers were putting improper pressure on their clients to plead guilty."[124] Both the president of the Law Society (the organization of solicitors) and the chairman of the Bar (the organization of barristers) published letters in national newspapers attacking the research prior to its publication. The chairman of the Bar wrote to the Home Secretary stating that "in my view it would be directly contrary to the public interest that the book should be published in its proposed form at this stage"; a member of the House of Commons posed a question to the Home Secretary about the pending publication, and this led to a lengthy written reply.[125]

One objection to the research was its heavy reliance on interviews with defendants. One High Court judge "likened legal research that consists of interviewing defendants to medical research that canvasses the opinions of flies that buzz round wounds."[126] Partly in response to these critiques, another researcher undertook a replication and extension of the earlier study that included interviews with the defendants' lawyers.[127] This study, which differed in design from the first study in several important respects,[128] found few instances of pressure from lawyers and concluded that defendants usually plead guilty because they have no way to contest the charges against them. Does this mean that there is no plea bargaining in England, or does it simply indicate a more complex guilty plea system than that associated with the common image of plea bargaining? The latter is probably the case.

As in the United States, there is much less give-and-take than the image suggested by the term *bargaining*. The process is more one of trying to clarify what the appropriate sanction is through an effort to understand the nature of the actions and the nature of the actor, what one American researcher

124. Spencer, supra note 14, p. 263.

125. Baldwin and McConville, supra note 123, p. viii.

126. Spencer, supra note 14, p. 263. Baldwin and McConville were unable to interview barristers as part of their larger research project owing to resistance from the Bar; see Baldwin and McConville, supra note 123, pp. 23–24.

127. Robert D. Seifer, "Plea-Bargaining in England," in William F. McDonald and James A. Cramer (eds.), *Plea-Bargaining* (Lexington, Mass.: Lexington Books, 1980), pp. 179–197.

128. The second study involved only defendants sentenced to prison, while the first involved both imprisoned defendants and those who received sentences not involving imprisonment. While the first study focused on those who entered late guilty pleas, the second study took a random sample without regard to when the guilty plea was entered. Third, the later study included those sentenced by magistrates as well as those sentenced in Crown Court.

called "settling the facts."[129] Other researchers have likened the process more to that of a supermarket with fixed prices (which one can take or leave) than to the bazaar where one specifically bargains over prices.[130] Increasingly, researchers have come to refer to a "guilty plea process" rather than to "plea bargaining."

Structurally, there is an implicit guilty plea system built into the English criminal justice system, at least for either-way offenses (which comprise the majority of cases sent to Crown Court). The sentencing authority of magistrates is limited to a term of imprisonment of six months, plus a range of fines.[131] A defendant who wants to plead not guilty and be tried before a jury must request committal to the Crown Court, whose sentencing authority includes more severe sanctions. This institutionalizes in an unstated but quite formal way the threat of more severe sanctions for those who demand a jury trial for most common offenses.[132] All that a solicitor must say to a defendant who says he or she wants a jury trial is something to the effect of: "You know that if you plead guilty here at Magistrates' Court you will almost certainly get at most six months imprisonment, and quite likely you will get off with a fine; if you insist upon a jury trial, and even if you then decide to plead guilty, you could go to prison for much longer." It is easy to see why most defendants plead guilty before the magistrates.

Beyond the *implicit* threat of more severe sentences for those who insist on a jury trial, there was for some years an acknowledged system of sentence discounts for defendants who pleaded guilty in the Crown Court. The Court of Appeal had endorsed a 25–30 percent discount on the sentences of those who pleaded guilty, and most Crown Court defendants were aware of the discount.[133] This discount applied only to those who enter a guilty plea before the trial starts. In 1994 Parliament explicitly authorized such discounts for defendants who plead guilty at an early stage in the court process.[134]

CRIMINAL JUSTICE AS A POLITICAL ISSUE

How then do crime and criminal justice enter into the political arena? Several types of interactions between politics and the criminal justice system that

129. Pamela Utz, *Settling the Facts: Discretion and Negotiation in Criminal Court* (Lexington, Mass.: Lexington Books, 1978).

130. Peter F. Nardulli, James Eisenstein, and Roy B. Flemming, *The Tenor of Justice: Criminal Courts and the Guilty Plea Process* (Urbana: University of Illinois Press, 1988).

131. Spencer, supra note 14, p. 272.

132. Of course, this does not apply to offenses that must be dealt with in Crown Court, but the number of defendants accused of such offenses is a very small proportion of the total number of defendants who stand accused of indictable offenses.

133. RCCJ, supra note 101, pp. 110–111. See also Alex Samuels, "Discount for Guilty?" *Solicitors Journal* (Oct. 15, 1993), p. 1029; and Zander and Henderson, supra note 102, p. 146.

134. The Criminal Justice and Public Order Act 1994, §48.

occur in the United States do not occur in England. For example, many American chief law enforcement officials are either directly elected (in the case of county sheriffs) or are appointed by elected officials such as mayors; in some communities it is common for the election of a new mayor to result in the appointment of a new police chief. While there is some local influence on the selection of chief constables, that selection is largely the responsibility of officials in the Home Office in London, who do not make their decisions in direct response to electoral results. In the United States, most trial judges must periodically face the electorate (to win office initially, to win re-election to office, or for retention in office), and the judge's handling of criminal cases can arise as an issue in the election. Also, in most states, the person responsible for prosecuting those accused of criminal acts is an elected official (usually with the title district attorney, but sometimes called the states' attorney). As discussed above, in England neither the judges nor the prosecutors are directly involved in the electoral process.

Crime as a political issue is likely to arise only through parliamentary politics or through local governmental elections. In the former, crime-related issues are most likely going to concern the structure, operation, and funding of the criminal justice apparatus. In the latter, the issue is likely to be more limited, focusing primarily on local police operations (over which local authorities have quite limited control) and possibly on the local Magistrates' Courts. From the mid-1970s to the mid-1990s the primary arena has been parliamentary, through crime and criminal justice as an electoral issue or criminal justice reform on the parliamentary agenda.

Criminal Justice as a Public Concern

To gauge the concern of the British public regarding crime, over many years the British Gallup Poll has asked (on almost a monthly basis) "What would you say is the most urgent problem facing the country at the present time? . . . And what would you say is the next most urgent problem?" (see figure 3.2).[135] As the most important problem, law and order usually fluctuates in

135. In this section I refer to Britain because the Gallup data do not isolate England and Wales from Scotland. The monthly *Gallup Political & Economic Index* (prior to 1991 the title was the *Gallup Political Index*) has reported the percent responding with something concerning "law and order" to the first question and to the two questions combined. Prior to April 1973, only the most important problem was ascertained; law and order was first identified as a category in June 1973. When the percentage falls below some unstated threshold, Gallup omits law and order from its reports; for purposes of coding, I have presumed the figure to be one-half of 1% for the most important problem and 1% for the two most important problems. On rare occasions, Gallup has skipped a month; these are considered as missing except when there were two surveys in a prior month or succeeding month that allowed me to get twelve readings for the calendar year (when there were more than twelve readings in a year, I average appropriate pairs).

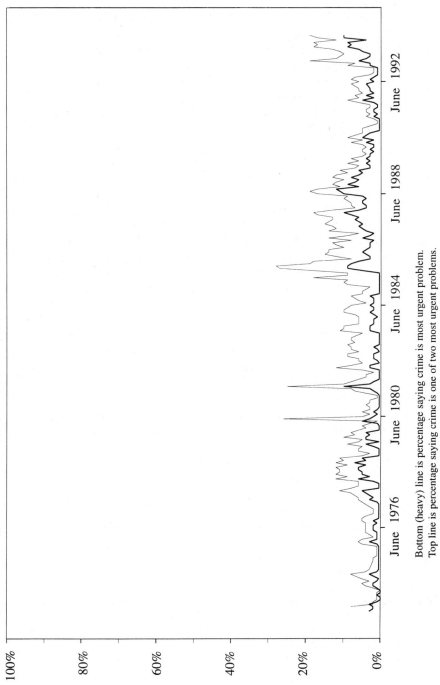

Bottom (heavy) line is percentage saying crime is most urgent problem.
Top line is percentage saying crime is one of two most urgent problems.

Figure 3.2. Concern about Crime in Britain

the 5 percent and under range; the major exceptions are 1987–89 (and briefly in late 1985) when it rose to 12 percent, and the second half of 1993, when it rose to the 8–10 percent range. The trend for the two most urgent problems parallels that for the most urgent problem. Except for 1985–89 and the second half of 1993, it usually fluctuates in the 5–10 percent range. Overall, the low percentage who identify law and order in response to Gallup's query indicates that the issue is of secondary concern.

However, this does not mean that the public does not have a strong concern about crime. Gallup has also occasionally (between 1975 and 1988) asked, "Do you think any of these are a very serious social problem in Britain today?" Included in the list of possible problems were crimes of violence, juvenile crime, rape, and organized crime. The percentage of respondents who said that each of these is a problem has been high throughout the survey period, and has increased over the years. For example the percentage saying that crimes of violence are a serious problem went from 76 percent in 1975 to 96 percent in 1988. The corresponding figures for juvenile crime are 70 percent and 93 percent (although this fluctuated between 70 and 80 percent for most of the time period) and from 49 percent to 92 percent for rape.

One can also see the concern of the British public about crime in the responses to questions asked during the months prior to the 1989 election about the importance of various issues. Throughout the period that Gallup asked the question the percentage of respondents saying that "maintaining law and order" was "very important" hovered around 80 percent; some months, it had the highest percentage of "extremely important" responses (surpassing all of the economic issues), but this lead was never by more than a percentage point or two.[136]

We can also see an increase in the responses to the question, "Is there any area right around here, that is, within a mile, where you would be afraid to walk alone at night" (see figure 3.3). The level of fear, as measured by this question, is greater in Britain than it is in the United States where Gallup has asked a virtually identical question.[137]

How does the pattern of public concern in England compare to that in the U.S.? The Gallup Poll in the United States has asked a question similar to the question, "What do you think is the most important problem facing this country today?" and with only occasional exceptions, Gallup has reported a

136. *Gallup Political Index*, June 1979, p. 11.

137. The question in the United States is, "Is there any area near where you live—that is, within a mile—where you would be afraid to walk alone at night?" The figures are from *Gallup Poll Monthly*, March 1992, p. 51. As Jacob pointed out in chapter 2, there are substantial variations by size of city in the United States, with fear considerably higher in the largest cities (e.g., New York, Chicago, Detroit, Miami, Los Angeles) than in the second-tier cities (Boston, Dallas, Seattle, etc.).

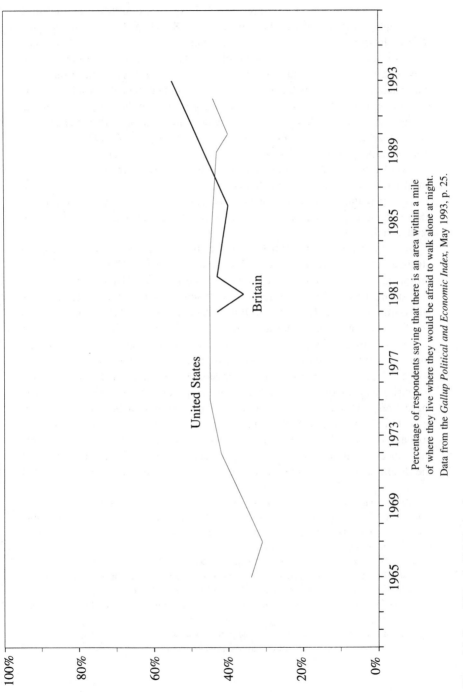

Percentage of respondents saying that there is an area within a mile of where they live where they would be afraid to walk alone at night. Data from the *Gallup Political and Economic Index*, May 1993, p. 25.

Figure 3.3. Fear of Crime in Neighborhood

single response to this (see figure 3.4).[138] Prior to 1994, crime as the most important problem peaks at 29 percent in 1968 (when it was a major issue in the election campaign). During that time, only the war in Vietnam surpassed it as the "most important problem." The first corresponding data for Britain is for 1973, and through about 1978 the level of concern in the U.S., while not as high as in the late 1960s, was higher than in Britain. As the data show, from 1978 through 1993, crime has been in the 2–6 percent range in the U.S., but has fluctuated more widely in Britain, with some periods higher than the U.S. and others lower. In the latter part of 1993, the proportion of respondents identifying crime as the "most important problem" facing the United States skyrocketed, rising to 16 percent in September 1993, and then to 49 percent in late January 1994;[139] there was no corresponding change in Britain. As Jacob discussed in chapter 2, this sharp increase probably reflects the amount of media coverage the crime issue received in the second half of 1993.

We can also compare British attitudes vis-à-vis crime as a public issue to attitudes in other European countries. Since the early 1970s a series of coordinated surveys among the countries of the European Union (Eurobarometer studies) from time to time have included questions that relate to crime and criminal justice. In 1988, the Eurobarometer asked, "These days, which are for you the most important topics and events?"[140] Respondents were encouraged to give more than one reply. One of the categories that was used for coding British responses to this question was "law and order/crime/etc."; about 7.5 percent of the British respondents mentioned crime-related issues. In only seven of the other twelve countries participating in the survey was there a response category that captured crime, criminal justice, law and order, as a topic of importance.[141] Compared to the other seven countries, Britain appears to fall in the middle regarding concern about crime. Countries where the concern is higher include Italy (14 percent), Belgium (10 percent), and the Netherlands (9 percent); a lower level of concern is found in Ireland

---

138. All data are taken from *The Gallup Poll Monthly* and its predecessor the *Gallup Opinion Index* (Gallup's monthly report on its general public opinion questions). In 1973, there were several occasions when Gallup reported the "next most important" as well, or in combination with the "most important."

139. The figure stood at 37% in mid-January 1994.

140. The figures in this section are computed from data contained in Karlheinz Reif and Anna Melich, *Euro-barometer 30: Immigrants and Out-groups in Western Europe, October–November 1988* (Ann Arbor, Mich.: Inter-University Consortium for Political and Social Research, 1991).

141. In one other country, West Germany, there was a response that dealt with "internal security," but this appears to focus on terrorism rather than routine crime.

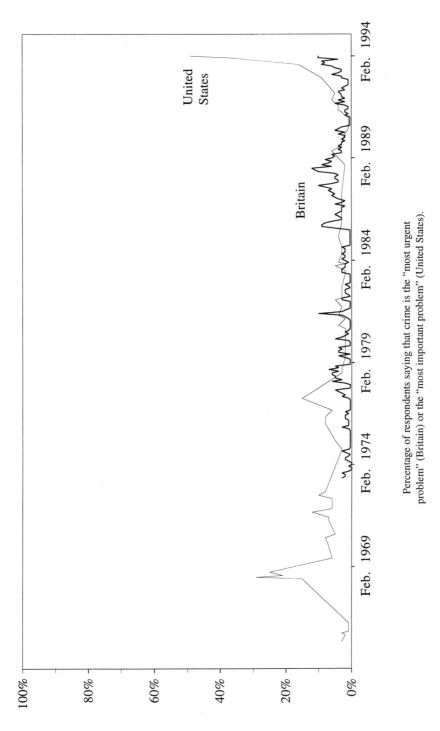

Percentage of respondents saying that crime is the "most urgent problem" (Britain) or the "most important problem" (United States).

Figure 3.4. Concern about Crime in Britain and the United States

(2 percent) and Denmark (4 percent); and a similar level is evident in France (8 percent) and Spain (7 percent).[142]

Overall, the public opinion data suggest that Britons worry about crime, and see it as a problem, particularly when prompted. However, when put in the context of the economic problems in Britain in the past two decades, crime is clearly a second-order concern.

Crime as an Electoral Issue

There are several ways to examine the role of crime in the electoral arena. One is to try to assess its importance in the voting decisions of the electorate. The Gallup poll survey after the May 1979 election showed that, despite some emphasis on law and order by the Conservative Party, few voters identified law and order themes as one of the two most important issues in their voting decision.[143] Another indicator is the inclusion of crime-related questions in postelection surveys. While the 1983 election study included a cluster of crime-related questions, crime does not emerge as a major issue more generally from the perspective of voting behavior research. In a summary of trend data from the British election studies between 1963 and 1987, the only crime-related issue asked sufficiently often to warrant mention was capital punishment.[144]

This does not mean that political parties have not tried to make law and order an issue in election campaigns. This is evident both in the party platforms (called "manifestos" in Britain) and in campaign activities themselves.[145] One finds that the Tories (the Conservatives) have spoken to the law and order issue at least since 1964 (the earliest manifesto I looked at) when they stated, in a section titled and subtitled "Freedom and Order" and "Upholding Law": "We shall continue to build up the strength of the police

142. For similar results in the late 1970s, see Jacques René Rabier and Ronald Inglehart, *Consumer Attitudes in Europe* (Ann Arbor, Mich.: Inter-University Consortium for Political and Social Research, 1978), pp. 83–94.

143. Gallup asked respondents the following open-ended question: "Think of all the urgent problems facing the country at the present time. When you decided which way to vote, which *two* issues did you yourself consider most important?" Only 11% responded with law and order related themes, compared to 42% inflation, 27% unemployment and jobs, and 20% strikes and industrial relations (*Gallup Political Index*, June 1979, p. 11).

144. Ivor Crewe, Neil Day, and Anthony Fox (eds.), *The British Electorate 1963–1987: A Compendium of Data from the British Election Studies* (Cambridge: Cambridge University Press, 1991). Other issues that might be seen as law related include abortion, pornography, racial and sexual equality, treatment of strikers, and nationalization of major industries.

145. For an analysis of news coverage of the law and order issue in the context of one election campaign, see Alan Clarke and Ian Taylor, "Vandals, Pickets and Muggers: Television Coverage of Law and Order in the 1979 Election," *Screen Education* 36 (1980), pp. 99–111.

forces." The 1964 Labour manifesto does not speak explicitly to the law and order issue.

The Tories have consistently made more of the law and order issue than the Labour Party over the last quarter century. Based on all the Labour and Conservative manifestos between 1964 and 1992, the Tories usually devoted more lines to law and order than did Labour (see figure 3.5).[146] There is a clear increase in attention to the law and order issue over time. In 1992, the Conservative manifesto had 117 lines dealing with law and order; for about fifteen years the count had been about one-third to one-half of this, which in turn constituted a substantial increase compared to the 1960s. In contrast, the Labour Party has tended to refer to the law and order issue without going into substantial detail. The greatest attention was in 1983, and much of the discussion was of undoing actions the Tories had taken during the previous four years and challenging a major proposal to increase the powers of the police.

It is striking that the Conservatives have made so much of crime, even as crime rates shot up during their long period of control of the British government.[147] One explanation for this seeming paradox is that Tories focus on crime in order to shift attention away from the economic retrenchment that occurred during the 1980s. Perhaps by diverting attention to crime in the streets and away from the unemployed in the streets, the Tories could get the electorate to overlook the problems associated with (Labour would say, "caused by") policies put in effect under Margaret Thatcher. Some analysts have argued that Thatcher came to power in 1979 with the interrelated goals of "replac[ing] socialism with a market economy, reduc[ing] State involvement in the field of welfare provision, and break[ing] the power of the trade unions."[148] As part of this goal, the Tories sought "to develop a strong State in the arena of law and order." A related explanation is that the Conservatives sought to maintain a strong state but had to find an area in which to do this as they reduced the role of the state in the economy. One analyst argues that strong central authority over education, the weakening of local government, and the strengthening of the authority of the police replaced state management of major elements of the economy.[149]

146. The manifestos are usually included in the *Times Guide to the House of Commons,* published after each election. The 1970 manifestos are taken from F. W. S. Craig (ed.), *British General Election Manifestos, 1900–1974* (London: Macmillan, 1975), pp. 324–366. In counting lines, I did not include terrorism, Northern Ireland, or drug abuse.

147. See Loveday, supra note 40, and Brake and Hale, supra note 40, pp. 94–115, for specific discussions of how crime has inexorably increased despite the Tory policies intended to bring it under control.

148. Brake and Hale, supra note 40, p. 2.

149. Loveday, supra note 40.

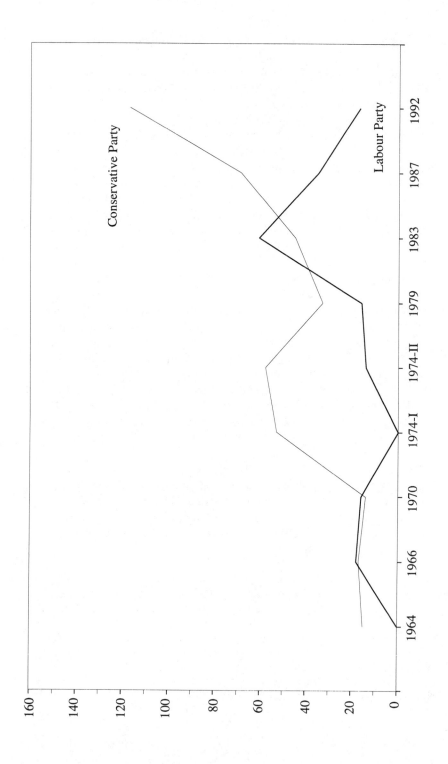

Number of lines of text concerning crime appearing in party manifestos.

Brake and Hale suggest a third line of argument (which is not entirely distinct from the others): "Law and order [as a political issue] . . . has developed in response to social anxieties felt by 'respectable' elements of British society about a Britain which has difficulties in coming to terms with its position in a changing world. It is no longer possible to maintain a Little England attitude in the new European community. Contemporary Britain is a multi-ethnic, multi-racial, culturally diverse society. It is no longer dominated by established tradition, or established religious beliefs; it has new populations with new sets of consciousness."[150] Thus, law and order has become a metaphor for resistance to change, although this linking of law and order to tradition was evident even before Thatcher became the leader of the Conservative Party.[151] In a fundamental sense, the Conservatives have continued to stress law and order because in England it has come to be a metaphor for the traditional English social structure.

Law and Order as a Parliamentary Issue

While the public has not made law and order a primary issue, it has been an important and controversial issue in Parliament over the past fifteen years.[152] This is evident in the changes wrought by the Criminal Justice Act of 1982, the Police and Criminal Evidence Act (1984), the Public Order Act (1986), the Criminal Justice Act of 1986, the Criminal Justice Act of 1988, the Criminal Justice Act of 1991, and the Criminal Justice and Public Order Act (1994). The various criminal justice acts were generally concerned with the sentencing and sanctioning process. For example, the 1982 act was directed primarily toward the handling of juvenile offenders, particularly whether and under what conditions they should be incarcerated, partly in response to the extremely high recidivism rate among juveniles. This act sharply increased the number of young persons in custody, with no apparent decrease in recidivism.[153] Some of the acts dealt with procedural matters, such as the abolition of the peremptory challenges of potential jurors in the 1988 act.[154]

The most controversial of the acts is the Police and Criminal Evidence Act of 1984 (PACE). This act required that persons give their name and address to a police officer when asked. It extended the right of the police to engage in searches and to make seizures. It authorized the holding for questioning of a person for up to ninety-six hours without charge (although the police must bring the person before a magistrate within thirty-six hours). It

150. Brake and Hale, supra note 40, p. 168.
151. See, for example, the 1974 Conservative Manifesto.
152. See Lord Windlesham, *Responses to Crime: Penal Policy in the Making* (Oxford: Clarendon Press, 1993), pp. 1–3.
153. Blake and Hale, supra note 40, pp. 70–72.
154. See Zander and Henderson, supra note 102, p. 174.

authorized the taking of fingerprints and samples of hair or blood without consent. When the initial draft of the act was released in 1982, a strong negative public response forced the government to agree to a wholesale list of amendments. Even with the changes, the government was not able to push the proposal through before the 1983 election. The spurt of attention to criminal justice in the 1983 Labour manifesto was in significant part a response to the then-proposed Police and Criminal Evidence Act. Support came from law enforcement professionals and from groups on the right of the political spectrum, while opposition came from the civil liberties groups and groups on the left. When the Thatcher government won the 1983 election, it was able to push through a version of the bill, but one about which the Association of Chief Police Officers was less than enthusiastic.[155]

In 1991, in response to a series of controversial miscarriages of justice, in which police had fabricated or concealed evidence, the Home Secretary announced the creation of the Royal Commission on Criminal Justice. In July 1993, the commission issued its report with hundreds of specific recommendations for change.[156] Some of the proposals were highly controversial, including one that would effectively eliminate the accused's right to demand a jury trial in either-way offenses.[157] Other proposals included specifically authorizing sentence discounts for pleas of guilty, allowing judges to comment to juries about a defendant's decision to remain silent, establishing an independent tribunal to review alleged miscarriages of justice (with the power to refer cases to the Court of Appeal for formal action), and rules concerning disclosure of evidence by both the prosecution and the defense.[158] Civil libertarians, senior judges, and others immediately attacked many of the proposals (in particular regarding jury trials and the right to remain silent), and violent demonstrations occurred as Parliament was considering specific proposals.[159]

In the fall of 1994, Parliament narrowly passed what is known as the Criminal Justice and Public Order Act of 1994, which did not include most of the more controversial proposals of the Royal Commission. The new law provided courts with more and tougher sentencing alternatives for youthful offenders, gave the police additional powers of search and seizure, added restrictions on the right to bail, provided sentence discounts for early pleas of guilty, and allowed judges or juries to draw inferences from a suspect's

---

155. Brake and Hale, supra note 40, pp. 41–43.

156. *RCCJ*, supra note 101, pp. 188–219.

157. This would be accomplished by giving the Magistrates' Court the option of rejecting a defendant's request that he or she be committed to Crown Court.

158. *Times* (London), July 7, 1993, pp. 4–5, 35.

159. "Justice Bill Protest Ends in Violence," *Guardian Weekly*, Oct. 16, 1994, p. 10.

decision to remain silent.[160] The last of these is one of the most controversial: previously, persons accused of criminal offenses had the right to remain silent similar to that provided by the Fifth Amendment of the U.S. Bill of Rights. Where under the provisions of PACE, police told suspects something like, "You do not have to say anything unless you wish to do so, but what you say may be given in evidence," the police now say: "You do not have to say anything. But if you do not mention now something which you later use in your defense, the court may decide that your failure to mention it now strengthens the case against you. A record will be made of anything you say and it may be given in evidence if you are brought to trial."[161]

The intriguing question is whether any of the latest changes will make much difference. As pointed out by Jacob in his discussion of American crime control efforts in the previous chapter, the policy variations tried in the U.S. have had little practical effect on crime. Rather, they have served more symbolic, rhetorical functions. Much the same is true of crime control efforts in England. The key difference is that the centralized political system has led to more centralized efforts, with crime being seen as less significant on the local political agenda because the tools of crime control are out of the hands of local officials.

CONCLUSION: CRIME AND JUSTICE ON
THE ENGLISH POLITICAL AGENDA

In this section, I have not examined questions of internal politics (politics within the prosecution service or the police forces, including the political implications of recruitment and advancement practices). I do not mean to suggest, by this omission, that such politics do not exist. Rather, I have chosen to focus on the interaction of politics with the criminal justice system.

The structure of the English criminal justice system eliminates some types of the explicit political interactions found in the U.S. The fact that judges and prosecutors are chosen through a nonelectoral process has implications for how such actors respond to political pressures (or fail to respond). In the U.S., a judge who hands out sentences that the voters see as too lenient is likely to be voted out of office; an English judge need have no such fear. However, Parliament has devoted significant time to policies regarding crime control, and the party manifestos make it clear that crime has been an issue in the electoral arena. Public opinion trends show that most Britons say that crime is a very important issue when asked directly; however, when asked

160. "Criminal Justice and Public Order Act 1994," Home Office Press Release, Reuter Textline, Nov. 3, 1994.

161. William E. Schmidt, "Silence May Speak Against the Accused in Britain," *New York Times,* Nov. 11, 1994, p. A17.

in an open-ended fashion what is *most* important, few people mention law and order issues. Moreover, the proportion naming law and order issues as most important has not risen even as the amount of reported crime (measured in terms of crime rates) in England has doubled, then doubled again, and then doubled yet again over the past forty years.

Given this sharp rise in crime, and the efforts of the Conservative Party to play on the issue of law and order, why has crime not emerged as a major issue in British politics? The most obvious, and most important, reason is that the economic difficulties facing Britain, and the controversial nature of the economic reforms pursued by the Tories starting in 1979, have overshadowed all other issues. However, there is a second reason that concern about crime has remained secondary: the metaphorical quality of the crime issue.

The fact that crime has been a significant issue in American politics during the past thirty years and has been less important to British politics reflects the link between race and crime, and the centrality of the race issue in the United States during this period.[162] The crime-race linkage is evident in Britain as well;[163] in particular, urban disorders (such as the Tottenham riot that led to the Winston Silcott case) and the portrayal of muggers as mostly young black males in the late 1970s have had racial overtones.[164]

However, crime has been linked less to *race* than it has to *change*, as represented by the involvement of immigrant groups more generally. In part this reflects that crime is hardly new to English society; one only needs to harken back to Dickensian images of London. As stated in 1983 by the head of the Metropolitan Police: "Throughout London there are locations where unemployed youth—often black youth—congregate; where the sale and purchase of drugs, the exchange of stolen property and illegal drinking and gaming is not uncommon. The youths regard these locations as their territory. Police are viewed as intruders, the symbol of authority—largely white authority—in a society that is responsible for all their grievances about unemployment, prejudice and discrimination. They equate closely with the criminal rookeries of Dickensian London."[165] What makes crime today different is that it is not the working-class English "bloke" who pinches a few wallets

---

162. The link between race and crime in the United States was dramatically illustrated in late 1993 by comments· made by Rev. Jesse Jackson. Jackson said that he is "relieved" when he realizes that a person following him on the street is white and not black; "An Older Grimmer Jesse," *Newsweek,* Jan. 10, 1994, p. 24.

163. See, for example, Roger Hood, *Race and Sentencing: A Study in the Crown Court,* A Report for the Commission for Racial Equality (Oxford: Clarendon Press, 1992).

164. See Brake and Hale, supra note 40, p. 47.

165. Quoted in ibid., p. 160.

rather than work in some dreary factory or some bleak coal mine. Rather, crime is associated with groups that are visibly non-English, even though the vast majority of crime in England is committed by persons who are ethnically English, and less than 20 percent of persons incarcerated in England in 1989 were members of ethnic minorities.[166]

More generally, England has ceased to be a relatively homogeneous society (although it was always a highly differentiated and stratified one). England is increasingly heterogeneous, with significant and distinct communities of persons from the Caribbean, Africa, South Asia, East Asia, and the Mediterranean (particularly Cyprus and Greece). Added to this is the uncertainty associated with closer economic, political, and geographic ties to the Continent. Crime is a form of disorder that amplifies uncertainty and fear, and the criminal justice system is the government's effort to respond to the public's need for social control to counter that uncertainty and fear.

The Personal Plight and the Politics of Redress
ENGLAND: A NONLITIGIOUS SOCIETY?

In the face of adversity, whether the dreary climate or personal misfortune, for most English people life goes on without blaming, complaining, or claiming. An American journalist who resided in England for several years observed: "the most striking characteristic of the British . . . is their stoicism, or what the novelist Anthony Burgess calls their 'patient and philosophical resignation.' They will put up with anything and seldom do much by way of redress except to write a peevish letter to the Times of London. . . . They consider it the height of bad manners to make a fuss about anything, even if they have legitimate ground for complaint."[167] An English journalist, writing in the wake of the capsizing of an English Channel ferry that resulted in almost two hundred deaths, described "the English temperament [as one] . . . that abhors panic": "Faced with disaster, or the threat of it, the English would a hundred times rather under-react than over-react."[168]

Because of this image, commentators frequently cite England as an example of a society that is less litigious than the United States. While this image is only partly accurate, there are deep-seated differences in the societal orientations of England and the United States, and the political and social responses to the day-to-day problems and misfortunes of individuals reflect these differences.

166. Hood, supra note 163, p. 3.

167. Ray Mosely, "Deep in the Heart of England: Why Can't the British Be More Like Us?" *Chicago Tribune Magazine* 26 (Aug. 7, 1988), p. 28.

168. John Hooper, "How North Sea Oil Puts Government Policy over a Barrel," *Guardian*, June 18, 1987, p. 26.

Reactions to Problems

While the image of extreme stoicism reflects stereotypes, those stereotypes may have bases in behavior patterns.[169] One leading British legal scholar cites evidence suggesting that the volume of tort claims is significantly lower in Britain than in the United States.[170] For example, the estimated tort lawsuit rate in Britain is about one-quarter that in the United States.[171] There are problems using information on actual lawsuits because most claims for redress are resolved far short of such actions; that is, lawsuits constitute the peak of the "dispute pyramid."[172] This pyramid has at its base the problems that can lead to court action, with resolutions short of formal legal action falling between the base and the peak. We need to examine the entire range of responses to understand how people in England respond to the broad category of personal plight problems and how Parliament has structured judicial and quasi-judicial institutions to handle such problems.

Comparisons of British and American data on responses to personal injuries sustain the argument that, at least in this arena, Britons are more likely to "grin and bear it." In an extensive comparison based on a variety of American and British data sets, I found that, after taking into account whether or not the injured person attributed fault to someone else, the rate of claiming in the U.S. exceeded that in Britain. Interestingly, the claiming gap appears to be relatively small in situations where the injury victim blames someone else.[173] For those who do not blame others, or do so only partially, the gap is larger, with the rate of claiming two to three times higher in the United States. Attribution of fault thus appears to be a more influential factor in claiming behavior in Britain than is the case in the United States. In Britain, it appears that the dominant principle is "when in doubt, don't claim" while in the United States, it is "when in doubt, consider claiming." Of equal significance are differences in patterns of blaming. Particularly for injuries arising from traffic accidents, Americans are more likely than Britons to blame someone else. In Britain, injury victims tend to accept at least part of the blame or to attribute the accident to fate.

169. Richard E. Miller and Austin Sarat, "Grievances, Claims, and Disputes: Assessing the Adversary Culture," *Law & Society Review* 15 (1980–81), p. 527. For a more general discussion of the issue of dispute avoidance, see William L. F. Felstiner, "Influences of Social Organizations on Dispute Processing," *Law & Society Review* 9 (1974), pp. 63–94; "Avoidance as Dispute Processing: An Elaboration," *Law & Society Review* 10 (1975), pp. 695–706.

170. P. S. Atiyah, "Tort Law and the Alternatives: Some Anglo-American Comparison," *Duke Law Journal* (1987), pp. 1004–1009; Atiyah's data are limited to England and Wales.

171. This is Miller and Sarat's metaphor; see supra note 169, pp. 545–546.

172. Herbert M. Kritzer, "Propensity to Sue in England and the United States: Blaming and Claiming in Tort Cases," *Journal of Law and Society* 18 (1991), pp. 452–479.

173. Kathleen M. Zahorik, "Consumer Problems in Three Countries," paper presented at meetings of the Law & Society Association, Berkeley, Calif., 1990.

Routine consumer grievances constitute a second area where we have good information on the response to problems. An American study found that 75 percent of the consumers who had problems with services or products complained to the provider; British data show a rate of 76 percent.[174] Neither study placed minimums or maximums on the amount of money that might have been involved in the problem. An earlier study of purchase-related problems involving at least five pounds, conducted in several low-income boroughs in London, reported a complaint rate of 86 percent.[175]

Contrasting the patterns for personal injury with those for consumer problems suggests that simple generalizations about the relative willingness of Britons to seek redress for problems are probably incorrect. Nonetheless, important commonalities help us understand the disparate patterns.

Alternative Presumptions of Redress

To understand the handling of personal plight problems in Britain, we need to use another country as a contrast, and the discussion in Chapter 2 makes the United States the obvious choice. One temptation is to rely upon a "hyperlexis" argument:[176] Americans are overly rights conscious, overly litigation prone, and just too contentious. To support this line of argument one might cite anecdotes about the kinds of cases brought into the courts of the United States, the liability insurance crisis, or the words of Alexis de Tocqueville: "Scarcely any political question arises in the United States that is not resolved, sooner or later, into as judicial question."[177] Although this explains higher levels of claiming and blaming in personal injury cases, it fails to account for the lack of differences between Britons and Americans in seeking redress for consumer problems.

We can trace the difference in the case of injury problems, and the similarity in the case of consumer problems, to a common underlying element which structures choices. The core difference between Britain and the United States is where each country lodges fundamental responsibility. The United States has built its structure for handling personal plight problems around

174. Jack Ladinsky and Charles Susmilch, "Community Factors in the Brokerage of Consumer Product and Service Problems," in Gerald D. Suttles and Mayer N. Zald (eds.), *The Challenge of Social Control: Citizenship and Institution Building in Modern Society: Essays in Honor of Morris Janowitz* (Norwood, N.J.: Ablex, 1985), p. 204. Office of Fair Trading, *Consumer Dissatisfaction: A Report on Surveys Undertaken for the Office of Fair Trading* (London: Office of Fair Trading, 1986), p. 21.

175. Brian Abel-Smith, Michael Zander, and Rosalind Brooke, *Legal Problems and the Citizen: A Study in Three London Boroughs* (London: Heinemann, 1973), pp. 125–126.

176. Bayless Manning, "Hyperlexis: Our National Disease," *Northwestern Law Review* 71 (1977), pp. 767–782.

177. Alexis de Tocqueville, *On Democracy*, trans. Henry Reeve, rev. Francis Bowen (New York: Alfred A. Knopf, 1945), 1:280.

individual action, which I label "individualization of redress." This pattern arises from a variety of phenomena, ranging from the ideology of the rugged individualist through the vigilantism of the frontier to the emphasis on a kind of rule of law that requires individual action for enforcement. In contrast, in Britain, the antecedents are the paternalism of the Crown and the landed gentry; the result is a social duty of care and protection. Thus, in Britain the inclination is to move problems into the public arena rather than to privatize them. Two examples of this are responding to major injurious events with public inquiries and commissions rather than a barrage of lawsuits and the criminalization of consumer protection law. Another way to contrast the two is to describe the American response as a bottom-up response (some might say market-oriented) versus the British top-down response (which, for lack of a better term, I label paternalism).

HANDLING COMMON TYPES OF PERSONAL PLIGHT
PROBLEMS IN ENGLAND

Everyday Problems and the Legal Order

In describing the types of personal plight problems people experience and how the legal system deals with those problems, either one can start with the legal system and describe what people bring to the system, or one can start with those who experience the problems and ascertain the mechanisms through which they choose to deal with those problems. In this section, I do a bit of both.

Torts

To most Americans, the archetypical noncriminal legal problem is one arising out of personal injury or property damage caused by someone else. The High Court and the local County Courts share jurisdiction over tort cases. All personal injury cases involving £50,000 or less commence in the County Courts. The High Court normally tries cases involving more than £50,000, the County Court tries those involving less than £25,000, and those in between may go to either, depending upon the complexity of the case.[178] Only a very small fraction of those experiencing injuries initiate action in the courts. I estimate that there are about 50,000 to 60,000 personal injury cases annually in England,[179] out of perhaps 3 million persons experiencing injuries

178. Lord Chancellor's Department, "High Court and County Courts Jurisdiction Order 1991," *Statutory Instruments 1991*, No. 724.

179. In 1991, 10,278 personal injury cases were filed ("writs issued") at the Royal Courts of Justice (*JSAR 1992*, p. 31); Multiplying by three to estimate the total for the High Court gives a figure of about 30,000. A study done for the Lord Chancellor's Department estimated a total of 55,000 personal injury cases per year, of which 31,000 were from the High Court and 24,000 from the County Court; see INBUCON, *Civil Justice Review: Study of Personal Injury Litigation* (London: Lord Chancellor's Department, 1986), p. 1.

each year (200,000 from road accidents and 350,000 from work-related events, and the balance from household and recreational accidents), and another 250,000 make claims through the tort system without ever initiating formal court proceedings. The remainder, many of whose injuries or illnesses are not compensable through the tort system, obtain compensation from sources such as social security, occupational sick pay, and private insurance.[180]

Cases in England involving only property damage seldom require formal court action. In traffic accidents, the victim's own insurance company usually compensates for property damage—even when someone else is at fault. This does not arise from statutes or court decisions but from an insurance industry practice called "knock for knock"; specifically, insurance companies figure that fighting among themselves over property damage liability will cost more than it is worth, given that losses should average out. Furthermore, this allows insurance companies to discourage many small damage claims by a system of "no claims bonuses"; insureds receive an increasing discount for each year they do not file a damage claim with their own insurer, and they lose this bonus if they file a claim, even if someone else was clearly at fault.[181] There are no figures from the High Court indicating the number of property damage cases, and none from the County Courts.

Overall, taking both the personal injury and the property damage cases, most Britons resolve those cases without resort to the courts. This is by no means unique to Britain, but it is likely that the percentage handled by the courts in Britain is at least somewhat lower than in the United States, and probably somewhat higher than in countries such as Japan that (see chapter 6), which have mechanisms that divert disputes that might arise in the wake of routine injury or damages.[182]

Consumer Problems

Consumer problems are a routine part of modern consumer culture. In competitive market economies, manufacturers and sellers have incentives to go to substantial lengths to maintain consumer loyalty. This creates expectations on the part of consumers that when they bring a problem to the attention of a manufacturer or a seller that person or organization will make an effort to satisfy the consumer. Given this, it is not surprising that

---

180. Lord Chancellor's Department, *Civil Justice Review: Personal Injury Litigation* (London: Lord Chancellor's Department, 1986), p. 7.

181. In the U.S., higher rates follow insurance claims, but not typically if the other party was clearly at fault (i.e., you collect from your own insurance company because the other driver was uninsured).

182. See Miller and Sarat, supra note 169. Also see chapter 6 on Japan.

patterns of consumer complaining in the United States and Britain are similar. As in the United States, there are large numbers of consumer complaints on the order of 25–30 million per year, very few of which ever get into the judicial system.[183] A study of small claims cases in England found that only 13 percent involve consumer complaints,[184] about 5,000 to 6,000 cases per year. This works out to about 2 out of every 10,000 consumer problems.[185]

Divorce and Debt

There are two types of personal plight problems that regularly come to court in Britain and the United States: divorce and debt. The single largest portion of cases in both the County Courts and the High Court are those filed by creditors against individual debtors.[186] As elsewhere, many such cases are uncontested and result in a judgment by default through a simple clerical process. In other cases, the initiation of court proceedings leads the debtor to pay the sum without any formal court action. In still others, the debtor appears but does not challenge the validity of the creditor's claim, leading to a "judgment by admission."

The other type of personal plight cases frequently coming to court involve family law. As in the United States most divorces in Britain occur by consent of the parties; formal court action consists almost exclusively of approving an agreement worked out in advance of the court appearance. For example, 180,000 petitions for dissolution of marriage were filed in 1991; only 153 cases were scheduled for trial in the High Court's Family Division (the County Court disposing of the rest), and 71 of those ended without actually completing a trial (settling before or during the trial).[187]

183. See Office of Fair Trading, *Consumer Dissatisfaction: A Report on Surveys Undertaken for the Office of Fair Trading* (London: Office of Fair Trading, 1986), p. 2; Office of Fair Trading, "Annual Consumer Dissatisfaction Survey (November 1989)," *BeeLine* (published by the OFT) 90.2 (1990), pp. 21–23.

184. Touche Ross, *Study of Small Claims Procedure* (London: Lord Chancellor's Department, 1986), p. 23.

185. This estimate is consistent with unpublished figures from the Office of Fair Trading's surveys of consumers; unpublished letter from S. G. Linstead of the Office of Fair Trading to Richard Thomas of the National Consumer Council (dated 15 May 1985), provided to the author by OFT.

186. In 1985 approximately two million debt cases were filed in the County Courts (which constitutes more than 90% of the caseload), and 150,000 were filed in the High Court (about two-thirds of the caseload of the High Court's Queen's Bench Division); Lord Chancellor's Department, *Civil Justice Review: Enforcement of Debt* (London: Lord Chancellor's Department, 1986), p. 3.

187. Ibid., p. 51.

Housing

The law concerning the ownership and occupancy of property differs radically in England from that in the United States. Historically, owner-occupancy of housing is much less common, and even the definition of ownership differs. About 5 percent of "homeowners" actually have only a long-term lease on the property (a leasehold) that they purchased from a previous occupant and can sell to another occupant if they so choose.[188] Most other homeowners have a "freehold" arrangement that closely resembles the type of ownership that exists in the United States.

As of 1990, two-thirds of the households of Britain lived in owner-occupied housing.[189] Most of the rest of the population were tenants, either in privately owned buildings or in "Council"-owned units (what Americans would call public housing). British law concerning the rights of owners and tenants is quite elaborate: landlords have very specific responsibilities concerning the upkeep of the property, levels of rents are controlled on many properties, and tenants of unfurnished premises can possess a "controlled or regulated tenancy," which makes it difficult or impossible for the owner to force the tenant to leave and allows the tenancy to be passed to other members of the tenant's family.[190] As one might imagine, this system produces substantial conflict between property owners and tenants over questions such as amount of rent, whether the tenant has violated the terms of the tenancy (and hence can be forced to give up possession of the premises), and whether the landlord has properly maintained the property.

Disputes involving residential property most often revolve around rent: the amount that can be charged under the Rent Control Act, and whether or not the landlord can evict the tenant for nonpayment. An administrative tribunal, the local Rent Assessment Committee, usually deals with questions of what is a fair rent.[191] Payment problems, leading to eviction (or attempted eviction), constitute a type of debt case, but one with greater significance than the typical debt claim, since it can lead to the loss of housing. The County Courts handle these debt cases, issuing eviction notices called "orders for possession."

188. Computed based on a total of 66.3% of 23,301,000 dwelling units being owner-occupied (Central Statistical Office, *Annual Abstract of Statistics 1994* [London: HMSO], p. 48) and 750,000 households in England and Wales occupying their residences under leasehold arrangements (*New York Times,* Mar. 21, 1993, p. E4).

189. Central Statistical Office, *Annual Abstract of Statistics 1994.*

190. Jackson, supra note 17, p. 139.

191. Council on Tribunals, *Annual Report 1992–93* (London: HMSO, 1993), p. 85, henceforth COTAR.

Employment Cases

British employment law differs substantially from American employment law. The governing doctrine in the U.S. is "employment at will," and American employers have broad latitude to hire and fire in the absence of a formal contractual relationship and as long as hiring and firing is nondiscriminatory.[192] In contrast, in most other advanced industrial countries, including Britain, employers can dismiss individual employees of longstanding only for just cause.[193] Under British law the dismissal of an employee without just cause constitutes "unfair dismissal," which is compensable.[194] The coverage of the law is broad; in one case, a wealthy American living in London fired the couple who worked for him as butler and housekeeper and was ordered to pay $26,000 in compensation.[195] In addition, British law provides specific protections against racial or sexual discrimination and guarantees of equal pay. Industrial tribunals decide cases covering a variety of employment-related issues, including compensation arising out of unfair dismissal (the majority of cases), discrimination, and unequal pay claims.[196]

Immigration Cases

Immigration cases are a significant legal and political issue in Britain. An important legacy of the British Empire is very large populations that at one time had a right of immigration into Britain. Since about 1960 there have been periodic waves of immigration into Britain, typically either from former British colonies in Africa or from the Indian subcontinent; substantial numbers of immigrants have also come from the Caribbean and from the Mediterranean. The political response to these waves of immigration has been to try to stem the tide by abolishing rights to immigrate for many groups and to limit in other ways who may and may not reside in Britain. Immigration adjudicators hear appeals of decisions of the immigration officers at ports of entry; appeals from these officials go to the immigration appeal tribunal.

192. See Jacob's discussion of job termination in the United States in chapter 2.

193. See Erhard Blankenburg and Ralf Rogowski, "German Labour Courts and the British Industrial Tribunal System: A Sociolegal Comparison of Degrees of Judicialisation," *Journal of Law and Society* 13 (1986), pp. 67–91; the comparison of England and Germany will be specifically discussed in chapter 5.

194. See Hugh Collins, *Justice in Dismissal: The Law of Termination of Employment* (Oxford: Oxford University Press, 1992).

195. "The Jeeves of Today Remains Loyal—to Himself," *New York Times,* Jan. 23, 1993, p. 4:2.

196. COTAR 1992–93, p. 80. For a sketch of the broader system, see Linda Dickens, Michael Jones, Brian Weeks, and Moira Hart, *Dismissed: A Study of Unfair Dismissal and the Industrial Tribunal System* (Oxford: Basil Blackwell, 1985), pp. 1–28.

Social Benefits Cases

Britain's social welfare system provides many benefits, including industrial injury benefits, allowances for severe disability and mobility problems, maternity benefits, funeral expenses, and a variety of income supplements. While many of these programs are more or less automatic, others depend on discretionary decisions.[197] Either the Social Security appeals tribunals or medical appeals tribunals handle appeals of negative decisions by agencies administering social benefit programs. Unlike the United States, where unhappy appellants regularly appeal decisions of administrative law judges about denial of welfare benefits to the courts (about 7,500 Social Security cases in the Federal District Court in 1990, down from a high of about 30,000 in 1984),[198] the English courts rarely deal with such cases.

Tax Cases

The tax system in England, as applied to individuals, has both similarities and differences to the American system. As in the United States, the British government derives revenue from taxes on purchases (but in the form of a value-added tax rather than a sales tax), income tax, and tax on real property. The structure of the income tax in England results in relatively few disputes: it is withheld by the payer of the income such as the employer or the financial institution generating interest or dividends; only persons with self-employment income or investment income not subject to direct payment by the payer of the income regularly have to file a tax return in the form familiar to Americans.[199] Producers and sellers of goods and services pay the value-added tax directly to the government and pass the cost on to the consumer. The income tax and the value-added tax are principal sources of revenue for the central government.

For most of the twentieth century, a system of property tax (both on residential and commercial property) known as "rates" was the primary source of revenue for local government services. This system and its successors have generated significant tax disputes involving individuals. "Rates," payable by both owner-occupiers and tenants, tied the amount of tax to the value of a property. In the late 1980s the Conservative government abolished

197. See Roy Sainsbury, "Administrative Justice: Discretion and Procedure in Social Security Decision-Making," pp. 295–329 in Keith Hawkins (ed.), *The Uses of Discretion* (Oxford: Clarendon Press, 1992).

198. *Annual Report of the Director of the Administrative Office of the United States Courts* (henceforth cited as *AOUSC*), *1990* (Washington, D.C.: GPO, 1991), p. 140; *AOUSC 1985*, p. 283.

199. Inland Revenue, *Inland Revenue Statistics 1994* (London: HMSO, 1994), p. 18; only about 9 million of the 56 million persons in the United Kingdom file income tax returns in a given year (letter from Paul M. Heggs, Inland Revenue, to author, Dec. 6, 1994).

the system of rates for residential property and replaced it with what amounted to a "head tax" (a tax per adult based simply on residence) which the government named the "community charge" and which opponents (and almost everyone else) immediately dubbed the "poll tax." While this theoretically might have eliminated many disputes that arose under the rates system, the number of disputes rose with the implementation of the poll tax, revolving principally around the question of who was liable for it and where. The situation did not improve when the storm of protest over the poll tax led to its replacement in 1993 by a graduated "council tax"—a per-person tax depending upon the valuation of the property. This has led to disputes over both the liability and the amount of the liability. Historically, if a ratepayer could not resolve a dispute over rates by negotiating with the local valuation officer, the case went to a local tribunal known as the local valuation panel (or, more commonly, the local valuation court).[200] Ratepayers dissatisfied with the decision of the local valuation court could appeal to the lands tribunal, but few did so.[201]

With the change to the poll tax, the number of contested assessments quadrupled, at least briefly. Where the local valuation courts had been running 150,000 or so listed cases each year, in 1990 the number skyrocketed to 712,000 cases listed with the renamed (in 1989) valuations and community charge tribunals, but dropped back to 194,000 in 1991.[202] With the new council tax in operation, the name of the tribunal changed yet again (valuation tribunals), but the caseload held steady in 1992 at 195,000 cases.[203]

Summary

Simple generalizations about seeking redress—that Britons are willing to tolerate many problems about which Americans complain—are unwarranted.

200. John Baldwin and Sheila Hill, "Settled Without a Hearing: The Disposition of Rating Appeals in England and Wales," 1987 *Public Law*, 400–425. John Baldwin and Sheila Hill, "Rating Appeals Heard by Local Valuation Courts in England and Wales," *Civil Justice Quarterly* 7 (1985), p. 111; John Baldwin and Sheila Hill, "Tribunal Membership: The Role of Local Politics in Recruitment of Local Valuation Panels in England and Wales," *Civil Justice Quarterly* 6 (1987), pp. 130–141.

201. Less than 1,000 cases (813 in 1985) a year ever made it to the lands tribunal, and 75% or more of those would be settled or withdrawn (630 in 1985) before the tribunal could act; see John Baldwin and Richard Young, "Appeals from Local Valuation Courts to the Lands Tribunal," *Civil Justice Quarterly* 7 (1988), p. 344.

202. COTAR 1991–92, p. 67; see also Tim Moloney and Richard Young, "Community Charge Appeals: A Major Problem?" *Civil Justice Quarterly* 10 (1991), p. 206.

203. COTAR 1992–93, p. 82. The Local Government Finance Act 1992, which created the council tax, does not permit appeals to the Lands Tribunal (the only appeal permitted is to the High Court, on a point of law). See Council on Tribunals, supra note 191, p. 33.

Regarding tort cases, significant numbers of Britons who might seek compensation fail to do so; in contrast, there is no apparent unwillingness to complain about consumer problems, and there does not appear to be any significant difficulty in obtaining redress. Furthermore, there are areas, such as unfair dismissal and setting of rents, that occasion little disputing in the United States but produce tens of thousands of cases in Britain.

Varying structures exist for dealing with personal plight cases. Most cases never come to formal dispute-processing institutions; in many the person with the grievance does not seek redress, in many the source of the problem promptly grants redress, and in some informal intervention by third parties takes care of the problem. Of those disputes that do reach formal institutions, lower-level courts (the County Courts and for some types of situations the Magistrates' Courts) handle some cases, with the High Court considering a small number. The English system diverts many more cases out of the formal court system to a system of administrative tribunals; while the majority of cases dealt with by administrative tribunals involve conflicts between individuals and governmental agencies (housing authorities, immigration authorities, social security authorities, tax authorities, and the like), these tribunals also deal with significant numbers of private cases (particularly in the employment arena).

To deal with this complex mix of problems, England has three levels of judicial and quasi-judicial institutions that vary in formality: administrative tribunals handle most routine problems, particularly those involving governmental agencies; County Courts (and to some degree Magistrates' Courts) decide minor problems involving debt, personal injury, property damage, contracts, and family relations; the High Court hears cases involving more serious or complex problems. In addition, citizens can obtain assistance from both lawyers and nonlawyers, many of whom are volunteers, or can seek intervention by government agencies, which adds two tiers to the English system for dealing with personal plight problems: assistance, advice, and possibly intervention by nonprofessional government-funded advisors (for example, Citizens' Advice Bureaux) and direct intervention by governmental agencies, particularly consumer protection offices. While this is a multi-tiered system, it is not clearly hierarchical; one does not appeal from tribunals to the County Court to the High Court.

SOURCES OF ASSISTANCE

Americans with personal plight problems such as those described above might choose to attempt to resolve the problem without seeking assistance. However, an American who uses assistance is very likely to go to a lawyer. As discussed in chapter 2, there are two major reasons for the primacy of legal professionals as sources of assistance. First, for problems involving the payment of a sum of money, lawyers accept as compensation some percentage of the payment that they ultimately obtain for the client. While it is common to call these fee arrangements "contingent fees" (no win, no pay), they are actually a very specific type of arrangement that we can understand better as a kind of commission system. For the lawyer's client, the commission system has the obvious advantage of requiring no up-front payment and eliminating the client's fear of confronting a bill from the lawyer if the lawyer fails to resolve the problem by getting a payment from the other side.

Second, and equally important, the American legal profession has taken an expansive view of what activities constitute the practice of law and has jealously sought to exclude nonlawyers from those activities. Essentially, the legal profession deems all advocacy (with a particular emphasis on advocacy where a client is likely to be in a position to pay a fee or where situations that virtually require the client to have an advocate) to be the practice of law. Legal advocacy is not limited to the courts; it includes representation before administrative "courts" or agencies, such as those bodies that decide disputes over workers' compensation, disability payments, welfare benefits, taxes, and so on.

The situation in Britain differs sharply. First, rules of practice have not permitted solicitors to accept "contentious work" from private individuals on a commission basis, although solicitors can take debt cases, a type of quasi-contentious matter normally dealt with on behalf of business clients, on that basis.[204] To some degree an extensive system of government-funded legal aid mitigates the absence of commission fees (see below), and changes that permit other forms of "no win, no pay" fee arrangements, to be called "conditional fees," were authorized in 1990 and went into effect in 1995 for insolvency, human rights, and personal injury cases. Under this system, solicitors may enter into an agreement with their clients to forego a fee if there is no recovery, and to receive their normal fee plus an "uplift" of as much as 100 percent (but no more than 25 percent of the damages recovered) if the case is successful.[205]

The second major difference is the definition of what constitutes the practice of law for purposes of the legal profession's right to exclude others. In England there are no limitations on who may give legal advice or on who may assert a claim on behalf of someone else *until that claim matures into litigation in a court of law*. Thus, there are no restrictions on representation

204. See Law Society, *Memorandum on Maintenance and Champerty: Claims Assessors and Contingency Fees* (London: The Law Society, 1970), pp. 8–9.

205. Courts and Legal Services Act of 1990, Part II, Section 58, Conditional Fee Agreements. Michael Napier, "Now More Can Afford to Go to Law," *Times* (London), July 11, 1995.

before the many administrative tribunals described above, and there is no monopoly of representation in seeking to settle a claim short of initiating a court action. Moreover, nonlawyer representatives are not subject to the restriction on commission-based fees. While this has permitted a variety of sources of assistance and representation to develop, it has not (with one exception) resulted in a wide-open fee-for-service market in representational services.

Citizens' Advice Bureaux

The single largest providers of assistance and advice in personal plight problems are Citizens' Advice Bureaux (CABs). CABs exist throughout Britain, with full-time offices in larger towns and cities and at least part-time offices in many smaller towns.[206] Local governments typically finance the CAB operations, which include a paid staff of managers and supervisors. Trained volunteers provide most of the client services. Most CABs have arrangements with some local solicitors who volunteer advice on a rotating basis.

There is virtually no limit on the matters about which the CABs will provide advice, and the number of inquiries is very large: more than seven million in 1987–88. About one-quarter of the inquiries relate to social benefits programs, 20 percent to consumer problems (including consumer debt), 11.5 percent housing and real property, 9.5 percent family and personal, 9 percent employment, and 7 percent "administration of justice."[207] Some CABs will, in some circumstances, send a representative with a client to a hearing before an administrative tribunal.

In a study of representation before tribunals, Genn and Genn found that, other than friends and family, CABs were the most common source of representation before social security appeals tribunals, appearing on behalf of 40 percent of the represented appellants (54 percent if one does not count representatives who were a friend or family member).[208] CABs play a smaller role before industrial tribunals or no appreciable role before immigration tribunals or mental health tribunals. While CABs cannot provide representation in County or High Court cases, they may be present and assist a litigant in the small claims part of County Courts.[209] While permissible, there is no

206. In the late 1980s, there were 910 bureaus, Spencer, supra note 14, p. 467.

207. Judith Citron, *The Citizens' Advice Bureaux: For the Community by the Community* (London: Pluto Press, 1989), pp. 25–26. Both the volume and mix of inquiries to CABs have changed sharply.

208. Hazel Genn and Yvette Genn, *Effectiveness of Representation at Tribunals: Report to the Lord Chancellor* (London: Queen Mary College, 1989), p. 19.

209. The person providing this assistance is called a "McKenzie" man, after the case which established that such assistance was permissible; *McKenzie v. McKenzie* 1970 Weekly Law Reports 472 (Court of Appeal, Civil Division).

indication that this constitutes a major source of representation or assistance in court.

Specialized Advice Services

In addition to CABs, several sources of advice specialize in particular areas. Probably the most used of such services are Consumer Advice Bureaux operated by local offices responsible for enforcing laws related to consumer protection. In addition, organizations concerned about welfare rights, either generally or for targeted groups, such as the elderly, provide representation for about 6 percent of social security appeals where there is representation.[210] Separate agencies, such as a marriage guidance council, provide marriage counseling and advice.[211] Representation for immigration appeals comes from the government-funded United Kingdom Immigration Advisory Service (UKIAS) and the private Joint Council for the Welfare of Immigrants (JCWI). According to one study, UKIAS provides representation in 50 percent of immigration appeals hearings,[212] with JCWI appearing in 2 percent of appeals.

Social Service Agencies and Units

It is not uncommon for various types of social service agencies and units to provide assistance in some circumstances. For example, persons involved in social security appeals can seek help from specialized units within the social security bureaucracy ("tribunal units"), or from sources with knowledge about obtaining benefits, such as social service agencies and probation officers. A significant proportion of the representatives appearing before social security appeals tribunals come from such sources.[213]

Unions

British trade unions provide many benefits to their members, including assistance with a wide range of personal plight problems, both work related and not work-related. Six percent of the representatives before social security appeals tribunals come from the trade unions, as do 25 percent of the representatives before industrial tribunals.[214] While these figures do not count lawyers retained by the trade unions on behalf of union members, one of the most important services unions can provide is to retain a solicitor (and bar-

210. Genn and Genn, supra note 208, p. 19.
211. See Barbara Harrell-Bond and Alan Smith, "Dispute Treatment in an English Town," in Maureen Cain and Kálmán Kulcsár (eds.), *Disputes and the Law* (Budapest: Akadémiai Kiadó, 1983), p. 59.
212. Genn and Genn, supra note 208, p. 33.
213. See ibid., p. 19.
214. Ibid., pp. 19, 46 (some computations by the author).

rister if necessary) on behalf of the member to assist with a personal plight problem. One study found that 44 percent of the representatives who appear at industrial tribunal hearings are barristers and solicitors;[215] unions provided many, if not most, of these. While the most common situations where unions provide a solicitor are work related, unions will often provide representation for a member for problems that are not work related.

Law Centres and Legal Aid

In the United States, low-income persons can seek legal assistance from government-funded legal services organizations regarding matters that do not lend themselves to commission-type fee arrangements. Salaried attorneys employed by an agency associated with the Legal Services Corporation provide most such services. Much less common is a "judicare" type system in which government pays private attorneys to provide legal services to low-income citizens.

In Britain, the situation is essentially reversed. "Law centres" with salaried attorneys provide only a small portion of the professional legal services available to low-income persons. Attorneys working in law centres generally restrict their services to those issues where private attorneys, either retained on a private basis or through legal aid, choose not to work.[216] The effect is to focus on areas that are more "political," such as consumers' rights, housing, social security—particularly if a case is likely to benefit a group (for example, tenants) rather than a single individual or family.

Private attorneys working in conjunction with government-funded legal aid provide most low-income legal services. Legal aid, administered by a board chosen by the Lord Chancellor,[217] offers funding for legal advice and for "matrimonial" (i.e., divorce) and other litigation. Legal aid does not provide funds for representation at most administrative tribunals or other forums open to advocates other than solicitors and barristers; legal aid does provide funds for advice to persons considering an appeal to a tribunal, but few persons eligible make use of such assistance.[218] Furthermore, there is some evidence that private practice solicitors are not generally interested in areas such as welfare benefits work, even if the solicitor does a lot of legal aid work. This is in part because few solicitors have any expertise in the area,[219] and there is no incentive to invest the resources to acquire that ex-

215. Ibid., p. 46.

216. Jackson, supra note 17, p. 555.

217. Until the late 1980s, legal aid was administered by the Law Society, which is the professional association of solicitors.

218. See Genn and Genn, supra note 208, p. 1.

219. See John Baldwin, "The Role of Citizens' Advice Bureaux and Law Centres in the Provision of Legal Advice and Assistance," Civil Justice Quarterly 8 (1989), p. 26.

pertise. The lack of interest in this type of work, and "administrative law" work more generally, may be reflective of a more deeply ingrained view regarding the appropriate spheres of work for lawyers, both on the part of the profession and on the part of government officials.[220] Some solicitors' firms do handle large volumes of legal aid welfare benefits cases, but these firms tend to rely on paralegals to do much of the actual work.[221]

The system for providing legal advice is largely self-administered by the solicitors providing the service. The solicitor determines the client's eligibility. If the client is eligible, then the solicitor may provide up to two hours of advice without prior approval from the legal aid authorities.[222] If the cost of the services exceeds this initial amount, the solicitor must obtain clearance from the local Area Legal Aid Committee before proceeding. For actual litigation (either matrimonial or something such as personal injury), the solicitor must obtain authorization before commencing the action. Solicitors involved in contentious work do not particularly like dealing with legal aid because it results in delays while waiting for clearance to proceed from one step to the next, and it may involve a reduction in the solicitor's fee. There is some evidence of solicitors proceeding on what amounts to a contingency basis: they recognize that if the action is unsuccessful they will not receive compensation for their services.[223]

Legal aid interacts in crucial ways with the traditional rules regarding who bears the expense of litigation. Britain relies on the principle that the loser should pay the legal fees of both sides. This "English rule" regarding the costs of litigation differs from the "American rule," under which each side pays its own legal fees regardless of who wins and who loses. The "loser pays" principle does not normally apply to a litigant with legal aid. In areas such as personal injury, the governing principle is that, if the party with legal aid could not afford to pay his or her own legal fees, how can one expect them to pay the other side's fees in the event that the action is unsuccessful? Furthermore, why should the legal aid fund pay fees to a prevailing party such as a liability insurer that has substantial resources and can readily absorb the costs of the litigation?[224]

220. Susan Sterett, "Legality in Administration in Britain and the United States: Toward an Institutional Explanation," *Comparative Political Studies* 25 (1992), pp. 195–228; see also Herbert M. Kritzer, "Abel and the Professional Project: The Institutional Analysis of the Legal Profession," *Law and Social Inquiry* 16 (1991), pp. 542–543.

221. Neville Harris, "Judging the Quality of Welfare Benefits Work by Firms of Solicitors," *Civil Justice Quarterly* 10 (1991), p. 319.

222. Legal Aid Board, *Report on the Operation and Finance of the Legal Aid Act 1988 for the Year 1991–92* (London: HMSO, 1992), p. 20.

223. See Hazel Genn, *Hard Bargaining: Out of Court Settlement in Personal Injury Actions* (Oxford: Clarendon Press, 1987), pp. 88–90, 109–110.

224. Ibid., pp. 90–91.

One final point about legal aid is that the proportion of the population that is eligible to receive legal aid has sharply declined. A 1991 study commissioned by the Law Society showed that the percentage of the population eligible for in-office assistance under a system administered by the solicitors themselves had dropped from two-thirds of the population in 1979 to 37 percent in 1990. Eligibility for legal aid in personal injury claims fell from 81 percent of households in 1979 to 51 percent in 1990.[225] In April 1993, the Lord Chancellor implemented a radical change in eligibility that resulted in an immediate sharp reduction in the numbers eligible for civil legal aid. Some senior members of the judiciary attacked this move, and the Law Society unsuccessfully filed suit in the High Court claiming that the Lord Chancellor had exceeded his powers.[226] The moves by the Lord Chancellor reflected the rapidly rising cost of legal aid to the British treasury.[227] The net result of the tightened eligibility rules is to reduce access to the courts where legal representation is a necessity; however, there is no indication to date that the number of cases brought to court has actually declined because of these changes—such a decline would be difficult to identify given the various other changes that have taken place over the past several years.

Other Fee-for-Service Providers

In Britain, there are two other potential fee-for-service providers of services for personal plight problems. The first of these are accountants, whose purview in Britain is substantially broader than in the United States. Most of that difference is relevant only for corporations, but a person operating a small business could turn to his or her accountant to help with problems for which an American businessperson would use a lawyer (incorporation, forming a partnership, and so on).[228] There is no information on the roles played by accountants who serve small businesses, but recent movement in the direction of permitting some types of joint professional practices between solicitors and members of other professions suggests that the lack of clear

225. *Times* (London), Mar. 28, 1991, p. 5. See also "Legal Aid—Decline and Fall," *Law Society's Gazette*, Mar. 19, 1986, pp. 839–840; and "Eligibility Drops by 14 Million," *Law Society's Gazette*, Oct. 11, 1989, p. 7.

226. "Lord Chief Justice Deplores Mackay's [the Lord Chancellor] Legal Aid Reforms," *Times* (London), Feb. 4, 1993. "Solicitors Sue Lord Chancellor," *Guardian Weekly*, Apr. 18, 1993, p. 3.

227. "A Survey of the Legal Profession," *Economist*, July 18, 1992, p. 16. Between 1989 and 1994, the annual expenditure on legal aid doubled, even as eligibility was decreasing; Legal Aid Board, *Annual Report 1993–94* (London: HMSO, 1994), p. 3.

228. "Chartered" accountants are currently (1995) seeking authorization to handle probate cases, an area currently restricted to solicitors because of the formal role of the courts; see *Law Society's Gazette*, June 9, 1993, p. 6.

boundaries probably has significant implications for the various professional groups.[229]

Because of the lack of restrictions on representation outside of court and the provision of legal advice, there is nothing to prevent nonprofessionals from offering their services. In fact, in the area of personal injury damages, claims (or loss) assessors are available to assist persons negotiating settlements with insurance companies; moreover, loss assessors normally work on a commission basis (typically 15–25 percent of the amount recovered). There is no systematic information available about the volume or source of work done by loss assessors, the nature of experience and training brought to that work, or the degree of success achieved.[230] One result of the more limited eligibility for legal aid may be an increase in the number of cases handled by loss assessors; one franchise-based group, Independent Legal Practitioners, is reported to have handled £1 million worth of work during an eighteen-month period.[231]

The sources of assistance for persons in England with legal problems differ sharply from the sources in the U.S. Whereas one has to look hard to find American sources of assistance other than lawyers, in England such sources are readily available and frequently are more easily accessible than lawyers. The difficulty of hiring lawyers—because of the declining availability of legal aid and, at least until recently, the lack of a no-win, no-pay fee structure for legal services—and the ready availability of other types of assistance directs many types of disputes and problems away from the courts; the reason for this is that, with some very specific exceptions, nonlawyers cannot assist persons with cases in court. Only time will tell if the availability of no-win, no-pay fees for legal services will change the way that persons in England with personal plight problems turn to institutions for redress.

INSTITUTIONAL VENUES FOR RESOLVING
PERSONAL PLIGHT PROBLEMS

Magistrates' Courts

Three types of English courts deal with civil matters of one type or another: the Magistrates' Court, the County Court, and the High Court. With regard

229. Law Society, *Multi-Disciplinary Partnerships and Allied Topics* (London: Law Society, 1987); Lord Chancellor's Department, *The Work and Organisation of the Legal Profession* (London: HMSO, 1989), §12(A).

230. From interviews I conducted in 1987, it appears that some of the loss assessors previously worked as claims inspectors (what in the United States are called claims adjusters) for liability insurers. Others started out limiting their work to property-only cases that do not involve third party damages (i.e., the victim of the loss is seeking compensation from his or her own insurance company and there is a question of the value of the loss).

231. Sean Webster, "Age of the No-Win, No-Fee Outfits," *Times* (London), Oct. 4, 1994.

to civil cases, the role of the Magistrates' Court is limited to certain matrimonial matters: spousal maintenance, child support, and paternity. When dealing with such cases, the magistrates sit as a domestic court.[232]

This aspect of the court's jurisdiction is interesting considering the structure of the Magistrates' Courts. When lay magistrates sit as a domestic court, the three-person panel normally includes at least one man and one woman.[233] Only magistrates who are members of a special domestic panel can sit as a member of a panel in domestic court, and the magistrate must undergo special training to be a member of this panel.[234] Most judges of the County Courts, the other likely venue to handle these types of matrimonial cases, are male. These judges live mostly in larger metropolitan areas and have little knowledge (or experience) of the local social or economic experiences of those coming to court with domestic cases. In contrast, the magistrates know the local situation (including local pay levels, rents, and the other factors that might affect both what is needed for maintenance and support and what a wage earner could be expected to pay).[235]

County Courts

Parliament established the County Courts in the middle of the nineteenth century to provide a local jurisdiction for debt enforcement and other minor civil matters, leaving the High Court to handle more significant issues. In raw numbers, debt cases still dominate the caseload of the County Courts,[236] but over the years Parliament has increased the definition of what falls within the County Courts' jurisdiction. By the mid-1980s, the basic jurisdictional limit of the County Courts had risen to £5,000, with a special informal "arbitration" procedure available for contested small claims cases (£1,000 or less as of July 1991).[237] In addition, the County Courts handle matrimonial

232. This matrimonial jurisdiction is primarily a result of the historical role of magistrates' courts in a number of administrative matters, particularly the administration of the poor laws, which included the power to punish those who failed to support their dependents; see Spencer, supra note 14, p. 317.

233. In mid-1995, a major review of the civil justice system, headed by a senior judge, Lord Woolf, was under way. An interim report, *Access to Justice* (London: Lord Chancellor's Department, 1995), proposes a number of major changes in procedure that may significantly alter the system. There is no way of knowing which, if any, of the proposals will become part of the final plan and which will eventually be adopted. Many changes advanced by the previous review, less than a decade earlier, were never put into place.

234. Jackson, supra note 17, p. 328.

235. Spencer, supra note 14, p. 319.

236. Jackson, supra note 17, p. 330.

237. See Maureen Cain, "Where Are the Disputes? A Study of a First Instance Civil Court in the UK," in Cain and Kulcsár (eds.), supra note 211, pp. 119–133.

matters not going to Magistrates' Courts, especially divorce cases as well as many domestic violence cases. Circuit judges preside in the County Courts; district judges handle uncontested and small claims matters in the County Courts.

High Courts

The High Court, which is based at the Royal Courts of Justice in London, deals with major civil matters. The High Court has three divisions: Chancery, Family, and Queen's Bench. With regard to personal plight matters, the latter division is most relevant. The Queen's Bench is a "general jurisdiction" court, considering a range of contentious matters, particularly money claims, breach of contract, negligence (such as personal injury), libel, and disputes over goods and services. The Family Division hears complex matrimonial matters, but such cases are rare. The Chancery Division deals with some personal plight matters, such as difficult landlord-tenant cases, some disputes over property, and contested probate; however, the numbers of such cases are relatively small. The more important role of the Chancery Division is in commercial and business-related disputes. The High Court hears cases either in London or at one of approximately twenty-five first-tier centres around England and Wales. Any of the district registries located at many County Courts can handle the High Court's pretrial work. Technically, a litigant can file and pursue cases within the jurisdiction of the County Courts in the High Court, but the rules discourage this by limiting the costs that a successful litigant can recover to those the litigant would have received in County Court.

As the result of a major review of the civil justice system undertaken by the Lord Chancellor's Department in 1986–87, Parliament modified the relationship between the High Court and County Court by the passage of the Courts and Legal Services Act of 1990. This act authorized the Lord Chancellor to redistribute jurisdiction between the County and High Courts, which he did in 1991, abolishing financial limits on the jurisdiction of the County Courts, giving substantial concurrent jurisdiction to the two types of courts, requiring that personal injury cases involving damages up to £50,000 start in the County Courts, and establishing flexible criteria for the allocation of proceedings between the two courts. The goal of these actions was to allow the High Court to deal expeditiously with the more substantial and important cases requiring the attention of the senior judiciary.

Procedures in the Civil Courts

The handling of personal plight problems (and other civil matters) in the British courts differs from the procedures that are familiar to Americans, which has important implications for the manner of resolution of personal plight problems both in and out of court.[238]

Juries and Awards

In the United States there is an expectation that, if a case goes to trial, a lay jury will assess both responsibility (liability) and damages. In Britain, civil juries are rare and play a significant role in the civil justice system only in libel and slander cases. The use of juries began to decline in the late nineteenth century, and the right of a jury trial in most other civil matters effectively ended in 1933.[239]

The impact of this on damage awards is difficult to quantify, but it almost certainly has a major effect. Juries return large awards in libel cases with some regularity. For example, in 1987 a jury awarded British novelist Jeffrey Archer £500,000 for libel committed by a popular London tabloid; the largest libel award by an English jury was £1.5 million.[240] However, aside from libel cases, the British courts do not offer the opportunity for winning the large, "jackpot" verdicts that are the stuff of the American liability debate.[241]

Moreover, the presence of the extensive social welfare system (national health insurance, extensive disability and assistance benefits, and so on) in Britain substantially reduces damage awards in personal injury cases. Damages customarily consist of both "special damages," which cover the measurable pecuniary loss (for example, medical bills and lost wages) and "general damages"—more commonly called "pain and suffering." In Britain the welfare state automatically pays much of what constitutes special damages, and there are substantial limits on general damages.[242]

Uncertainty

Case precedents guide the decision-makers—professional judges—in determining the "quantum" of damages; a standard reference work referred to as

238. As with small claims procedures in the United States, the idea of the informal arbitration procedure is to create a setting in which litigants do not need to retain a solicitor to prosecute or defend a claim.

239. Jackson, supra note 17, p. 84.

240. *New York Times*, July 25, 1987, p. 4. "No End to Libel Roulette," *Law Society's Gazette*, Dec. 6, 1989, p. 19.

241. An example of an exception to this observation occurred in 1993 when a boy who survived having his ventilator turned off soon after birth, resulting in severe handicaps, was awarded £960,000 (almost $1.5 million) by a High Court judge; *Guardian Weekly* Dec. 5, 1993, p. 11.

242. Atiyah, supra note 170, p. 1023.

Kemp and Kemp provides a compilation of these precedential cases.[243] Experts on personal injury, particularly barristers who specialize in personal injury work, use these cases to estimate likely damage awards. The degree of reliance on accepted standards for establishing damages, particularly in fairly routine cases, is substantial: I have heard reports of barristers advising solicitors to reject settlement offers as too low when the gap between the offer and the barrister's evaluation of quantum was on the order of only 10 percent.

This is not to say that there is no uncertainty in litigation. Complex personal injury cases may involve combining damages in ways not covered in *Kemp and Kemp,* and even in routine cases, solicitors are often uncomfortable estimating quantum.[244] The rule that reduces a plaintiff's damages according to his or her contributory negligence further increases this uncertainty.[245] More important, rules controlling the sharing of information before trial (the process of discovery) can restrict the ability of the parties to predict the determination of liability. Where we can think of the American system as akin to playing poker with all, or almost all, of the cards face up, in the British system one plays the litigation game with all, or almost all, of the cards face down; "trial by ambush" is the governing expectation.[246] In the United States, essentially everything is "discoverable." In Britain, only medical and other documentary evidence are automatically discoverable, and the rules requiring that a witness reveal the substance of his or her testimony prior to trial applies only to directly involved parties. The parties need not even provide the names of witnesses other than the parties themselves before trial. All this combines to create the potential of substantial uncertainty on issues of liability.

Costs

A final difference between civil litigation in the U.S. and England is the rules governing the "costs" of litigation. As noted previously, in principle, the loser-pays rule governs the British system. In practice legal aid and third-party sponsorship (primarily by unions, but also through some private legal expense insurance programs) substantially mitigates this rule. Nonetheless, the general *expectation* is that if you initiate a legal action and you lose, you will incur significant costs; this creates disincentives. In an

---

243. David A. M. Kemp, *Kemp and Kemp: The Question of Damages in Personal Injury and Fatal Accident Claims* (London: Sweet & Maxwell, 1986).

244. Genn, supra note 213, p. 75.

245. The British term is *contributory negligence,* which is called comparative negligence in the United States.

246. Genn, supra note 213, p. 32.

extreme example, an actress who lost a libel action faced legal bills estimated to be £400,000.[247] Furthermore, the declining eligibility of legal aid makes more potential litigants subject to the threat of the loser-pays rule, and the recent movement toward no-win, no-pay fee arrangements for solicitors does nothing to counteract the powerful disincentives of this rule, although several plans in development may provide insurance against the risk of costs to litigants who have employed their solicitors under the conditional fee arrangement.[248]

One additional component of the loser-pays system allows a defendant who expects to be found liable (and who would thus expect to pay the plaintiff's costs under the loser-pays rule) to shift at least part of the threat of costs. The defendant makes a formal offer to settle known as ''payment into court'' for a specific amount and deposits that amount with the court. If the plaintiff rejects the offer, and at trial obtains a judgment less than the offer, the winning plaintiff must pay any costs incurred by the *losing* defendant after the date of the payment into court. In theory, this provides a powerful tool that defendants might use to their advantage in settlement negotiations. In practice, it appears that defendants actually use it relatively infrequently.[249] However, it remains a potent threat for the litigant with modest resources.

Routinization of Personal Plight Problems

As discussed above, the programs of the welfare state divert out of the legal system many types of compensation issues that arise as part of personal plight problems. Effectively, compensation becomes routinized in a way that mitigates the need for conflict-based mechanisms for dealing with those problems.

Of course, the welfare state generates its own conflicts, usually over entitlements and compensation levels. The British response has been to construct a fairly elaborate system of administrative tribunals. The principle of operation of these tribunals is supposed to be informality and fairness. The tension between these principles has led to an increasing concern about the need for experienced representatives to assist appellants before the tribunals. Evidence indicates that represented appellants are more likely to succeed in their appeals to tribunals than are unrepresented appellants.[250] Unrepresented appellants report feeling unable to effectively present their case, and feeling

247. "Actress Loses Libel Case," *Guardian Weekly*, Feb. 8, 1994, p. 9.
248. "Litigation Protection Launches Rival to Law Society's Insurance Scheme," *The Lawyer*, July 18, 1995, p. 2.
249. See Genn, supra note 213, pp. 111–112.
250. Genn and Genn, supra note 208, p. 243.

"intimidated, confused by the language, and often surprised by the formality of the proceedings."[251] The failure of the legal aid system to provide representation before administrative tribunals limits the fairness of adjudication that occurs in those settings.

Diversion through Criminalization

Britain has adopted another solution for consumer problems: moving them from the civil arena to the criminal arena. Consumer protection laws, which establish responsibilities of sellers of goods and services, provide for criminal penalties for merchants who violate the law. For example, the Property Misdescriptions Act, which came into effect in April 1993, provides for fines against real estate agents who make "false or misleading statements about property matters in the course of estate agency business and property development business."[252] Violators face fines of £5,000 or more.[253]

Citizens' knowledge of their rights as consumers probably account for the high likelihood that citizens will lodge complaints over consumer problems. The national Office of Fair Trading (OFT) collects data from local governmental offices responsible for enforcing the consumer protection laws. In the first quarter of 1990, more than 160,000 consumers lodged complaints with these local authority offices,[254] totaling on the order of 600,000 to 700,000 complaints per year. The ability of these offices to resolve the complaints, either by convincing the consumer that the complaint lacked merit under the law or by convincing the provider to offer some form of redress, results in the virtual absence of consumer cases in the County Courts.

Criminalization extends to other areas as well. For example, under Britain's system of protected tenancies (where tenants effectively have an ownership right to occupy a property), a property owner sometimes harasses a tenant to vacate. British law criminalizes such harassment.[255] Thus, withdrawal of services by a property owner, or acts that interfere with the peace or comfort of the occupant, can constitute criminal harassment.[256]

---

251. Ibid., p. 241. My own experience observing hearings before several "administrative tribunals" in the United States is consistent with this: unrepresented appellants are seldom prepared to present their case in an effective manner. The success of efforts by decision makers to draw out the necessary details to decide the case in a way similar to what would occur with high quality representation is spotty at best.

252. "Act Puts Block on Agent-Speak," *Times* (London), Mar. 28, 1993.

253. *Guardian Weekly,* Apr. 11, 1993, p. 3.

254. *Beeline,* 90/2, August 1990, p. 40.

255. See, for example, Section 29 of the Housing Act of 1988.

256. For more on this, see "New Rights for Harassed Tenants," *Law Society's Gazette,* June 28, 1989, pp. 18–20.

SUMMARY: ACCESS TO REDRESS

The overall picture that emerges from this discussion of personal plight in Britain is that, whether through intentional policy decisions, cultural inclinations, or coincidence, Britain has channeled away from the courts options and opportunities for redress. The resulting variety of alternatives, barriers, and limitations discourages bringing court actions or mitigates the need for such actions.

The relative lack of interest in litigation work by most general practice solicitors further encourages this orientation away from court action. There are specialists in personal plight litigation, particularly personal injury specialists, who know the system and have developed a systematic and efficient operation to process large numbers of claims in a way that is profitable.[257] However, as long as solicitors possessed a monopoly on handling the transfer of real property ("conveyancing"), "contentious work" was less profitable than conveyancing. With the demise of the conveyancing monopoly (and the resulting decline in fees for conveyancing work),[258] there is evidence of increasing interest by solicitors in seeking out clients with personal plight problems. This is clearly evident in the reversal in the Law Society's traditional opposition to contingent fees.[259] In 1987, the Law Society published proposals to provide for something that, from the perspective of the client, looked very much like a commission-fee structure, combined with insurance against having to pay the opponent's costs if the legal action was unsuccessful.[260] The system was designed to allay the fears of potential clients with regard to the costs of losing and to encourage more potential clients to come forward.

Scottish law has for some time permitted lawyers to accept cases on a "speculative" basis that amounted to a no-win, no-pay arrangement. As noted previously, the Courts and Legal Services Act of 1990 authorized the Lord Chancellor to permit a similar arrangement, called "conditional" fees, in England; under a conditional fee, solicitors can accept cases with the understanding that they receive no fee if no compensation was obtained, and that they receive their normal fee plus an "uplift" (an extra amount) if compensation is obtained. This system finally went into operation in July 1995.

The interest and willingness of solicitors to seek out contentious work are most important in those arenas where legal representation is key to obtaining redress *through the legal system*. In the Britain the clearest example is personal

257. See Genn, supra note 213, p. 41.

258. See Herbert M. Kritzer, "A Comparative Perspective on Settlement and Bargaining in Personal Injury Cases," *Law & Social Inquiry* 14 (1990), p. 176.

259. This opposition is clearly documented in a 1970 Law Society paper, *Memorandum on Maintenance and Champerty: Claims Assessors and Contingent Fees.*

260. Law Society, *Improving Access to Civil Justice* (London: Law Society, 1987). The plan is referred to as a contingent legal aid fund.

injury. As noted previously, the welfare state provides for much of the compensation that an injured person would typically seek through the American tort system such as medical expenses, part of the lost wages, and so on.[261] In theory, however, the injured person can seek significant additional compensation, both for intangibles such as pain and suffering and for expenses not otherwise compensated.[262] However, if the claimant does not have legal representation, it is very unlikely that a British insurer will pay tort-based compensation. One study found that direct settlements between an injured party and an insurer occur in only 8 percent of personal injury tort claims in Britain.[263] One might speculate that insurers refuse to deal with unrepresented claimants to discourage claims, and, as long as solicitors were relatively uninterested in contentious work, such a practice benefitted the insurer. Solicitors essentially serve as the gatekeepers to tort-based compensation.

Sometimes limitations in the system largely foreclose individually based action. For example, in 1987, the English ferry *Herald of Free Enterprise*, departing from Zeebrugge, Belgium, for England, capsized when water came through the doors used for loading vehicles onto the ferry, resulting in almost two hundred deaths. The crew member responsible for closing the doors was asleep at the time of departure, and no senior officer checked to ensure that the doors were closed prior to departure. Despite this clear negligence, the ferry company (and its insurer) paid very little in damages to the families of those who died. Treaty agreements limited damages to a maximum of £39,000 for each fatality (a total of £7.6 million if every fatality were compensated at the maximum amount); the total payout came to only £6 million, which covered more than six hundred claimants.[264] Compare this to the aftermath of the 1988 bombing of Pan Am flight 103 over Lockerbie, Scotland, in which 270 persons died; victims' families filed multiple lawsuits in New York, one of which led to a $9 million verdict.[265]

In addition, the drift of British policy regarding personal plight problems is to direct such problems away from the type of individually oriented solutions typically provided by litigation and toward societally oriented solutions that create governmental structures to ameliorate many problems. For example, the welfare state heads off the need for compensation in many

261. See Peter Cane, *Atiyah's Accidents, Compensation, and the Law*, 4th ed. (London: Weidenfeld and Nicolson, 1987), pp. 405–409.

262. Some types of compensation can be received both through the social welfare system and through the tort system; ibid., pp. 406–408.

263. Donald Harris, Mavis Maclean, Hazel Genn, Sally Lloyd-Bostock, Paul Fenn, Peter Corfield, and Yvonne Brittan, *Compensation and Support for Illness and Injury* (Oxford: Oxford University Press, 1984), p. 81.

264. *Times* (London), Feb. 3, 1988, p. 3.

265. *New York Times*, July 23, 1992, p. A7.

situations, and the consumer protection laws head off the need for a great deal of private consumer-oriented litigation. However, problems and disputes come up regardless of the type of system. Closed avenues of redress suppress some of these; the state handles others directly, and administrative tribunals with norms of informality and nonadversarialness deal with others.

When major problems or events occur, the state responds rather than leaving the problem to individually based action through litigation. The *Herald of Free Enterprise* disaster is a good case in point. A formal government inquiry, headed by a High Court judge, led to a series of safety recommendations to avoid a repeat occurrence and disciplinary action against the ship's captain. In the wake of the inquiry, the director of public prosecutions instituted criminal proceedings, both against three company directors and four crew members for manslaughter and against the ferry company itself for "corporate manslaughter."[266] However, the charges did not lead to criminal convictions for any of the defendants.[267]

Even when individuals seek redress through the legal system, there is likely to be some type of social response.[268] Later in the same year as the Zeebrugge tragedy, a fire at the King's Cross underground station in London resulted in thirty-one deaths. Investigations determined that smoking materials (most likely a lighted match) ignited the fire, probably by falling through an exit escalator into an accumulation of grease and debris underneath. Although authorities had banned smoking in the underground after a 1985 fire at another station, smoking was common, particularly as persons rode the escalators from the train level to the street level. The inquiry into the fire determined that while the precipitating cause of the fire was illegal smoking, the failure to maintain the escalator properly permitted the fire to start and spread quickly.[269] The inquiry led to the resignation of the head of London Transport and to a promise by the government to invest substantial sums to upgrade safety on the underground. Unlike the Zeebrugge tragedy, treaties did not place limits on damages, and about one hundred victims (or their families) and firefighters initiated claims and legal actions; some of these claimants succeeded in obtaining tort-based compensation.[270] Families of the

266. "Ferry Chiefs and Crew Face Zeebrugge Charges," *Daily Telegraph,* Dec. 19, 1989, p. 3.

267. "Court Acquits P&O European Ferries and Seven Former Employees," *Guardian,* Oct. 20, 1990.

268. See Atiyah, supra note 170, pp. 1032–1033.

269. Desmond Fennell, *Investigation into the King's Cross Underground Fire* (London: HMSO, 1988).

270. *Times* (London), June 27, 1990, p. 2; Feb. 21, 1991, p. 4; Dec. 19, 1990, p. 3. The family of one fireman received £250,000 in damages from London Transport; *Times* (London), June 27, 1990, p. 2.

victims of the fire also considered instituting a private prosecution for corporate manslaughter.[271]

One can overstate the limiting and channeling of redress. For example, there is a well-established pattern in England of using the tort system to obtain compensation for asbestos-related disease. In the United States, asbestos litigation has risen to crisis levels in the federal (and some state) courts and is marked by unpredictability, huge caseloads, denial of responsibility and stiff defendant resistance, high transaction costs, corporate bankruptcies, and failed solutions of various types. In contrast, asbestos litigation in England (and the rest of the United Kingdom), has settled into a pattern involving a relatively high degree of predictability, manageable caseloads, acknowledged responsibility, and relatively low transaction costs. Unlike several Continental countries, England has chosen not to channel asbestos-related injuries out of the courts.[272] The reliance on tort-based remedies in this arena flows from a combination of factors: the law clearly establishes the legal responsibility of employers to provide a safe and healthy work environment; trade unions' important role in supporting members' legal claims short-circuits the disincentives of the English civil justice process; and a well-established group of specialist plaintiffs' solicitors handles cases efficiently and profitably on what amounts to an hourly fee basis.[273] While observers frequently argue that tort-based compensation paid in England is far below that paid in the U.S., the *net* difference (after taking into account the costs and fees paid to the plaintiffs' attorney by the claimant in the U.S.) between English and American compensation to asbestos claimants is relatively small.[274] Still, there is some indication that fewer potential claimants seek compensation than in the United States, but simple explanations such as cultural differences or procedural differences are insufficient to account for the lower claiming rates in England.[275]

CONCLUSION

Within the British social and legal system, one finds a set of complex arrangements to provide avenues of protection, compensation, and redress. The

271. *Times* (London), Nov. 19, 1989, p. 13.

272. For example, the Netherlands has adopted a social insurance approach rather than a tort-based approach; see Harriet Vinke and Ton Wilthagen, "The Non-Mobilization of Law by Asbestos Victims in the Netherlands," paper presented at meetings of the Law & Society Association, Philadelphia, May 28–31, 1992.

273. See Tom Durkin, Robert Dingwall, and William L. F. Felstiner, "Plaited Cunning: Manipulating Time in Asbestos Litigation," paper presented at meetings of the Law & Society Association, Oakland, Calif., June 1990.

274. See William L. Felstiner and Robert Dingwall, "Asbestos Litigation in the United Kingdom: An Interim Report," American Bar Foundation Working Paper no. 8807 (1988).

275. See Tom Durkin and William L. F. Felstiner, "The Meaning of Propensity to Sue Rates: A US–UK Comparison," unpublished paper, American Bar Foundation, 1990.

key to understanding the matrix of mechanisms in Britain is that it builds on an assumption of social responsibility rooted deeply in the highly stratified, socially differentiated nature of British society.

Rather than relying on individuals asserting rights, demanding damages, and otherwise seeking redress, Britain provides a broad net of social programs to mitigate many of the inevitable misfortunes of modern life. Furthermore, for most of the latter half of the twentieth century, British housing and employment policy provided a more secure environment that lessened some of the problems that might otherwise have occurred. Finally, by shifting consumer protection into the criminal arena, Britain has lifted the responsibility for insuring fair dealing from the individual consumer and placed it in the hands of a government agency. The impact of this set of policies is to establish a collective pattern of redress and prevention that contrasts sharply with the individualistic-based set of presumptions that dominate in the United States.

Elites, Institutions, and the Judicial Process in England

In this section I turn to government officials and institutional (including corporate) actors, whom I will call "elites." What role do the courts play in public and private administration beyond the routine handling of individual cases? Do the courts provide a check on the actions of elites and government agencies? What effect do the courts have on the relationships among elites?

The relevant courts are generally the High Court, the Court of Appeal, and the House of Lords. The High Court normally serves as the point of entry for significant disputes involving elite actors (although some cases start in an administrative tribunal, and occasionally as a criminal matter in the Crown Court). Two of the High Court's three divisions are important here: the Queen's Bench (which has general jurisdiction) and the more specialized Chancery Division (which hears matters dealing with probate disputes, bankruptcy, ownership and use of land, trusts, partnership issues, and copyright and patents). The Queen's Bench includes the Commercial Court and an Admiralty Court, which hear disputes between major commercial entities and cases arising out of maritime affairs, respectively. The judges chosen to sit in these courts normally have expertise that allows them to deal fairly and efficiently with often highly technical (and high value) cases.

The High Court also has appellate jurisdiction. For example, several judges of the Queen's Bench sit as a panel to constitute the Divisional Court, which exercises what is called "judicial review" over the actions of administrative tribunals and governmental officials.[276] In the United States the term *judicial review* is generally reserved for a court's determination of whether

---

276. Spencer, supra note 14, pp. 152–163; however, judicial review can also be exercised by a single judge of the High Court.

a law is constitutional; thus, in the U.S. judicial review is synonymous with constitutional review. English courts use the broader meaning of the term— the review of actions of governmental bodies (that is, the legislative and executive branches) by a court.[277] In fact, in England, there is no constitutional review by the courts, limiting judicial review to questions about the legality of the actions of government officials in carrying out their duties.

In an ordinary appeal, the issue raised is normally whether a court misconstrued facts or applied law inappropriately in a particular case. If an appeals court finds an error, the court may enter a new decision in the case. Judicial review is more limited; the question is whether the previous decision maker, which can be either a tribunal or a government official acting in his or her official capacity, has "acted upon an error of law,"[278] for example, by taking into account irrelevant considerations or failing to consider relevant factors. If the court finds error, it may throw out the decision, but it may not enter a new decision; the case must go back to the decision maker for a new decision.[279] As I will discuss in some detail below, the English version of judicial review is of increasing importance because, rather than simply ensuring that administrators and bureaucrats obey the will of Parliament, the courts have taken an expansive view of judicial review, building up "a body of judge-made law that the courts deem to apply to all public authorities unless clearly and expressly excluded by the relevant legislation." The courts have been resistant to efforts of Parliament to rein in the exercise of judicial review, interpreting such phrases as "any decision of . . . shall be final" as reflecting finality of fact but not finality with regard to errors of law.[280]

Appeals from the decisions of the High Court (as well as from the County Courts) normally go to the civil division of the Court of Appeal.[281] Some types of cases (and those with certain amounts of potential damages) have a right of appeal to the Court of Appeal, while others require leave to appeal,

277. See Maurice Sunkin, "The Incidence and Effect of Judicial Review Procedures Against Central Government in the United Kingdom," pp. 143–156, in Donald W. Jackson and C. Neal Tate (eds.), *Comparative Judicial Review and Public Policy* (Westport, Conn.: Greenwood Press); Susan Sterett, "Judicial Review in Britain," *Comparative Political Studies* 26 (January 1994), pp. 442.

278. Spencer, supra note 14, p. 154.

279. Specific procedures for judicial review are a relatively new phenomenon, having been introduced primarily by a change in the rules of procedure (in response to a recommendation of the Law Commission) in 1977; Jack I. H. Jacob, *The Fabric of English Civil Justice* (London: Stevens & Sons, 1987), p. 181. However, the practice of judicial review by the English courts is far from new, dating back to at least the middle of the nineteenth century; see Hartley and Griffith, supra note 5, pp. 326–331.

280. Hartley and Griffith, supra note 5, p. 365.

281. Appeals from a small number of specific administrative tribunals go directly to the Court of Appeal; see Spencer, supra note 14, p. 93.

either from the trial judge or from a judge of the Court of Appeal. The Court of Appeal functions as a collegial court of judges deciding cases in groups rather than sitting alone, with most matters involving a panel of three judges. Traditionally, the Court of Appeal conducted its business with all information read out or orally argued in court, and the Lords Justices orally stating their decision either individually or as a decision of the Court. Clerks record and transcribe those decisions. While the oral style of decision is still the norm, the Court of Appeal also relies increasingly on written documents. In cases decided by a judge rather than by a jury at trial, the court may reverse the finding of the trial judge; in practice, the Court of Appeal does not rehear the entire case but relies instead on the written record of the lower court. Nor does it very often second-guess the trial judge's finding of fact.[282] Nonetheless, consideration by the Court of Appeal constitutes real review; from 1952 to 1983, the Court of Appeal reversed about 35 percent of the decisions appealed to it.[283]

The top of the judicial hierarchy is the Judicial Committee of the House of Lords,[284] consisting of ten to fifteen Lords of Appeal in Ordinary (Law Lords). Law Lords are usually professional judges, with life appointments to the House of Lords; other members of the House of Lords are excluded from the Judicial Committee, except for occasional situations involving a member who happens to be a barrister. The Law Lords are given life peerages in order to exercise the House's appellate function. Other members of the House who have held high judicial office, such as former Lord Chancellors, also serve as members of the Judicial Committee.[285]

Formally, the Lord Chancellor, as the presiding officer of the House of Lords, heads the Judicial Committee; in practice, the Lord Chancellor sits with the Judicial Committee only sporadically.[286] Members of the Judicial Committee normally sit as an Appellate Committee consisting of five Law Lords, in contrast to the U.S. Supreme Court, which always hears cases en banc—all members sitting together. Cases come to the House of Lords by leave of either the court below (which grants only about 10 percent of re-

282. Ibid., p. 92.

283. Burton M. Atkins, "Interventions and Power in Judicial Hierarchies: Appellate Courts in England and the United States," *Law & Society Review* 24 (1990), p. 83. For comparison, Atkins reports the reversal rate for U.S. federal appeals court, which from 1977 to 1987 averaged 16 percent—about half the rate of the English Court of Appeal. See also, Burton M. Atkins, "Party Capability Theory as an Explanation for Intervention Behavior in the English Court of Appeal," *American Journal of Political Science* 35 (1991), pp. 881–902.

284. The description here is from Spencer, supra note 14, pp. 93–95.

285. Jacob, supra note 279, p. 242; and Griffith, supra note 28, p. 55.

286. Regarding the Lord Chancellor's actual activity as a judge, see Anthony Bradney, "The Judicial Activity of the Lord Chancellor, 1946–1987: A Pellet," *Journal of Law and Society* 16 (1989), pp. 360–372.

quests for leave to appeal) or by leave of a committee of the Law Lords (the Appeal Committee grants 25–35 percent of the requests it receives).[287] While the Law Lords do not normally participate in the legislative proceedings within the House of Lords, they do on occasion join in debate and speak, particularly when the issue at question concerns a relatively technical issue of law or the operation of the court system; on occasion, a Law Lord may even introduce a bill.[288]

The number of cases typically heard each year by an Appellate Committee is small, sixty to eighty.[289] In form, the proceedings of the Appellate Committee panels maintain some of the fiction that the House of Lords in its legislative capacity makes decisions. The "House" formally decides cases when the Law Lords sit as the House of Lords rather than as the Appellate Committee, and each member of the panel of the Appellate Committee presents a "speech" rather than rendering a "judgment," although the speeches are not actually read out. The rate of reversal in the House of Lords has been running around 35 to 40 percent in recent years, but has fluctuated during the latter half of the twentieth century.[290]

ACTIONS INVOLVING THE GOVERNMENT

Observers often hold England out as an example of a country that, in contrast to the United States, leaves the running of the government to the legislative and executive branches rather than to the courts.[291] While this may have once been true, and while English courts have avoided getting involved in the kind of day-to-day oversight of government action that has been much written about in the United States,[292] English courts are increasingly willing to tell the government officials, at both national and local levels, that their action is wrong.[293]

287. See Burton M. Atkins, "Alternative Models of Appeal Mobilization in Judicial Hierarchies," *American Journal of Political Science* 37 (1993), p. 785; See *JSAR 1993*, p. 8, for the 1993 figures.

288. See Griffith, supra note 28, pp. 55–58.

289. In 1993, the Law Lords decided 84 cases (76 from England and Wales); *JSAR 1993*, p. 9. This was up from 63 cases in 1992; *JSAR 1992*, p. 10.

290. See Atkins, supra note 283, pp. 90–91.

291. See Fred L. Morrison, *Courts and the Political Process in England* (Beverly Hills, Calif.: Sage Publications, 1973), pp. 217–224.

292. See, for example, Donald L. Horowitz, *The Courts and Social Policy* (Washington, D.C.: Brookings Institution, 1977); Jeremy Rabkin, *Judicial Compulsions: How Public Law Distorts Public Policy* (New York: Basic Books: 1989).

293. See Jerome Waltman and Priscilla H. Machado, "Postindustrialism and the Changing Face of Administrative Litigation in England, 1960–1985," *Social Science Journal* 29 (1992), pp. 185–198. "Ministers Feel the Long Arm of the Law," *Financial Times*, Nov. 12–13, 1994, p. 5.

Government Actions Affecting Individuals
Judicial Review

A first example involves the actions of immigration officials. Because it is an island, Britain has been able to exercise relatively stringent controls on entrance into the country. As noted previously, Britain has in recent years tightened criteria for entry, in particular for persons from former British colonies who at one time had virtually a right of entry and settlement. In a 1993 case, authorities deported a teacher from Zaire who was seeking political asylum in Britain, even though an official of the Home Office, which is responsible for immigration matters, had stated in court that the teacher would not be deported pending a renewed application for judicial review in the Divisional Court. An action for contempt was brought against the Home Secretary because he had ordered the deportation. The Home Secretary claimed that he could not be cited because he was acting on behalf of the Crown, and he enjoyed the sovereign immunity that protected the Queen from being brought into court. The House of Lords ruled that the Home Secretary could be found in contempt.[294]

The ruling was significant in two ways. First, it made clear that members of "Her Majesty's government," acting in their capacity as members of the Cabinet, are subject to the courts performing the judicial review function. Second, it strengthened the hand of the courts in reviewing immigration matters, which comprise one of the two largest sets of cases brought for judicial review in the Divisional Court.[295] Furthermore, this strengthening of the courts came while the caseload of the Divisional Court was dramatically increasing. From 1963 to 1993, the Divisional Court caseload went from 190 cases to 3,635 cases, a 1,813 percent increase; the increase from 1992 to 1993 was about 18 percent.[296] Most of the cases are applications for leave to apply for judicial review.[297] The court grants about half of the applications, and in about half of the cases decided on the merits the court "allows" the

294. *M. v. Home Office,* 3 All ER 537 (1993); see *Times* (London), July 28, 1993, *Guardian,* July 28, 1993, p. 2.

295. Together with housing, immigration constitutes about half of the matters brought for judicial review; see "Dearth of Expertise on Judicial Review," *Law Society's Gazette,* June 23, 1993, p. 5.

296. *JSAR 1993,* pp. 15–16. Most of the increase, particularly in judicial review, came after 1980. See Maurice Sunkin, "What is Happening to Applications For Judicial Review?" *Modern Law Review* 50 (1987), p. 435; Maurice Sunkin, "The Judicial Review Case-load, 1987–1989," *Public Law* (1991), pp. 490–499; Maurice Sunkin, Lee Bridges, and George Mészáros, *Judicial Review in Perspective: An Investigation of Trends in the Use and Operation of the Judicial Review Procedure in England and Wales* (London: Public Law Project, 1993).

297. See Sunkin et al., supra note 296.

review (finds that the action of the government official or tribunal violated the law).[298]

Groups and individuals can use judicial review. An example of group action involves several interest groups' challenge to the government on matters relating to homelessness. Interest groups working to alleviate homelessness originally brought cases in the County Court, as an action for damages. A decision by the House of Lords foreclosed the County Courts as an avenue of redress in matters concerning the homeless. The interest groups then shifted to bringing cases as applications for judicial review.[299]

An example of individual action involving the disciplining of a head teacher (principal) of a school in London who had allegedly made a racist remark arose in the 1980s. The educational authority suspended the teacher pending review of the matter. After the governing body of her school had "acquitted" her of the charge of having made the remark, the council of the local borough (the governmental unit in London, as there is no citywide government) initiated its own disciplinary proceedings. The court granted the head teacher's application for judicial review and issued an injunction barring the council from rehearing the case while the court considered whether it was lawful for the council to conduct such a rehearing. The court eventually ruled that the case could not be tried twice, thus upholding the action of the school's governing body. After initially refusing to reinstate the head teacher and expressing the intention to appeal to the Court of Appeal, the council backed down and reinstated the teacher.[300]

The courts have become involved not just in "administrative" matters but also in matters of broader policy. In the summer of 1993, as Parliament was preparing to vote on ratification of the Maastricht treaty, which dealt with the integration of the European Community, the former editor of *The Times* filed an application for judicial review with the High Court, explicitly challenging the ratification process but implicitly challenging the treaty itself. The High Court granted the application for judicial review, throwing the ratification process into turmoil. However, after hearing the challenge, the High Court rejected it and allowed the ratification vote to proceed.[301]

The outcome was different when the government announced in 1992 that state-owned British Coal was going to shut down thirty-one coal mines, leaving fewer than twenty in operation and putting 30,000 miners out of work. Conflict between the Conservative government and the coal miners had been intense. The government had successfully resisted a strike by miners in 1984–

298. *JSAR 1993*, p. 15.
299. See Harlow and Rawlings, supra note 3, p. 141.
300. See *Guardian*, Oct. 23, 1986, p. 1; Nov. 5, 1986, p. 1; Dec. 16, 1986, p. 1.
301. *Guardian Weekly*, July 25, 1993, pp. 1, 9; *New York Times*, July 31, 1993, p. 3.

85, but after that strike British Coal had established a consultative procedure to be followed whenever it wanted to shut down a mine. The procedure granted mine workers and their unions the right to refer proposed closures to an independent advisory body.

In 1992, the government was anxious to get British Coal into a financial condition that would allow its sale to private owners. To accomplish this the government wanted to close mines that it believed were not sufficiently profitable and decided to dispense with the consultative procedure. Three mining unions successfully filed an application for judicial review. The High Court ruled that the government's plan to close the mines was unlawful; the court ordered the government department with responsibility for the mines, the Department of Trade and Industry, and British Coal to pay more than £500,000 to the three unions to cover the unions' costs in bringing the action. The mines had to stay open,[302] at least until British Coal had completed the requisite procedures, but many of the mines were eventually closed.

Clearly the English courts have become increasingly involved in the day-to-day operation of the English governmental system. In her memoirs, Margaret Thatcher noted a concern at one point that judicial review might undermine plans for limitations on spending by local governments.[303] Government departments have had to devote significant energies to the problem of anticipating and avoiding court review of their actions.[304] In 1987, authorities published a pamphlet entitled *The Judge Over Your Shoulder* to provide guidance to civil servants on how to avoid having their actions and decisions overturned by the courts; a revised version was published in 1995.[305]

"Ordinary" Court Actions against Government

Groups of individuals can also challenge the government through ordinary civil actions claiming damages. A dramatic example of this occurred in the community of Cleveland County (in northeast England) in the spring of 1987. A new physician in the community began employing a method of diagnosing child sexual abuse that immediately led to a sharp increase in the number of such diagnoses; a colleague adopted the same technique. Between February and July 1987, the two doctors diagnosed 121 children from 57 families as

302. *Guardian Weekly,* Dec. 27, 1992, p. 3.

303. Margaret Thatcher, *The Downing Street Years* (New York: HarperCollins, 1993), p. 665.

304. See Maurice Sunkin and A. P. Le Sueur, "Can Government Control Judicial Review?" *Current Legal Problems* 44 (1991), pp. 161–183.

305. Anthony Barker, "Judicial Review in Whitehall," paper presented at 1995 meeting of the American Political Science Association, Chicago, p. 10.

sexually abused.[306] Such a diagnosis allowed authorities to remove a child from parental custody immediately, possibly along with other children of the family, to be placed "in care." The inquiry into the events in Cleveland found that many of the children had been victims of abuse, but others had not.[307]

The events in Cleveland County received widespread coverage in the media. The image presented was that of physicians overly reliant on a single diagnostic procedure that was needlessly disrupting families. The *Sunday Times* featured an account of a girl, aged ten, and her two brothers, aged twelve and fourteen, who were removed from their family after being diagnosed "as victims of 'regular and frequent abuse.'. . . The children were interviewed six times by police and social workers and each time denied they were abused. Anatomically-correct dolls were produced in the hope the children would talk about their bodies; still they said it wasn't true. . . . A care order was obtained from magistrates and the children could not go home. Since then an independent examination has found that two *have not* been abused and in the third child's case the result is inconclusive." The children were still "in care" in the hospital.[308] Later investigations related the stories of children who had been abused, some by immediate family members and some by others.[309]

The local member of Parliament became involved, voicing harsh criticism of the physicians and urging parents to consult solicitors.[310] The day after the *Sunday Times* report, several families, with a total of seventeen children in care, went to the High Court seeking orders returning their children. The High Court immediately returned some children to their parents, and additional hearings over the following weeks led to the return of others.[311]

The controversy resulted in an official inquiry (headed by one of the few women on the bench of the High Court). After publication of the inquiry report, a number of families initiated legal actions for damages against the doctors and the local government.[312] About half (twenty-eight of fifty-seven) of the families involved in the events of 1987 settled out of court with the

---

306. Elizabeth Butler-Sloss, *Report of the Inquiry into Child Abuse in Cleveland 1987* (London: HMSO, 1988), p. 21.

307. Ibid. See also Carol Smart, *Feminism and the Power of Law* (London: Routledge, 1989), pp. 62–63.

308. *Sunday Times* (London), June 28, 1987, p. 11. See Butler-Sloss, supra note 306, pp. 30–31, for another account of the experience of this family; eventually, a High Court judge held that sexual abuse had not occurred, and returned the children to the custody of their parents.

309. See Butler-Sloss, supra note 306, pp. 25–35.

310. *Guardian*, June 27, 1987, p. 32.

311. *Guardian*, June 29, 1987, p. 1; July 1, 1987, p. 1.

312. *Times* (London), July 7, 1988, p. 6; July 8, 1988, p. 5.

local government, the local health authorities, and the two physicians, receiving a payment of £1 million (£7,500 to £10,000 per child).[313]

Civil Liberties Cases in the House of Lords

The absence of a bill of rights historically limited the role of the English
courts in the area of civil liberties.[314] However, this situation may be changing. The role of civil liberties cases on the Law Lords' agenda has increased:
in 1960 it comprised less than 10 percent of the cases decided each year but
by 1990 was more than 30 percent.[315] There are a variety of possible explanations for this change; the most likely are the growth in interest groups
willing to pursue their goals through courts and the increasing availability of
legal aid to pay for civil liberties litigation.[316] The growing influence of
European law and courts (discussed below) may also be an important factor.
Over time, this may change judges' attitudes about their appropriate role.[317]

Business Challenges to Government Policy

Businesses and corporations have also used the courts to challenge government policy. Take the example of Laker Airways' efforts to establish a low
cost transatlantic service in the 1970s.[318] In 1972, Laker obtained a license
from the British Civil Aviation Authority (CAA) to operate service between
London and New York. About eighteen months later, an administrative law
judge at the United States' Civil Aeronautics Board (CAB) issued a report
endorsing the granting of a permit. The full CAB, however, opposed the
permit, and so recommended to President Richard M. Nixon (who was the
final decision maker because of the international implications). While Laker
was awaiting presidential action, the board of rival British Airways asked the
British CAA to revoke Laker's license, claiming that there had been both an

313. *Times* (London), Oct. 16, 1991, p. 4.

314. For a general discussion of the systems that do promote and protect civil liberties in
England, see David Feldman, *Human Rights and Civil Liberties in England and Wales* (Oxford:
Oxford University Press, 1993); for a detailed discussion of the status of various civil liberties
issues, see Christopher McCrudden and Gerald Chambers (eds.), *Individual Rights and the Law
in Britain* (Oxford: Clarendon Press, 1994).

315. Charles Epp, "Constitutional Courts and the Rights Agenda in Comparative Perspective," Ph.D. diss., University of Wisconsin, 1995, chapter 2.

316. Ibid.

317. David Rose, "UK: Silent Revolution—Judges with Radical Views," *The Observer*,
May 9, 1993; David Feldman, "Public Law Values in the House of Lords," *Law Quarterly
Review* 106 (1990), pp. 246–276.

318. This account of Laker Airways is taken largely from Howard Banks, *The Rise and
Fall of Freddie Laker* (London: Faber and Faber, 1982), supplemented by a variety of newspaper
reports.

increase in cost and a decrease in traffic on the route. In July 1975, the Trade Secretary, the cabinet minister responsible for the CAA, announced plans to reverse the prior decision granting Laker a license; the American CAB then withdrew the license that was sitting unsigned on the president's desk. The following year, the Trade Secretary announced the terms of the guidelines that would govern CAA's issuance of permits for long-haul scheduled service, which included a provision effectively giving the board of British Airways veto power. Parliament approved these guidelines as required by the Civil Aviation Act.[319]

Laker initiated action in the High Court, claiming that the Trade Secretary had exceeded his powers. Specifically, Laker claimed that granting the British Airways board a veto conflicted with the terms of the Civil Aviation Act of 1971, which mandated that the CAA encourage privately owned airlines (British Airways was at the time owned by the government) to provide passenger services.[320] In July 1976, the High Court ruled in favor of Laker.[321] The decision rejected the government's guidelines as violating the Civil Aviation Act, even though both Houses of Parliament had approved the guidelines. The judge noted that only a statute can amend a statute, and the guidelines were a policy statement, not a statute. The government had also claimed that it had acted under the prerogative of the Crown in granting the license to Laker and could use that same prerogative to revoke the license. The Court held that the Civil Aviation Act had restricted the Crown's prerogative with regard to revoking the designation during the term of the license (which was ten years) or until international agreements governing international air service were terminated.

The government took the case to the Court of Appeal because of the importance of what the High Court had said regarding the prerogatives of the Crown (in effect, the powers of the government). The panel hearing the case was headed by the Master of the Rolls (the chief judge of the Civil Division of the Court of Appeal), who issued a blunt decision upholding the High Court's support for Laker.[322] The decision, going beyond simply enabling Laker to start its Skytrain service, explicitly made clear the Court's view of the limits of the government's power, going so far as to cite a 1611 case decided after King James I attempted to govern by proclamation, in which the courts declared that the king had no prerogative except that granted by the law of the land.[323] The government initially planned to appeal to the

319. See Griffith, supra note 28, p. 136.
320. Quoted in Banks, supra note 318, p. 34.
321. *Laker Airways Ltd. v. Department of Trade* 121 S.J. 52 (1976).
322. *Laker Airways Ltd. v. Department of Trade* 2 All ER 182 (1977).
323. Banks, supra note 318, p. 52.

House of Lords but decided not to do so in light of prior decisions in the Lords.

ACTIONS AGAINST AND AMONG NONGOVERNMENTAL INSTITUTIONS

The courts in England have an important impact on the relationship of the government to the governed. What is the role of the courts in the private relationships of institutional actors, both among themselves and with regard to customers and constituents? How important are the courts in maintaining relationships among major commercial entities?

Business Disputes

The common wisdom in the United States is that businesses have sought to avoid using the courts to govern their relationships with one another. In the early 1960s, Macaulay found that businesses relied upon informal mechanisms, as the critical continuing relationships are not well served by the dispute-processing mechanism of formal adjudication.[324] Research provides contradictory evidence on whether the role of courts and formal adjudication in the relationships among business entities in the United States has been increasing.[325]

In England, the courts have long accommodated the needs of businesses. In 1895, the judges of the Queen's Bench Division of the High Court set up special procedures to handle cases arising out of commercial transactions.[326] A specialist judge took responsibility for the Commercial List, as it was then known, both in screening cases and in processing the cases on the list. In 1970, the Commercial List became, by statute, the Commercial Court; this court is still part of the Queen's Bench Division, but cases now come to the court by designation or request of one or both parties, unless the commercial judge rejects the case as inappropriate for the court.

The jurisdiction of the Commercial Court includes the carriage of goods, contracts related to ships and shipping, insurance and reinsurance, banking

324. Stewart Macaulay, "Non-Contractual Relations in Business: A Preliminary Study," *American Sociological Review* 28 (1963), pp. 59–76.

325. Terence Dunworth and Joel Rogers, "Corporations in Court: Big Business Litigation in the U.S. Federal Courts, 1972–1990," paper presented at Conference on Changing Patterns of Business Disputing, Institute for Legal Studies, University of Wisconsin Law School, Nov. 19–20, 1993; Ross E. Cheit, "Corporate Ambulance Chasers: The Charmed Life of Business Litigation," *Studies in Law, Politics, and Society* 11 (1991), pp. 119–140.

326. This discussion of the Commercial Court is taken from Spencer, supra note 14, pp. 44–46, and from the Lord Chancellor's Department, *Civil Justice Review Consultation Paper No. 3: The Commercial Court* (London, Lord Chancellor's Department, 1986), henceforth *Commercial Court*.

and commercial credit, commercial contracts, and the purchase and sale of commodities. Judges with specialized experience in commercial and business affairs staff the Commercial Court, and the court makes special efforts to resolve urgent matters speedily. The goal is to provide, where possible, quick resolution so that commercial affairs and relationships can return to normal.

Little information on the work of the Commercial Court has been compiled, but there is some evidence that the caseload doubled from 1979 to 1984,[327] as business-related litigation was rising more generally. One analysis of the cases handled in the Commercial Court showed that about half were shipping cases (for example, failure to deliver on time, loss of goods); the other half of the Court's work involves a variety of types of cases (banking, insurance, debt, contracts, and so on.[328] As is true in most courts, few cases get to trial—about 10 percent.

While most of the work of the Commercial Court deals with routine disputes that arise in the course of commercial relationships, the court can also find itself embroiled in cases with far-reaching implications. In the early 1990s, the court was at the center of an insurance crisis involving Lloyd's of London. Losses of as much as £2.1 billion (about $3 billion) led to charges and countercharges and strained the Lloyd's system of underwriting insurance risk. That system relies on what are called Names—wealthy individuals or families who pledge their assets as insurance against losses in return for premiums paid to them through Lloyd's. Historically, this has been a way of generating a tidy payment with little risk (and no outlay of money, which meant that Names could simultaneously invest the assets elsewhere and earn a double return). In the early 1990s, however, losses started to mount, and Names had to pay out significant sums of money, in some cases essentially wiping out their assets. Lloyd's filed cases in Commercial Court against Names who did not pay, and Names filed cases charging negligence against underwriters and directors.[329] The exact number of cases has not been reported, but the prospect is for the litigation to take years to resolve, in part because it will be some years before the full depth of the losses is clear. The long-term implications for Lloyd's are uncertain, although in one 1994 decision the Commercial Court found in favor of the Names, with a decision that was estimated to cost Lloyd's potentially £500 million or more.[330]

---

327. See *Commercial Court*, supra note 326, p. 4. See Peter Vincent-Jones, "Contract Litigation in England and Wales 1975–1991: A Transformation in Business Disputing?" *Civil Justice Quarterly* 12 (Oct. 1993), 337–358.

328. See *Commercial Court*, supra note 326, p. 11.

329. "The Lloyd's Names Litigation," *The Law Society's Gazette*, June 30, 1993, p. 2.

330. "Lloyd's Names Win £500m," *Guardian Weekly*, Oct. 16, 1993, p. 9.

Business Disputes between Groups of Individuals and Institutions
Many of the personal plight problems discussed earlier pit individuals against institutions, both public (governmental agencies) and private (insurance companies, landlords, financial institutions, and the like). In this section, I focus on disputes involving aggregates of individuals who have joined together on an ad hoc basis to pursue a grievance against a private institution. In the United States, groups pursue such actions either through formal mechanisms such as class-action suits and "multidistrict litigation" (MDLs) in the federal courts, or through informal alliances involving what Galanter has called "case congregations."[331] It is more difficult to bring such cases in England because the formal mechanisms of case aggregation are generally not available. Lawsuits are firmly embedded in an "individualist model" of action.[332] The result is that informal aggregation is the primary vehicle by which a group of similarly situated persons bring actions against private defendants. However, even informal group actions face major obstacles in the English system, as illustrated by the Opren litigation.[333]

Opren was a medication for treating arthritis developed and marketed by the American pharmaceutical giant Eli Lilly. After Opren had been on the market for about two years, Lilly removed the drug because of reports of significant negative side effects. Widespread litigation arose, leading to large judgments against Lilly in the United States, including at least one punitive damage award of $5 million. However, the decision of an American judge barred English Opren "victims" from suing Lilly in American courts. A group of solicitors' firms, acting in concert with an organization of victims' families (the Opren Action Group) developed plans to bring legal action in the English courts. A key problem facing the solicitors and their clients was that of costs: under the English losers-pay rule, litigants ineligible for legal aid faced a threat of losing everything they had if Lilly were to prevail and the plaintiffs had to pay Lilly's costs (which would probably come to hundreds of thousands, if not millions, of pounds).

The solicitors sought to structure the action so that a case involving a legal-aid plaintiff (who would not be liable for the costs) would be the "lead action"and resolve key common questions of law or fact, such as whether Opren had the side effects alleged by the plaintiffs. If these matters could be

331. Marc Galanter, "Case Congregations and Their Careers," *Law & Society Review* 14 (1990), pp. 371–395.

332. See Harlow and Rawlings, supra note 3, pp. 124–128.

333. In 1995 the Legal Aid Board granted legal aid to 200 people with lung cancer and other smoking-related illnesses. This grant covered preliminary investigation, and how far the matter will proceed is not clear. See Clare Dyer, "Tobacco Firms Face Mass Legal Action," *Guardian*, Feb. 1, 1995, p. 20.

answered in the positive, the issue for the individual plaintiffs would become whether they had suffered any of the side effects, and, if so, what damages Lilly should pay. The variety of alleged side effects required twenty separate lead actions. Because of the number of lead actions, the strategy of using a legal-aid plaintiff for the lead action failed, and the judge handling the litigation ruled that all plaintiffs relying upon the lead action should contribute to the costs incurred in litigating those actions. Those plaintiffs directly at risk for Lilly's costs and those with more marginal claims (whom the legal aid authorities would be reluctant to back) were inclined to withdraw from the litigation. Many of these plaintiffs had experienced the types of side effects that Lilly had agreed to pay damages for in the United States, but the English legal system had given Lilly a much stronger hand than it had in the U.S. courts.

The action of "a fairy godparent" (in the words of one judge) rescued the Opren victims: a wealthy property owner agreed to underwrite the costs of those plaintiffs without legal aid (up to £2 million). Complicated negotiations then ensued. An initial settlement involving 1,250 plaintiffs called for a payment of £2.25 million in compensation; some plaintiffs attacked the settlement as inadequate, and controversy erupted when it was found out that Lilly had agreed to pay £4 million in legal costs and secured an agreement from the solicitors representing plaintiffs involved in the settlement that they would not represent any future Opren plaintiffs. However, most of the plaintiffs accepted the £1,800 average payment, many owing to the withdrawal of legal aid because the legal aid authorities considered the settlement adequate and were unwilling to underwrite further litigation.

Similar examples of group litigation in England are relatively rare.[334] The combination of the lack of a class-action mechanism and the threat of costs against a losing litigant who is not represented by legal aid creates strong disincentives for group action against corporations and organizations that are likely to use the procedural rules zealously to their own advantage. The resources available to corporations, and the absence of an entrepreneurial legal profession, reinforce the individualist mode of action inherent in the English system of private litigation.

THE GROWING ROLE OF THE EUROPEAN COURTS

Throughout this essay I have largely ignored one important fact of legal life in England during the last twenty years: England's growing ties to continental Europe. There are two major European courts to which English courts must look in a number of situations: the Court of Justice of the European Com-

---

334. My discussion of the Opren example is taken largely from Harlow and Rawlings, supra note 3, pp. 116, 130–135, 186–191.

munity (CJEC; known more commonly as the European Court of Justice) which deals with matters arising under the treaties creating and governing the European Union (originally called the European Economic Community or EEC), and the European Court of Human Rights (ECHR) which considers matters arising under the European Convention on Human Rights. Several observers have noted that England (and the United Kingdom more generally) has surrendered major elements of its sovereignty, particularly to the European Union (EU).[335] This has had the effect of introducing some elements of a written constitution that limits Parliament's power to change *any* law that it believes the courts have interpreted improperly.[336]

The two European courts differ in their authority over English law and courts. England is treaty-bound to accept the decisions of the European Court of Justice; the authority of the European Court of Human Rights is more based on morals than on a formal treaty. The United Kingdom is a signatory to the European Convention on Human Rights but has never taken the steps that would bind it to defer to decisions of the European Court of Human Rights. Regardless of the basis of authority, both courts will become even more important in England in the years to come. Before assessing the impact of the courts on England, let me briefly describe each.

The European Court of Justice adjudicates issues arising between member states of the European Union and issues arising from the internal administration of the EU. It is the former that is of primary importance for English courts. Cases involving England can come to the European Court in essentially two ways. First, Article 177 of the Treaty of Rome provides that if a question of European Community law arises during an ordinary lawsuit in a national court of a member state, that national court can apply to the CJEC for a preliminary ruling. The second way cases get to the CJEC is through "direct actions": one or more member states (or the European Commission itself) brings an action against another member to the Court if the respondent member is alleged to be violating its obligations under the EU treaties.[337] In these actions, which resemble judicial review in England, it is not necessary for the initiating party to demonstrate any actual injury or harm. Alternatively, individuals can bring cases against member states alleging violations

335. See P. P. Craig, "Sovereignty of the United Kingdom Parliament after Factortame," *Yearbook of European Law* 11 (1991), pp. 221–271; Martin Shapiro, "The European Court of Justice," in Alberta M. Sbragia (ed.), *Euro-Politics: Institutions and Policymaking in the "New" European Community* (Washington, D.C.: Brookings Institution, 1992), p. 126.

336. Ferdinand Mount, *The British Constitution Now: Recovery or Decline* (London: Heinemann, 1992), p. 223. Hartley and Griffith, supra note 5, pp. 174–175.

337. Mary L. Volcansek, *Judicial Politics in Europe: An Impact Analysis* (New York: Peter Lang, 1986), p. 5.

of obligations under the treaties, but only if the individual can demonstrate individual harm.[338]

The Court itself consists of thirteen judges (one from each member state, plus an additional one drawn in rotation from France, Germany, Italy, the United Kingdom, and Spain),[339] plus several "advocates general," who effectively serve as investigators for the Court.[340] Judges are expected to have top-notch legal credentials (persons qualified for appointment to the highest courts in their home countries), and whose independence "is beyond doubt."[341] Selection of judges is by unanimous agreement among the member states, although after selection the judges do not represent their home countries.[342] Judges serve for six years and may be reappointed. The court, based in Luxembourg, operates in a series of "chambers," consisting of either six or three judges;[343] this allows the court to hear cases as panels rather than en banc.

Through 1993, the United Kingdom (there are no separate statistics for England) was party to 55 direct actions (20 as the initiator and 35 as the respondent), out of 3,146 actions (for comparison, Germany was involved in 115, and France, 164). Courts in the United Kingdom obtained 162 preliminary rulings, out of 2,690 (for comparison, courts in Germany obtained 857, and France, 665).[344] Most cases involve tariffs, agricultural subsidies, quotas, and the like.[345] However, others involve issues such as employment discrimination (equal pay for equal work), the rights of migrant workers, eligibility of foreign workers for social security, and various issues of social policy.[346]

The European Court of Human Rights (ECHR) is part of the institutional structure associated with the European Convention on Human Rights, which

338. Shapiro, supra note 335, pp. 124–125.

339. L. Neville Brown and Tom Kennedy, *The Court of Justice of the European Communities*, 4th ed. (London: Sweet & Maxwell, 1989), p. 18.

340. The model here is similar to that of Continental courts rather than to English courts; see the chapters on France and Germany that follow.

341. Brown and Kennedy, supra note 339, p. 46.

342. See Shapiro, supra note 335, p. 124.

343. Brown and Kennedy, supra note 339, p. 37.

344. Ibid., pp. 414–419; see also Christopher Harding, "Who Goes to Court in Europe? An Analysis of Litigation against the European Community," *European Law Review* 17 (1992), pp. 107–125.

345. For general reviews of the work and impact of the European Court of Justice, see Shapiro, supra note 335; Volcansek, supra note 337; Hjalte Rasmussen, *On Law and Policy in the European Court of Justice* (Dordrecht: Martinus Nijhoff Publishers, 1986); Gordon Slynn, *Introducing a European Legal Order* (London: Stevens & Sons/Sweet & Maxwell, 1992).

346. Brown and Kennedy, supra note 339, pp. 416–421.

has been in force since 1953.[347] The convention provides what amounts to a bill of rights, although it is not binding upon a signatory unless the signatory has effectively incorporated the convention's provisions into domestic law. While many countries have so incorporated the provisions of the convention, the United Kingdom has not, and English courts, including the House of Lords, have ruled that government ministers need not take the Convention into consideration in their actions.[348] Still, observers have described the English courts as "not relying on [the convention] to direct their judgments, but taking full account of them and trying as far as possible to establish a kind of consonance between the provisions of the Convention and the law of England."[349]

The absence of a domestic "bill of rights" has made the government of the United Kingdom a popular target for actions under the terms of the convention. One observer asserted that "the United Kingdom has been found in violation of the European Convention on Human Rights more often than any other signatory and that it has consistently been the subject of more applications for alleged breaches than any other State."[350] Through September 1985, the United Kingdom had been a party to fourteen cases that resulted in judgments of the ECHR and lost twelve of those cases.[351] The United Kingdom has been the target of challenges in the ECHR over property rights (rights of tenants and landlords), the rights of trade unionists, public morality (laws concerning homosexuality), freedom of speech and freedom of the press, rights of family members (rights of parents vis-à-vis access to children in the care of the government), privacy, detention, treatment while in custody, in addition to several cases arising from the conflict in Northern Ireland and the British government's attempts to respond to and control that conflict.[352]

The European Court of Human Rights is the last step in handling alleged violations of the European Convention on Human Rights. A person or group may bring a complaint about a violation of the Convention to the European Commission on Human Rights. The commission is an administrative body that investigates complaints, seeks to mediate among parties where possible,

347. Andrew Drzemczewski, "The Growing Impact of the European Human Rights Convention upon National Case Law," *The Law Society's Gazette,* Feb. 25, 1987, p. 561.

348. Ibid., p. 562. "Ministers Unfettered by Euro Convention Lords Rule," *The Law Society's Gazette,* Feb. 13, 1991, p. 4.

349. Mount, supra note 336, p. 230.

350. See Françoise Hampson, "The United Kingdom Before the European Court of Human Rights," *Yearbook of European Law* 9 (1989), p. 121; note that Hampson is not making this assertion but pointing out that others have made it.

351. Spencer, supra note 14, p. 430.

352. Ibid., pp. 139–146, 151–156.

and issues reports concerning its judgment about the validity of the complaint. If the parties fail to reach a resolution, the complaint may go to the European Court of Human Rights in Strasbourg. The court consists of one judge from each member state, chosen in a manner similar to that for judges of the European Court of Justice. A panel of judges normally hears cases, although the court can choose to sit en banc.[353] The court conducts its proceedings orally, using the inquisitorial approach of Continental courts (see chapters 4 and 5 on France and Germany, respectively) rather than the more adversarial style of English and American courts.[354]

The Impact of the European Courts on England and English Courts

We can measure the growing importance of European law in England in a variety of ways. One simple measure is the amount of discussion of European law in the English legal press. The *Legal Journals Index* began publishing in 1986, and entries for "EEC Law" between that year and 1992 rose from 355 to about 1,400. Taking together the entries for "European Court of Justice," "European Convention on Human Rights," "European Commission on Human Rights," and other variations, the count goes from 17 in 1986 to 94 in 1992 (after peaking at 110 in 1991).

A second approach is to look at the frequency with which British courts cite CJEC and ECHR cases. Through the end of 1993 Lexis located 478 cases citing CJEC and 83 cases citing ECHR.[355] The frequency of these citations increased from fewer than ten per year during the 1970s, to 10–20 per year during the early 1980s, to 20–40 during the mid-1980s, and to 40–60 during the early 1990s (rising to 82 in 1993).

Of course, these increases may simply represent improved case reporting or higher caseloads generally (the more cases, the more citations). To check for this, I obtained a similar time series of citations to House of Lords cases.[356] Figure 3.6 shows the trends for both the House of Lords and the combined trend for the European courts. Part of the increase in citations to the European courts probably reflects general trends in citations, but the growth pattern for citations to the European courts is much clearer than the pattern for the House of Lords.

A 1992 survey carried out in Britain and the other countries of the European Community provides a glimpse of how Britons perceive the European

353. Ibid., p. 430.

354. See Hampson, supra note 350, pp. 128–129.

355. The Lexis Library used was "ENGGEN"; the search was for citations to "ECR" (*European Court Reporter*) or to "EHRR" (*European Human Rights Reporter*).

356. I specifically limited this to House of Lords cases dealing with English law; the citation searched for was HL(E).

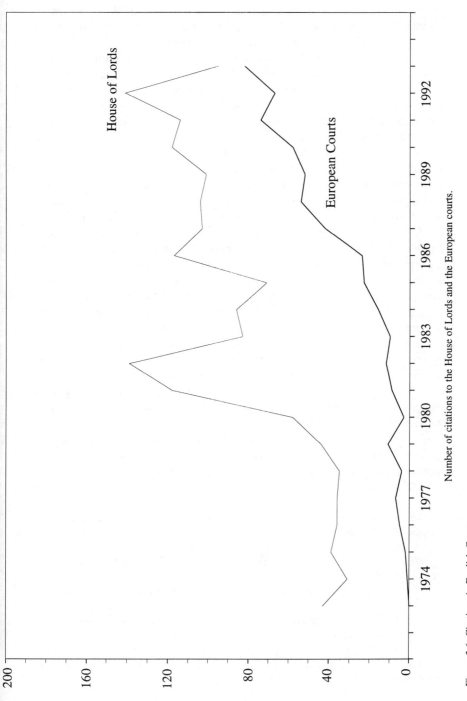

Figure 3.6. Citations in English Courts

Court of Justice.[357] Fifty-two percent of Britons reported having heard "something recently" about the European Court of Justice, compared to 63 percent who had heard something recently about the House of Lords.[358] Compared to respondents in other countries, Britons' responses fell near the median on awareness of and attentiveness to the European Court of Justice. Similarly, when asked questions about their support for the European Court of Justice, Britons were in the middle, compared to respondents in other countries, in their level of general support and their willingness to accept a decision that they did not like.

In summary, in thinking about the English courts one must consider developments in the broader European context. How significant these changes will be ultimately for the intersection of law, courts, and politics in England will depend on legal and political developments. If the English courts assert increasing authority, the treaty obligations entered into by the British government may provide legal toeholds for the courts. For example, in a widely publicized 1994 case brought by the Equal Opportunities Commission (a government agency) against the government of John Major, the House of Lords struck down a 1978 law that limited certain rights of part-time workers. The Law Lords ruled that the law breached European law because it discriminated against part-time workers (a disproportionate number of whom are women).[359] News reports speculated that this ruling would lead to a "significant increase in the number of politically controversial cases brought against the government by pressure groups and others," with one report declaring "Britain may now have, for the first time in history, a constitutional court."[360] A few weeks later, an industrial tribunal awarded £300,000 to a woman whom the army had dismissed in 1981 after she became pregnant; the European Court decided a similar case involving a private employer in England three months later.[361] These cases became possible after a European directive stating that employers, including the military, must treat men and women equally at work, and the European Court of Justice removed an £11,000 ceiling on claims.

357. See James L. Gibson and Gregory A. Caldeira, "The European Court of Justice: a Question of Legitimacy," *Zeitschrift für Rechtssoziologie* 14 (1993), pp. 204–222.

358. The intention of this question was to ask about awareness of the nation's highest court; it is not clear that the survey clearly distinguished between the House of Lords as a judicial body and the House of Lords as a legislative body.

359. "Law Lords Give Full Rights to Part-Time Workers," *Guardian Weekly*, Mar. 13, 1994, p. 8.

360. "UK Part-Time Work Rules in Breach of EU Law," *Financial Times*, Mar. 4, 1994, p. 6; "Profound Judgment," *The (London) Times*, Mar. 5, 1994.

361. "Sacked Woman Officer Wins Fight," *Guardian Weekly*, Apr. 17, 1994, p. 9; this case was actually decided by a Scottish tribunal. "Pregnant Women Gain Protection," *Guardian Weekly*, July 24, 1994, p. 8.

Some observers have called on the Parliament to incorporate the European Convention on Human Rights into British law.[362] If the Parliament did this, the English courts' reliance upon decisions of the European Court of Human Rights would surely increase; more important, the role of the courts in England more generally would probably increase. The frequency that the ECHR has found the British government to be in breach of the convention may create pressures on the government to consider seriously incorporating the convention, and members of Parliament have introduced bills to accomplish this.[363]

Courts, Politics, and . . .

In this chapter, I have examined a variety of ways in which the judicial system in England functions within the broader legal and political landscape of that country. The structure of various aspects of English public life diverts issues out of the courts, either by avoiding the need for court-based remedies (by providing remedies through the social welfare system) or by providing forums outside the court system (through administrative tribunals) to resolve routine and recurring individualized issues. Courts continue to provide a modicum of oversight in these areas, and litigants have increasingly asked the courts to use the mechanism of judicial review to direct governmental offices and officials to execute their duties in a manner that is consistent with legal obligations. My discussion does not by any means settle the question of whether there is a difference in the litigiousness of Americans and the English; to the degree that rates of litigation differ, it may reflect that life is structured in England in ways that decrease the need for the types of remedies that litigation provides.

On the criminal side, while there are variances in process and organization, there is probably more similarity than difference. In both countries crime and criminal justice have been significant political concerns, although I have argued that the crime issue has been less central in England, not necessarily because crime is less of a social problem but because of continuing focus on economic issues within the English political system. The centralized nature of the English judiciary and criminal justice system focuses the responsibility more clearly on political leaders in London, so that Parliament has been the focus of policymaking and legal change regarding criminal justice.

In addition to staffing and operation of judicial institutions, U.S. and English institutions differ in the roles they play in the larger political system in two ways. First, while the English courts exercise a function called judicial review, they have no functional equivalent to the American version of judicial

362. See Mount, supra note 336, pp. 230–232.
363. See Spencer, supra note 14, p. 431.

review, which is actually constitutional review. Second, the courts in England have been unwilling to exercise the kind of direct control over other governmental institutions that courts in the U.S. have done repeatedly over the past several decades.

The simple explanation for the limited form of judicial review in England is the absence of a written constitution. Parliament is supreme, limited only by tradition and popular will. While observers often hold out the U. S. Supreme Court's power to declare acts of Congress unconstitutional as what makes the Court unique in its role and influence, the English system is actually the unusual structure.[364] Most developed democracies have a court that serves as a constitutional check on the legislative and executive branches.[365] In most systems outside the United States, the constitutional tribunal stands apart from the courts that handle "routine" matters. The selection process for members of these tribunals is often explicitly political (unlike the judges of the "ordinary" courts); many members of these constitutional tribunals had extensive parliamentary experience. The function of these courts is to "protect civil and political liberties" which reflects the realization that, even with popular sovereignty, in a free democratic system "the legislative and executive are . . . likely to abuse their powers."[366]

England has provided a mechanism whereby the courts can check the abuse of power by the executive, the English version of judicial review, and the courts have made it clear that the reach of this power extends, through the power to hold Cabinet members in contempt, to the prime minister's cabinet. However, the English courts have no control over the actions of

364. It is also worth noting that the few of the cases decided by the U.S. Supreme Court actually speak to the constitutionality of acts of Congress. Outside of criminal procedure, most of the Supreme Court's docket involves cases of statutory interpretation and review of the actions of federal agencies; see Herman Schwartz, "The New East European Constitutional Courts," *Michigan Journal of International Law* 13 (1992), p. 748.

365. Such courts exist in Germany, Austria, Canada, Australia, Italy, Belgium, Portugal, Spain, and many emerging democracies of Eastern Europe. Louis Favoreau, "American and European Models of Constitutional Justice," in David S. Clark (ed.), *Comparative and Private International Law: Essays in Honor of John Henry Merryman on his Seventieth Birthday* (Berlin: Duncker & Humblot, 1990), p. 106; André Bzdera, "Comparative Analysis of Federal High Courts: A Political Theory of Judicial Review," *Canadian Journal of Political Science* 26 (1993), p. 6; Alec Stone, "The Birth and Development of Abstract Review: Constitutional Courts and Policymaking in Western Europe," *Policy Studies Journal* 19 (Fall 1990), pp. 81–95; Christine Landfried (ed.), *Constitutional Review and Legislation* (Baden-Baden: Nomos Verlagsgesellschaft, 1988); and Schwartz, supra note 364, passim. I omit France from this list although some observers (including Stone) include it. For more about constitutional review in France, see chapter 4 in this volume.

366. Schwartz, supra note 364, p. 747 (paraphrasing *The Federalist Papers,* numbers 38 and 50.

Parliament. This does not mean that the courts are totally subordinate to Parliament. Rather, it would probably be more appropriate to say that the English system divides the realms of Parliament and the courts into separate spheres. The principle of *sub judice* prohibits members of Parliament from discussing and acting upon matters pending before the courts;[367] the Speaker of the House of Commons vigorously enforces this rule.

Even without the power of constitutional review, court decisions in England have led to significant social and political change, and court decisions regularly have political consequences.[368] Historically, the most dramatic example of this is probably the court decision in *Somerset v. Stewart*, which was interpreted as ending slavery in England. An English court wrote and handed down this opinion in 1772, four years prior to the American Declaration of Independence. While the abolition of slavery in Britain was complete when the Scottish courts made a similar ruling six years later, it took another sixty years for the Parliament to pass an Act for the Abolition of Slavery, which ended slavery in the British colonies.[369]

There are a variety of possible reasons for the courts' unwillingness to become involved in the detail of administration and operation of public institutions. Does this reflect limitations on the courts in England? Would Parliament respond negatively to such actions by the courts? Or might it have something to do with the staffing of the courts? The latter explanation is intriguing. The Lord Chancellor selects most judges of the English courts from the ranks of experienced barristers, who work within a structure that limits their opportunities for gaining experience in political affairs or public administration. A barrister who accepts a government post (other than as a member of Parliament) must give up his or her right to appear as an advocate before the upper courts, effectively disqualifying that barrister from consideration for appointment to the judiciary. It is fair to say that the Lord Chancellor draws the judges of the courts of England from among the best active barristers (although at least some of the *very* best might decline offers appointment because they would have to give up too much income if they went onto the bench).[370]

Contrast this to the staffing of courts, particularly federal courts, in the United States. Those who select federal judges do not look to the elite of the legal profession, but rather to the best of the lawyers who combine political and legal careers.[371] Many judges on the U.S. federal bench have had exten-

---

367. See Harlow and Rawlings, supra note 3, pp. 178–182.

368. See John Griffith, *Judicial Politics since 1920: A Chronicle* (Oxford: Blackwell, 1993).

369. Harlow and Rawlings, supra note 3, pp. 12–16.

370. On the backgrounds of appellate judges, see Tate, supra note 34; and Morrison, supra note 281, pp. 70–91.

371. Donald Dale Jackson, *Judges* (New York: Atheneum, 1974), p. 225.

sive experience in both legislative and administrative roles. In England, a judge who is a former barrister with no direct experience in political administration might be very reluctant to make a decision that resulted in having to deal with the day-to-day operation of a prison or a school district or a mental hospital. On the other hand, this might look much less forbidding to an American judge who had previously been a governor or a party chairperson or a staff counsel to a member of Congress.

Some argue that English judges are becoming less reluctant to get involved in governmental oversight,[372] and there have been specific changes in recent years that reduce judges' isolation from politics. However, as long as few judges have had significant experience in the rough-and-tumble world of governmental operations, it is unlikely that the courts will involve themselves beyond the current practice of judicial review, although the willingness of judges to try to secure reform of government practices through this mechanism may continue to expand. The willingness of the Lord Chief Justice and other judges to oppose publicly and vociferously such changes in criminal and court process as rights of audience for solicitors, unit fines, and restrictions on the right to a jury trial makes clear that today's English judges speak out on matters where they believe they have expertise. Furthermore, English judges are now willing to hand down decisions that make law, either by changing exist law or dealing with new issues. In 1991, the House of Lords overturned the principle that a husband could not be criminally sanctioned for raping his wife, and in 1993 established guidelines on the nature of physician's responsibility vis-à-vis keeping an unconscious person alive when there was no chance of that person regaining consciousness.[373]

Only time will tell whether this apparent increase in lawmaking represents a major change in the role of the courts in England. If it does represent a change, it will be interesting to see whether positions on the bench become more attractive to legal professionals with substantial political experience. The limited role of judges in England through much of the twentieth century may explain in part the absence of those with political experience from the bench: politically active barristers may not have seen a judgeship as a position from which they could exercise influence on policy and government. This might well be changing.

372. See Joe Rogaly, "Why Judges are Jumping," *Financial Times*, Nov. 2, 1993; Rose, supra note 317.

373. See Anthony Lester, "English Judges as Law Makers," *Public Law* (Summer 1993), pp. 269–290. These two cases are *R. v. R.*, 4 All ER 481 (1991), and *Airedale NHS Trust v. Bland*, 1 All ER 821 (1993).

4

Courts in the Political Process in France

D O R I S M A R I E P R O V I N E

To the French, a striking characteristic of the American system of government is our deference to judges. Constitutional government, American-style, envisions the judiciary as a coequal branch of government with power to determine whether the legislature and executive have strayed beyond their proper authority. The relationship between branches includes, not just a judicial veto power, but a gap-filling role in which judicial opinions lend substance and clarity to open-textured legislation. In this tendency to blur the distinction between judicial policymaking and judicial dispute resolution we resemble Britain and other nations that are members of the Anglo-American legal family. The Anglo-American legal tradition, which has been the focus of chapters 2 and 3, teaches that a little judicial lawmaking is an inevitable part of the process of applying law to particular cases, especially when individual rights are at stake.

France operates on a different model, one that challenges Americans to rethink familiar assumptions about the relationship between rights, law, and courts. In France, as in other countries that follow a civil law tradition, courts are not a coequal branch of government. The principle of constitutional review by courts never took root as it did in America's early decades of nationhood. The role of courts in protecting individual rights is debatable in France, and their power to review legislation or executive orders for constitutional defects is highly suspect. The courts were on the losing side of the French Revolution, and they suffered a tremendous loss of power and prestige in its aftermath. Two centuries later, their commitment to independence from the other branches is still in doubt. Courts in France are not known for standing up to other government officials, and no one expects them to play an active role in governance. A look at French government textbooks confirms this impression. André Tunc's introduction to a 1959 text on American courts for French readers remains accurate: "No authority, writing on the

French government, would think of devoting a chapter to the Court of Cassation (France's highest court) and to the court system."[1]

France has a curious double standard about courts. While it refuses to authorize its own judges to intrude into legislative or executive domains, it supports supranational courts that have that power, and it accepts a form of constitutional review outside its regular court system. France's complicated stance on the question of constitutional review can be explained in part by historical circumstance. Before 1950 the concept that courts might thwart legislative action on constitutional grounds was poorly understood in France and in Europe generally. European liberal thought saw an unfettered democratic process as the best guarantee to liberty, a position that prevailed for more than a century. The experience of World War II, however, encouraged European nations to rethink this stance. Most of them invested their top appellate courts with the power to declare law incompatible with constitutional obligations. As Edward McWhinney observes: "Court-based testing and ultimately control, on 'higher law' constitutional grounds, of executive and legislative action is one of the more striking trends in constitutionalism and constitution-making of the post–World War II era."[2]

France participated in this movement, to a point. It joined with other countries in western Europe in creating the Council of Europe and in drafting the European Convention for the Protection of Human Rights and Fundamental Freedoms, to be enforced by a new European Commission and Court on Human Rights. The idea was to use litigation by individuals and governments to increase European vigilance on behalf of individual rights. In a clear departure from European tradition, a set of fundamental legal principles became the basis for guaranteeing liberty, in opposition to the democratic process, if necessary.[3] France also participated in the creation of the World Court and the Court of Justice of the European Communities. Like the Commission and Court on Human Rights, they have become more active in monitoring the activities of member states, and in the process have helped to change French consciousness about the role of courts in society.

The theme of Europeanization and its impact on beliefs about courts runs through the sections that follow. The influence of the new supranational courts, which has been felt most in the areas of criminal justice and economic regulation, is an important part of this story. But the impact of European-

1. Reprinted in Dallis Radamaker, *The Political Role of Courts in Modern Democracies* (London: Macmillan, 1988), p. 129.

2. Edward McWhinney, *Supreme Courts and Judicial Law-Making: Constitutional Tribunals and Constitutional Review* (Dordrecht, Netherlands: Nijhoff, 1986), p. 1.

3. Cynthia Vroom, "La liberté individuelle au stade de l'enquête de police en France et aux Etats-Unis," *Revue de science criminelle et de droit pénal comparé* (1988), p. 489.

ization on French attitudes toward judicial power also encourages comparison with the other countries in the region, including comparisons about individual freedoms. This has increased pressure on French judges to be more attentive to the liberties of citizens and to demonstrate their independence from other organs of the state. Other public institutions are also under pressure to respect rights and to justify their initiatives, sometimes in constitutional terms.

France now accepts the idea that individual rights enjoy constitutional protection, but not the idea that ordinary courts should perform this function. France's solution to the problem of protecting constitutional values has been to develop alternatives to American-style judicial review. The most significant of these institutions is its Constitutional Council, a body that reviews legislation before promulgation for adherence to legal and constitutional requirements. The council is part of the legislative branch but acts much like a court in reviewing proposed legislation for consistency with the constitution.

France's continued adherence to the old idea of legislative supremacy sets it apart from most other European nations. What can we learn from France's effort to safeguard constitutional values by other means? More fundamentally, can French exceptionalism help explain what drives the worldwide movement toward constitutionalism and judicial review? France's subordination of courts to the other branches of government also has a nonconstitutional dimension. In the aftermath of the French Revolution, legislators sought to avoid all forms of judicial policymaking. The idea that judges might cite their own precedents to justify a decision was firmly rejected. This places courts in an awkward position in applying legislation to unanticipated circumstances. How have French judges dealt with this problem?

This chapter begins with a close look at the legal institutions French people rely upon to protect their rights. The differences between France and America are significant. The issue of abortion, controversial in both societies, offers an illustration. In France the debate centers on moral issues and political strategy, but not on legal rights or predictions of what courts will do. A decision as famous as *Roe v. Wade,* which established the parameters of the abortion debate in the United States, would be unthinkable in a French context. Courts in France do issue rulings in some abortion-related cases, but their influence is limited both by the scope of their authority and by the expectation that other institutions, including Parliament, will consider the liberty issues at stake.

Rights consciousness, which in the Anglo-American context implies a readiness to resort to courts, is not highly developed in France. The institutional limitations on judicial policymaking have undoubtedly discouraged activists from enlisting courts in their efforts. Legal tradition also discourages political discourse based on rights. France builds on a civil-law tradition common to the nations of Europe. That tradition makes a sharp distinction between law and politics and assigns judges no role in the development of law.[4] The application of law to unanticipated situations is the province of legal scholars, who claim to understand law's internal logic and overall coherence. The great competitor to the civil-law tradition, as noted in chapter 1, is common-law jurisprudence. In common-law countries like England and the United States, law is conceived in more pragmatic terms, and it is understood that judges have a hand in lawmaking when they adjudicate cases. This is true even in England, where there is no judicial review. The legal pragmatism characteristic of common-law countries leaves room for a popular sense of rights-consciousness to develop. In a civil-law jurisdiction like France, on the other hand, rights consciousness and litigiousness run against the historical grain.

The relatively restrained political role assigned to courts has an impact on the way crime is pursued and punished in France. France gives the police broad powers to pursue criminal wrongdoing, and the courts have not in general challenged the exercise of this authority. Critics charge that the judiciary is progovernment in prosecuting crime. In ordinary cases this criticism suggests an insensitivity to the rights of the individuals the government investigates or charges with crimes. In cases where the government's own activities are subject to investigation, the progovernment criticism implies judicial willingness to whitewash official wrongdoing. This section investigates both aspects of the claim that French criminal justice should be more independent of the executive branch through a discussion of the controversy over the government's handling of an AIDS-infected blood supply.

The next section of this chapter considers the role of courts in resolving "private disputes," that is, disputes between individuals and with businesses. France has developed an impressive network of accessible, affordable administrative courts to deal with citizen complaints against enterprise. Its legal profession provides representation at a reasonable price. Alternative dispute resolution is available for disputes between neighbors and associates. This approach to civil justice emphasizes the resolution of specific disputes rather than the development of legal doctrine that can be extended to new problems. French caution in expanding remedies is evident in Parliament's reluctance

4. In this respect, as John Bell and other observers have pointed out, American and French legal writing is sharply at odds: "French writers are frequently engaged in formulating a rather exaggerated contrast between law and politics, starting from a rather rigid conception of the separation of powers. On the other hand, the American commentators . . . come from a tradition where law and politics are very closely tied together in the role of the Supreme Court" (John Bell, *French Constitutional Law* [Oxford: Clarendon Press, 1992], p. 230).

to revise its civil code, now two centuries old. Courts have been ingenious in adapting the code to current circumstances in spite of the revolutionary-era mandate that judges make no law. By American standards, however, liability law is underdeveloped in France. There is, not surprisingly, little fear of a litigation explosion.

The final section of this chapter considers the role of courts in regulating the private enterprises and organizations that help to sustain France's economy. Nations vary in the extent to which they admit courts into this domain. France has traditionally preferred a nonjudicial approach to regulation. In France, technocrats and bureaucrats have close relationships with business, and they are shielded from judicial review and public scrutiny. How well does this approach work in a period in which workers expect protection from market forces, discrimination, and environmental harm? How, for example, does France deal with citizen pressure to ensure safe operation of nuclear reactors? What happens when enterprises have grievances against government?

Figure 4.1 provides a summary view of the French court system. The sections that follow will discuss most of these tribunals and the relationships between them. However, this system is not strictly hierarchical, and, as figure 4.1 indicates, no single court sits atop the whole judicial apparatus. The disaggregated pattern would be even more striking if the diagram had included the Constitutional Council, which is not, strictly speaking, part of the court system, despite its constitutional-review function. Even in this rough diagram, one can discern French distrust of a strong, unified, administratively centralized judiciary. The section that follows explores the consequences of this perspective for the protection of the constitutional rights of individuals against state encroachment.

Constitutional Review in France

The differences between French and American legal traditions were apparent to Alexis de Tocqueville, who voyaged to America in 1831, shortly after the fall of Charles X ended his aspirations for a judicial career. The shift in regimes had the unanticipated consequence of encouraging de Tocqueville to study the American political system, and to probe its differences from the European and English examples of representative government with which most educated French people were familiar.

Not surprisingly, de Tocqueville was much impressed with the independence of American judges and their ability to play a significant political role without anyone questioning their authority. The difference between the two countries was not evident in the day-to-day work of courts, the makeup of the judicial branch, or in the physical appearance of courtrooms. In these and

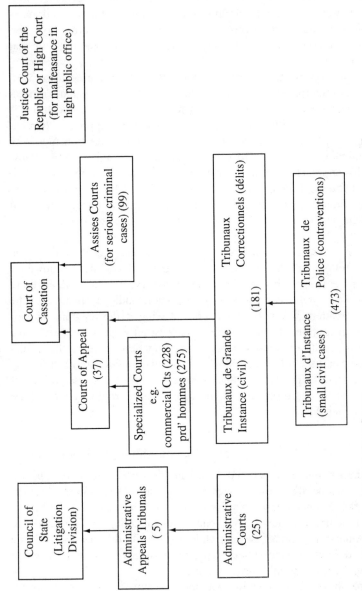

Figure 4.1. Structure of French Court System

many other respects, French and American judicial systems were similar. In the France of de Tocqueville's day, for example, judges also tended to be politically well-connected. In France, however, judicial decisions carried no weight beyond the particular case, and judges enjoyed no special prestige. Nor did French judges have life tenure, a right guaranteed by the United States Constitution to all federal judges.

America's greater tolerance for judicial policymaking, de Tocqueville believed, could be explained by each nation's attitudes toward its constitution. Americans considered theirs to be amendable; in France, the constitution was thought, incorrectly as it turned out, to be immutable: "In France the constitution is also the first of laws, and the judges have the same right to take it as the ground of their decisions; but were they to exercise this right, they must perforce encroach on rights more sacred than their own: namely, on those of society, in whose name they are acting. In this case reasons of state clearly prevail over ordinary motives. In America, where the nation can always reduce its magistrates to obedience by changing its Constitution, no danger of this kind is to be feared."[5]

Other observers attribute the relative weakness of French courts to the rigidity and overcentralization of the French state.[6] In their determination to create a coherent and rational government in the aftermath of the French Revolution, according to this perspective, French political leaders incorporated courts into the executive branch and subjected them to the authority of the Minister of Justice, a presidential appointee. France did draw clear boundaries between the judiciary and other governmental functions, but only to prevent courts from intruding into the executive or legislative sphere.

Preoccupation with the rationality and coherence of legal rules was well entrenched, even before the revolution. The monarchy had devoted considerable energy to creating a single legal system that might help to unite the country. The effort began in the sixteenth century when the government asked Charles du Moulin, a legal scholar, to make sense of France's welter of local customs in terms compatible with principles derived from the Roman law.[7] Neither he nor those who followed him in this work succeeded in persuading local communities to give up their own legal standards. Thus more than sixty different inheritance and property laws existed in 1790 when the Constituent Assembly first voted to take up the task of codifying French law. Later, at

5. Alexis de Tocqueville, *Democracy in America*, vol. 1 (New York: Knopf, 1945), pp. 105–106.

6. Radamaker, supra note 1, p. 149.

7. Thomas H. Reynolds and Autro Flores, *Foreign Law: Current Sources of Codes and Basic Legislation on Jurisdictions of the World* (Littleton, Colo.: Rothman, 1991), vol. 2, pp. 3–4.

Napoleon's insistence, the assembly turned the project over to scholars, and the result was a set of influential codes that finally imposed a single, uniform set of legal principles on the French people.

The French republicans also accepted the monarchy's claim that government needs no special authorization from the people in order to govern. The debate was between those, following Voltaire, who wanted a strong executive, and the Rousseaueans, who believed that the legislative assembly represented the will of the people. Neither side was willing to assign significant power to the judiciary or sacred status to the constitution. The idea that judges might use the constitution to monitor and correct the government's performance thus could gain no purchase. As Xavier Blanc-Jouvan and Jean Boulouis observe: "It is hardly possible to talk of a true *judicial* 'power' since such a constitutional recognition would not have been in keeping with the tradition of the French Revolution."[8]

The 1958 constitution, France's ninth since the revolution, represents a modest departure from this tradition. The new constitution, for the first time, specifies limits to Parliament's lawmaking authority and insulates the judiciary from arbitrary dismissal. The 1958 constitution also provides a clear constitutional basis for the protection of fundamental individual rights. These changes were part of a broader reorganization of government in which Parliament lost power to the President and to executive agencies. Charles De Gaulle demanded these changes as a condition for his return to power after the war in Algeria brought down the Fourth Republic. These changes in the relationship between Parliament and the President, however, were not intended to revisit the issue of constitutional review by courts. France, in theory at least, remains committed to the idea that courts are basically an administrative organ of the state.

France's failure to give courts the power to review legislation for conformity with the constitution has long been regarded by most scholars and some politicians as unfortunate. The nation's leaders, these critics suggest, should pay more attention to the individual's relative powerlessness in the face of government authority and allow constitutional challenges in course of ordinary litigation. Periodically, presidents of France have attempted to move the nation in this direction. In 1990, for example, President François Mitterrand introduced legislation to provide judicial review in French appellate courts. In a televised address to the nation, he cast the issue in terms of the freedoms French people should enjoy to challenge their government: "It would be great progress in democracy, returning to basics, to permit each Frenchman not to turn to intermediaries, but to say to himself: 'My funda-

8. Xavier Blanc-Jouvan and Jean Boulouis, "France," in *International Encyclopedia of Comparative Law* (London: Oxford, 1991), p. F–48.

mental rights—to liberty, to equality, to everything which has been recognized in the great principles inscribed in the Constitution—has been misunderstood, transgressed, and so I demand justice myself."[9] The provision, which would have allowed litigants to raise constitutional objections in the course of lawsuits brought for other reasons, passed the National Assembly. It was defeated in the Senate, which considers itself a strong advocate of civil liberties, by conservatives who resorted to the traditional rallying cry for opponents of judicial review: "Gouvernement des juges."[10]

The issue of judicial review would be more pressing if France had no other means of discouraging government overreaching. The executive and legislative branches, however, each exercise significant internal checks on their own authority. Supranational courts provide additional safeguards. The organization of the legal profession and law practice also offers some insulation against unwarranted governmental intrusions, though to American eyes the profession seems ill-organized to confront government on behalf of the individual. The remainder of this section considers each of these checking institutions in turn.

ADMINISTRATIVE REVIEW AND THE COUNCIL OF STATE

France has a large, powerful administrative apparatus, a legacy of the monarchy that survives because it suits France's desire to be a strong, welfare-oriented state. The 1958 constitution clarified and solidified the dominant position of the administration in government by limiting Parliament's power to oversee the executive branch and by giving the administration power to pass laws related to its own domain (*pouvoir reglementaire*). Ninety percent of French legislation becomes law by this route, including even major initiatives, such as the revision of the code of civil procedure. Parliament lacks sufficient staff and resources to discipline the administration effectively. Public inquiries about administrative wrongdoing usually go nowhere, as exemplified by the fact that Parliament has disciplined only thirty government officials since World War II.

Government bureaucrats also operate without fear of interference from the judiciary. French law has been clear on this point for two centuries. In the words of one revolutionary-era law that is still in effect: "The judicial functions are and will remain forever separate from the administrative functions.

---

9. Quoted in Louis M. Aucorn, "Judicial Review in France: Access of the Individual Under French and European Law in the Aftermath of France's Rejection of Bicentennial Reform," *Boston College International and Comparative Law Review* 15 (1992), p. 455.

10. The term appears to have originated with Edouard Lambert's 1921 book, *Le gouvernement des juges et la lutte contre la legislation sociale aux Etats-Unis*. The United States experience with judicial review, particularly in times of stress, helps sustain French opponents of judicial review.

The judges will not be allowed, under penalty of forfeiture, to disturb in any manner whatsoever, the activities of the administrative corps, nor to summon before them the administrators, concerning their functions."[11]

To help implement the theory of total separation between administrative and judicial functions, Parliament established a Tribunal of Conflicts, a court that took its present form in 1872. The sole purpose of the court is to resolve issues of jurisdiction between the administrative sector and the ordinary courts. The membership of the tribunal reflects its purpose of differentiating between judicial and administrative business. Three of its nine members are elected by members of the Council of State (the apex of the administrative sector), three from the Court of Cassation (the highest court), with two additional members elected by these six individuals. The Minister of Justice presides.[12]

France's determination to protect government administration from judicial oversight distinguishes it from the American and English legal systems. The Anglo-American tradition of checks and balances requires that independent judges have an opportunity to review administrative action for conformity with authorizing legislation and the constitution. Judges who operate within this tradition may defer to administrative expertise, but they are in a position to determine when this is and is not desirable. In the 1930s, for example, the United States Supreme Court made clear its hostility to business regulation by declaring many key New Deal statutes unconstitutional. American courts have also taken strong positions in such areas as broadcast regulation, antitrust, and environmental standard setting, scrutinizing administrative action for conformity with authorizing law and constitutional strictures. British courts have also taken a strong position on their authority to keep administrative action in line with legal requirements (see chapter 2). The French system avoids the problem of conflicting perspectives by preventing ordinary judges from reviewing administrative action, relying instead on a system of review based in the administrative sector.

Do these two approaches to administrative review produce startlingly different results? An empirical answer to this question is beyond the scope of this chapter, but at least one commentator claims that the two systems of review have tended to converge over time. Rivero argues that British judges, purporting to build on ancient common-law principles, now reach results consistent with French administrative law, which has been constructed by

11. Quoted in Bernard Rudden, *A Sourcebook on French Law* (Oxford: Clarendon, 1991) p. 142. See also Henry Abraham, *The Judicial Process*, 6th ed. (New York: Oxford, 1993), p. 256.

12. All elected members of the tribunal serve for three-year terms. The caseload is not heavy. Since its establishment in 1872, the tribunal has heard about 2,000 cases.

executive personnel from code principles. What he finds "incredible" is that each nation nevertheless proclaims its consistency with its own historical traditions.[13]

The brains of the French administrative state is the Council of State, a venerable institution with an enviable record of stability, prestige, and power that extends back to the earliest days of the French republic. The council attracts the most talented, most ambitious graduates of France's Ecole Nationale d'Administration, an exclusive graduate school of public administration that educates virtually all of the government's top administrative officials and many of its politicians. The Council of State is a sought-after assignment because of its centrality and significance to the national government. It is an inside player, assisting the President, and sometimes Parliament, in preparing legislation and examining it for constitutional defects. It is secretive and influential in this aspect of its operations.

The Council also oversees the government's huge public sector, which grew to nearly one-third of the workforce in the early 1980s. Since then it has shrunk slightly as France has privatized some industries, but the rate of public employment in France remains almost twice that of the United States. The public sector is also more centralized in France, with most employees working at the national level, rather than in local or regional agencies, as in the United States.[14] This vast bureaucracy requires direction and an opportunity for civilians to resolve complaints against bureaucratic action.

In accordance with the principle of strict separation between administrative and judicial functions, the Council of State, rather than the courts, deals with complaints against bureaucrats. This process of administrative review began in 1799 and has always been regarded as a basic right of French citizens. Administrative review, it was hoped, would be sufficient to protect the rights of French citizens against the arbitrariness of the much-resented bureaucracy. The idea was to provide a fast, fair, and inexpensive remedy for government error. The Council would appoint a rapporteur to investigate each complaint and then report to members of the Council, who, together with the rapporteur, would resolve the problem and provide damages where appropriate. When necessary, the Council would put on its executive hat and make policy to prevent a recurrence of the situation that caused the citizen to complain. The whole process could be set into motion without a lawyer or payment of large fees. Most matters, in fact, could be handled by an exchange of relevant documents.

13. Jean Rivero, *Administrative Law et Droit Administratif* (Paris: Pichon and Durand-Auzias, 1986), p. 139.

14. Donald C. Rowat (ed.), *Public Administration in Developed Democracies* (New York: Marcel Dekker, 1988), p. 445.

This orderly method for handling citizen dissatisfaction with administrative decisions has attracted the admiration of some American commentators. Henry Abraham, for example, claims that: "To the French—and to many careful observers in the Anglo-Saxon world as well—theirs is the only logical system of supervising the administrative branch of government, not only because of its rapid, convenient, and efficient adjudicatory process, but also because of the expertise inherent in the judicial personnel that staff its administrative courts."[15]

The system does not, however, appear to be as problem-free as Abraham suggests. The Council has always had difficulty acting in a timely fashion. In 1953 the Council had a backlog of 26,000 cases and was eight years in arrears. The solution was to create twenty-four regional administrative tribunals, saving the Council for an appellate role. By 1987 the Council, with the capacity to review only about 8,000 appellate cases a year, had again fallen into arrears, with 25,000 cases awaiting review. The most recent effort to resolve the caseload problem has been the creation of yet another layer of review consisting of five specialized administrative appeals tribunals to hear tax, contract, and work-related disputes. At this point the administrative review apparatus looks much like a court system, with layers of review and a corps of administrative judges who enjoy the right of *inamovibilité,* which protects them from involuntary transfer. The litigation division of the Council of State takes appeals on a discretionary basis, overseeing both the new appellate tribunals and various specialized agencies, such as the Court of Budgetary and Financial Discipline, the Senate Audit Office, and the Superior Council of National Education. The latest reforms also allow the Council to guide the lower administrative tribunals with an *avis* or memorandum on applicable administrative principles. Currently about 100 of the Council's 263 members work on administrative cases.

The system can nevertheless be criticized for ineffectiveness in resolving citizen complaints, which still takes years. The damages offered are often grossly inadequate. Policy changes do occasionally result from complaints, but the system has done little to make the French bureaucracy more palatable to citizens. As Yves Meny notes: "Paradoxically, from the excessive dogmatism which dominates the philosophy of the administration has emerged an almost cynical pragmatism which allows a rule to be made without any conviction that it will be applied. . . . The absence of illusion on the part of administrators has its parallel among the administered: they detest the state but ceaselessly demand its intervention. Relations between bureaucrats and the public are often appalling and characterized by a mutual hatred which only the impotence of those confronting one another can justify; the irritation of the citizen, who finds

15. Abraham, supra note 11, p. 265.

himself lost in the administrative maze, is matched by the frustration of the public official, who is the prisoner of the rules he must apply.''[16]

The Council of State's benchmark in resolving disputes has always been applicable statutes and, where ambiguity remains, general principles of law, a vague term for an amorphous jurisprudence deriving from statutes, customary law, and constitutional guarantees. It has created a very significant body of case law that guides its decision making. The Council also displays considerable independence in its decisions and has even interpreted its responsibility to include correction of the President himself. Thus the Council declared illegal President de Gaulle's decision to set up a special military tribunal to try terrorists during the Algerian war, a decision that so angered de Gaulle that he even considered abolishing the Council of State. The Council, however, continues to claim authority to review all executive acts for conformity with the general law, including principles noted in the preamble to the 1958 constitution.

This evolution reveals a specialized version of constitutional review that bears some resemblance to judicial review as practiced in general jurisdiction courts in the United States and in many western European nations. While investigation of the impact of these different approaches is beyond the scope of this chapter, this brief overview of developments in the French administrative sector suggests that, even in a nation that distrusts judges, a growing sensitivity to fundamental rights demands procedures for evaluating constitutional claims.

The sense of constitutional mission that animates the Council of State has a metanational aspect. Article 55 of the French constitution requires that France give precedence to its treaty obligations when they conflict with domestic legislation. France is bound to respect the decisions of the European Commission and Court on Human Rights and to defer to certain directives emanating from the offices of the European Union in Brussels. Membership in the European Union also requires that France adhere to the decisions of the Court of Justice of the European Union in Luxembourg and that it refer cases there that involve interpretation of the EU treaty. The Council of State at first avoided making such referrals, citing the proposition that questions with obvious answers do not need to be referred to the Court of Justice in Luxembourg, the so-called *acte clair* doctrine. The Council also took a rather narrow view of the power of the EU in instances where Parliament adopted an inconsistent statute subsequent to the treaty. The Council, however, reversed itself in a 1989 case and now accords the treaty full effect in all instances.[17]

At the other end of the administrative review spectrum, in the local tribunals that resolve most disputes, there is also reluctance to accept arguments that take

16. Yves Meny, "France," in Rowat, supra note 14, p. 290.

17. *In re Nicolo*, Oct. 20, 1989, Conseil d'Etat, 1990 *D.S. Jur.* 35 (Fr.).

administrators beyond familiar bureaucratic territory. The conservatism of the administrative tribunals was an issue, for example, in a 1992 dispute over a Toulouse hospital's decision to destroy two frozen embryos. The plaintiff argued that a court, rather than an administrative tribunal, should hear the case because it "touches fundamental individual rights." An administrative tribunal was unlikely to appreciate the fundamental human rights dimension, even though it is bound to take account of the European Convention for the Protection of Human Rights and Fundamental Freedoms in its judgments. The narrow-mindedness of the administrative courts, this litigant suggested, would force her to wait for the European Court of Human Rights to take up the case after all appeals within the French system were exhausted. She would be required to run "a judicial marathon" to protect her rights.[18]

The situation is not necessarily as bleak as this litigant claimed, however. In 1993 the Council of State overruled an administrative court's decision that the wearing of headscarves by Islamic girls and their unwillingness to participate in certain high school sports (like swimming) required their expulsion from public school. An administrative appeals court had upheld the original expulsion, but the Minister of Education, Lionel Jospin, requested further review. The Council of State reversed the decision, permitting the students to wear headscarves on religious grounds, but only to the extent that they did not interfere with school administration. The administrative tribunals below, the Council said, had not paid enough attention to the religious liberties students enjoy, even in a school setting. The school was wrong to forbid this religious expression without investigating how disruptive the scarfwearing would be. The timing and manner of a religious display are crucial, the Council said, in a reasoning reminiscent of U.S. Supreme Court jurisprudence on this subject.[19]

The Council of State's role in constitutional interpretation extends beyond the occasions in which it must resolve a dispute. The Council also advises the government on the compatibility of all bills with the constitution and existing law. This advisory role became more important in the 1970s, with the rise of a new player in French politics, the Constitutional Council. The section that follows describes this agency and its work.

THE CONSTITUTIONAL COUNCIL

France's legislative process, according to some observers, has become "judicialized."[20] Political opponents in Parliament score points against each

---

18. "Embryons Congelés," *Dernières nouvelles d'Alsace*, Oct. 8, 1992, p. 7.

19. Paul Sabourin, "Notes de Jurisprudence," *Droit public et de la science politique en France et à l'étranger* 109 (1993), 220–231.

20. See Alec Stone, *The Birth of Judicial Politics in France* (New York: Oxford, 1992) and Vroom, supra note 3.

other with legal arguments; the whole process looks toward constitutional review. How can this be in a country so reluctant to embrace the principle that judges should examine legislation for constitutional defects? The answer lies in the emergence of the Constitutional Council, which has the power to review proposed legislation for incompatibility with the constitution and other legal defects. Upon referral, the Council examines the law and either allows it to stand as is or requires revisions. This body, a uniquely French invention, has successfully carved out a niche for itself as "guardian of the constitution."

The Constitutional Council is a product of the 1958 constitutional revision. De Gaulle, author of this reform, did not anticipate that the council would become an arbiter of fundamental constitutional guarantees. His primary objectives were to reduce Parliament's involvement in the administration of law, thus allowing the executive to act with a freer hand, and to limit Parliament's freedom to revise "organic law" (Parliament's internal procedures and the electoral law). The idea was to create a very distinguished body that would, upon request, declare whether a proposed law exceeded Parliament's proper sphere. The council was to be made up of all of the ex-presidents of France able and willing to serve, plus nine other prominent individuals, with three selected by each chamber of the Parliament and the three by the President. Each member serves for a nine-year term and cannot hold another government post while on the council. Giscard d'Estaing, for example, was obliged to withdraw from the council when he was elected to the National Assembly in 1984. The Constitutional Council at the outset could act only upon referral by the president, the prime minister, or the chief of either chamber of the Parliament, and it was expected to pass judgment within one month.

The council succeeded in attracting a distinguished membership, some with backgrounds in law, others in politics. In the first twenty years, eight members came from the Council of State, five were attorneys, and five were professors. One-third were graduates of the Ecole Nationale d'Administration.[21] During most of this period the council did almost nothing; it received only nine referrals during the first fifteen years of its existence. In 1974, however, Parliament modified the constitution to change the rules for bringing proposed legislation to the council. Any faction or party able to get sixty members of either chamber to agree could henceforth request review. This small change had dramatic effects.

The council immediately became attractive to minority coalitions within Parliament, who discovered that they could block or delay new initiatives by referring legislation to the council before promulgation. The rate of referral increased dramatically, from an average of one proposed law per year to

21. McWhinney, supra note 2.

thirteen, reaching a rate of sixty-six laws per year between 1974 and 1981. The rate of referral continued to rise throughout the 1980s.

As the council's workload increased, so did its willingness to correct the Parliament. During the 1980s, for example, the council struck down major initiatives related to reimbursement for nationalization, regulation of the press and electronic media, and the right to strike. Now nearly every law that evokes significant controversy in Parliament goes to the Constitutional Council for pre-promulgation review and, as one member of the National Assembly has observed: "The Council is behind every parliamentary debate, is present even inside the political groups."[22]

Knowing that any major initiative will probably have to undergo council scrutiny, members of Parliament and the administration have begun to incorporate the council's perspective into their thinking. They consult experts, including the Council of State, to help frame bills that will pass review. Factions extract compromises from majorities by threatening a referral. In a 1993 debate over immigration restrictions, for example, the Socialist minority called the government's new law "segregationist," and the debate turned to whether the government's proposal was in conformity with the constitution.[23] To resolve the impasse, the government commissioned a National Advisory Commission on Human Rights to render an opinion on proposals.

In determining what constitutional norms to apply to proposed legislation, the council has adopted a surprisingly expansive approach. A crucial turning point came in 1971 when it found relevant principles in the preamble to the ·1958 constitution, which refers to and incorporates the 1946 constitution, which in turn refers to the 1789 Declaration of the Rights of Man and "republican principles of government." This group of principles has become known in France as the *bloc de constitutionnalité*. The framers of the 1958 constitution, it should be noted, expressly denied that the preamble to the document, which affirms a general commitment to these principles, was to be given constitutional status.

The council's approach to constitutional interpretation invites comparisons to the United States Supreme Court. Like the Supreme Court, the council ranges widely in search of applicable standards, and, like a constitutional court, the council sometimes cites its own precedents to help justify or explain its decisions. These interpretations sometimes play a role in subsequent litigation, and when they are relevant, they are binding on all French courts. The council also reassembles the Supreme Court in exercising its veto power with circumspection. The council rarely challenges Parliament directly with

22. Quoted in Vroom, supra note 3, p. 318.

23. "Immigration: Débat ouvert à l'assemblée," *Dernières nouvelles d'Alsace*, June 16, 1993, p. 1.

an outright veto of a proposed law (*angulation*). It prefers to critique parts of a law instead, often offering corrective wording to deal with its "amputation" of problematic language. Its caution has helped the council maintain an aura of neutral constitutional guardianship. To date, Parliament has accepted every revision the council has offered, often copying its suggested revisions word by word.

It would be a mistake, however, to go too far in analogizing the Constitutional Council to a court exercising the power of constitutional review. The council evaluates proposed legislation, not signed laws that have gone into effect. It does not resolve disputes between citizens or take appeals from any source. It has no power to check the way courts interpret legal rules or to supervise the implementation of its decisions.

Pre-promulgation review has certain advantages. Early review prevents implementation of unconstitutional legislation. The process is rapid, usually occurring within a matter of weeks after referral, and it is more often than not oriented toward revision, not reversal, of legislative judgment. But this efficient process may occur when public emotions are at a peak. Consider, for example, the problem of state support for private schools, always a volatile issue in France. In January 1994, while major demonstrations were occurring in the streets of Paris, Parliament referred a controversial law on school funding to the council. Not surprisingly, questions arose about the capacity of the council to be impartial in such a political climate.[24]

In effect, the Constitutional Council is a forum of last resort for minority voting blocs in the Parliament. The Council members' long terms of office mean that the party that is out of office may still have strong support. In 1986, for example, France was in a period of "cohabitation" between a Socialist president and a nonsocialist Parliament and prime minister. President Mitterrand appointed his former minister of justice, Robert Badinter, to be president of the Constitutional Council. This gave the Socialists the council leadership, which was supplemented by three other loyal Socialist votes on the nine-member council. The new Chirac government had to compromise on many initiatives to avoid unfavorable action in the council. Even with these efforts, the council amputated or annulled twice as much legislation as it approved. "The legislature," François Léotard complained, "legislates under the shadow cast by the Council." The Socialists, it might be noted, could have said the same thing when they were in power and appointees from the Chirac government blocked many of their initiatives.[25]

24. Franck Lefillatre, "The French Constitutional Council: The Rise of a Constitutional Jurisdiction," unpublished manuscript on file with the author.

25. Alec Stone, "In the Shadow of the Constitutional Council: The 'Jurisdiction' of the Legislative Process in France," *West European Politics* 12 (1989), p. 19.

The discussion so far suggests a nation amenable to constitutional review, as long as it does not occur in an ordinary courtroom in the course of an ordinary lawsuit. A look at France's highest appellate court, the Court of Cassation, confirms this impression. Parliament created the Court of Cassation in 1790 to replace the pre-revolutionary *Conseil du Roi*, one department of which had overseen judicial affairs. The legislators recognized the need for a single central court that could render final decisions, but they wanted to limit this power as much as possible. So they made the new court an adjunct to Parliament and they forbade it from going beyond legal analysis to resolve the underlying disputes brought before it.[26] Judges were elected for four-year terms and were required to conduct all their deliberations in public.

Judges are now appointed and may deliberate in secret, but their mission remains nearly as narrow as it was at the outset. The court has power to quash (*casser*) judicial decisions because they mistakenly interpret the law, but the judges must decide only the specific points of law referred to them, and they must render their decision as narrowly as possible. The court rarely issues rulings on the proper outcome of cases and provides only the skimpiest of decisions to instruct the lower courts on the applicable law. If the panel of the Court of Cassation disagrees with the reasoning of the lower court, it typically sends the matter, not to the original court, but to another court at the same level (generally one of the regional courts of appeal). The new court can decide the facts as it sees fit and, remarkably, is not bound by the legal views of the panel of the Court of Cassation that sent it the case. Until recently, only decisions of the full bench (which rarely sits together) could bind a lower court, and its decision was binding only on the legal issues at stake.

The court is organized along bureaucratic lines. There are eighty-four judges, all of whom sit in Paris, supplemented by about forty *conseillers référendaires* who vote on cases on which they have worked. The judges are organized into five specialized chambers, each of which considers a particular type of appeal. Appointment tends to come toward the end of a judicial career: the average age is over sixty. The first woman was appointed to this bench in 1946, but it remains overwhelmingly male. This court must consider a caseload in excess of 12,000 cases per year, about two-thirds of which are appeals from civil judgments; the remainder are criminal appeals.

26. In the words of a 1790 decree: "Sous aucun prétexte et en aucun cas, le Tribunal de cassation ne pourra connaître du fond des affaires," quoted in Bellet, "France: La Cour de Cassation," in Pierre Bellet, André Tunc, and Adolph Touffait, "La Cour Judicaire Suprême: Une enquête comparative," *Pans economica* (Paris: 1978), p. 93. Roughly translated, the passage reads, "Under no circumstances is the Court of Cassation to rule on the substance of the matter in dispute."

The gargantuan caseload, the limited review power, and the large, sub-divided bench discourage efforts to create a coherent jurisprudence. The vast majority of decisions are summary affirmations of the judgment below. Most are not even published. When a panel of the court does commit its thoughts to writing, they are in the form of a syllogism. The decision begins with applicable principles, moves on to a citation of selected facts, and concludes with a result that appears to follow ineluctably from what precedes. Judges rarely address the economic or social consequences of a choice, and they make no effort to clarify or explore the legal principles they rely upon. If judges have any doubts about the applicable law, they are not expressed in the decision; dissents and concurrences are unknown. This style fits the civil-law mythology that judging is a technical and deductive skill, with no creative or subjective component.

This style of rendering decisions has many critics in the French legal community. Its formality and aloofness, they charge, prevent the court from playing an effective leadership role. As Touffait and Tunc note: "The decisions of the courts in France, especially of Cassation, is a little like the mass in Latin. It keeps a respectable tradition going, but it also repeats formulas that many don't understand and that permit the spirit to go where it wants to."[27] These authors recommend a much more open discussion of the issues at stake, with dissenting opinions, as appropriate.

Critics of the Court of Cassation would also drastically reduce the number of cases it is obliged to decide. Given the rarity of a reversal, it is likely that many cases are filed simply to delay an inevitable negative final judgment. One study estimated that 70 percent of appeals to the Court of Cassation were primarily for purposes of delay and without any realistic hope of reversal.[28] Requiring a decision in every case also has a negative effect on the institution—it gives the misleading impression that the purpose of review in the Court of Cassation is error correction, rather than the development of a coherent response to contemporary legal issues.

The U.S. Supreme Court provides an alternative approach to appellate review that is much admired by some French scholars. André Tunc, for example, describes the discretion to refuse jurisdiction on prudential grounds, a power the U.S. Supreme Court uses to good effect to keep its caseload to manageable proportions, as one characteristic of an "ideal supreme court." Tunc's ideal court would also resemble the Supreme Court in having law clerks, oral argument, separate signed dissenting and concurring opinions, and a reasonably coherent jurisprudence.

27. A. Touffait and André Tunc, "Pour une motivation plus explicite," *Revue trimestrielle de droit civil* (1974), p. 287.
28. See Bell, supra note 4, p. 105.

Since the 1980s the Court of Cassation has moved a little closer to the position that it can, in an appropriate case, consider constitutional rights and liberties in evaluating a legal claim. Perhaps the most notable example was a decision on April 25, 1985, that referred to the constitution for guidance in determining the susceptibility of the acts of certain police officers to court review. As the government's prosecuting attorney argued in that instance: "The judge must seek a juridical solution to problems in light, not only of specially written texts, but also of the great principles of law, whose very obviousness often allows them to escape codification."[29]

The effects of a system so reluctant to allow judges a role in interpreting the constitution are mixed. One need not be concerned, for example, that the legislature or executive will defer to the judiciary in grappling with tough policy issues. French politicians know they are responsible for political hot potatoes like church-state relations and racism in police ranks. Citizens know they can influence these debates by taking to the streets to let their views be known. Perhaps this is why street demonstrations are much more common in France than in the United States or England.

Exclusion of the judiciary from constitutional review and administrative oversight, however, also has a negative side. Many people complain about the power of government functionaries to do whatever they want, as long as they can find a rule. In a system without meaningful external review, rules abound. Crossing the border, for example, can mean one set of requirements on one day, and other requirements the next. Cynicism about the capacity of the bureaucracy to respect the rights of citizens, not surprisingly, is widespread in France.

EUROPEAN COURTS IN FRENCH LAW

In France a hard-fought lawsuit or administrative proceeding does not necessarily end at the Court of Cassation or the Council of State, the nation's traditional terminus points for legal action. European courts may also be available. Business disputes that touch upon economic interests protected in the European Union (EU) can be brought before the Court of Justice of the European Union, which sits in Luxembourg. Cases that raise issues covered by the European Convention on the Rights of Man, the document that sets forth the norms of the Council of Europe, may be taken to the European Commission on Human Rights and ultimately to the European Court on Human Rights, both of which sit in Strasbourg, France. These judicial bodies support larger governance projects, one economic in focus, the other, social and political. Their relevance to this discussion lies in their power to declare a member nation's policy inconsistent with community norms. Member states, in turn, are obliged to respect these judgments.

29. DS Jur. at 333, 1985.

Chapter 3 described the makeup and functions of the Court of Justice of the European Union and the Commission and Court on Human Rights in the context of their relationship to the EU and the Council of Europe. Subsequent sections of this chapter consider the significance of these supranational courts in the French political process. The vantage point for detailed consideration will be particular disputes. At the outset, however, it seems useful to ask a more general question: how has France adapted to the new reality of supranational courts empowered to review, and perhaps overturn, its own domestic policies? This aspect of the European union, which is fundamental to its success, clearly runs counter to the French tendency to subordinate the judiciary to the lawmaking and executive branches.

France has accepted European judicial intervention in its domestic affairs, but reluctantly. It took France twenty-three years to ratify the European Convention of the Rights of Man, a document it helped to draft in 1950. France delayed even longer in making itself amenable to suit by individuals, finally permitting these suits in 1981, but with the qualification that it might revisit the issue after five years. This embarrassingly long period of delay in allowing suits stemmed more from opposition to the idea of judicial oversight than from opposition to the principles themselves. Indeed, ordinary courts and even the administrative tribunals and the Council of State were occasionally incorporating references to the European Convention on Human Rights in their decisions by the mid-1970s.

The European Commission and Court have since become familiar endpoints in the appellate review process and reference points throughout the French system. The guarantees of individual rights that France lacks at the national level are to a significant degree available through this supranational route. The problem, as noted earlier, is the degree of sophistication such litigation requires. French courts are not inclined toward broad interpretations of human rights guarantees under the European Convention, but suitors must nevertheless frame their claims in these terms from the outset or risk dismissal for failure to exhaust national remedies. Another problem is the slow movement of litigation through layers of national review. Indeed, it typically takes six or seven years to carry a case through all national appeals to the Commission on Human Rights, which has a growing backlog of cases awaiting review. A decade can easily elapse before the case reaches the commission, and more time may be necessary if the European Court on Human Rights takes up the issue. Despite these obstacles, France has one of the highest rates of petitioning the commission among member states.

The Court of Justice of the European Union becomes involved at a much earlier stage of an economic dispute. A business can sue to prevent enforcement of a policy that might violate the EU treaty, and the domestic court or tribunal that hears the case is then obliged either to apply the treaty itself or to refer the case to the EU court for clarification.[30] The reference procedure thus puts European judges in a position to veto the economic policies of the French parliament or administration. But the treaty indirectly also enhances the power of French judges, providing them with grounds to set aside administrative rules or legislation in resolving the disputes it does not refer to the EU court.

The difficult political issue, initially, was whether French courts would ever send cases to the EU court for review. The issue arose in the context of a general ambivalence about the powers of the EU. French anxieties did not seem to be relieved by the fact that two of the organization's principal architects, Jean Monnet and Robert Schumann, were French citizens. In keeping with this general reticence, the courts at first took the same approach as the Council of State, employing the acte clair doctrine to avoid sending issues arising under the treaty for interpretation by the EU court. The Court of Cassation relied on this doctrine until 1967 and made no referrals. Two years later, however, the court of appeal in Colmar, a regional appellate court, explicitly recognized all of the decisions of the European Court of Justice as binding and went on to apply one of these decisions to the dispute at hand.[31] A pattern of cooperation soon evolved, references becoming commonplace from throughout the court system. As noted earlier, the Council of State also began to adopt a more conciliatory attitude in the 1970s, examining the consistency of French legislation with treaty obligations with a more critical eye than it had in the past.

These changes in the courts and administrative sector reflect a more general acceptance of the obligations of membership in the European community. European standards have become a point of reference in French political debate, and the pronouncements of the courts associated with the EU and Council of Europe are now seen to contribute to that discussion. French law students and legal scholars study their decisions for guidance in domestic disputes. In a 1992 prosecution of a conscientious objector, for example, the defense lawyer claimed that a longer term of service for objectors contravened the European Convention on Human Rights. Counsel for the government disagreed, citing a 1989 decision by the Court of Cassation that had considered this issue. The reference to fundamental rights was accepted by all parties as a normal aspect of the proceeding.[32]

---

30. Treaty obligations, under the 1958 constitution, clearly take precedence over conflicting domestic legislation. The problem at first was in deciding what aspects of the Treaty, Regulations, and Directives must be applied by the national courts. The European Court of Justice has taken a generous view of the EU mandate as it applies to national courts. See especially *Costa v. ENEL,* ECR 585 (1964).

31. *Saarknappschaft v. Freund* and another, *Cour d'Appel de Colmar,* (1969) CMLR82, 84.

32. "Le double procès de l'objecteur," *Dernières nouvelles d'Alsace,* Feb. 18, 1993, p. 3.

RETROSPECT, A CONSTITUTIONAL REVOLUTION?

Sensitivity to individual rights is clearly on the increase in France. The Constitutional Council has had a significant influence on legislative debate and executive initiatives. The Council of State has assisted in this process and has accepted the power of the new European courts to make binding policy. The domestic courts, working within a framework that prohibits judicial review, have reached decisions that are sensitive to rights by other means, including reference to the European Commission and Court on Human Rights. These trends can be expected to continue as the Court of Justice of the European Union and the European Commission and Court decide more cases and build on the precedents they have already established.

Developments in France are part of a broader European movement to accept judicial guardianship of fundamental rights. Austria in 1945, Italy in 1948, and Germany in 1949 each adopted a written constitution that included basic rights, limited government, and judicial power to enforce constitutional guarantees. Realizing that they were entering into a new and potentially dangerous era of big government, these nations sought to bolster the protections afforded citizens, typically by establishing a single constitutional court with the power of judicial review. In the words of legal scholar Mauro Cappelletti: "The modern constitutions, their bills of rights and judicial review are the elements of a 'positive higher law' made binding and enforceable: they represent a synthesis of a sort of legal positivism and natural law. They reflect the most sophisticated attempt ever designed to 'positivise' values without, however, either absolutizing such values or relinquishing them to the mutable whims of passing majorities."[33]

France, a leader in the initial stages of European unification, was more reluctant than most western European nations to give its own judges new powers. Cappelletti is critical of this approach: "The dramatic history of Continental Europe in the last two centuries, where the ideal of civil libertarians was for too long one of strict separation of powers, rather than of reciprocal checks, is very instructive. Strict separation brought . . . a weaker judiciary, essentially confined to 'private' (civil and criminal) adjudication; it brought about an unchecked legislature, and, as long as a separate branch of administrative courts did not succeed in emerging, an unchecked executive as well. Only a balanced system of reciprocal checks and balances can combine, without dangers to freedom, a *strong* legislature with a *strong* executive and a *strong* judiciary as well."[34]

The United States, Cappelletti asserts, got this right; France got it wrong, but is moving toward what Cappelletti calls "quasi-judicial review" in which

33. Mauro Cappelletti, *The Judicial Process in Comparative Perspective* (Oxford: Clarendon Press, 1989), pp. 209–210.
34. Ibid., 23.

other institutions take up constitutional review functions that could be more effectively handled by ordinary courts. France's progress, however, has been slowed by the diffuse, unmanageable organization of its courts, by the lack of discretion in appellate courts over case selection, by the absence of stare decisis, and by the way judges and lawyers are trained to think about the law.[35] This suggests that the availability (or inavailability) of judicial review is only one dimension of a broad-based relationship between a society's legal system and its politics. France's determination to keep a lid on judicial power, for example, helps to reinforce the political regime's tendencies toward centralization and control by experts. One can also see a connection between France's long-standing political commitment to a welfare state and a legal system that offers many entry points for citizens who seek greater benefits. The institutional weakness of French courts, however, diminishes the political payoff that might otherwise be associated with accessible dispute resolution because judges tend to be seen as government officials, rather than as independent guardians of the rights of citizens.

The dynamic relationship between courts and politics can also be explored by looking at the biographies of judges. Nations differ in the degree to which judges have experience or connections with politics. Many judges at every level in the United States, for example, have had experience in politics or personal connections with the politicians who helped to put them into office. In England, judicial appointments tend to be less politicized, but the English House of Lords, a segment of which hears final appeals, is still a legislative body. France has followed a different path, drawing its judges from the ranks of those educated specifically for judicial posts. The judges at the top of the judicial pyramid have seniority in the system and perhaps more ambition and better connections than others, but they have not typically had political careers or political sponsors. The only exception to France's system of a politically insulated bench is the Constitutional Council, the one body with authority to reverse the legislature. Even in a nation that aspires to keep judging and politics separate, some positions are simply too sensitive to fill with people who do not have a political track record.

The difference between nations that insulate judges from politics and those that do not, however, is more than strategic—at stake are fundamental beliefs concerning the role of litigation in developing the law. In other words, how a nation prepares and selects its legal personal depends on prevailing principles of jurisprudence. As noted above, France differs fundamentally from common-law nations like the United States and England in the position it

35. Stare decisis is a rule American courts have developed to make judicial policymaking more consistent and more credible. It provides that judges will follow the logic of past decisions unless they become convinced that the earlier court had misapprehended the applicable rule.

takes on the origins of law and the role of judges. We should therefore expect France to differ from the United States and England in how it educates its lawyers and judges.

As we have seen in earlier chapters, common-law countries tend to see law practice as a valuable preparation for a judgeship, indeed as a capstone for a legal career. The idea prevails that law is a craft and that judging too is a creative process in which the wise judge subtly helps to keep law up to date. Civil-law tradition takes a much more matter-of-fact view of practicing lawyers and of judges, and locates law's dynamism, not in the practical world of legal practice and litigation, but in the academic community.

The scholarly community helps to keep law up to date in two ways. One is by explaining the law in treatises, legal encyclopedias, and textbooks. These volumes are organized to reveal what is believed to be the deep structure and overall coherence of law. Legal academics are also expected to play a role in drafting legislation. Indeed, Napoleon turned to scholars to draft the civil and criminal codes that helped to make France famous among civil-law nations. In Merryman's words: ''The civil law is a law of the professors.''[36]

The ideology of legislative supremacy seems to co-exist easily with a disposition to venerate legal scholars over practitioners, whether the pratitioners be courtroom lawyers, judges, or even legislators. Thus French judges often cite academic authority to explain their decisions, and it is not unusual for French lawyers to cite scholarly opinion in their briefs. In common-law jurisdictions the lines of influence tend to run the other way, with academics studying judicial opinions and judges basing their decisions on the arguments that practicing attorneys frame for their consideration.

The influence of the scholarly community upon legal practitioners is guaranteed by the French method of legal education, which stresses legal principle over practical education. Case law tends to get short shrift, in part because French legal scholarship does not honor the principle of stare decisis, but also because the necessary indices of reported cases do not exist. French law professors do not typically write case books, as American law professors do, and French academics tend to disdain any identification with advocacy in their academic work. Many never join a local bar association. Even those who do practice law draw a sharp distinction between this work and their teaching and scholarly research.

Law is taught as a science, with an emphasis on deriving basic principles. Scholars evaluate legal documents for the extent to which they conform to

36. John Henry Merryman, *The Civil Law Tradition*, 2d ed. (Stanford, Calif.: Stanford University Press, 1985), p. 56.

the principles the schools teach. A comment by Christian Atias captures the attitude: "Much depends upon the extent to which the lawmakers of civil statutes are aware of the science which they must acquire, the choices which they must make, the many objectives they have to pursue, and the various techniques which are available to them."[37]

Law is an undergraduate specialty in the university. The program lasts four years, but a student can get a general studies degree after two, and a *licence en droit* after three. Many flunk out after the first year. The basic four-year degree is the *maitrise en droit,* but those who stay on an additional year can earn a national diploma, which is a prerequisite for the doctoral degree.[38] Students who desire a doctorate must find a mentor among the established professors. The doctoral student becomes the professor's assistant and remains closely associated with the professor throughout his or her career, a system that gives great authority to the more senior professors. Professorships are scarce and, not surprisingly, highly competitive. To be eligible, a prospect must not only complete the doctorate, but also pass a rigorous national exam.

Students who major in law do not necessarily intend to take up the field professionally, however. Law is a popular major among students who have no intention of going on in any legal field, as I found in lecturing in a first-year law class in Strasbourg. No one in a class of about forty students had plans to be a lawyer or judge, a pattern of disengagement from career ambitions that a law teacher would never expect in the United States. France clearly encourages public knowledge about legal norms and ideals without teaching respect for lawyers or judges. The key to this difference may be that France, like other civil-law countries, tends to mythologize law as a set of coherent principles that citizens are well-advised to learn, while Anglo-American countries tend to mythologize the work of courtroom advocates and judges.

The route to a judgeship in France and other civil-law nations is ordinarily through specialized education. Schooling begins with an initial undergraduate university degree in law. After graduation, at about age twenty-three, candidates take a competitive examination to enter the Ecole Nationale de la Magistrature in Bordeaux. The government established the school in 1958

---

37. Christian Atias, *The French Civil Law: An Insider's View* (Baton Rouge, La.: Louisiana State University Press, 1987), p. 40.

38. The hierarchy of degrees in law is the same used to measure levels of preparation in other professions (except medicine, which follows its own pattern): (a) after two years of study, the Diplôme d'études universitaires générales (DEUG); (b) end of the third year, licence en droit; (c) end of fourth year, matrise en droit; (d) end of fifth year, Diplôme d'études approfondies (DEA) or Diplôme d'études supérieures specialisées (DESS); (e) after successful completion of thesis: Doctorat d'état.

(as the National Center for Judicial Studies) in connection with other reforms designed to boost the independence of judges. It operates under the Ministry of Justice, but is financed separately from that agency. At first, applications were few—only a few hundred people expressed interest in the 1960s. But since the mid-1970s, the number of applicants has increased sharply to more than one thousand a year for about two hundred positions.

Coursework is divided between formal studies in law and psychology and internships in various courts. This process of qualification by education has helped to produce a bench that includes a significant proportion of women, persons from working-class backgrounds, and persons from former colonies, such as Algeria. By the early 1980s, 21.4 percent of all judges were women; among those under thirty-four, the proportion was 43.8 percent.[39] By 1990, women outnumbered men at the lowest ranks, but held less than ten percent of the top posts.[40]

The effort to ensure the independence of French judges extends to matters of appointment, promotion, and discipline. Initial appointments are made on the basis of examination scores, with those receiving the highest scores getting first choice at available positions. Promotion depends on seniority, on one's success in impressing the senior judge in the local bench, and on willingness to relocate. One could anticipate appointment to high judicial office, in short, only after considerable time in a lower judicial post. The whole process is overseen by the Council of the Judiciary, a body of judges drawn from various levels in the judicial hierarchy and operating under rules that have been the source of considerable controversy. The degree to which the president dominated the process was criticized, as was the power of a senior judge to influence a young colleague's career. France reorganized these procedures in February 1994 to respond to the criticisms of executive domination and exclusion of lower-court judges from the Council of the Judiciary, but the impact of these changes on the independence of judges remains to be seen.[41]

Efforts to enhance the qualifications and independence of judges have not been accompanied by higher pay and other job enhancements. The French judicial system has long been underfunded by the standards of other western

39. Henry W. Ehrmann and Martin A. Schain, *Politics in France*, 5th ed. (New York: HarperCollins, 1992), p. 158.

40. "La justice," *Cahiers de la documentation française* 25 (1991), p. 63.

41. Administrative judges finally won the right of *inamovibilité* (irremovability for failure to be willing to accept a transfer or other arbitrary reason) in 1986 with other legislative changes designed to enhance their status. At this point, some scholars argue, administrative judges enjoy more job security than ordinary judges. See, e.g., Françoise Dreyfis and François d'Arcy, *Les institutions politiques et administratives de la France*, 4th ed. (Paris: Economica, 1993).

European nations. Less than 1 percent of the national budget currently goes to support the Ministry of Justice, which pays most expenses associated with the court system. A big problem in many courts is lack of judicial personnel, the number of judgeships having failed to keep pace with the growth of caseloads.[42] Nor have French judges escaped their earlier status as quasi bureaucrats.

Working conditions and the fact that judging is not regarded as an elite profession in France have encouraged a unionization movement among judges. This movement began in 1968 when a group of judges formed the Syndicat de la Magistrature (SM), a move that resulted in disciplinary action from the government. The union survived and still attracts many of the younger judges. The largest and most representative union, however, is the Union Syndicale de la Magistrature (USM). A third union, Association Professionelle des Magistrats (APM), was formed in 1981 and remains the smallest of the three.

The difficulties French judges have had in gaining independence and salaries commensurate with their responsibilities suggests that the profession is not held in particularly high public esteem in France. It is certainly true that France, lacking a tradition of the judge as lawmaker, lacks famous judges. America, in contrast, seems to have more than its fair share: John Marshall, Oliver Wendell Holmes, Earl Warren, and Thurgood Marshall are almost father figures to a public that accords the Supreme Court a place in the nation's moral development. England also has its great lawgivers, such as Mansfield. But the difference between French and American attitudes extends further, into beliefs about ordinary judges. In France the judiciary is widely regarded as an occupation for those who lack the ambition to be practicing lawyers or academics, and many people identify judges with the government, an impression that is reinforced by the frequency with which prosecutors become judges. Indeed, the term *magistrat* refers to both judges and prosecutors. Polls consistently give the judicial system poor ratings for efficiency and independence.[43] French judges are thus in a bind, enjoying little of the public prestige that might help insulate them from pressure to conform to the Ministry of Justice's bureaucratic initiatives.

The tendency to overlook courts as an important source of legal or moral leadership can be seen in the reaction to an incident that occurred while I was teaching in Strasbourg. During the 1992 electoral campaign, the right-wing politician Jean-Marie Le Pen decided to campaign in Strasbourg and requested space in one of the city's large public halls. The mayor refused on

42. Ibid., p. 51.

43. Alan Katz, "France," in Katz (ed.), *Legal Traditions and Systems: An International Handbook* (Westport, Conn.: Greenwood, 1986), p. 118.

political grounds, and Le Pen sued, winning an injunction in an administrative court. The mayor defied this ruling, attracting no particular criticism from the area newspapers, who were hostile to Le Pen. In the end he came to Strasbourg anyway, but he was forced to speak outdoors, behind police barricades. A year later Le Pen visited the area again and was again refused a public hall. This time he hired space in a local hotel, and, rather than suing again, led his supporters in a demonstration before the prefecture.[44]

The practicing bar, a natural ally of the judiciary in the Anglo-American system, is not well-organized to represent the shared interests of bench and bar in France. There is no mass-membership organization like the American Bar Association to engage the nation's attention on controversial legal issues important to lawyers, though beginning in the 1970s, some lawyers did form trade unions. French bar associations are local, with each attached to a particular court. Law firms also tend to be small, and many practitioners work alone. Nor has the legal profession succeeded in carving out a particularly lucrative niche in the national economy. *Notaires,* who are trained separately from lawyers, do some of the work that American lawyers do. They draft wills, mortgages, and other documents; they certify materials to be used as evidence in court; and they often become a family's trusted legal advisor. Often they advise all sides in the legal transactions in which they are involved. There are 55,000 notaires in France, which makes them more numerous than lawyers.[45]

For courtroom advocacy, one must hire an *avocat,* a subdivision of the profession that specializes in courtroom work.[46] There are about 31,000 avocats in France, but they do not enjoy the prestige (and notoriety) that litigators in common-law nations do. The organization of the courts, particularly the absence of juries, does not allow for the type of flamboyant advocacy associated with the American criminal defense or civil plaintiff's bar. Nor can French courtroom lawyers lay claim to the exclusivity associated with the English barristry or to the incomes associated with corporate practice in the United States. The contingent fee, an arrangement that makes civil litigation affordable and occasionally very profitable for American lawyers, does not

44. "Le Pen manifeste à la préfecture," *Dernières nouvelles d'Alsace,* Mar. 10, 1993, p. 3.

45. Ibid., p. 112.

46. This is a simplification. Before 1971, France had three types of lawyers who could plead in courts, *avocats, agrées* (who plead in commercial courts), and *avoués* (who plead in appellate courts). The 1971 legislation attempted to fuse the three groups by giving broader powers to avocats. But the effort at reform has not been entirely successful because magistrates in the appellate courts prefer avoués over avocats (Katz, supra note 43, p. 112). Until recently, some of these groups also competed with *conseils juridiques,* practitioners who now take the same courses and exams avocats do. Other specialists, *greffiers* (numbering about 1,000) and *huissiers* (numbering about 3,000), are attached to particular courts.

exist in France. To take a percentage of damages for a fee would be considered a shocking departure from appropriate professional practice. Instead, lawyers are paid at a state-set rate for representing clients, and they are entitled to charge an additional (unregulated) fee for their services. There is controversy over whether local bars should suggest suitable fees or hourly rates, a matter that remains unresolved because of concern that suggested fees will be set too low.[47]

State-regulated rates for common legal services and free legal counsel for people charged with crimes help to explain why access to attorneys is not a controversial issue in France. France's system of comprehensive health care and its network of administrative tribunals to hear workplace and other small-scale disputes also tends to lessen the demand for legal services because these tribunals are informal and people often represent themselves. Free state-sponsored mediation and conciliation services similarly help reduce demand for lawyers. The emphasis on available mechanisms for dispute resolution coexists, as noted earlier, with a de-emphasis on the development of legal doctrine through litigation. The decentralization of the legal profession into regional bars and distinctive specialities and the relatively low status of courts reinforce this tendency.

The next section considers the social-control function of courts in the French context. The control of crime is a serious political issue in France, as it is in the United States and England. Fear of crime appears to be growing even more rapidly in France than the crime rate. The French judiciary plays a largely facilitative role in the criminal justice system, as one might predict from its historical association with executive authority. The idea that judges might take an active role in protecting the rights of defendants against overweening state authority is much less well established. In France, primary responsibility for bringing the law into harmony with evolving standards of justice is conceived to lie outside the courts. This presents an anomaly for anyone raised on a diet of judicial review. How does France, with its strong executive and reticent judiciary, provide a sense of due process in the prosecution of crime?

Criminal Justice in France: An Overview of the Process

This section describes the process of investigation, prosecution, and trial of criminal cases in France, a framework that is significantly at variance with Anglo-American norms and traditions. It is tempting to conclude that the French system is less protective of individual rights, and, in a sense, that is

---

47. Anne Boigeol, "The French Bar: The Difficulties of Unifying a Divided Profession," in Richard Abel and Philip Lewis (eds.), *Lawyers in Society*, vol. 2 (1988), pp. 278–279.

true. But to focus solely on the weapons individuals can employ to contest state authority may be to ignore practical differences in people's capacity to advocate their interests. France downplays advocacy in favor of careful investigation by authorities, a strategy that has virtues that the English and American criminal justice systems lack. The approach has been dubbed "inquisitorial," in contrast to the Anglo-American "adversarial" tradition. Its weaknesses are most evident, not in the prosecution of ordinary crime, but when government officials themselves are the wrongdoers.

Crime is a preoccupation in France. Local newspapers always carry a detailed account of the previous day's criminal violence and news of ongoing investigations and trials. As in the United States, the media focus their attention on accusations against the famous and on the everyday crimes that are especially vicious or daring. The crime rate itself seldom made news until 1991, when it took an unexpected leap of 7.2 percent, the largest increase in a decade.[48] Thefts make up more than two-thirds of this total.[49]

France stands between the United States and Japan in rates of reported crime (see chapter 5). This rough marker of criminal activity, however, masks a distinction between France and the United States that bears noting. On the one hand, rates of crime against property in the two nations are rather similar. In 1990, for example, France reported 5.2 motor vehicle thefts per thousand population, while the United States reported 6.5 per thousand. Rates of violent crime in the two countries, however, are another matter. Assuming that police records in each nation bear a roughly comparable relationship to actual criminal activity, homicide in France occurs about half as often as in the United States. Armed robbery, which hit a high of 9,393 incidents in France during 1991, is still almost fifteen times less frequent than in the United States. Rape, which is also on the rise in France (at 5,068 in 1991 compared to 2,937 five years earlier), occurs one fifth as often.

The French government's response to crime is highly differentiated. Most juvenile, military, maritime, and workplace crimes go to specialized divisions of the trial courts. In recent years France has seized on possibilities for diverting other minor civil and criminal cases to nonjudicial forums like mediation centers. The government sponsors an association for research into dispute resolution alternatives, and the Ministry of Justice has been active in establishing centers, often as a court-provided service.[50] Diversion from the regular system is also the norm in the relatively rare instances where the

48. "Crimes et délits en expansion," *Dernières nouvelles d'Alsace* (May 12, 1992), p. 3.

49. Institut National de la Statistique et des Etudes Economiques, *Annuaire statistique de la France, 1991–92* 96 (1992), p. 810.

50. Marie-Clet Desdevises, *Revue de science criminelle et de droit pénal comparé* (1993), 45–61.

charge is misfeasance in high public office, such as parliament or the presidency. All such cases used to be heard in the High Court, a tribunal established shortly after the French Revolution. Failure of this court to effectively control misbehavior in office at lower levels, however, recently precipitated creation of a new tribunal, the Justice Court of the Republic. This system still leaves many cases of ordinary crime for the regular court system. Such cases are classified by their degree of seriousness and processed accordingly (see figure 4.1 for the basic dimensions of this system).

The least serious of the cases that go into the regular court system are *contraventions*, minor infractions like speeding or hunting out of season. Contraventions are punishable by fines up to 6,000F (about $1,200) and up to two months in jail. They are triable before a single judge in one of the nation's 473 police courts. These tend to be part-time tribunals whose judges also typically preside over civil cases; in such circumstances they operate as *tribunaux d'instance*.[51]

The type of criminal activity that would be a misdemeanor or a low-grade felony in the U.S. court system is a *délit* in France. Délits are heard in the nation's 181 correctional tribunals. These three-judge courts, like the police courts, also double as civil courts (*tribunaux de grande instance*) and as appellate tribunals (for appeals from police courts). Punishments range from two months to ten years. There is no right to a jury trial in these cases, but there is a right to appeal to the next court up in the judicial hierarchy, one of the regional courts of appeal.[52]

The most serious transgressions, such a murder and armed robbery, are *crimes*, some of which are punishable by life imprisonment. These cases are triable in the nation's ninety-nine regional *assises* courts. These are specialized courts with no function other than to try serious criminal cases. The assises court operates with a three-judge panel and a jury of nine lay persons. There is no appeal from the court's judgment, except by way of a *pourvoi en cassation*, a petition to the nation's highest court to affirm or annul the application of law in the case.[53] The distinction between findings of fact, which are deemed final after trial, and application of law, which is subject to appeal, is similar to Anglo-American procedures. France, however, has no equivalent to the ancient writ of habeas corpus, an English tradition incorporated into the U.S. Constitution that permits prisoners to petition for release on grounds of illegal imprisonment.

51. Xavier Blanc-Jouvan and Jean Boulouis, "France," in *International Encyclopedia of Comparative Law* (New York: Oxford, 1991), p. F–54; and see Institut National de la Statistique et des Etudes Economiques, *Annuaire statistique de la France, 1991–92*, 96 (1992), p. 807.

52. Ibid.; and see Ministry of Justice, *Guide des droits des victimes* (Paris: Gallimard, 1982), pp. 17–18.

53. Ministry of Justice, supra note 52, p. 37.

There are also important differences between French and Anglo-American approaches to the investigation and prosecution of crime. France draws a sharp distinction between investigation and trial, and involves the judiciary deeply in the investigatory phase. A special judge, called a *juge d'instruction* (examining magistrate), is in charge of the criminal investigation and is responsible for filing a report on its progress. This report goes to the chief judge of the panel that will try the case. The report furnishes the trial judge with the information he or she will need in order to question witnesses, including the defendant. This system provides French citizens with surprisingly little protection against police intrusions pursuant to an investigation. The issue is not simply the failure of the examining magistrate to exercise authority to prevent police and prosecutorial abuses, but the attitude of the law itself.

THE PRESUMPTION OF INNOCENCE IN FRENCH LAW

French law makes no promise to citizens that they can remain at liberty absent reliable evidence that they are guilty of a crime. Instead, the law requires citizens to cooperate with reasonable police investigations. The duty to cooperate involves submitting to police inquiries about one's identity and other matters, and may also include detention at police headquarters for up to twenty-four hours for more extensive questioning. Prior judicial approval is not necessary if police suspect a person may have committed a crime. The period, called *garde à vue*, can be extended another twenty-four hours on a prosecutor's say-so.

The emphasis on police investigation over citizen rights has a long history in France. Napoleon relied heavily on police forces to consolidate and centralize his power, and spying and violent repression were commonplace during that era. Secrecy and strict discipline remain hallmarks of the police, as does the idea that the police represent government, not the people.[54]

The organization of police forces in France reflects a preoccupation with protecting central authority against disorder. One branch of the police, the Gendarmerie Nationale (GN), is part of the Ministry of Defense, while the other, the Police Nationale (PN), is under the Ministry of the Interior. Both the GN and the PN have elite units trained to control riots, and members of the GN's Gendarmerie Mobile live in barracks and undergo paramilitary training for that purpose. The GN is also likely to be involved when terrorism threatens. The 1994 arrest of the long-time fugitive terrorist Carlos, for example, was the work of the Groupe d'Intervention de la Gendarmerie Nationale, a branch of the GN.

54. Erika Fairchild, *Comparative Criminal Justice Systems* (Belmont, Calif.: Wadsworth, 1993), p. 67.

Even in areas unrelated to terrorism and riot control, France emphasizes centralized authority in policing. France gives its national police forces much more enforcement authority than the United States does, for example. Housing regulation, work on the census, health code enforcement, and other matters Americans would leave to administrative agencies come under police authority in France. France also makes a sharp distinction between its central cities and outlying areas, assigning the PN to Paris and the cities, and the GN to the rural areas. But the PN also has duties that involve officers in urban problems. Within the PN, the operational divisions (*police judicaire*) are responsible for investigating crimes. They work under the supervision of the court system. Most references in this chapter are thus to the police judicaire.

Judicial controls on police are significantly less than in the United States, not so much because of organizational factors, but because the rules demand less sensitivity to the rights of citizens. Until 1994, for example, police did not even need evidence that a prospective detainee was guilty of a crime. The procedure could be invoked against anyone believed to have relevant information. Police were entitled to hold such persons virtually incommunicado, which meant no calls for up to twenty-four hours to family members, to an attorney, or even to summon medical assistance. The law prohibited and punished physical abuse, but not psychological intimidation. This broad power to detain is curiously at odds with the much narrower right of the police to search private property in the course of a criminal investigation.[55]

Parliament modified the authority of the police to detain persons on their own authority when it revised the code of criminal procedure in December 1992. Witnesses who are not implicated in crimes can no longer be held in garde à vue absent unusual circumstances, and those who are in custody have a right to call their families and to summon medical help at the onset of detention. Consultation with a lawyer is also permitted, but only for thirty minutes. This last reform was introduced gradually. No change was to occur in the first months after promulgation; after March 1993, the right to see a lawyer took effect after twenty hours of questioning. Not until January 1994 did one have the right to see a lawyer immediately, except in cases involving suspected terrorists, where the law provided for up to forty-eight hours without seeing counsel. It remains unclear whether lawyers will actually be available to detainees who cannot afford counsel—the government has made no arrangements to compensate attorneys for visits to garde à vue.

Other sections of the new law revise France's arraignment and pretrial detention procedure, which had become an embarrassment to the government. Under the old system, the prosecutor could prolong a suspect's de-

---

55. Vroom, supra note 3.

tention long after garde à vue by making a case for detention before the examining magistrate, who often followed the state's recommendation. In 1990, for example, more than 40 percent of those incarcerated were being held in pretrial detention; 11 percent of these people were eventually acquitted of all charges.[56] The average detention period had grown steadily since 1970, and by 1990 it had reached three and a half months, with 35 of every 100,000 inhabitants being held (see figure 4.2). France, critics note, leads Europe with more unconvicted people behind bars than Turkey or East Germany before unification.[57] The situation was even worse a decade earlier (see figure 4.2). In the early 1980s over half of those confined were awaiting trial, a rate that only Italy exceeded among the nineteen member states of the Council of Europe.[58]

The new law attempts to establish a presumption of innocence in the early stages of prosecution, a principal objective being to make it more difficult to incarcerate people before trial. The examining magistrate no longer has the authority to decide whether or not detention is necessary. The legislation vests this decision with the *président* of the court during the first year after promulgation, and then with a three-member panel composed of a judge (other than the examining magistrate) and two lay persons who have no ongoing relationship with the court. The detainee will have a right to go before a judge every three and a half months for a hearing and to request exculpatory investigations. Those who are being investigated but who have not been detained are entitled to notification that they are suspects.

Police groups and judicial associations opposed many of these changes. Opposition from examining magistrates has been particularly intense. Some judges have criticized the requirement that they notify persons under investigation, warning that this may allow criminals to escape or to intimidate witnesses. Judges have also expressed concern that the new law will allow seasoned criminals to act with impunity and that the reforms neglect the rights of victims.[59] The vice president of one of the national judges associations, Jean-François Richard, complained that with the new law France had created a system of ''deux vitesses'' (two speeds)—one for the rich and powerful, the other for the poor. In the weeks following promulgation, 127 of the nation's approximately 600 examining magistrates demanded that they be relieved of their duties.[60]

56. ''Des transformations plus que des bouleversements,'' *Le Monde*, Dec. 23, 1992, p. 10.

57. ''Les juges ne décolèrent pas,'' *Dernières nouvelles d'Alsace*, Jan. 13, 1993, p. 4.

58. André Ortolland, ''La justice,'' *Notes et études documentaires* (1985), p. 117.

59. ''Les juges ne décolèrent pas,'' supra note 57.

60. ''La jacquerie des juges,'' *L'Express,* Feb. 4, 1993, p. 15; and see ''Les juges ne décolèrent pas,'' supra note 57.

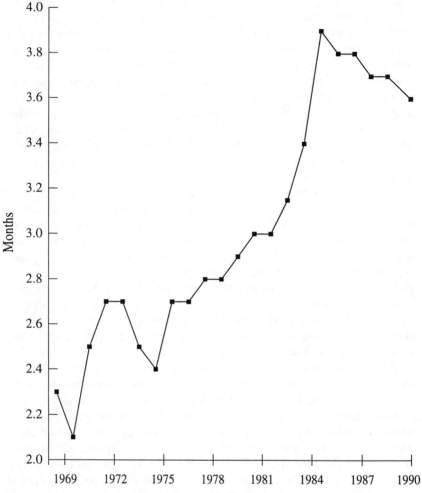

Figure 4.2. Average Length of Pretrial Detention in France

Their reaction to the new law suggests that many examining magistrates identify themselves more with law enforcement than with protection of the rights of the accused. Daily interaction with police and prosecutors may well condition examining magistrates to favor the long-term interests of regular participants over those of the accused, a problem Blumberg has identified with the criminal justice system in the United States.[61] The difference is that

61. Abraham Blumberg, *Criminal Justice: Issues and Ironies*, 2d ed. (New York: New Viewpoints, 1967).

in the United States, the focus of concern has been the independence of counsel for the defense, while in France, concern focuses on the independence of the examining magistrate.

The significance of the examining magistrate in the pretrial process in France points to a fundamental difference between civil-law nations like France and common-law jurisdictions like the United States and England. In Anglo-American systems, the crucial event is trial, and the appropriate metaphor is combat, with defense counsel taking primary responsibility for articulating the interests of the accused. The civil-law alternative that France represents envisions a more cooperative relationship between participants, with careful investigation at the heart of the criminal process. Plea-bargaining is not part of the process because of the expectation that trial will occur, whether or not the defendant confesses.

Active judicial involvement in the preparation of the case for trial also tends to reduce the role of defense counsel in protecting the defendant's rights. The examining magistrate, who is responsible for assuring the quality of the investigation that underlies the prosecution, enjoys sweeping powers. In serious cases the magistrate directs the investigation personally, ordering any potentially relevant witnesses to appear and authorizing searches of premises, seizure of financial records, examination by experts, and viewings of physical evidence as he or she sees fit. The examining magistrate can delegate some investigatory decisions to the police, but the responsibility lies ultimately with the magistrate.

As broad as these powers are, they are not unbounded. At the initial appearance, the magistrate is required to tell defendants of their right to remain silent and to offer free counsel to defendants who can not afford to hire their own. Failure to do so nullifies any subsequent statement provided by the accused. At no point in the investigation may the accused be called as a witness. In examining other witnesses, the defense enjoys at least a limited right to influence the direction of the investigation: it can ask the examining magistrate to pose certain questions; refusal to do so must be explained in writing and is subject to appeal. Nor does the examining magistrate have sole discretion over whether or not to send serious cases forward for trial; an indicting chamber performs a role similar to that of an American grand jury in assises cases.[62]

CRIMINAL TRIALS

The trial provides an additional check on the quality of the pretrial investigation. At the trial the examining magistrate retires from the scene, and the

62. G. E. P. Brouwer, "Inquisitorial and Adversary Procedures—A Comparative Analysis," *Australian Law Journal* 55 (1981), p. 215.

chief trial judge takes over. Many of the safeguards we associate with criminal trials in the United States operate in France as well. The trial is public, and the state carries the burden of proof for every element of the crime. Witnesses are put under oath and questioned. The state wins a conviction in the most serious cases only by persuading a jury of laypersons (and judges) of the defendant's guilt. The lay participants are selected with the participation of counsel. Even in less serious cases, a panel of three judges must be persuaded.

A criminal trial in France, however, is in many respects a continuation of the pretrial investigation. A judicial officer (this time the chief judge) continues to dominate the process, asking or approving all questions presented to witnesses, who testify at length, without interruption by counsel. There is no cross-examination. The trial also features a lengthy interrogation of the accused by the chief judge. The accused can remain silent, but because negative inferences will almost certainly be drawn from this strategy, the accused usually testifies. The examination ranges widely into the defendant's past, probing attitudes toward schooling, early relationship with parents, drug use, and other matters related to the defendant's character and potential for rehabilitation. Character assessment, in fact, is the sole objective of this interrogation in many cases because guilt is not really at issue. To encourage frank disclosure, the accused is not put under oath and cannot be prosecuted for perjury.

Throughout the trial the jury sits arrayed on both sides of the chief judge and the two associate judges. Together they form a long, impressive bench at the front of the courtroom. Jurors can pass notes to the chief judge with questions they would like to have posed, but they do not question the witnesses themselves. The French jury includes nine laypersons drawn from a panel of twenty-seven local residents. Selection occurs at the outset of the trial, when the chief judge draws names from a large urn. The names are provided to defense counsel a few days beforehand. Both the defense and the prosecution have the right to challenge (that is, object to) particular jurors, though they must do so without the detailed inquiry into a candidate's background and beliefs that has become typical in seating a jury in the United States. The defense can prevent up to five potential jurors from sitting; the prosecutor, up to four. Neither side is obliged to explain its reasons for rejection.

Judicial input into the trial continues when the jury retires to deliberate because judges are part of the jury. During deliberations, which are held in secret, the judges may be active participants. They cannot entirely dominate the process, however. Votes on guilt and sentencing are taken by secret ballot, and balloting rules require a majority of eight in deciding the defendant's guilt. Three like-minded judges would have to persuade at least five jurors in order to convict. Sentencing decisions are by majority vote. When all of these decisions have been made and recorded, the jury returns to the court-room and the chief judge announces its decision.

Criminal trials in France are distinctive, not only in leaving much to the chief judge, but in providing assistance to the crime victim. France allows victims to seek damages through the criminal process, the *partie civile* joining the action at the outset. So-called moral damage, such as loss of a loved one, is a sufficient ground for seeking damages, which will be assessed by the jury at the end of the criminal trial if there is a conviction. The victim also has the option of suing for damages in civil court, but piggy-backing on the criminal trial is ordinarily much easier.[63] The victim can use this process even if the prosecutor decides not to pursue the case. In this situation the victim becomes the moving party and the examining magistrate provides the necessary assistance.[64]

The right of private parties to join a criminal action can occasionally propel a case or a cause into the public spotlight. Representatives of feminist organizations, for example, became parties civiles when France began to prosecute immigrant parents and the persons they hired to perform genital mutilation on their infant daughters. GAMS, a group dedicated to the abo-lition of sexual mutilation, estimated in 1984 that 23,000 girls were at risk in France. The legal issues in these cases centered on whether genital muti-lation is a crime and, if so, at what level it should be prosecuted. The penal code, not surprisingly, is vague on the subject, and the government was in-clined to treat these cases gingerly. The first case, filed in 1979, was tried in police court before a magistrate. The feminist organizations appearing as parties civiles exercised their right to appeal, and the higher courts declared genital mutilation to be a crime (using the specific French meaning) prose-cutable in the assises court before a jury. Some of the defendants also got political mileage from these cases, engaging expert "ethnopsychiatrists" to argue that the women charged were not criminally responsible because their subordination to custom and to their husbands was analogous to an irresistible force, a defense to prosecution under the penal code.[65] The litigation thus

63. The civil party does have a problem if there is an acquittal in the criminal case. An acquittal in criminal court is also binding in a subsequent civil action, according to a 1921 decision of the Court of Cassation. The decision has encouraged legislative efforts to allow indemnification of victims even in cases where there is no conviction. See Michèle-Laure Rassat, *Droit pénal* (Paris: Presses Universitaires de France, 1988), 367–368.

64. Ministry of Justice, supra note 52, pp. 26–33.

65. The history of the prosecutions and the political debate is recounted in detail in Bronwyn Winter, "Women, the Law, and Cultural Relativism in France: The Case of Excision," *Signs* 19 (1994), 939–974.

highlighted a long-simmering debate over the assimilation of immigrants into French society.[66]

The French approach to criminal justice avoids many of the pitfalls associated with the more adversarial approach to trial in England and the United States. French witnesses do not have to deal with punishing cross-examinations or complex hearsay rules, which are frequently arbitrary in application. The accused gets to speak at length and on subjects like childhood abuse that may encourage the jury to be lenient. Victims, represented throughout the trial and eligible for damages, are guaranteed their own day in court. The chief judge does not have to deliver a lengthy formal speech charging the jury, an exercise that creates opportunities for appellate reversal, and, frequently, confusion in the jury. Judicial participation in jury deliberations reduces mistakes and discourages improper racial and other biases.

It is probably impossible to determine, in the abstract, which system is more likely to uncover the truth of allegations against a defendant. France relies on the quality and professionalism of its magistrates. The United States and England place significantly more responsibility on defense counsel and on the capacity of an adversarial contest to uncover the truth. Rudolph Schlesinger highlights this difference by suggesting that if you were guilty and could choose between a trial on the French model or an adversarial contest based on Anglo-American principles, you would be wise to choose the French variety and select the worst lawyer you could find to defend you. This strategy would be certain to arouse the court's sympathy and best efforts in your behalf.[67]

The French approach to criminal justice tends to reduce disparities of treatment attributable to a suspect's wealth. The active role of the judge during investigation and trial tends to minimize the impact of whatever advantage there may be in hiring expensive private counsel. The state's power to detain suspects also has an equality-enhancing aspect. Lacking the escape-hatch of bail, France detains rich and poor alike when this seems necessary to an investigation. When professional soccer player Bernard Beffy was implicated in a recent corruption scandal, for example, he remained subject to interrogation despite the protests of his lawyer, Thierry Herzog, that his client "had become a hostage."[68] Beffy was in a position to air his dilemma in a national newspaper, but not to purchase his freedom.

66. See generally Patrick R. Ireland, *The Policy Challenge of Ethnic Diversity: Immigrant Politics in France and Switzerland* (Cambridge, Mass.: Harvard University Press, 1994).

67. Quoted in W. Zeidler, "Evaluation of the Adversary System: A Comparison," *Australian Law Journal* 55 (1981), p. 390.

68. Dino Dimeo and Christian Jaurena, "Affaire om-va: Une journée qui rebondit," *Libération*, June 30, 1993, p. 26.

The debate over the new criminal procedure law suggests the significance the French attach to the value of equality in the criminal justice
process. The decision to allow the defense more input into the detention
decision evoked fears that France is moving toward a system of justice
with one type of justice for rich or well-connected defendants with out-
spoken lawyers, and another type of justice for the obscure and the poor.
The debate over the new law also shows that the French realize that there
is a downside to a judge-dominated system. Trial judges, supporters of the
new law have argued, defer too often to examining magistrates in sentencing, sending those who have been held for long periods in pretrial detention to long prison terms on the grounds that they must be dangerous.
It is significant that France dealt with this problem, not by curtailing sentencing authority, but by reducing the discretion of the examining magistrate to order pretrial detention.

THE PROBLEM OF RIGHTS

In both France and the United States, judges are entrusted with the protection
of rights of persons who fall under the suspicion of authorities, but there are
significant differences in what each country expects judges to do. Americans
have grown accustomed to the idea that courts will play an active role, not
just in applying procedural rules, but also in shaping those rules to bring
them into line with constitutional requirements. Appellate judges, especially
those sitting on the U.S. Supreme Court, do much of the constitutional stan-
dard-setting. The project continues even with the appointment of ostensibly
less activist justices and judges. Indeed, one could say that the United States
has responded to the problem of rights in criminal justice by constitutional-
izing every step of the process.

France has taken a more pragmatic approach, using legislation to build
specific protections into criminal investigation and prosecution. Examining
magistrates take hands-on responsibility for the rights of the individual under
investigation. Trial judges work directly with juries. Appellate judges provide
after-the-fact review, but without attempting to craft broad policy guidelines
to cover every eventuality. Legal tradition encourages judicial reticence. Critics charge that the judiciary has not done nearly enough to control police
excesses, which, they claim, are an everyday reality in France.[69] Is this criticism justified? Or do such critics assume, wrongly, that the only effective
way to protect the individual against overweening state authority is to establish judicial review on the American model?

69. Michel Masse, "Protection procédurale contre les abus de la police et droit français,"
in Hélène Dumont and Michel Moreau (eds.), *Public Administration in Developed Democracies*
(New York: Marcel Dekker, 1988), p. 245.

The criticism that French appellate courts have not been active enough in protecting individuals is, in at least one sense, unjustified. Lacking a tradition of policy-oriented intervention, the courts can hardly be expected to step out of character and begin to fashion a panoply of enforceable rights from constitutional guarantees. French appellate courts *have* taken some tentative steps in this direction, but this movement is no stampede, and it is not likely to gather much momentum without political support.[70] And such support does not appear to be forthcoming. In the contemporary debate over criminal justice reform, for example, one does not hear arguments that France could solve its problems by investing its judges with a broad review power. Nor was there appreciable support in 1990 when Mitterrand proposed to rewrite the constitution to provide for judicial review.

France's historical reluctance to let its courts construe the constitution does have consequences for contemporary French people. The state's tepid response to widespread criticism of garde à vue illustrates the problem. Pretrial detention is a political bombshell—a police practice that is at once resented and accepted as a necessary element in the effort to fight crime. In 1994 alleged police excesses in apprehending and detaining immigrants provoked mass demonstrations in Paris. In the United States, courts sometimes rescue a legislature faced with such ticklish issues, fashioning a controversial policy in their role as interpreters of the constitution. This is not possible in France. The problem for the French parliament is not simply that it cannot turn the matter over to courts, but that it cannot rely on judicial precedent to bolster support for legislative policies that are politically risky.

In assessing the capacity of the French system of criminal justice to protect individual rights, it is important to recognize that the American version of constitutional review has these dual functions. It is both a check (on the other branches) and a deposit (of authoritative argument on the meaning of the constitution and its applicability to contemporary problems). It is easy to overlook this second process of accumulating a body of relevant precedent. Scholars tend to dwell on the turning points, those the cases in which a court first claims a new power. The overall record, which would indicate the degree of oversight being exercised, may be ignored.[71] But a look at the political history of constitutional courts indicates that judicial review becomes politically meaningful only by increments: a record of constitutional interpretation is essential if a court is to play a significant political role.

A comparison of due process protections that focused only on judicial decisions interpreting constitutional rights would thus be seriously misleading, not only because France is in a period of change, but because the two

70. Cappelletti, supra note 33.
71. See ibid.

systems differ in the degree to which they rely on this means of checking state authority. As noted above, the United States, for historical reasons, has placed a great deal of faith in the capacity of its courts to maintain individual rights, while France has taken a more diversified approach. We have already discussed the role of the Constitutional Council, which reviews most criminal justice legislation for constitutional defects. There are significant checks built into the process of investigation and adjudication. The examining magistrate is in a position to oversee police activities during the pretrial process. The system of administrative courts also provides some protection against police and prosecutorial excesses. At the same time, the system encourages a degree of professionalism in prosecutors, whose education and status are equivalent to that of examining magistrates.[72] Most of these checking mechanisms do not exist in the United States.

The two countries also differ in their willingness to allow external review of their procedures for dealing with accused persons. The European Convention for the Protection of Human Rights and Fundamental Freedoms provides a detailed set of criminal justice norms for all signatory states to follow. Criminal defendants from all over Europe have not hesitated to invoke these norms to challenge their convictions. The Commission and Court on Human Rights, having considered more cases in this area than in any other, have produced a rich and nuanced jurisprudence on criminal due process. These bodies have rendered several significant decisions that put France on notice that it will have to reform high-handed police and prosecutorial practices to bring itself in line with European standards. As early as 1984, just three years after France made itself amenable to individual petition, French judges had applied the Convention in more than three hundred of their reported cases.[73] Of the cases that eventually went to the Commission and Court for final resolution, perhaps the most notorious is the *Tomasi* case, decided on August 27, 1992. Félix Tomasi was acquitted of charges of murder after spending five years and seven months in pretrial detention. The Strasbourg court obliged France to pay Tomasi a million francs for his legal costs and damages.[74]

72. In France prosecutors are the *magistrature debout*, literally, the standing judiciary, while judges are the *magistrature assise*, or the sitting judiciary. The prosecution, both the office itself and its representatives, is also referred to as *le parquet*, a reference that dates back to pre-revolutionary days when the prosecutor had a fixed place to stand on the wooden floor of the courtroom.

73. See Raymond Leglais, "Constitution française, Convention Européenne des Droits de l'Homme et protection des personnes contre les abus policiers," in Hélène Dumont and Michel Moreau, *Droits de l'individu et police* (Paris: Editions Themis, 1990), p. 240.

74. *Human Rights Reports* 15 (1993), p. A/241-A.

It is hard to imagine an equivalent willingness in the United States to submit domestic practices to outside review and revision. The prevailing belief in the United States has been that the Constitution is an adequate source of rights and that our own domestic courts are an adequate source of interpretative authority. The consequence for criminal justice is that U.S. courts, particularly the Supreme Court, have become a lightning rod for public frustration with the shortcomings of law enforcement. The American approach to rights may even have the perverse effect of reducing public scrutiny of the system's day-to-day activities. The complex process of implementing judge-declared procedural rights tends to dampen the government's enthusiasm for trial, and no countervailing considerations encourage this form of public participation. The adversary tradition, in fact, discounts the public's stake in criminal justice. The prosecutor and the defense have sole discretion over whether the case will be aired in public and submitted to laypersons for judgment. The result is ironic: most cases in the United States are disposed of in secret, by plea-bargaining, with little oversight by judges and none by the public.

The French criminal justice system, in short, is paternalistic and, frequently, intrusive. An aggressive criminal defense lawyer in France will find fewer protections for a client than are available in the American system. But it is also likely that the average criminal will receive more considerate treatment in France than in the United States—the full airing of life circumstances that France prescribes inclines the system toward lighter penalties. In serious cases, such as prosecution for murder, the differences are particularly dramatic. It is not unusual, for example, for a murderer to receive a five-year sentence in a French court.

What happens when the tables are turned and citizens accuse the state of criminal activity? If government does not respond effectively to claims that it has acted criminally, the legitimacy of the regime will be cast in doubt. But a country that does not stress limits on legitimate government authority is unlikely to instill strong protections against government malfeasance. Public cynicism about the capacity of the government to cleanse itself can be anticipated. The recent struggle to assess criminal liability for the French government's distribution of blood contaminated with the AIDS virus illustrates this problem.

CRIMES BY THE GOVERNMENT: THE SIDA SCANDAL

Between July and October 1985, French public health officials allowed at least 1.6 million units of blood to go into circulation, knowing they were probably contaminated with the AIDS (in French, SIDA) virus. This decision resulted in the infection of approximately one thousand people, most them hemophiliacs and many of them children. Three hundred of these people had died by 1993.[75] In the Paris region, 60 to 90 percent of hemophiliacs are infected, probably a world record.[76]

France's course of action was risky in several respects:

- Officials delayed approval of a U.S.-produced test for the presence of the AIDS virus.
- They prohibited importation of treated blood and exported untreated blood products.
- They continued to gather blood from prisons, even in the face of evidence that a high proportion of the prison population was HIV positive.

In all of these decisions, economic considerations outweighed concern for public health. The scandal provoked a political crisis that helped to drive the ruling Socialists from power. It also created a legal crisis.

Fateful Choices

The scientific world became aware of the relationship between blood and AIDS only gradually. Most of the initial diagnoses of AIDS involved male homosexuals, which had encouraged speculation that sperm was the sole vector. Not until January 1982 did the U.S. Centers for Disease Control confirm a case of AIDS in a hemophiliac. Suspicions that blood might be an agent of infection grew as the number of such cases accumulated. A March 1983 article in *Transfusion,* a well-known journal among hematologists, noted eight American cases and warned that blood transfusions were the probable source of infection. By June of that year the Pasteur Institute claimed to have discovered the retrovirus that causes AIDS.

At this point there was no way to be sure whether or not existing blood supplies were contaminated with the AIDS virus, or even the extent of infection among hemophiliacs. It was clear, however, that modern methods of treating hemophilia vastly increased the risk of some blood-borne diseases. Hemophiliacs lack coagulating-inducing proteins, the most common of which is called factor 8. The early treatment, transfusion of whole blood, provided an inefficient means of introducing the essential proteins. Scientists later discovered a procedure for pooling blood supplies, freezing the plasma, and isolating factor 8 in the sediment. As many as 5,000 specimens may be pooled in this procedure, which creates a product that can be dried and shipped in convenient powdered form. The disadvantage of the new procedure is that one donor with an infectious disease, such as hepatitis, can con-

---

75. Mark Hunter, "Blood Money," *Discover* 14 (August 1993), p. 71.

76. Michel de Pracontal, "La dernière parade du docteur Garretta," *Le Nouvel Observateur,* July 30, 1992, pp. 12–15, p. 13.

taminate the entire lot. The HIV virus, scientists eventually realized, posed the same risk.

France was nevertheless committed to this procedure. The government licensed seven regional centers to produce factor 8 from blood donated at these and other government-approved collection points. At the hub of this system and larger than the rest is the Paris-based National Center for Blood Transfusions (CNTS), which supplies about half of the nation's blood needs. In 1982 the Ministry of Health gave CNTS a monopoly on the importation of foreign blood supplies and provided loans to increase the center's productive capacity. The ministry made its long-term objective clear: to move France toward self-sufficiency in supplying its blood needs by 1985.[77] Locally collected and processed blood, it was felt, would be cheaper and purer than what could be purchased on the world market.

In France, as elsewhere, concerns that blood supplies might be at risk had encouraged efforts to produce a reliable test of potential donors and a means of "cleaning" donated blood. By the fall of 1984, a scientist at the Pasteur Institute had developed a prototype test for screening donors. Others in France and abroad were experimenting with ways to isolate and destroy the HIV virus in factor 8 and other blood products. The method of choice by 1984 was heat, which apparently killed the virus. This approach was much discussed at the July 1984 meeting of the International Blood Transfusion Society in Munich. By the end of the year, both the U.S. Centers for Disease Control and associations of American hemophiliacs were recommending that unheated blood products be avoided.

French public health officials were aware of these developments, although for a long time they discounted the risk to French blood supplies. The government even stepped up its program to collect blood from prison inmates in January 1984. Officials reasoned that France, which did not offer payment for blood, would be protected by the public-spiritedness of its blood donors. Only nations that bought blood, like the United States, need fear contamination through donation by high-risk groups like drug addicts. As Jean Ducos, president of the consulting commission on blood transfusion, explained: "In the United States, accidents tend to happen where donors are paid. These people tend to live in miserable conditions, and they are often homosexuals, drug addicts, and Haitian immigrants."[78] Ducos did not realize that the free sandwiches and coffee handed out at French collection centers attracted many addicted donors.[79]

77. "Le sang contaminé," one of a series of articles, most without individual authorship, *Libération Spécial Sang*, May 1993, p. 18.

78. Ibid., p. 34.

79. See Hunter, supra note 75, p. 72. Jacques Roux, director general of health, was something of an exception to the general rule of bland optimism. On June 20, 1983, Roux wrote the

Some French AIDS researchers, concerned about the dangers, did contact journalists during this period. *Libération* began to cover the story, but met with stonewalling from CNTS officials. Their persistence precipitated a July 8, 1993, counterattack from top officials in the Pasteur Institute, who argued that the press should show more respect for their expertise. The institute finally sued *Libération* for its July 7 article entitled "Four Bodies in the Cupboard at the IPP" (the Pasteur Institute). The Institute won a one-million franc judgment and a temporary reprieve from adverse news coverage.[80]

Evidence that France's supply of factor 8 and other blood products were contaminated nevertheless began to accumulate. Many CNTS researchers were aware, for example, of a study of 133 French hemophiliacs which showed a high incidence of AIDS. A March 13 in-house conference at CNTS included a presentation of this research. The agency also heard from Dr. François Pinion, chief of hematology at one of the largest hospitals in Paris. Pinion called CNTS and the Ministry of Health on December 12, 1984, to voice his concern about the results of tests he had conducted on his hospital's blood supplies. The tests showed high levels of contamination in the factor 8 supplies that CNTS had provided the hospital. Pinon's alarm must have confirmed what some in the CNTS hierarchy already believed. Jean-Pierre Allain, the center's research chief, had for some time taken pains to import heat-treated products for a young hemophiliac he had taken into his home.[81]

The July 1984 Munich meeting marked France's first tentative steps toward eliminating contaminated blood products. Michel Garretta, then assistant director of CNTS, used the occasion to initiate negotiations about heat treatment with Immuno, an Austrian firm.[82] Garretta closed this deal in February 1985. The problem was that Immuno could not begin production for several months. The only safe solution was to import heat-treated blood products until Immuno could catch up with the domestic demand. This, however, would be costly and would put CNTS behind in the effort to minimize dependence on imported products.

Concern for the safety of those who depend on blood products also required that CNTS withdraw nonheated blood supplies from circulation.

---

nation's collection centers to warn them to be wary of donations from known risk groups, but no one seems to have taken this letter very seriously. (See Hunter, p. 76 and *Libération Spécial Sang*, supra note 77, p. 22.) The letter was not sent to prison administrators. Nor did Roux take further steps to warn of the danger. He was later convicted for his role in the blood scandal.

80. Josette Atlia, "Ceux qui ne voulaient pas savoir," *Le Nouvel Observateur*, Nov. 12, 1992, p. 31.

81. Hunter, supra note 75, p. 76.

82. This was not the first such proposal Garretta had entertained. On May 10, 1983, an American company, Tavenol, had proposed a method of heat-treating French blood supplies. Garretta turned down Tavenol.

Safety, it turned out, was not the primary consideration in Garretta's calculations. Garretta was concerned about the cost of destroying existing stocks of factor 8 and other blood products. He calculated these costs and deemed them prohibitive. It would be necessary, he decided, to work out a "compromise," using up contaminated blood stocks until domestic production of safe blood products became sufficient to satisfy demand. He recommended using the old, contaminated stocks for a few more months. Imported heat-treated blood would be banned, and requests to use heat-treated blood would be discouraged.[83] This decision was made with a clear understanding that the existing blood stocks were contaminated, and it was not made alone. Garretta discussed the problem at a May 29, 1985, meeting with representatives of the relevant ministries and other CNTS officials. The notes of this meeting, later published in the media, indicate that CNTS officials estimated the rate of contamination at 100 percent.

Cost considerations also played a role in a French decision to delay approval of an American test that could identify AIDS-infected blood donors. On February 11, 1985, the American firm of Abbott requested French approval of its test, which was in the final stages of the licensing process in the United States. The American test would be half as expensive as a French prototype that was not yet in production. The dilemma was whether to approve the American test and lose the French market to foreign competition, or to delay long enough to let the French catch up. A domestic market of 91 million francs ($11 million) was at stake.

Once again, officials put cost ahead of human lives. Abbott renewed its application in April, which provoked a letter from Robert Netter, director of the National Laboratory of Health, that "to delay much longer runs the risk that someone will seek recourse in the Council of State." The problem was discussed at a May 9 meeting that included representatives of Prime Minister Laurent Fabius, and representatives from the ministries of health, commerce, social affairs, and finance. Their decision to delay Abbott's approval a bit longer did protect the French market. Had they quickly approved the Abbott test, however, up to 2,210 lives would have been spared.[84] Fabius, who was later to deny any knowledge of the decision to delay approval of the American test, gave its French competitor a boost when, on June 19, he announced that testing of blood donors would soon be compulsory. The French test became available two days later. Abbott's test, on the other hand, did not win approval until July 25.[85]

83. *Libération Spécial Sang*, supra note 77, p. 18.

84. Annie Kouchner, "Un test français sinon rien," *L'Express*, Nov. 8, 1991, pp. 21, 16.

85. *Libération Spécial Sang, supra* note 77, p. 16. France is not the only nation where public health officials have been obliged to explain why they discounted the AIDS threat. In

The Criminal Process

This series of events created what one reporter dubbed "a French SIDA-gate."[86] AIDS-infected hemophiliacs brought criminal proceedings against Garretta (who had assumed the directorship of CNTS), his associate director, Jean-Pierre Allain; Netter; and Jacques Roux, director general of health. The outraged hemophiliacs also sought to implicate three members of Mitterrand's cabinet: Laurent Fabius; Georgina Dufoix, minister of social affairs; and Edmond Hervé, secretary of state for health. Bringing the ministers to justice proved more difficult than prosecuting the doctors.

All the initiative in both cases came from hemophiliacs. Many victims also filed administrative claims for compensation, and a few brought civil suits, naming CNTS and other transfusion centers as defendants. The government's role in the criminal case against Garretta, Allain, Netter, and Roux was more complicated. Victims, as injured parties, have a right to initiate a criminal prosecution in French law, as noted earlier. When this happens, the government usually undertakes prosecution of the case on behalf of the civil parties and on behalf of the citizenry at large. But in this instance, the state prosecutor at first played a surprisingly passive role "like a stranger to the case."[87] The prosecutor's reticence paralleled that of other government representatives. The media's revelations of official misconduct initially brought forth no official apologies, no internal investigations, and no offers of compensation. Not until it became clear that its liability for damages would be immense did the government finally did offer compensation: 100,000 francs (about $20,000) to victims and their families in return for a promise not to sue. More than 1,000 of the 1,200 victims accepted this offer. Many were desperate for funds to deal with their escalating health problems and fearful of the time and expense of civil litigation. Those who did bring such suits received much more than the government had offered in settlement, some collecting as much as two million francs (about $400,000).

The victims filed their first complaint in the correctional tribunal in Paris, a court that hears délits. Examining magistrate Sabine Foulon took charge of what turned out to be a four-year investigation. The initial problem was in

---

Switzerland the Red Cross has been sued for negligence in protecting blood recipients. In Germany the Minister of Health has been asked to resign after conceding that at least 373 patients in German hospitals were given transfusions of blood infected with HIV. The Ministry claims that most of these transfusions occurred before 1985 (i.e., before the danger was known), while critics charge that improper risks were taken because of ties to the pharmaceutical industry (Stephen Kinzer, "Blood Gives AIDS Virus to over 300 Germans," *New York Times*, Oct. 10, 1993, p. 8).

86. Gérard Badou, "Sang: Le dossier du scandale," *L'Express*, Nov. 8, 1991, p. 14.

87. Gérard Badou, "Crimes de sang," *L'Express*, July 3, 1992, p. 19.

determining what crimes might have been committed. The difficulty, as one observer noted, is that "AIDS spreads faster than the code of criminal procedure can be elaborated."[88] Roux and Netter were finally cited for failure to assist a person in danger, a délit that carries a penalty of three months to five years. The examining magistrate charged Garretta and Allain with fraud in not signaling the risks involved in using a product, a crime that parliament established in 1905 to deal with misconduct in the food industry. The maximum penalty for this crime is four years' imprisonment. Sabine Paugam, lawyer for some of the hemophiliacs, complained that they were forced to pursue the poisoners with "a law made for spoiled mustard and yogurt."[89]

Garretta and the others maintained their innocence throughout the investigation and trial, which finally began on June 22, 1992. They claimed not to have understood the gravity of the AIDS threat at the time crucial decisions had to be made.[90] If they were guilty, they argued, so were hundreds of others who similarly underestimated the risk. Lawyers for the defendants focused particularly on the culpability of the three cabinet ministers, who appeared likely to escape prosecution entirely.

All but Netter were nevertheless convicted on November 4, 1992, with chief judge Louis Mazières delivering a 191-page judgment in the case. The court rejected the victims' attempt to charge the defendants with poisoning and involuntary manslaughter, reasoning that the necessary elements of intention were absent.[91] Roux, charged with failure to render assistance to a person in danger, received a suspended sentence. Allain, like Garretta, was convicted under the 1905 product law. He received a two-year sentence and a substantial fine. Garretta received the maximum penalty of four years, but before final sentencing, he fled to Boston with his family, where he accepted a post with a Boston biotech firm, Heamonetics. He returned to France three months later, and was promptly jailed. Garretta complained bitterly that he had been made a sacrificial lamb in this case.

Among the defendants, only Allain appealed, seeking a more lenient sentence. The civil parties filed a new complaint for poisoning. The state then filed its own appeal, asking for a retrial of all four defendants, a request that is not considered double jeapordy under French law. Nevertheless, the state's move was surprising in light of the trial court's judgment, which was favor-

88. Ibid. p. 18.

89. Gérard Badou, "Sang: Le procès de la honte," *L'Express*, July 10, 1992, p. 28.

90. *Libération Spécial Sang*, p. 54.

91. Poisoning, the judge reasoned, envisions an intent to use a relationship of trust to harm another, a degree of malevolence that was absent in this case. Involuntary manslaughter requires a simple cause and effect relationship between the action taken and the harm caused. The defendant must be in a position to make a simple probability calculation of the danger to be answerable for this crime.

able to the prosecution in all significant respects. The second trial began in May 1993 before the Paris Court of Appeals, which ruled that a poisoning charge is not appropriate absent an intent to cause death.

The fact that the three cabinet members had not been charged in this case did not prevent them from being excoriated by the press. For a time it looked as if the case against them might be tried in this milieu, with charges and denials being exchanged in television broadcasts, letters to the editor, and speeches before parliament. These exchanges also brought the French judicial system under fire, particularly its procedure for handling crime by high officials. The 1958 constitution protected officials from prosecution in the ordinary courts for crimes committed in office. Such cases were triable only in the ancient High Court, which could be convened only by following a complicated procedure that created substantial bulwarks against prosecution. The clear objective was to make sure that prosecution of public officials occurs only upon solemn and carefully considered occasions in which a large majority of both houses of parliament agree.[92] The necessary level of agreement had never occurred during the thirty-two years in which these provisions had been in effect.

Parliament would have preferred to maintain this record of inaction because a prosecution of the ministers could "open the floodgates" for other claims against government officials.[93] Public opinion, however, ultimately forced the politicians to act. Press coverage of the criminal case against Garretta and his colleagues had been critical. Journalists had taken up the defense contention that the government was using the case against the doctors to draw attention from the misdeeds of members of the ruling elite. The magazine *L'Express,* for example, carried headlines like "The Murderous State" (July 31, 1992) and "Homicide" (July 10, 1992). Act-Up, an activist AIDS-awareness organization, demonstrated outside the courthouse throughout the trial.

The ministers themselves did nothing to relieve growing public sentiment against them. They were vigorous in their own defense, appearing on tele-

92. The procedure requires one tenth of the membership of one house to formulate a specific charge of criminal activity punishable under the penal code. If the necessary facts can be verified, the assembly and the senate must each elect fifteen members to an ad hoc commission that will vote to indict. Then, in plenary session, each house must pass on the accusatory instrument, with an absolute majority of all members voting for identical provisions. At this point a delegation of five judges designated by the court of cassation investigates the case, taking the role that an examining magistrate assumes in ordinary prosecutions. When it concludes its work, the case goes before the high court, which is composed of twenty-four politician/judges, twelve from each house. Each house elects its judges by an absolute majority in secret balloting. The twenty-four member court hears the case and renders its decision on the guilt or innocence of the minister(s) by a secret vote. There is no appeal from its judgment.

93. *Libération Spécial Sang,* supra note 77, p. 64.

vision and even invoking the good offices of Mitterrand, who asserted the innocence of his prime minister. Fabius' only crime, he declared, was to be a man of the left.[94] Laurent Fabius himself claimed at first that he should not be tried because he had done nothing wrong. Later he suggested that he should be brought before a "jury of honor" rather than the high court. Edmond Hervé blamed his own inaction on the scientific experts who advised him. Georgina Dufoix declared herself "responsible but not punishable," a phrase that came to symbolize the arrogance of the governing elite.

Parliament finally overcame its reluctance to invoke the High Court, urged on by politicians from the far right like Le Pen. In December 1992 both houses voted, by enormous majorities, to charge all three ministers with failure to render assistance to a person in need. The first prosecutorial effort got as far as the investigatory stage, which empowers a delegation of five judges appointed by the Court of Cassation in the role of an examining magistrate. The judges did not take long to throw out parliament's charge. Prosecution for actions taken in 1985 was barred, they declared, by the code of criminal procedure's three-year statute of limitations. Only a charge with a continuing aspect, such as involuntary homicide, could survive this jurisdictional defect.

The court's February 5, 1993, decision came at an awkward time for the Socialists, whose electoral support had been fading as the March elections approached. To avoid the political disaster of letting the case disappear on a technicality, the Senate decided to reinstate the charge of involuntary homicide that it had rejected earlier. The case is again pending, with uncertain prospects for an eventual decision on the merits. Meanwhile the legal foundation on which this prosecution rested has changed. Just before the Beregoveoy government fell in 1993, it proposed a new court to deal with the actions of ministers, one more in keeping with the judicial procedures to which other citizens are subject. The constitution has now been amended to create a new Justice Court of the Republic to replace the old High Court. In September 1994, a three-judge commission of inquiry from the new court made headlines when it charged the three ex-ministers with conspiracy to poison, a crime that allows a prison term of up to thirty years.

Pressure from French victims, particularly hemophiliacs and their families, has been unrelenting at every level. Angry parents greeted the ex-ministers when they appeared to testify, and parents have pressed, unsuccessfully so far, to join as parties civiles in the action against the ministers. In other forums as well, victims continue to press their claims against the government,

94. "La mise en accusation de M. Fabius, de Mme. Dufoix et de M. Hervé est jugée recevable par le Bureau du Sénat," Le Monde, Nov. 18, 1992, p. 7.

petitioning administrative tribunals at every level and, in some instances, taking their cases to the European Commission on Human Rights. An estimated 2,500 victims have received compensation so far. The government at first sought to resist these claims, but later provided procedures for compensation. The case of Alain Vallée is illustrative. A hemophiliac, Vallée was infected with the HIV virus during blood transfusions between November 1984 and June 1985. In 1989 he applied to the Ministry of Health for compensation, which was refused a few months later. The following summer he applied to the Versailles Administrative Court; Vallée's petition was consolidated with four hundred other applications in the Paris Administrative Court, which held the state liable to hemophiliacs infected between March and October 1985. A government commissioner recommended compensation but referred the case to the Council of State because Vallée had pursued a parallel claim before a government compensation fund. The council issued a ruling in October 1993, but not before Vallée had taken the matter to the European Commission in Strasbourg on the grounds that under the Convention the state had taken excessive time to render its decision. The Commission agreed and set the matter for further proceedings.

Suits by other victims are also possible. Greek and Italian prosecutors are considering lawsuits as they explore the damage France caused in continuing to export untreated blood products after the AIDS danger was known. Litigation may also be in prospect for damages caused by the government's decision to continue to collect blood from prisoners in the face of clear evidence that many prisoners were HIV positive. Here again, government documents indicate a decision made with an eye to maintaining the quantity, rather than the quality, of blood supplies.

The SIDA Scandal as Moral Drama

The SIDA tragedy became a rallying point for political reform. Changes have been implemented in procedures for collecting, testing, and distributing factor 8 and other blood products. Public pressure also sensitized parliament to the need to develop a less cumbersome method for holding public officials accountable for their actions. Some have even suggested vesting jurisdiction in the ordinary courts, as in the United States. This would be a huge step in a country that is accustomed to insulating the executive from judicial oversight. The concern, even among the journalists who helped bring the scandal to light, is that the public will develop a thirst for vengeance that could paralyze government. As Jean-Michel Tenard, a contributor to *Libération,* wrote: "The SIDA affair taught us that government institutions will have to accept the responsibility for their own acts, and, will, without doubt, have to allow their ministers to be tried in the ordinary courts. But it will also be necessary to find ways to contain the 'collective hysteria' that can develop, which can render government responsible for doing everything, and in the process, prevent it from doing anything effectively."[95]

The SIDA affair is a reminder that political careers depend on sensitivity to the public's standard of moral responsibility, which does not necessarily reflect the official view. Indeed, politicians like Georgina Dufoix inadvertently provided a rallying point for the public's discontent with her disingenuous remark that she was "responsible but not punishable." Her continued presence in the government was evidence that the Socialists, in fact, accepted no responsibility for the SIDA tragedy.

The SIDA affair also teaches that when politicians attempt to avoid liability for their actions, victims will invoke the law, even when it does not appear to be up to the task of moral vindication. In this instance there were no criminal statutes that quite fit the circumstances and prosecutors were reluctant to pursue the victims' allegations. The awkward, time-consuming procedure for invoking the high court's jurisdiction provided an even more formidable bulwark against public accountability. Under the pressure of determined litigants and public indignation, however, none of these barricades proved insurmountable. Whether or not any high public official eventually serves time for his or her part in the SIDA scandal, the affair has already offered astute politicians a lesson.

Finally, this case teaches that courts offer a safety valve in modern societies, providing a legitimate route for outrage with the actions of public officials. They offer an alternative to the politics of violence, sabotage, and street riots, though not to eventual defeat at the polls. Intriguingly, this function does not depend on the availability of judicial review or on a high degree of rights consciousness in society. Instead, the concept of the rule of law that is essential for the operation of liberal, capitalist, democratic states may be the foundation for the expectation that courts can somehow set the moral compass right when officialdom will not.

Civil Justice

The realm of civil justice, where injured parties sue their injurers, seems more insulated from the political fray than criminal adjudication. Private individuals, not the state, decide whether to seek judicial assistance. No one goes to jail or pays a fine. The sense of moral condemnation that goes with prosecution in the name of the entire community is absent. Civil disputes are mostly over private wrongs and the objective is usually restitution, not public vindication of the community's moral code, though moral standards do determine what injuries are actionable and how much injurers must pay. The

95. *Libération Spécial Sang*, supra note 77, p. 64.

role of government is to provide a framework for evaluating behavior and a neutral forum for hearing claims.

To conclude that civil litigation is basically a private affair, however, would be a serious mistake. Citizens expect their government to help them deal with the injuries of social living—the broken promises, car accidents, ruined reputations, failed marriages, and other unfortunate events that are part of contemporary human experience almost everywhere. And government plays a part in producing these injuries, authorizing behavior that has the predictable consequence of causing injury to some.[96] The solution, typically, is to offer injured individuals the right to sue their injurers and recover money damages for the harm, a form of government-sanctioned combat that has attracted many venerable critics, from Dickens to Daumier.

Civil suits allocate values just as authoritatively as the welfare and tax systems do, as chapter 1 reminds us. This publicly ordained distribution of private monies occurs under procedural and substantive rules that may be the subject of intense political conflict. In the United States, for example, debate over tort reform has long engaged the interest of state legislators, who hear regularly from doctors, litigators, the insurance industry, and consumer groups concerned about liability for defective products and similar issues. Even at the national level, where the capacity for legal reform is more limited, occasional spectacular jury awards and the regular complaints of insurance companies and manufacturers have caught the attention of political leaders. President George Bush appointed a task force to study the alleged crisis in civil litigation, putting Vice President Dan Quayle in charge of the inquiry. The costs and delays of civil litigation became a campaign issue in the 1992 presidential election.

Governments must also decide how they will respond to injuries their own agents inflict in carrying out their duties. Most begin with a concept of "sovereign immunity," a right to be immune from civil suit that kings once claimed as a royal prerogative. Modern democratic governments justify exemption from the ordinary processes of assessing and paying damages on the grounds of separation of powers, citing the need for executive action unconstrained by the prospect of debilitating lawsuits for injuries caused in the scope of government's legitimate activities. The rise of the welfare state, with its promise of government guardianship against virtually any peacetime injury, has forced governments to abandon the idea of immunity and to offer compensation, but typically through administrative tribunals, rather than the ordinary courts.

96. Guido Calibresi develops this idea in *Ideals, Beliefs, Attitudes and the Law* (Syracuse, N.Y.: Syracuse University Press, 1985). The argument that injuries represent social choices supports a broad-based, generous approach to remedies.

The French position on civil justice is consistent with its traditional suspicion of judicial power: Every effort is made to minimize the capacity of
courts to influence public policy in the course of resolving civil suits. The
issue in France is how to provide adequate relief for injuries without turning
too much of the task over to judges. In the area of civil justice, the official
position on this point has been clear since 1804, when France adopted a
comprehensive civil code designed to respond to every contingency with a
rule. Codes of civil procedure, commerce, criminal procedure, and penal law
soon followed.

THE CODE CIVIL

The idea behind codification was that law could be made simple and clear
enough to be reduced to a popular handbook that would take its place next
to the Bible on each family's bookshelf.[97] Lawyers would become redun-
dant, and judges would simply apply the gapless law to the facts of the
cases, like technicians. The process of codification, in short, was a highly
ideological, indeed, utopian, effort that should not be confused with the
tiresome task of imposing some order on related but separately enacted
statutory provisions that is called "codification" in common-law jurisdictions.

The *Code Civil* and its four companion codes achieved somewhat less
dramatic results than the idealists expected. Most of the work was done by
established legal scholars, not by revolutionary spokespersons. For the most
part, the codes consolidated prior customary law, much of which had a basis
in the earlier Roman law.[98] The codification of French law is less important
as a break with pre-revolutionary norms than the harbinger of a changed
attitude toward courts. The clarity and simplicity of the codes did make law
more accessible to the French masses and did signal a decision to reduce the
power of judges. René David and Henry de Vries note: "The Civil Code
became in the nineteenth century the symbol of the desirability and effectiveness of creating law exclusively through representative assemblies rather
than through the courts. . . . The judiciary, under a statutory duty since the
Revolution to express reasons for their decisions, found their most satisfactory starting point in the articles of the Codes."[99]

The belief that the codes provided an answer to every question began to
wane, David and de Vries suggest, toward the end of the nineteenth century.
Literally applied, their provisions began to seem incompatible with the social

97. Merryman, supra note 36, p. 28.
98. Katz, supra note 43, p. 107.
99. René David and Henry P. de Vries, *The French Legal System* (New York: Oceana,
1958), p. 15.

and economic values that developed as industrialization and urbanization progressed.[100] Unanticipated questions arose. Proposals for comprehensive reform of all five documents were considered as early as the 1830s. The sheer complexity of the codification effort, however, discouraged piecemeal changes. The 1804 Code Civil, remarkably, still survives recognizably intact.[101]

Parliament's failure to keep the codes up to date gave scope to judicial creativity. Judges began to rely on their own authority to extend provisions to new situations and lawyers learned to search for relevant precedents and use them in their arguments.[102] The brevity and generality of the Code also encouraged judicial elaboration, as Tomlinson explains:

> The nature of the Code itself accentuates the interpretative role of the courts. The Code is not a piece of special interest legislation designed to address a particular problem. Rather, like our Constitution, it is the product of a public-spirited effort to state basic principles to govern people's affairs for an indefinite period. Not surprisingly, French courts treat these basic principles as starting points for reasoning by analogy and for developing over time subordinate rules that best meet present-day needs. American courts have occasionally done the same thing when interpreting open-ended statutes such as the post–Civil War Civil Rights Acts and the Sherman Antitrust Act. In recent years scholars have encouraged courts to interpret such statutes "dynamically" in light of contemporary needs.[103]

Despite the movement to elaborate the code with judicial rules built on cases, and despite the incursions in recent years of special statutes modifying code provisions in enumerated circumstances, French legal scholars remain quite devoted to the idea that their code lays out a coherent, comprehensive approach to the problem of legal responsibility. This passage from *French Civil Law: An Insider's View* illustrates a common perspective: "The coherence of the civil law is not any less characteristic than its inspiration. The civil law is a whole in which everything is intrinsically tied; any reform of one element has a repercussion on all the others and the knowledge of one solution presupposes the examination of those solutions surrounding it. The

---

100. Ibid.

101. The evolution of the codes from Roman law days is discussed in Arthur T. von Mehren and James Russell Gordley, *The Civil Law System* (Boston: Little, Brown, 1977) pp. 3–53, esp. 48–53.

102. Merryman, supra note 36, p. 47; Atias, supra note 37, pp. 53–54.

103. See, generally, Edward A. Tomlinson, "A Study in Judicial Lawmaking," *Louisiana Law Review* 48 (1988), pp. 1358–1359.

rules of the civil law . . . contribute to a certain extent to the definition of the citizen—and this definition must have its logic."[104]

The inclination of judges and scholars to interpret the language of the code with imagination and a sense of modern conditions is particularly important in the area of torts, which the code deals with in only five short articles, four of them unrevised since their 1804 enactment.[105] In these and other negligence cases, judges generally begin their analysis with Section 1382, the basic statement on liability for acts that injure another: "Every act of whatever human agency that causes damage to another obliges him by whose fault it happened to repair it." This principle will sound familiar to anyone schooled in the Anglo-American law of negligence. So will the concerns French judges discuss in the cases: damage sufficient to cause legal injury; the adequacy of the causal connection; the scope of one's duty to others.[106] As in Anglo-American law, the judges have developed a behavioral norm of reasonableness and qualifying doctrines like comparative negligence, assumed risk, and force majeure. Damages are available for pain and suffering as well as material damage.

Judicial creativity in shaping the code to modern conditions, however, has no clear jurisprudential foundation. France does not accept the Anglo-American concept of equity, which encourages judges to be imaginative in finding ways to avoid unjust results. Nor does it recognize the Anglo-American principle of stare decisis, which allows judges to cite their own prior decisions as authority for principles of law, a doctrine that got its start in the eleventh century when England proved too isolated for its Norman conquerors to govern at the local level. There was no comparable break with central authority in France.

The French codifiers opted for an approach they believed would be simpler, more uniform, and more democratic. The French experience shows not just that such efforts at finality are futile, but that judges may fill gaps in a code in a manner reminiscent of the incremental, precedent-oriented, common-law method of adjudication. Martin Shapiro notes the Anglo-American tendency to develop rules of interpretation to explicate the broad principle of liability for negligence and argues that French judges followed a similar ap-

104. Atias, supra note 37, p. 38.

105. In Tomlinson's words: "The French legislature has retained these meager articles basically unchanged despite the political, economic, and social upheavals that France has undergone since the time of Napoleon. On four occasions the legislature amended article 1384, but those changes only affected special cases of liability and not the basic principles" (supra note 103, p. 1300).

106. F. H. Lawson, A. E. Anton, and L. Neville Brown, *Amos and Walton's Introduction to French Law* (Oxford: Clarendon Press, 1967), p. 207.

proach: "Most of the actual decisions about who had to compensate whom were determined by these more specific rules rather than the principle standing alone. No such rules were given in the French code. How did the French judges do without them? They didn't. They too invented them. Potential rules were proposed, elaborated, and tested and then were accepted, rejected, and/ or modified, in a mixture of academic writing, arguments before courts, and court decisions.'' Although French legal education and judicial opinions often omit references to case precedents, this is more a matter of style than substance. French practicing lawyers study cases and cite them in their briefs. Judges rely on case-based reasoning in their decisions, even when they fail to justify decisions in these terms.[107] The movement toward stare decisis and innovative decision making has been furtive, Jestaz suggests, because the concept of judicial policymaking is anathema for leaders from either end of the French political spectrum: "The question of whether a judicial decision is or is not a source of law becomes a quarrel for theologians. The question doesn't progress because the right and the left stick to the idea that the law must be simply totally obeyed—the right fears disorder and the left wants the welfare of the people. They agree on denying reality when it contradicts their dogmatism. So, in other words, and according to another well-known formula, caselaw is a source of law, but one must not say it too loudly.''[108]

This tension between the practical need for rules and commitment to an ideology of judicial passivity encourages French judges to mask judicial creativity whenever possible. One can see this in the style in which decisions are rendered. Tomlinson notes: "What differentiates the French case-law system from the common law is primarily the formulaic method adopted in France for stating case-law rules. French judges do not struggle to extract holdings from prior cases, but to formulate as precisely as possible the applicable case-law rule. . . . The French system gives more weight to what judges do over time, while the common-law approach overemphasizes what the judges do when *first* confronted with an issue.''[109]

ACCESS TO COURTS, LAWYERS, AND REMEDIES

The French tendency to downplay the policymaking role of courts can also be seen in the structure of the French remedy system. The network of tribunals for resolving civil disputes is more highly compartmentalized than in

107. Martin Shapiro, *Courts: A Comparative and Political Analysis* (Chicago: University of Chicago Press, 1981), pp. 137–145.

108. Loosely translated by Kahn-Freund from P. Jestez, "La jurisprudence, ombre portée du contentieux," in Bernard Rudden, Otto Kahn-Freund, and Claudine Levy, *Sourcebook on French Law*, 3rd ed. (Oxford: Clarendon, 1991), p. 252.

109. Tomlinson, supra note 103, p. 1357.

England or in the United States. About 40 percent of the civil disputes that might be considered by courts of general jurisdiction in the United States, for example, go to specialized tribunals: labor courts hear labor cases; commercial courts hear cases between merchants and consider bankruptcy petitions; rural rental commissions handle disputes over farm leases; the National Health Insurance system has an administrative board to handle grievances. Some tribunals are staffed by people whose expertise is the activity in dispute, not law.[110] Cases involving government facilities are handled through the administrative court system—the ordinary courts have no jurisdiction to grant judgments against the state.[111]

Injury cases that have a criminal aspect, like some serious automobile accidents, are usually handled in conjunction with the criminal proceeding. The victim notifies the prosecutor and becomes a partie civile in the action, collecting damages at the same time the jury returns a finding of guilt. The state makes this process as easy as possible. The government conducts the investigation necessary to establish guilt; the victim is obliged only to prove damages. In a simple case a victim can get an initial judicial reading of the amount of damages that will be available. If the prosecutor decides to withdraw the action before this point, the partie civile becomes the moving party and the state-sponsored investigation continues. The state compensates victims and their witnesses for their time and travel incident to the investigation, and government even assists in the effort to collect damages, garnishing ten percent of a prisoner's holdings and earnings while in prison to pay the victim's damages. A victim can sue for moral injuries, such as death of a loved one, as well as for personal physical suffering. The Ministry of Justice publishes a guidebook entitled *Guide des Droits des Victimes*, which outlines the procedure for collecting damages as well as the criminal penalties that can be assessed against the injurer.

The policy of channelling cases away from the civil courts includes the facilitation of pretrial settlements. Efforts at conciliation once were required before most suits could be brought. The contemporary approach is to encourage the parties to settle on their own. Conciliation and mediation services

110. See Heleen F. P. Ietswaart, "Evolutionary Trends in Litigation in French County Courts, 1970–1984," paper presented at the 1986 annual meeting of the Law and Society Association, Chicago. Manuscript in possession of the author. A French version of this paper has been published: "L'évolution du contentieux civil aux tribunaux d'instance, 1970–1984," *Rapport de Recherche* (Vaucresson, France: Centre de Recherche Interdisciplinaire de Vaucresson, 1986).

111. France makes a distinction between official acts and *fautes personnelles*, which can be the subject of litigation in the ordinary courts because they are against the individual, not against the government. If the court second-guesses a litigant and declares an act to be a *faute de service* rather than a personal error, the litigant must re-file the action in an administrative tribunal.

are widely available and free. Some insurers have set up their own private dispute resolution procedures. Companies that insure car owners took this approach in the 1970s, with the consequence that traffic accident torts—once the most numerous type of case in the *tribunaux d'instance,* have now practically disappeared from the courts.[112]

France also employs rules of interpretation that discourage plaintiffs from seeking relief in the courts. Where there is a contract between the parties, prevailing doctrine dictates that the plaintiff's rights are limited to what the document provides, a rule that advantages institutional defendants over injured individuals. In the same vein, victims of medical malpractice must show that they did not consent to the treatment provided. Vicarious liability rules also tend to be strict: a French hospital, for example, is not responsible for the negligence of its resident physicians.[113]

In civil disputes that go on to become full-blown lawsuits, procedural rules help to keep plaintiffs from seeking precedent-setting judgments. In this respect, the differences between France and the United States could hardly be greater. The United States system encourages civil suits by allowing contingent fees, which permit injured plaintiffs to sue on the promise of sharing the recovery. In France, as noted earlier, this arrangement is considered shocking and inappropriate. American rules are liberal in allowing new defendants to join an action, in permitting amendments to complaints, and in encouraging wide-ranging inquiry into factual information held by an opposing party. These pretrial practices allow plaintiffs to build a case against a defendant as they proceed. France is stricter in allowing amendments and much less willing to allow plaintiffs to use discovery to investigate wrongdoing. The U.S. system also differs from the French in allowing punitive damages, sums assessed simply to punish the defendant for what a jury considers to be outrageous behavior. An example is the recent $42 million judg-

112. See Ietswaart, supra note 110, p. 18. Note that the same courts hear civil and criminal cases for the most part. The *tribunaux d'instance* hear smaller cases, generally up to 30,000 francs, or about $6,000 at 1995 exchange rates. Cases can be appealed only if the judgment exceeds 13,000 francs. These courts also hear landlord and tenant cases. The *tribunaux de grande instance* hear most divorces, adoptions, and other family cases, as well as debt and tort cases that are not under the jurisdiction of another court or administrative tribunal. Appeals go before the regional courts of appeals, where they are decided by panels of judges who specialize in civil litigation. Specialists within the Court of Cassation take up appeals based on error of law in much the same fashion as they examine criminal appeals. Ietswaart (supra note 110) describes this system briefly, as do von Mehren and Gordley, in *The Civil Law System,* 2d ed. (Boston: Little, Brown, 1977), chapter 2: "Institutions Exercising 'Judicial' Functions."

113. See *International Encyclopedia of Comparative Law,* vol. 2, ch. 12, section 52, "Complex Liabilities," by Tony Weir. This immunity does not extend to the nursing staff. See also ibid., "Professional Liability," by Panayotis J. Zepos and Phoebus Christodoulou.

ment against Domino's Pizza for damages arising from an automobile accident that one of its employees caused in rushing to make a delivery. The injury was not particularly serious, but the jury apparently punished the company for an advertising campaign that stressed rapid delivery over driver safety.

French legal traditions help to explain why there is such reluctance to use the court's powers to help plaintiffs build their cases against defendants. In French jurisprudence, the judge in a civil case is a neutral umpire, with responsibility to respond to what the parties themselves produce and to decide the case within the limits they set for themselves.[114] The public interest in any case extends only to its peaceful resolution. It would be an unreasonable infringement of the rights of others, for example, to require non-parties who may know something about the facts to participate in the litigation. These are not unfamiliar ideas in an Anglo-American context. The problem is that the power of attorneys to conduct their own investigations of the facts is quite limited in French law. There are no "fishing expeditions" in French courts. Instead, James Beardsley complains, there is "a settled habit of fact avoidance." Where a factual issue cannot be avoided by the system's complex rules for presuming facts from documents or from affidavits, an expert is appointed to investigate or the magistrate conducts an *enquête* to hear testimony from relevant witnesses. The lawyers sit in the back of the room, passing notes with questions they hope the judge will ask. There is no cross-examination, and thus no mechanism to weigh the credibility of this evidence. Trial, when it finally occurs, proceeds largely by judicial examination of documents; there are no juries in civil cases in France.[115]

Consumer organizations, not surprisingly, have difficulty in using French courts to pursue their complaints against businesses. There is no public interest bar in France and no habit of public interest litigation. Civil justice tends to be conceived in individualistic terms, and career judges fear violating their responsibility to respect the separation of powers. Practical problems also prevent litigation brought to vindicate the public interest. Many cases are too financially insignificant to interest individuals in pursuing litigation, but mechanisms for aggregating their interests are poorly developed in France. Not until the 1970s were organizations permitted to sue on behalf of their members, and class actions could not be brought for another two decades until a new consumer code was adopted. An organization may be coun-

114. Peter Herzog, *Civil Procedure in France* (Hague: Martinus Nijhoff, 1967), Section 7.23: "The Role of the Court in Ascertaining Facts," p. 306.

115. See ibid., chapter 5, "Pre-commencement Activities," pp. 232–237. And see James Beardsley, "Proof of Fact in French Civil Procedure," *American Journal of Comparative Law* 34 (1986), p. 467.

tersued and be required to pay damages if it does not prevail on the merits. Nor do organizations get much cooperation from public prosecutors, who have power to act against consumer abuses on their own.

The obstacles France places in the way of civil suits should not be read as a wholesale rejection of the principle of access to courts to vindicate rights. France has taken considerable pains to keep the fees for civil litigation at a reasonable level. A 1991 law, for example, makes civil litigation free to those who cannot afford it. The system encourages laypersons to represent themselves, and a significant minority do, especially before administrative tribunals. Even when people do hire lawyers, self-imposed and court-imposed restrictions on the scope of their activities tend to keep the fees much lower than in the United States. What this system does *not* provide, however, is a check on the excesses of powerful institutions. The problem, as Cappelletti and Garth observe, is that "a right of individual access, however liberally granted, does not necessarily lead to the vindication of new rights on a very large scale."[116]

CONVERGING TENDENCIES

The French, like other Europeans, view American developments in liability law with some disdain. A report comparing personal injury awards in countries belonging to the European Economic Community expresses the common sentiment: "We oppose the suggestion that the U.S. tort system provides a worthwhile example for the European personal injury award systems to follow."[117] French reluctance to follow the American example, however, is unlikely to overcome certain centripetal tendencies.

In both France and the United States, statutes are supplanting the old liability rules. In the United States the change is from case law to statute law; in France the movement is from the brevity and generality of ancient codes to specific, detailed legislation. In both instances, judges and lawyers tend to be slow to see the direction of change. American law schools, for example, still overemphasize judicial opinions as a source of law.[118]

---

116. Mauro Cappelletti and Bryant Garth, *International Encyclopedia of Comparative Law*, vol. 16: *Civil Procedure*, pp. 1–83.

117. Gavin Souter, "Report Seeks Uniform Injury Compensation," *Business Insurance*, Feb. 11, 1991, p. 27. The report, prepared by a London-based law firm, puts France seventh (out of twelve) in the size of its awards compared to other EC countries.

118. American law schools, Mary Ann Glendon observes, "have remained extraordinarily court-centered. We rely mainly on cases in law teaching; we emphasize the judicial development of the law; we produce an enormous literature on the Supreme Court, and our legal philosophers concentrate heavily on the nature of the judicial process." "The Sources of Law in a Changing Legal Order," *Creighton Law Review* 17 (1984), p. 685. Glendon associates the new primacy of statutes with the rise of the welfare state and the decline of government's preoccupation with the rights of private property. See, generally, ibid., 663–698.

Another change that tends to bring these two systems of law closer together is the movement away from considerations of fault as criteria for
assessing liability for accidental injury. Most countries now compensate injured workers without regard to whether they are partly or wholly responsible
for their injuries. This tendency to adopt a strict-liability approach to workplace injuries also offers an attractive solution to the problem of high transaction costs in other areas of tort. Investigation and individualized processing
are inherently expensive, as proponents of no-fault insurance plans point out,
and individualized assessment is of uncertain value in preventing undesirable
behavior. Criminal sanctions might be a more effective way of controlling
egregious cases of dangerous behavior, and government can regulate or rely
upon the private market in insurance to deal with the costs from injuries that
occur in the course of dangerous activities that society values.[119] America is
the leader in the trend toward strict liability, but France and other European
countries are moving in this direction.

The movement toward greater generosity in providing compensation for
injuries may be encouraging French courts to scrutinize more carefully the
rules that relieve the government from liability for its actions. Two recent
cases illustrate the trend. One, a 1986 case before the Court of Cassation,
considered a widow's petition for compensation after the police shot the
husband accidentally in attempting to apprehend two armed criminals from
a crowded café. The case had been dismissed by the trial court for failure to
show gross negligence, the traditional standard for recovery against police
officers. The Court of Cassation said that the constitutional principle of equality of burdens for citizens should also be considered and remanded the case
for further consideration. The gross negligence standard in this instance prevented the appropriate sharing of the burdens of police errors.[120] The second
case arose out of the government's mishandling of the HIV-infected blood
supply. The family of two victims of an HIV-infected transfusion sued a
transfusion center and won a judgment, despite a French law which provided
indemnification for victims from public funds and despite a contractual agreement designed to exempt the center from liability. The court invoked *prin-
cipes généraux du droit* to allow recovery of damages. Here again, the im-
plication was that the courts must act when other agencies of government
fail to protect the basic rights of individuals.

These examples suggest a certain judicial resistance to a prescribed role
that divorces them from issues of public concern. French citizens injured by

119. John G. Fleming discusses this trend in a book review, "Comparative Law of Torts,"
in *Oxford Journal of Legal Studies* 4 (1984), 235–243. He describes these changes at greater
length in "Is There a Future for Tort?" *Australian Law Journal* 58 (1984), 131–142.
120. *Consorts Pourcel c. Pinier*, Cass. civ. 10.6, 1986, J.C. P. 1986, 20683.

government's initiatives and mistakes are likely to benefit from this trend. Courts in the United States, on the other hand, are under pressure to show more restraint in affixing liability. American courts, critics charge, hamstring both government and business with their readiness to support new theories of liability, their failure to defer to government regulators, and their tolerance for large damage awards.

Courts and the Regulation of Enterprise

The French regime's concern with the self-aggrandizing tendencies of courts is evident in its stance toward the large organizations that populate the French economic landscape and that help to organize its social life. These entities— businesses, labor unions, churches, interest groups—require state support and encouragement to survive. They also require state limits if individual freedom and democratic control are to be protected. Courts can play a more or less expansive role in this process of calculated nourishment. In France, not sur- prisingly, government has opted for limited judicial involvement in the reg- ulatory effort. But this policy of insulating domestic courts from the regu- latory domain has not prevented the French government from having to cope with the decisions of the Court of Justice of the European Union, which have become a significant force in France's regulatory efforts.

This section focuses on government's relationship with large business or- ganizations. Two aspects of this relationship will be considered here: the availability of the courts to employees and consumers who challenge business practices as illegitimate or illegal; and the availability of the courts to em- ployers who challenge government initiatives they find harmful to their in- terests. The issue in both types of cases is the degree to which courts will be counted among the decision makers who are relevant to the implemen- tation of policy. The answer, I suggest, depends on the level at which judicial intervention is sought.

INDIVIDUALS VERSUS BUSINESSES IN THE COURTS

Suits by citizens, employees, and community activists challenging business threaten to disrupt familiar relationships between government regulators and the enterprises they regulate. The suitor, in effect, acts as a private attorney general to vindicate public rights and to change government's regulatory practice and policy. France has discouraged such suits with the argument that government officials, informed by their technical expertise, are the appropri- ate guardians of the public interest. Courts have played a crucial role in support of this rationale for noninvolvement.

Challenges to the nuclear power industry provide an illustrative case in point. Activists in the United States and some other countries have had considerable success in getting their arguments heard by courts. This has not been possible in France, where the courts have applied strict rules of standing to make it difficult to challenge siting or construction decisions. Even when courts do consider the merits of claims, they tend to treat challenged decisions as beyond the capacity of non-experts to comprehend or criticize. This closed-door policy, Frank Baumgartner suggests, has helped to radicalize French antinuclear activists, turning some into eco-saboteurs.[121]

The consequence of the courts' hands-off policy is that French producers of potentially dangerous products like pharmaceuticals enjoy a significant advantage over American companies in the international marketplace. With no concern for jury awards, punitive damages, or liability doctrines that favor consumers, French companies can move faster and afford more risks than companies in many other nations. French companies do not need to fear judgments comparable to the $83 million payout in damages that followed release of the swine flu vaccine in the United States, for example.[122]

The French approach to litigation initiated by employees to vindicate workplace rights is more complex. Such suits can support, rather than confound, the government's pro-labor regulatory initiatives, but they run against a French preference for collective action over individual, winner-take-all litigation. Anita Bernstein's analysis of the French approach to sexual harassment illustrates the tendency to focus on the problematical workplace, rather than the injured individual: "While Americans see the problem of sexual harassment as either wrongful private conduct between two people or as sex discrimination, Europeans have shaped it as a problem of workers, and sited the problem in the workplace."[123] The government has set forth standards of behavior that employers are expected to monitor and has criminalized certain severe forms of sexual harassment, but it has so far resisted pressure to make harassment a civil wrong that would permit an individual to sue for damages.

Membership in the European Community has had an impact on the French approach to business liability. The EU has declared that French drug manufacturers must adhere to European product liability standards, which are more favorable to consumers than French domestic law has been. Sexual harassment and workplace equality are also subjects of EU interest. France's recent

121. Frank Baumgartner, "Independent and Politicized Policy Communities: Education and Nuclear Energy in France and in the United States," *Governance: An International Journal of Policy and Administration* 2 (1989), p. 61.

122. The liability issues surrounding AZT raise similar problems. See Ann E. Wells, "Regulating Experimental AIDS Drugs: A Comparison of the U.S. and France," *Loyola of Los Angeles International and Comparative Law Journal* 13 (1990), p. 407.

123. Anita Bernstein, "Law, Culture, and Harassment," unpublished manuscript on file with the author (1993), p. 10.

initiative that incorporated sexual harassment into the national code that governs the workplace may, in fact, be traceable to an EU study that began in 1991.

BUSINESS VERSUS GOVERNMENT

The French government has pursued a policy of forceful intervention in dealing with business. As Vivien Schmidt explains:

> Traditionally, France's pattern of industrial policymaking has been "statist," meaning that government decision-makers and decision-making organizations take a leadership role in policymaking and have primary control over structuring the "state-society relationship," dictating the pattern of interest representation and resisting the pressures of interests, whether organized or not, where they choose. At the formulation stage, this means that governments can undertake "heroic" programs in which government leadership remains paramount and consultation is often minimal. The most recent examples of these are the programs of nationalization under the Socialists in 1982 and privatization under the neoliberal right between 1986 and 1988.[124]

The government is able to maintain this interventionist posture, Schmidt argues, because it is willing to negotiate the details of implementation, creating exceptions where necessary to ease the pain of regulation. Others have noted a characteristically French willingness to accept the decisions of regulators because of their elite education and a cultural tendency to value expertise, including expertise in public administration. According to Feigenbaum: "It is no accident that the policy debate in France is narrowly defined. Perhaps no other political elite so enjoys the uniformity of shared perceptions that is characteristic of the French decision-making structure. The upper reaches of the French administration are populated by professional civil servants bound together by a powerful network of formal and informal ties. These are ties that are essentially a product of French education grafted onto a particular form of organization, the Grands Corps."[125] Sometimes cooperation is achieved, Feigenbaum points out, because the state really has no

---

124. Vivien Schmidt, "Upscaling Business and Downsizing Government: France in the New European Community," paper presented at the annual meeting of the American Political Science Association, Sept. 2–5, 1993, Washington, D.C. On file with the author, p. 7. For a more explicitly comparative view see Andrew Shonfield, *Modern Capitalism* (Oxford: Oxford University Press, 1965). See especially chapter 5: "The Etatist Tradition: France." Harvey B. Feigenbaum, building on this literature, probes the government's independence from the enterprises it regulates. See *The Politics of Public Enterprise: Oil and the French State* (Princeton, N.J.: Princeton University Press, 1985).

125. Feigenbaum, supra note 124, p. 101.

policy—it simply does what the largest business organizations want it to do.[126]

Litigation between business and government would be detrimental to this somewhat symbiotic relationship, and it is very rare in France. An exception is the saga of Edouard Leclerc, France's premier discount retailer. In 1949 Leclerc opened a general food store in his hometown of Landerneau in western Brittany. The building was spartan and the prices were low. Within a few years, Leclerc had expanded and opened several new stores. Local retailers began a decades-long effort to stop the discounting, later joining forces with national firms that did not want their prices undercut. They worked through local officials and the administrative tribunals all the way to the Council of State. They even filed suit in local court, winning victories here and there. Leclerc fought back with his own appeals to ministers, administrative tribunals, and the ordinary courts. One of his cases went as far as the Court of Cassation, which supported him. Meanwhile, government policy on price cutting vacillated. Had the government's own position on price-cutting been firm in this period, Leclerc's strategy would have failed. Even so, Leclerc's behavior was unusual enough to earn him scholarly attention.[127]

Leclerc's strategy of defiance and litigation eventually took him to the Court of Justice of the European Union. His first case challenged a 1981 statute that regulated book prices. Later he took on the government's procedures for regulating the wholesale price of gasoline. The European court supported Leclerc on both occasions. His success suggests an important change in the landscape of business disputing. The European Union, acting often through the Court of Justice in Luxemburg, has begun to have an impact on domestic economic policy. As Robert Keohane and Stanley Hoffmann observe: "No other international organization enjoys such reliably effective supremacy of its law over the laws of member governments, with a recognized Court of Justice to adjudicate disputes. . . . A recent study concludes that national administrations implement Community law about as effectively as they apply national law, and in its own analysis of such issues, the Commission has concluded that most national courts 'are collaborating effectively in the implementation of Community law.' Indeed, of all Community institutions, the Court has gone farthest in limiting national autonomy, by asserting the principles of superiority of Community law."[128]

126. Ibid., p. 94.
127. William J. Adams discusses his activities at length in *Restructuring the French Economy* (Washington, D.C.: Brookings Institution, 1989), pp. 223–243. His autobiography is entitled, appropriately, *Ma vie pour un combat*.
128. Robert Keohane and Stanley Hoffman, "Institutional Change in Europe in the 1980s," in *The New European Community: Decisionmaking and Institutional Change*, Robert O. Keohane and Stanley Hoffmann (eds.) (Boulder, Colo.: Westview, 1991), pp. 11–12. For a thoughtful

France, more than any other member nation, has been changed by its membership in the European Union, according to Vivien Schmidt. The formerly close, mutually supportive relationship has given way to one in which government leads less and business competes more.[129] It is likely that the Court of Justice will continue to play a significant role in shaping this new working relationship. Whether the Court's activism will encourage litigants to turn more often to the French courts, however, remains to be seen.

Conclusion

The political role of courts in France is changing. The transformation of the judiciary's function in criminal cases is clearest. The new code of criminal procedure puts pressure on the courts to protect the rights of the accused as never before, and decisions by the European Commission and Court on Human Rights have further expanded these duties. More changes appear to be in store. France is one of the leaders among the nations of Europe in the number of petitions its residents filed with the Commission. Decisions in some of these cases are bound to have an impact on French procedural law.

Membership in the European Union has also tended to broaden the framework French people use to consider rights issues. A European sense of human rights and economic liberties is developing, and cross-community comparisons have an impact on domestic politics. France's embarrassing position as "the champion of pretrial detention," for example, helps explain its recent willingness to revise the code of criminal procedure. As Denis Bredin, a French lawyer and scholar, explains: "The project isn't simple: it throws into question our oldest judicial traditions, our repressive social mentality, and our complicated relationship with the rights of man, which we are more interested in proclaiming than respecting, and also our legal and judicial connections with other European countries, because, if Europe is to become a reality, legal systems that remain vastly different from each other will coexist only with difficulty."[130]

---

description of the Court and its work see Martin Shapiro, "The European Court of Justice," in Alberta M. Sbragia (ed.), *Euro-Politics* (Washington, D.C.: Brookings Institution, 1992), pp. 123–151. The Court, these authors suggest, began to take a less active role in the mid 1980s as the commission's capacity for lawmaking grew. This trend, they believe, can be expected to continue.

129. Schmidt, supra note 124, p. 1. Government, she argues, has downsized and business has upsized in response to European integration (Ibid.)

130. Jean-Denis Bredin, "Libérons la justice!" (An interview with the author prepared by Sylvaine Pasquier and Sylvaine Stein), *L'Express*, Feb. 18, 1993, p. 40.

The sheer volume of pending claims in French courts creates another kind of pressure for change. Numbers of minor criminal violations and small civil claims are growing, further encouraging the already well-established movement to channel disputes away from the courts. The much-touted system of administrative courts is taking in more cases than it can dispose of each year.[131] Prisons are overcrowded, a situation that is provoking periodic strikes by guards. The whole court system, as Bredin notes, is at the point of "asphyxiation."[132]

Pressures for systemic change are likely to embroil France in a complex, unsatisfying, series of policy choices. The government is not in a good position to enact fundamental changes in its court system, even though reforms designed to enhance judicial capacity and independence could ameliorate concerns about the regime's legitimacy. Reducing the glut of cases will require either an infusion of substantial resources or a significant reduction in caseloads. With unemployment rates high and the social welfare system in crisis, neither type of relief is likely to be forthcoming. Any efforts to increase efficiencies in the system would be likely to run aground of the growing insistence on greater sensitivity to human rights.

The problem in France, however, goes deeper. The French are disillusioned with their government. The March 1993 elections represented a resounding defeat for the long-governing Socialists, forcing Mitterrand to "cohabit" with political enemies. A 1993 poll reported that 63 percent of French young people think politicians are chronically dishonest.[133] Its own unpopularity puts the French government under pressure to criminalize behavior that it cannot persuasively promise to control by other means.

Consider, for example, a case that in some ways eerily parallels the SIDA affair. The case involves an experimental treatment for dwarfism that uses human pituitary glands to manufacture human growth hormone. The technique, unfortunately, does not protect recipients from acquiring Creutzfeldt-Jackob disease, a long, debilitating, and ultimately fatal nerve disease. Doctors claim to have been unaware of this when, eight years ago, they treated twenty-four children with the hormone. Nineteen of the patients have died by 1993. The government has responded by charging the doctors with involuntary homicide.[134]

The government's vigor in pursuing these two doctors suggests that the political leadership has learned that vigorous prosecution can shore up sup-

131. "Crimes et délits," supra note 48, p. 4.

132. Bredin, supra note 130, p. 43.

133. "In a Time of Shared Hardships, the Young Embrace Europe," New York Times, Aug. 11, 1993, p. A12.

134. David Dickson, "Malpractice Denied," Nature 364 (July 1993), p. 372.

port for a shaky regime. The same conventional wisdom seems to be circulating in the United States, where convictions for public corruption have risen tenfold between 1980 and 1995.[135] This suggests a link between law and politics that de Tocqueville failed to anticipate in focusing on the American tendency to constitutionalize every political question. Were de Tocqueville alive today, he might be struck by a tendency to criminalize political questions, both in his own country and in the United States.

The strategy of using courts to legitimate the political regime has other facets besides invigorated prosecution of official wrongdoing. The effort to improve the accessibility of courts for minor dispute resolution is on-going, and consumer litigation can be pursued more easily than ever before. France has taken bold steps to accommodate constitutionalism, that sense of government's obligation to live up to legal standards that is felt everywhere. What Louis Favoreau says of Europe generally is increasingly true of France: "Constitutional norms are progressively impregnating all branches of law, thanks to the increasingly important jurisprudence of fundamental rights. Constitutional law is no longer just institutional law; it is also substantive law whose application has a direct effect on individuals. In this, the European systems incontestably approach the American system in breaking with the 'civil law tradition.' "[136] The French movement toward constitutionalism and fundamental rights is nevertheless distinctive in certain key respects. France remains devoted to its two-track justice system in which crimes and interpersonal disputes proceed through one court system, while a specialized corps of administrative judges resolves claims against government. Constitutional issues tend to be reserved for the highly specialized Constitutional Council. At every level there is reluctance to acknowledge the reality of judicial policymaking.

French institutional arrangements and legal traditions thus continue to discourage citizens from pursuing litigation as a solution for basic social problems. The American tendency to litigate is not admired in France, although activists sometimes participate in litigation to bring long-simmering issues to a boil, as when French feminist organizations became parties to the prosecution of Muslim fundamentalist parents for the practice of genital mutilation of their infant daughters. American rights consciousness and litigiousness are,

135. In 1975 there were 179 federal convictions for public corruption. By 1990, that figure had risen to 1,084. Indictments have increased at every level: federal, state, and local, but the greatest increases are at the federal level. See "Federal Prosecutions of Public Corruption: 1975 to 1988," in U.S. Department of Commerce, *Statistical Abstract of the United States, 1992.*

136. Louis Favoreau, "American and European Models of Constitutional Justice," from David S. Clark (ed.), *Comparative and Private International Law* (Berlin: Duncker and Humblot, 1990), p. 34.

of course, controversial in United States, as well, and many believe the United States has gone too far in permitting courts to shape public policy. France provides anyone concerned about these issues a fascinating alternative vision of the role of courts in society.

5

Changes in Political Regimes and Continuity of the Rule of Law in Germany

ERHARD BLANKENBURG

Germany presents itself today as a stable democracy with an established pattern of the rule of law. Its self-confidence became apparent after the unification of East Germany (German Democratic Republic, or GDR) and West Germany (Federal Republic of Germany, or FRG) when in 1990 the re-establishment of the Rechtsstaat was officially emphasized as part of a "German" identity which has survived more than one totalitarian regime. The West German legal profession took over the judiciary in East Germany in hope of demonstrating the superior traditions of their rule of law.

In this chapter I shall try to point out the calamities of this self-image. The judiciary in Germany has become a separate institution emphasizing autonomy from politics at the same time that it has gained considerable political power. Judicial review effectively binds public decision makers to the letter of the law; sometimes it does not allow them discretion and does not adhere to a sufficiently restrictive "political question doctrine" which would keep courts out of political controversy. Moreover, the ministries of justice exert tight control over legal education as well as judicial careers. The number of professional judges (relative to population) is among the highest in the world, and civil litigation rates compare with the high levels reached in the more urbanized states in North America. Litigation rates are especially high in a variety of specialized tribunals adjudicating labor, fiscal, social, and administrative matters. Coordinating the different branches of specialized public and private law tribunals—each with their own appellate and high courts—requires sophisticated institutional mechanisms. This chapter will show that due to the combination of a state-controlled legal education, the regimented career patterns of judges, and the differentiated system of specialized courts, the legal profession in Germany emphasizes professional autonomy rather than democratic legitimation.

As the evolving German Rechtsstaat has repeatedly stumbled over totalitarian aberrations, it is best analyzed as a reaction to its historical predecessors and in the light of the civil-law cultures of its neighbors. One ought not assume that democracy and rule of law necessarily re-enforce each other, but rather fear that in reaction to Germany's history judicial power prevails at the cost of democracy.

Political Domination and the Rule of Law

When Montesquieu said that the judiciary should be nothing but "the mouth of the law," he implied two ideas which shape the self-image of the legal profession in the Continental tradition of civil law countries: that the courts should be strictly bound by the statutes of the law, and that in interpreting and applying it they should be entirely autonomous.[1] Continental legal cultures therefore see the codes of law as a body of rules that gives judges an authority above politics, and they consider the professional training at university law schools and lifelong tenure of judges as the guarantees of that autonomy. Popular election of judges, and certainly campaigns to get votes, would in the eyes of a European judge bring about an unsupportable degree of political dependence. On the other hand, courts are expected to stay out of what are considered "political" decisions. Case law ideally should be nothing more than a concretization of what is "in the law" or at least implicitly recognizable as intention of the legislator. Democracy in this conception of the separation of powers comes *before* the law, but it does not belong *in* the law.

Such a simple formula serves normative purposes, partly because reality never quite conformed to the ideal. Montesquieu used his interpretation of the English constitution as a rhetorical instrument for his critique of the dependence of the courts on the kings and princes of the European continent. Prior to the French revolution the judiciary was thought to be part of the absolutist power, so the idea that courts could be used to control that power seemed revolutionary indeed. Nevertheless, when the enlightenment philosophy of the eighteenth century postulated that law was to be above political power, it had laid the groundwork for an institutional separation, which was codified in the nineteenth century. The exact balance between political dependence and professional autonomy has varied from one legal culture to another and over time. The tension between the two remained vital throughout the history of all European legal cultures.

Legal history in and around Germany provides excellent examples of the contingencies which affect legal cultures. Until the beginning of the nine-

---

1. Charles de Montesquieu, *De l'esprit des lois*, 1748.

teenth century, law had been a patchwork of jurisdictions sometimes based on locality and usually on status (such as whether a person was town burger, a member of a guild, or the gentry). During the eighteenth century there were attempts at detailed codification of substantive law (in Prussia and Austria, as well as other German princedoms), but it was the codification after the French revolution that created uniform law on the basis of egalitarian and individualistic values. It meant legislating not only substantive law codes, but also a system of procedural and organizational statutes (in contrast to the common-law tradition, which regulates organization and procedure by a hodgepodge of "rules of court"). The bourgeoisie used codified law on the Continent to establish a legalistic guarantee of juridical autonomy, which became the hallmark of the liberal state throughout postrevolutionary Europe.

But the universalism implied in the Napoleonic codes was superseded by national codifications. After the Congress of Vienna in 1815 Europe entered an age of nation building. Revising the codes according to native traditions became one of the central issues of national identity formation, but the system of codification, the structure of courts and other legal institutions, and much of the procedural law continued to be based on postrevolutionary French law. Colonial domination spread Austrian and German law to Eastern Europe. When forming national states, the emerging countries between the German-speaking and the Russian borders changed some substantive provisions, but they retained the overall codified structure. When in 1871 the twenty-five sovereign states became a unified Reich, uniform codification followed: a code of substantive criminal law in 1871, codes of criminal and civil procedure in 1877, a private law code in 1896, and commercial law in 1897.

While the codification movement in the nineteenth century established a "rule of law" free of political interference, it did not mean that the judiciary was rooted in democratic or egalitarian values. In Germany the ministries of justice supervised all legal education by state examinations, and they controlled the recruitment and the careers of prosecutors and judges. Mobility between the bar and the judiciary remained out of the ordinary, as judicial office was regarded in principle as a lifelong internal career ladder. Jews, for example, despite the emancipation edict of 1869, were discriminated against when they wanted to enter or be promoted within any part of the civil service (including the judiciary) until the end of the Kaiserreich (in 1918). Forming a substantial part of the legal profession, most Jews remained attorneys which offered them free access. Women were not admitted to state office until 1922. The Weimar Republic did away with such barriers, but it did not eliminate the antidemocratic attitudes among most judges.

The recognition of a mutual relationship between democratic ideals and the "rule of law" slowly gained ground among legal scholars and attorneys during the 1920s. The six-volume survey which the national high court

(Reichsgericht) issued at its anniversary is representative of the polarization of pro- and antidemocratic legal scholars; it included presentations of an authoritarian idea of the state on the one hand, and socialist concepts of an "economic democracy," on the other.[2] When the Nazis seized power in 1933, they ended the slow process of adaptation to democracy which the legal profession was undergoing. Statutory law in the Third Reich was either changed or replaced by prerogatives (*Maβnahmestaat*).[3] The Nazis increasingly used courts to legitimize the totalitarian rule including the extinction of political enemies and the genocide of everyone considered non-Aryan. Even though the Leipzig Reichsgericht tried to maintain some degree of judicial autonomy, especially with regard to direct political interference from the national-socialist party and the secret police, it had to yield its jurisdiction on political offenses, which were easily labelled high treason to a "Peoples' Court" (Volksgerichtshof) from 1934 onward. The high court continued to cede principles of law to political priorities throughout the twelve-year-rule of the Nazi regime. While the substance of law was transformed, the rule of law and the structure of judicial institutions were formally maintained.[4]

After the defeat of the Nazi regime, the institutions of justice were brought back to their pre-totalitarian tradition. While the basic codes of the Weimar Republic remained valid, the racist legislation of the Nazi period was nullified and much of the judge-made law of the high courts had to be "purified": those decisions which remained "in the continuity of the rule of law" stayed as valid law, those which were considered "racist" had to be invalidated as "aberrations from the true principles of law." The victorious Western allies provided the impetus to establish some of their own legal institutions: in Soviet-dominated East Germany this meant introducing a strong lay element, recruiting judicial personnel by vote of the political bodies, building a proletarian corps of the legal profession. and providing political guidance for prosecutors and courts. In West Germany a separate court for constitutional review was introduced which evolved into a judicial body of great authority and involvement in the political arena.

The East German communist regime made denazification of the legal profession a priority. In the first years after World War II they used special courts

2. O. Schreiber (ed.), *Die Reichsgerichtspraxis im deutschen Rechtsleben* (Jubilee edition of the German law faculties on the fiftieth anniversary of the Reichsgericht, Berlin: de Gruyter 1929). It includes contributions of Carl Schmitt (who later defended the "Führer principle"), on the one hand, and of socialist lawyers such as Hugo Sinzheimer, on the other.

3. Ernst Fraenkel, *The Dual State* (New York: Octagon Books, 1941).

4. Bernd Rüthers, *Die unbegrenzte Auslegung* (Tübingen: Mohr, 1968) rightly labelled the technique of perverting the substance of law while maintaining its form the "art of unlimited interpretation."

to try alleged Nazi members, and later the High Court of the GDR at Berlin took over the function of exposing former Nazis (especially those who had gained high office in West Germany).[5] True to the spirit of the Stalinist era, denazification was used for a number of show trials blaming the West Germans and legitimizing their own regime. Purges also dismissed bourgeois members from the courts without always proving their involvement in Nazi crimes. Without sufficient numbers of socialist and communist lawyers around, it took some time to replace prosecutors, judges, and attorneys with a proletarian background. Institutional reforms were introduced incrementally throughout the 1950s and 1960s. Soviet institutions superseded the Continental traditions with a twofold strategy: democratizing justice by introducing a strong lay element and at the same time establishing a central steering role for the prosecutorial power of the state. After the end of the Cold War, these socialist judicial institutions were replaced according to the Western model during the 1990s.

The lesson should be clear: politics has always determined courts and the law, but an undercurrent of judicial autonomy has been as pervasive as the iterative changes in political fate. The "theory of continuity" which the West German Federal High Court (Bundesgerichtshof) espoused in the last forty years is indicative of the identity crisis which changing regimes create for the idea of the "rule of law." Assuming that the rule of law (Rechtsstaat) is based on principles that are above current political considerations, the highest German court in civil and penal matters claims a continuity since 1879. Even the decisions of its predecessor, the Reichsgericht during Nazi times, are valid law in Germany unless the current court determines that they are based on racist or fascist ideas which, of course, are not viewed as in the tradition of the "true" law.

The end of the Cold War has simplified matters. The ideas and institutions of socialist law in East Germany and its ex-communist neighbors have been put on the shelves of history. According to the ideas of the West German "rule of law," they are yet another example of "false law" (*Unrecht*, in contrast to the true *Recht*). And indeed, not even idealist communists of the revolutionary generation deny that law in the communist countries (including the German Democratic Republic) had been used for political repression and secret surveillance. They, too, hold their "true" idea of law against a "false" reality, but in their case the political domination of the West has prevailed over their idea of "true law."

5. The famed "Weinheim trials" in 1950 were initiated by the Soviet occupation forces but taken over by East German authorities, trying some 1,500 prisoners in denazification camps, it sentenced and executed thirty-two. Among others who were involved in exposing former Nazis were the chief secretary of Konrad Adenauer's office, Hans Globke, and the West German Minister Theodor Oberländer.

LEGAL SYSTEM AND LEGAL CULTURE

German legal history makes clear what otherwise is hidden in the tradition of countries with fewer breaks in their history: the concept of "law" is multi-layered. Next to presumably universal ideas of law we talk about the valid body of law at a specific time and place, and we may contrast both with the observable practice of law. Following that distinction I shall call the bodies of law that are valid at a specific time and place (thus, the five countries compared in this volume in our times) the *legal system* and contrast them to legal practice. I consider this as a first step to comparing "legal cultures."

The frame of this book is the comparison of two common law countries, England/Wales and the United States, with three civil law countries, France, Germany, and Japan. Civil law is a system of codes which permits one to deductively infer the norms concerning a specific case, while common law is developed on the basis of case decisions inductively building up to a body of law. The language in which we describe our legal systems is shaped by these differences: discussing French or German legal institutions in the English language inevitably leads to incongruities. But the differences between these and the Japanese culture (which adopted German codes at the beginning of the twentieth century) are more extensive: the Japanese bureaucracy has established such tight control over the legal profession that the scope of law in social and economic life is radically limited compared to the legal culture of its German ancestors.[6] But while the training, access to, and composition of the legal profession forms an essential difference between families of legal systems, it can be seen as a cause as well as an effect of other elements of the culture. Comparative lawyers who focus on legal procedure more than on substantive law tend to emphasize the style of proceedings as distinguishing feature: common-law practice is supposedly more adversarial, based on the action of the parties and their lawyers, while Continental procedure is more judge centered and supposedly inquisitorial.[7] Again, while there is truth to such distinctions, there are also basic differences in procedural styles from one civil law or one common law country to the next. Legal systems throughout history have taken over elements of others' institutions and at the same time varied them by other elements of legal culture, resulting in individual entities characterized by clusters of variables on many levels.

The focus of this chapter is on the present German legal culture shaped as it is by West German institutional traditions. East German data from communist times are presented where appropriate in order to emphasize the features of the Western rule of law. Comparisons to the related civil-law cultures

6. Cf. chapter 6 on the role of the Legal Training Institute.

7. Cf. Mirjan Damaska, *The Faces of Justice and State Authority: A Comparative Approach to the Legal Process* (New Haven: Yale University Press, 1986).

of France and Japan are used to highlight German peculiarities among other civil law countries. Such comparisons clarify the difference between looking at "cultures," as opposed to "systems" of law, because even though these nations belong to the same family of closely related legal systems, their practice of law sometimes differs substantially. While a description of the legal culture must be based on at least cursory information about the valid body of law and the structure of legal institutions, its central focus is on behavioral data about people who use the law and of the ways it is implemented.

Comparisons within the civil law family show that similarity of formal legal systems (the laws on the books) is a bad predictor of how legal cultures actually work. While I employ the term *legal system* to describe only the characteristics of the formal institutions and the statutes of positive law, *legal culture* is here used to describe the actual application and invocation of law.[8] Legal behavior cannot be predicted on the basis of the rules of the legal system alone, but only on the basis of rules in the context of information about social factors determining when, how far, and by whom those rules are being used. Legal culture is thus a complex interrelationship of four levels:

- the body of substantive as well as procedural law and the rules of jurisdiction which traditionally form the subject of comparative law;
- institutional features such as the structure of the legal profession, the organization of courts and the infrastructure of access to them; legal training, scholarship, and the patterns of legal discourse.
- patterns of behavior that become visible in litigation or remain invisible such as avoidance of lawyers and courts;
- and the level of legal consciousness which signifies the values, beliefs, and attitudes toward law. For each of these dimensions, we need to take varying social characteristics into account. Especially when examining legal consciousness it makes a great difference whether we look at the general public, the legal profession, or specific subgroups.

Including an attitudinal layer of legal consciousness will enable us to make valid comparisons of legal cultures. More space than would usually be

---

8. I use the term *legal system* here in the sense of the comparative law literature, not to be confused with the concepts of "systems theory" in political science or sociology. Likewise, I do not follow the definition of *legal culture* among American law-and-society scholars who define this term as the "values, beliefs and attitudes with respect to law and legal institutions" (Lawrence Friedman, *The Legal System* [New York: Russell Sage, 1975]). While such conceptualization seems useful within the context of a single legal tradition, it is less plausible in the context of a comparative sociology of law.

granted in a work on the relations of courts and politics is devoted to access to courts, to the patterns of mobilization of lawyers and lower courts. As a concomitant of their lifelong career, the position of judges in lower courts on the European continent is usually not considered a matter of politics. In comparative perspective, however, the scope of cases, the party constellations, and the kind of disputes they bring forward is of undisputed political relevance. It shapes the borderline which is drawn between the realm of politics and that of the rule of law. In hinting at some comparisons with neighboring countries and with institutions familiar to American readers I shall try to characterize the specific features of the German legal culture. Contrary to common beliefs among American scholars, however, I do not assume that the explanation for cultural differences can first be found in popular beliefs and attitudes toward law. Unfortunately most of the data in the comparative literature are illustrative and present no more than impressions. But whatever variations of national attitude profiles have been found cannot explain the variety of behavioral patterns by which legal cultures differ from one country to the next.[9] Litigation behavior is one of the main sets of data which presents a challenge for explanation; neither traditional comparative law, nor the little information which we have on attitudes toward law would make us predict how different the scope of legal behavior is between Germany and its neighbors. It is even less plausible to expect that the radical changes of political regime in German history and the changing face of the rule of law would be explained by popular attitudes toward the rule of law. We will, rather, have to examine institutional structures of the German legal culture in order to explain continuities and changes of the role of the legal profession toward democracy and the rule of law.

Court Structure and Jurisdiction

German judicial institutions share basic formal features with other civil law countries. They have in common a legacy of Continental procedural traditions and court organization.[10] A two-tier system of first-instance courts handles criminal cases, with misdemeanors processed by local courts and more serious offenses heard by district courts.[11] Civil litigation is also processed by

9. Cf. Adam Podgorecki et al., *Knowledge and Opinion of Law* (London: Martin Robertson, 1973).

10. For a general introduction into the German legal system cf. Dieter Medicus, "Federal Republic of Germany," in *International Encyclopedia of Comparative Law* E, F1, F3–4 (Hamburg: Max Planck Institute, 1972); for the political context in which German courts function, P. M. Blair, *Federalism and Judicial Review in West Germany* (Oxford: Clarendon, 1981).

11. First-instance courts are roughly comparable to trial courts in England and the United States.

first-instance courts: the local courts handle small claims (presently up to DM10,000, approximately $7,000) as well as all matters of tenant law and family, and district courts hear cases with larger claims. The local courts also handle a number of noncontentious matters (such as registration of business failures and leaving church membership) and operate a summary dunning procedure for debt collection which will be tried in court only if there is an explicit objection by the debtor.

The main reason for segregating petty claims and dealing with them in a summary fashion is their high volume. As caseloads increased, the courts have repeatedly raised the threshold of what is "petty" as opposed to "serious." Criminal court prosecutors obtained increasing authority to handle routine cases without any judicial hearing, unless the accused objects. In civil cases the rising threshold has more than compensated for inflation in assigning local courts cases above what many people might consider small claims. The different tiers of judicial procedure—from the routines of pre-court and summary proceedings, to procedures with a hearing before a single judge, to hearings before various kinds of tribunals—provide an insight into the priorities with which the procedural and organizational codes allocate the time and effort spent on a case, thereby indicating its perceived seriousness.

The institutionalized perceptions of pettiness and seriousness reveal their policy implications most clearly with regard to the operation of criminal courts.[12] In criminal cases the prosecutor chooses between summary procedures and different benches according to the maximum possible sentence. Repeated streamlining reforms have enlarged the tier of pre-court summary procedures, so that the prosecutors' office handles the bulk of petty crime without formally charging before a court. Early in the Weimar Republic during its most liberal phase, a summary punitive order (Strafbefehl) was introduced as part of a general procedural reform. If a suspect consents, fines could be imposed without an oral hearing. Now prosecutors decide on these summary procedures on their own and a judge simply countersigns most of them. In an effort to streamline the judicial process since 1968, the use of summary procedures has been expanded to include such sanctions as invalidating a driver's license and imposing prison sentences of up to three months. In addition, prosecutors have been granted increasing authority to use their discretion not to prosecute or to drop charges if the defendant agrees to enroll in a diversion program. They may even grant dismissals in exchange for the defendant's making a "voluntary" contribution to a charity in order to get a petty case off the docket, a form of plea bargaining legalized in 1974.

12. For legal details cf. John Langbein, *Comparative Criminal Procedure: Germany* (St. Paul, Minn.: West, 1977).

If a case is not disposed of by one of these preliminary procedures, the prosecutor decides before which criminal court it will be brought. Sentences of up to one year in prison can be decided by a single judge at local courts and those of up to two years by a professional judge together with two lay referees (Schöffen). As sentencing in Germany is generally milder than in the United States, this covers most crimes. Very serious crimes with a possible prison penalty of two years or more are heard by a district court with three judges and two lay referees. Even though in practice the lay referees are often rather passive, they are expected to participate in the entire decision-making process at the hearing and the sentencing; thus they are not restricted to a verdict of guilty or not guilty like American juries predominantly are.

A special section of the criminal courts handles cases involving juveniles (from age fourteen to eighteen, and sometimes up to twenty-one). The law permits a wide range of educational measures and allows for dismissal from prosecution with or without referring the suspects to diversion programs.

In civil cases the jurisdiction of the court determines whether an attorney is needed as representative or not. Landlord-tenant cases are always before local courts, divorce before special family divisions with representation being compulsory. In all other civil cases, the competence of local courts ends at a rather arbitrary threshold which is set by statute (in 1995 at DM10,000, or $7,000). Parties can, however, channel their cases by agreement. Repeat players do this routinely by standard contract which makes local courts especially attractive to business litigants who routinely use courts for debt collection and similar routine procedures. The thresholds also have considerable consequences for the workload of appellate courts and for lawyers' litigation strategies. Disputants and their attorneys need considerable foresight about their likely success at one level or the other in deciding how much to claim because that determines which court they will appear before. Moreover, lawyer fees are computed on the basis of the value at stake. Contingency arrangements, like those in the United States, are considered unethical.

No one has blamed the arbitrary jurisdiction thresholds and the ease in circumventing them for their social consequences of favoring the repeat player and discriminating against the occasional litigant; however, they have repeatedly been criticized for their adverse effects in administering court caseloads. By focusing on internal organizational problems, the judiciary demonstrates that social effects are of secondary concern to them. The association of judges (Richterverein) has been much more concerned about procedural reform that impacts their internal work organization. The two-tier jurisdiction of local and district courts in civil cases used to make a difference on the bench: in the local courts, single judges decided, whereas in district courts, a bench of three professional judges was traditionally prescribed by law. Contemporary practice in district courts, however, has resorted to delegating simple cases, especially the taking of evidence, to a single judge who then reports to the bench. A storm of protest broke when an amendment to the procedural code in 1975 offered district courts a choice, and when reformers tried to abolish the multijudge bench in all first-instance civil cases. To the external observer it demonstrated that internal work arrangements arouse more judicial protest than any analysis of the social effects of the scope of civil justice outside the court building.[13]

SYSTEM OF APPEALS

In principle litigants in German courts can appeal first-instance decisions in a de novo proceeding (see figure 5.1). There are a number of explicit exemptions, however. Verdicts of district criminal courts can be appealed only under extreme circumstances such as in cases of alleged abuse of law—thus, strangely enough, while for minor misdemeanors a trial de novo can be admissible, verdicts on serious crimes and felonies are final. In civil cases appeal is generally available, except if the stakes are very small (presently appeal de novo is allowed for stakes above DM1,500, approximately $900). Appeals exclusively on points of law ("Revision") are treated by the Federal High Court, which examines the legal merits before admitting the case. If the value at stake exceeds DM 40,000, parties are entitled to be heard in appeal.

ADMINISTRATIVE TASKS OF COURTS

First-instance courts also perform a number of administrative and pre-trial tasks. Local courts handle several registries such as lists of registered associations and of church membership (which is used for levying a membership "tax" by which churches are financed). They also enforce the collection of child support and implementation of custody orders. District courts house the prosecution service that issues criminal charges and supervises the enforcement of criminal sentences. Formally, prosecutors can initiate cases and direct the police in their criminal investigations; in practice, however, they rely largely on the police for evidence and for the input of cases. Germany has no investigating magistrates such as exist in France.

SPECIALIZED COURTS

Public agencies have their own court system to handle complaints. The German tradition emphasizes the binding character of any administrative decision, with the consequence that every decision of a governmental agency is subject to re-

13. I refer to the discussion of introducing a single-tier court organization in 1972–74 and introducing a single-judge bench in district courts in 1984–86. Cf. the discussions in the journal of the judges' association, *Deutsche Richterzeitung* at those times. Survey evidence of the self-image of judges can be found in Raymund Werle, *Justizorganisation und Selbstverständnis der Richter* (Kronberg: Athenäum, 1977).

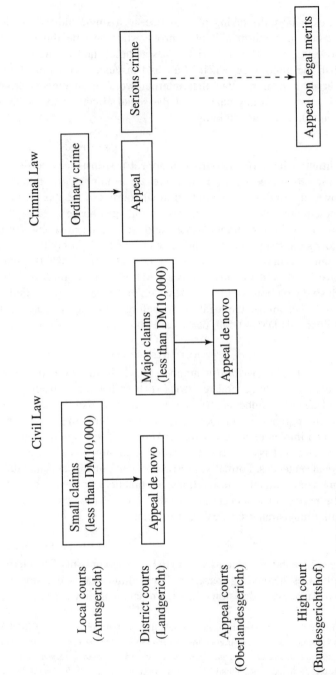

Figure 5.1. Appeals Process in Ordinary Courts

view by a court on the grounds of substance and due process. Complaints about decisions of federal, state, and local government entities have to first exhaust internal complaint procedures, and if this does not satisfy the plaintiffs they can invoke the general administrative courts. They consist of a first-instance court with a professional judge and two lay judges on the bench, with three professional and two lay judges in appeal. Even though many administrative complaints concern the implementation of policies at the state and community level, plaintiffs can often find legal points in federal legislation that are admissible for a second appeal before the Federal Administrative Court. The system thus provides four levels of proceedings, of which three are judicial: an original complaint, a judicial hearing in first instance, a de novo hearing before the state court of appeals, and a high court appeal on legal points.

Additional specialized administrative courts handle other disputes. Social security courts hear disputes arising from the administration of social insurance programs after the claimants have exhausted internal complaint procedures. As in the administrative courts, a bench of one professional and two lay judges hear cases originally, after which there are two levels of appeal. Fiscal courts hear disputes about taxes after the taxpayer has exhausted the internal complaint procedure.

Still another court system, in most states under supervision of the Ministry of Labor, handles labor disputes. Such labor courts were established in 1927 as a reflection of the corporatist ideas which bind trade unions and employers with representatives of the public interest in a tripartite legal framework. Socialist lawyers saw the right to strike, the institution of collective bargaining, and the tripartite bench in labor courts as elements of industrial democracy in the framework of an ''economic constitution'' which was to complement the ''political constitution'' of representative democracy. The courts were to force labor-management disputes into a procedural framework similar to the political process of party competition and parliamentary decision making. Labor courts provide two levels of appeal like most other courts, but their procedural code puts more emphasis on conciliation than do the regular courts. Labor courts hear individual as well as collective complaints about employment contracts. They decide on the basis of statutory law and on the provisions agreed upon in collective-bargaining agreements. Reflecting that dual source of substantive law, the procedure also contains a corporatist element because the judges who decide labor cases both at the original hearing and first appeal include one professional judge representing the state, one trade unionist, and one employer's representative. The parties are often represented by the lawyers of their union or business group rather than by independent attorneys.

Each of these specialized courts has its own federal court of appeals. Although lower courts are not bound by a stare decisis principle, they tend

Table 5.1. Number of Divisions (Senates) and Judges in
Diverse High Courts, 1990

	Divisions	Judges
Constitutional court	2	16
Federal high court		
civil senates	12	85
penal senates	5	37
Federal labor court	10	27
Federal administrative court	15	65
Federal social court	14	39
Federal fiscal court	11	60

Source: Jurisdiction regulations of the high courts, 1984, Bundesanzeiger 11.2.94. The federal court for registered patents is omitted here as it is a kangaroo court of the German Patent Office, comprised mainly of engineers and natural scientists, as are the federal disciplinary court and a number of senates for disciplinary matters of notaries, attorneys, and accountants, which are formed by judges of the various high courts.

to follow the decisions of higher courts. Table 5.1 shows the number of judges in each of the highest courts as well as the number of divisions (senates) by which they are organized.

The German Federal High Courts[14] are not a separate tier (like the U.S. federal court system), but rather the appellate level of a nationwide court system. However, local and district courts—whether general jurisdiction courts hearing criminal and civil cases or a specialized court hearing administrative, social insurance, or tax cases—are administered by the state (*Länder*) ministries of justice. Somewhat separate policies apply to labor courts, which are administered by the ministries of social and labor affairs in most states. The federal courts—which constitute the highest appellate level of each of the courts—are supported by the federal budget, but for personnel recruitment and in organizational matters, the joint commission of the federal and the state ministries of justice is the policymaking body. The federal constitutional court is governed by its own federal statute.

The many specialized courts, each with its separate appeal and high courts, cover a wider area of disputes than do American courts. In the Continental legal tradition, which upholds an ideal of consistency of terminology and

14. In some of the American literature the Bundesgerichtshof is translated as "German Supreme Court," and the diverse revision courts as Administrative Supreme Court, Supreme Court of Labor, etc. As this might encourage an association with the American Supreme Court, which has jurisdiction on constitutional issues as well as on points of statutory law, I use the term High Court indicating that these are the highest appellate level on points of law, not including constitutional review.

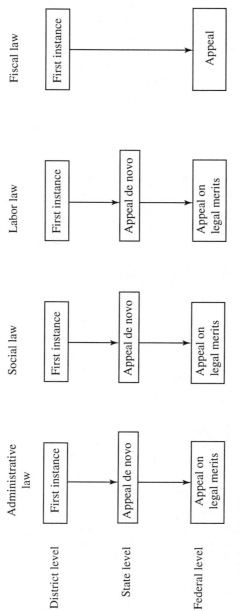

Figure 5.2. Specialized Courts

interpretations throughout the codified body of law, the diversity of appellate and high courts causes a potential problem of coordination. If decisions at the separate high courts at the federal level clash, for instance, when federal high courts employ inconsistent definitions of "violence" in criminal law, in tort law, and in labor law, they can be brought before a joint senate of judges of all the federal appeals courts chaired by the president of the federal high court. Each of the presidents of a high court can bring an issue of conceptual harmonization before the joint panel. In contrast to the American Supreme Court, which also functions as a constitutional court, the joint senate of the federal appeals courts only interprets within the boundaries of the statutory body of law.

With its many distinct court systems, each with its own trial courts, appellate courts, and federal high courts, with the further internal division of the federal high courts into specialized senates, the German judiciary has reached a degree of differentiation unsurpassed by any of its Continental neighbors. The federal high courts function as policymakers, innovating on the frontier of legal doctrine; their case decisions are intended to be in the interest of the law as much as to decide a conflict between two parties. As a result of the specialized courts and divisions within courts, the German judiciary encourages differentiation into autonomous fields of law. To elaborate further on an earlier example: the senate on strikes and lockouts of the federal labor court may develop a concept of what is legitimate use of violence that differs from one developed by the federal administrative court for political demonstrations, and both might need to be reconciled with the criminal law doctrine developed by the criminal senates of the federal high court. In order to coordinate such issues of doctrinal consistency and uniformity of law, each high court has an internal coordinating committee comprised of the chairs of the divisions, and together all the high courts form an overarching coordinating committee comprised of their respective chief judges (presidents). Comparing the size of the various German federal high courts (table 5.1) to the small club of judges in *cassation* in France or the British law Lords illustrates the considerable coordination problems of the German system.

Problems of specialization within each court system are aggravated by the distinct and closed career ladders of its judges. Federal court judges are recruited almost exclusively within their tier of either the ordinary lower courts or the respective administrative courts, including career civil servants from the departmental bureaucracies with whom they deal. Ideal candidates have some experience in a specialized administrative court and in the bureaucracy. The officials in the state ministries of justice who select federal court judges are committed to maintaining professional excellence within these courts. Thus they emphasize a sense of professional autonomy from party politics, but they also reinforce a strong sense of cohesion between government departments and the high courts.

Each of the specialized fields has developed its body of legal doctrine surrounded by its own controversy and consensus. A selection of the decisions of high courts is published in quasi-official collections in journals and on disk, usually prefaced by head notes (*Leitsätze*) formulated by federal appellate court judges. Interest groups publish and comment on the decisions and aspiring law professors write critical essays about them. The most influential collection of these decisions, however, are the continuously updated commentaries, which combine legal texts with short summaries and references to the "leading opinions." These are authored by federal appellate court judges and ministerial bureaucrats. Somewhat less authoritative are those written by law professors and attorneys.

Among the highest courts, the federal constitutional court (Bundesverfassungsgericht) stands out as the most political court. Its sixteen justices, who sit in two divisions, are elected by a commission of the two houses of the federal parliament. By statute, three of the eight members of each division must come from among the judges of the federal high courts; the other members are nominated by the parties represented in both houses of the federal parliament. Half of the justices are elected by a commission of the house of representatives (Bundestag), half of them by the senate house representing the governments of the states (Bundesrat). Both houses have to confirm by a two-thirds majority vote. The justices serve for twelve years. Even though it is not formally required, they are expected to have judicial experience, whether they are political nominees or career nominees. In fact, at least half of the Constitutional Court justices usually have followed a judicial career; the others are recruited from different backgrounds in the legal profession, mostly politicians and law professors. Party affiliations have always been apportioned according to quotas reflecting the political strength in both houses of the federal parliament, but they have seldom dominated the jurisprudence of the court.[15]

The complicated nomination process and the extraordinary majority needed for election favor the mainstream and exclude controversial politicians.[16] Usually public debate on the nominations is avoided. The committee

15. Cf. Christine Landfried, *Constitutional Review and Legislation* (Baden-Baden: Nomos, 1988).

16. A noticeable example was the refusal to nominate a highly qualified but controversial candidate from the Social Democratic party, Hertha Däubler-Gmelin, in 1993. After some party haggling, in 1994 a more middle-of-the-road Social Democratic (woman) candidate, Justice Jutta Limbach, was nominated in her place. Shortly after joining the court she was offered its presidency.

prefers to handle a fixed quota system with renegotiation only, if political majorities have drastically changed. The practice assures that the major parties are proportionately represented but renders it difficult for new parties to enter the club. Above all of the political criteria, however, there remains a basic professional prerequisite: candidates have to satisfy standards of professional excellence. The court has the reputation of standing above party politics and endeavors to speak with the authority of unequivocal law. This ambition also explains that in the first twenty-two years of its existence the court did not publish any dissenting votes on its decisions; since 1972 it has displayed more openness about internal conflict and dissenting opinions have become quite customary.

The Legal Profession
GROWTH AND COMPOSITION

Not only the high courts, but also first- and second-tier trial courts employ more professional judges (relative to the size of the population) than any of the neighboring countries and many more than England and the United States. A judgeship in Germany is usually a lifelong career, starting right after the completion of legal education.

As in other civil law countries, entry into the legal profession is not defined by the admission to the bar, but rather by attainment of educational degrees, which are earned by taking university courses together with a period of apprenticeship training and passing a state examination. In many civil law countries, distinct apprenticeship programs are offered for the diverse careers within the legal profession, thus splitting the profession into distinguishable occupational divisions. However, the German tradition maintains a uniform system of qualification for all careers in the legal profession by keeping examinations under control of the judicial administrations of the sixteen states (Länder). Their judicial examination offices choose the tests for the university examinations from among the professors' proposals, leaving little room for law school teachers to deviate from the prescribed course of learning. The examiners administer the compulsory judicial apprenticeship which rounds out the legal training. Some authors suggest that the bureaucratic control of legal education is related to the belief of German lawyers in the nonpolitical quality of professional standards of law.[17] One would have to add to this factor the belief of German law professors in the objectivity of "legal science" (rather than manmade "jurisprudence," as the English term suggests).

17. Wolfgang Weyrauch, *The Personality of Lawyers: A Comparative Study of Subjective Factors in Law Based on Interviews with German Lawyers* (New Haven: Yale University Press, 1964).

Legal studies take an average of six years at one of the (presently forty-one) law faculties of German universities, followed by two years of apprenticeship at courts, administrative agencies, and a lawyer's office. Both the university phase and the apprenticeship stage are completed by passing a comprehensive state examination. Half the examiners for the university phase are university professors, and half are judges and administrators nominated by the departments of justice. Occasionally an attorney is found among them. The second examination, taken after the apprenticeship, is entirely in the hands of the judicial administration.

The orientation of legal education toward judicial careers and public office (rather than private law practice) has been criticized for generations, without much success. Even in the early 1990s, when more than half of the law graduates entered private legal practice, this emphasis was institutionalized anew in the Eastern part of the unified country. However, to meet competition of more condensed law school education in other parts of the European Union, there are efforts to shorten the university legal education. Nevertheless, these attempts have so far faltered on the statutory provisions requiring all who want to enter a judicial career or practice as an attorney to pass both state examinations.[18]

While the statutory framework for the state examinations is uniform throughout the country, its administration is up to the individual states. This fits the general pattern of public administration in the Federal Republic, which in the fields of justice, education, and science leaves the implementation of national statutes to the states. In comparison to American federalism, the individual states have less leeway in determining policy and are much more constrained by detailed national legislation. In addition, uniform implementation rules are issued by the conference of the federal and all state ministries. This renders German federalism rather centralized: each ministry of the federal government forms coordinating conferences, while at the state level ministers and state secretaries (the highest career civil servant in a ministry) formulate implementation guidelines.[19] In the legal profession, the Statute on Judgeships (Richtergesetz) provides a tight framework for legal education; details such as the standards regulating state

18. In 1993 a law school at the rather young University of Lüneburg offered a training program in law without aiming at the full-fledged status of state-examined lawyers. It raised an uproar among the established legal profession; however, the much shorter training programs in other countries of the European community may soon break the monopoly of the traditional law faculties and the state examination requirements. So far, cram courses of private examination trainers ("repetitors") fill the gap which university schooling leaves.

19. Cf. Renate Mayntz and Fritz Scharpf, *Policy Making in the Federal Republic of Germany* (Amsterdam: Elsevier, 1975).

examinations are added by the coordinating conference of all ministers of justice. A single Land (state) cannot deviate from the statute or the coordinative implementation rules.[20]

Thus, becoming a full-fledged lawyer (Volljurist) in Germany requires a highly regimented education. For those who choose a judicial career, bureaucratic control will continue. A personnel file at the state ministry of justice which employs them will accompany them throughout their civil service. Aspiring judges begin their careers in a prosecutor's office or at a local court, and then follow a long trail of promotions to a district court, appeal court and—for the select few—possibly a high court position at the federal level. Temporary assignments of one or two years to an administrative position are usually helpful. The large number of potential candidates for higher judgeships gives much discretion to superiors in the hierarchy, and while they may base their preferences on general impressions of allegiance, political party preferences do not play a role. The co-optative element prevails, especially since 1970, when the Statute on Judgeship was amended to provide for collegial evaluation in the commissions deciding on judicial promotions.[21] In general, the commissions base their preferences on professional criteria rather than on affiliations with gender, religious denominations, and other identity groups or political parties.

For the more ambitious jurists, an appointment to one of the federal high courts may be the crown of their career. Most of the federal judges come from the ranks of the judiciary of the states, with the consequence that outside candidates such as private practitioners or lawyer-politicians are generally discouraged. In federal high courts party allegiance may play a role: nomination proposals by the state ministries of justice are apportioned to political parties according to their parliamentary strength. Not every applicant, however, may have a political affiliation or wants to make it known; in any case, the co-optative evaluation of the federal court judges generally supersedes political considerations with professional criteria.

Only on the constitutional court does party affiliation dominate recruitment criteria. Here career judges provide less than half of the appointments; the other half are determined by the two houses of the national parliament.

20. Termination was the fate of some "reform law schools" in the 1970s (notably at new universities such as Augsburg, Bremen, and Trier) which tried to integrate university learning with in-practice training. An amendment to the "statute on judgeship" had opened such possibility in 1970 for an experimentation phase of twelve years, but it was not renewed in 1982 as the national parliament had turned more conservative.

21. Some of the states (foremost Bavaria) still pursue a rather centralized recruitment and promotion policy, others (foremost in Northern Germany) rely more on co-optative committees, cf. David Clark, "The Selection and Accountability of Judges in West Germany: Implementation of a Rechtsstaat," *Southern California Law Review* 61 (1988), 1797–1847.

The fact that the recruitment of judges is determined largely by professional criteria increases the autonomy of the judiciary from politics. At the same time it diminishes the chance for democratic legitimation of the profession: in place of campaigning for a popular vote (as in many American states), German judges have to pay tribute to the pervasive administrative control throughout their career. The security of a tenured position at an early age provides little incentive to leave for other legal occupations, and at the same time it prevents entry of experienced lawyers from other parts of the legal profession. Civil service security and political autonomy of the German judiciary are achieved at the price of their separation from other parts of the legal profession. Despite the considerable size of the judiciary, they form a minority within the composition of the entire German legal profession (see figure 5.3).

Including law-trained graduates outside the judiciary and the bar the legal profession is even larger as is evident from indicator comparisons. As figure 5.3 shows, more than half the law graduates presently enter private practice. One third stay with it, but among the remainder, lawyers move between salaried positions in insurance companies or legal departments of corporations and associations. Many lawyers combine salaried positions with private practice, even though their admission to private practice is restricted, and they have to register in a special list of "syndicus lawyers." Finally, a sizable gray market of nonpracticing lawyers at the margins of the profession stay in for career flexibility, for status, and sometimes in order to profit from tax exemptions and pension benefits.[22]

Among private practitioners, the organizational setting is changing slowly. Compared to American law firms or those in London, Brussels, or Rotterdam, German attorneys still work in craftlike organizations with fewer than ten partners, and only a few are salaried lawyers. Until 1987 professional regulations forbade partnerships extending beyond one locale, but since then partnerships with branch offices in many parts of the country have been formed. East German attorneys in particular have sought West German partners since the unification in 1990, and as there appeared to be an overall shortage of Eastern lawyers, many West German law firms opened branch offices there. The number and size of law firms with more than ten partners still remains quite small (see table 5.3); they cluster around commercial centers like Frankfurt, Düsseldorf, Hamburg, and Cologne.

In the development of international law firms in the 1980s German lawyers have been laggards. Most attorneys still work as general practitioners for a

---

22. The Bar Association (Bundesrechtsanwaltskammer) when comparing their membership directory with that of the corporate income tax statistics comes up with about 30 percent not practicing members; considerably lower estimates are given by Michael Hartmann, *Juristen in der Wirtschaft* (Munich: Beck, 1992) who obtains his data by counting lawyers in salaried employment from a sample survey of companies.

Thousands

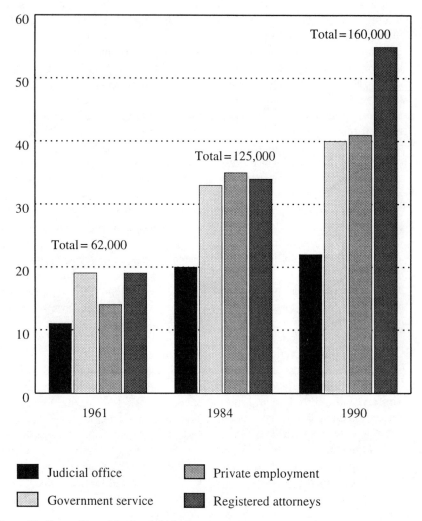

Figure 5.3. Composition of the Legal Profession

Table 5.2. Number and Size of German Law Firms

	1967	1980	1991
Number of registered attorneys	20,543	30,077	59,455
percentage in partnerships	26	38	39
estimated not in practice	25	30	25
solo lawyers in practice	49	32	36
Number of law firms with			
two to three partners	2,185	4,400	6,557
four to nine partners	149	704	1,429
ten or more partners	0	14	91

Source: Annual statistics, Chamber of Advocates, Bonn.

private as well as a business clientele. Exclusive specialization is rare and its advertising is statutorily limited to a few registered specialists in fiscal matters, administrative, social, or labor law.

As in many other postindustrial countries, there has been an explosive growth of the German legal profession since 1960 (table 5.2). The principal cause has been the extension of higher education. While in 1961 only 8 percent of all twenty-year-olds received a university education, in 1990 approximately 25 percent did so. As this growth of the educational system was accompanied by the formation of many new academic disciplines, the share of law students shows a long-term downward trend. However, in recent times legal education has risen in popularity with university students at the cost of the social sciences and pedagogical fields—this is clearly due to the labor market, which offers more chances for beginning lawyers than for teachers, social workers, or social scientists.

Nevertheless, fewer law graduates than ever find a salaried position at the beginning of their career. While previous generations were accustomed to choosing between tenure in the civil service and a judiciary position, or a more entrepreneurial career as private attorney or as counsel for a business enterprise, present-day jurists often have to start as private attorneys because no other employment is readily available. In the 1960s about one-third of all law graduates found positions in the civil service, only one-third entered private practice. In the 1980s less than 10 percent could count on public employment, and about 50 percent entered private practice.

The annual number of law graduates rose from 2,173 in 1960 to 7,419 in 1990. The size of the bar therefore has grown at a rate of approximately 6 percent per year. Part of the growth stems from greater enrollment of women in universities and their changing career opportunities. Women were first admitted to the bar in 1922, but they remained few and were excluded again during the Nazi period. Admitted once more after the Second World War,

Table 5.3. Representation of Women in Judicial Careers

	1973	1977	1981	1990
Law students	15%	25%	33%	45%
Judges on Probation	13	18	24	38
Judges in Tenured Position	9	11	14	18
Judges in Appeal Courts	—[a]	6	8	9

[a] no data

Source: Angela Hassels and Christoph Hommerich, *Frauen in der Justiz* (Cologne: Budesanzeiger Verlag, 1992).

their numbers nevertheless remained low until the 1980s. Since the beginning of the 1970s the gender gap started to lessen, slowly working its way up in the hierarchy of judicial careers (see table 5.3). However, even controlling for the generational gap by comparing age cohorts, women tend to be underrepresented among the higher positions.

INDICATOR COMPARISONS OF THE LEGAL PROFESSION

Judging by Continental standards, the German bar is quite sizable, but the judiciary stands out even more in international comparisons by its size (see table 5.4). Since 1984 when we collected comparative data in a systematic way, the number of judges has grown in a few countries by about 10 percent, as compared to the growth of attorneys in all countries on the Continent by an average of 50 percent.[23] Notably, the growth is paralleled in the United Kingdom and even surpassed by the United States. Japan is the one exception where the size of the legal profession is officially kept at a low level, so that the growing number of university graduates in law find their place in the salaried job market. Altogether, the rank order as shown in table 5.4 has remained the same. The situation in the former East Germany changed entirely with the change of regime: the bar is slowly catching up to the West German level; the judiciary in 1992 had reached about one-half the size of West Germany, but since then it has achieved a similar size within a few years.

Some of the differences of the size of the profession are due to different functional definitions of what judges and attorneys do. In continental countries such as France clerks handle the pre-hearing stage of procedures much more independently than in Germany, where judges reserve the privilege of handling preliminary procedures entirely. In England and Wales, justices of the peace who sit on courts that hear minor misdemeanor cases rely heavily on the preparatory work of court clerks. Thus, indicator comparisons of num-

23. Erhard Blankenburg (ed.), *Prozessflut: Indikatorenvergleich der Rechtskulturen auf dem europäischen Kontinent* (Cologne: Bundesanzeiger, 1989).

Table 5.4. Judges and Attorneys in West Germany, East Germany, France, Japan, England/Wales, and the United States (per 100,000 population)

	Attorneys	Professional Judges
West Germany (FRG 1992/1989)	94	28
East Germany (GDR 1989)	4	9
France (1992)	41	10
Japan (1984)	9	2
England/Wales (1992/1982)[a]	110	2
United States (1990/1987)[b]	320	12

[a]Judiciary including Puisne judges at high court, circuit judges, and recorders as shown in Judicial Statistics, p. 100. Does not include assistant recorders and chairpersons of tribunals.
[b]Includes state courts as well as federal and U.S. courts.

Sources: Attorneys 1992; Eurostat NACE 835. Japan: Statistical yearbook/ USA: ABA data on National Lawyer Population, 1993; England/Wales: barristers and solicitors. Judges: E. Blankenburg, *Prozessflut* (Cologne: Bundesanzeiger, 1989). United States: Klaus Röhl, *Gerichtsverwaltung und Court Management in dem USA* (Cologne: Bundesanzeiger, 1993).

bers of professional judges reflect only part of the judiciary; they are indicative only if interpreted in relation to the internal organization of courts and procedures.[24] Together with litigation data (see chapter 4), they present excellent starting points for a comparison of legal cultures.

Similar caveats have to be made with respect to what attorneys do. We should be careful when comparing the American rate of 320 lawyers per 100,000 of the population to the much lower rates of Continental attorneys because of the differences in profile. American lawyers perform a much wider array of legal services, which on the Continent are more often preformed by in-house legal departments and by other professions such as real estate agents or notaries. And even among Continental attorneys there are differences in the degree to which they are focusing on litigation services.[25] In Germany

24. Rates of professional judges as compared in table 5.4 would be thoroughly misleading, unless interpreted in relation to organizational factors. Especially the amount of delegation of judges' work to substitute judges, part time chairpersons and court clerks varies greatly from one system to another. The comparison, thus, should be used to point at those very characteristics: German courts stand out by strictly keeping to career judges on the bench, while British courts employ a great number of volunteer judges ("judges of the peace"), part-time lawyers ("assistant recorders"). Furthermore, a great deal of preparatory court work which Germans consider as being "strictly within judges' responsibility" is delegated in British and French courts to clerks (court clerks i.e., "greffiers").

25. Cf. Mieke Berends, "An Elusive Profession? Lawyers in Society," *Law and Society Review* 26, 1 (1992), 161–181.

the bar enjoys a statutory monopoly for legal advice and representation; they do not encounter any competition from other professions and paralegal services as they do in France or in common law countries, nor do they engage in conveyancing and other economic activities as do English solicitors or American lawyers. On the other hand, many trained German jurists are working in salaried positions in associations and big companies. The exclusiveness of the German Rechtsanwalt is not by far as extreme as that of the Japanese bengoshi, but the more limited scope of activities explains part of the difference in size of the legal professions.

COMPARISON OF WEST GERMANY TO EAST GERMANY

The comparison of litigation patterns below shows that West German (as well as Austrian and Belgian) legal practice is clearly more inclusive than the French, Danish, or Dutch. Even more striking is the insignificant role which law and the legal profession played in the communist countries.

Lawyers in communist countries were considerably less important as regulators of conflict than in the developed Western world. Both the small size of the bar and the number of attorneys relative to that of prosecutors and professional judges indicate a less comprehensive reach of the law in East Germany than West Germany. The quantitative relation of prosecutors to attorneys indicates which functions of law predominate in a regime. East Germany's repressive regime employed two prosecutors and as many professional judges per attorney; West Germany's liberal state had three attorneys for every judge (compared to about thirty lawyers per judge in the United States).

Communist authors used to argue that the many (59,000) lay judges in East Germany more than compensated for the small number of professional jurists. However, the role of the lay judges was mostly passive; their function was more to educate than to exercise a decisive influence in court procedures.[26] The explanation for the small number of professional jurists in East Germany is rather to be found in the relative marginality of litigation in the communist state. Almost half of the civil litigation concerned family matters, while cases of debt enforcement and civil liability (which keeps Western courts busy) were rare. Much economic activity took place in black markets, and disputes arising from it could not be litigated, as the only result would be that the prosecutor would charge both parties with illegal trading. Economic disputes between collective enterprises, on the other hand, were handled by an economic tribunal housed in the ministry responsible for the planned economy. The 120 "judges" on this tribunal were more involved in

26. Cf. Inga Markovits, "Pursuing One's Rights under Socialism," in *Stanford Law Review* 38 (1986), 689 ff.

bargaining than in deciding on cases. Review of administrative decisions, which occupies about one-third of West German judges in the specialized administrative, social, and fiscal courts, was entirely informal in East Germany, taking the form of "complaint letters." The East Germans also had disciplinary committees in most workplaces and in some neighborhoods ("societal courts"); these handled many petty offenses which in Western countries might partly be considered minor crimes, but partly would not be legally prohibited at all. The scope of informal disciplinary proceedings was wider in East Germany than the due process-controlled judicial proceedings in the West.

THE PURGE OF EAST GERMAN LAWYERS AFTER THE UNIFICATION

In anticipation of the unification at the end of 1989, many in the East German legal profession realized that their jobs might be terminated together with the political regime. The last GDR government replaced well-known communist jurists in high offices, and a number of law professors were asked to leave. Some of them quickly switched to private practice, but possibly not those who thought themselves to be apolitical.[27] Within the twelve months before unification, the number of registered attorneys in East Germany tripled due to an estimated 1,000 jurists who lost their government position and about 270 West German lawyers who saw a quick chance to get work in the "wild East."[28]

After unification, when West German law was imposed on East Germany, all law professors, judges, and prosecutors had to re-apply for their jobs. Questionnaires were handed out to every applicant with questions on party membership, activities in mass organizations, and participation in political trials.[29] Many former judges chose not to apply and became eligible for unemployment benefits; some accepted early retirement and a pension. About two-thirds of the former judges and prosecutors reapplied, but only about half of them were reinstated. Especially in Berlin, where Cold War sentiments still ran high, only 10 percent percent of the judges and prosecutors were reappointed;[30] in other

27. Cf. Inga Markovits, "Last Days," *California Law Review* 80 (1992), 55–129.

28. Own estimate on the basis of a count of the membership of the East German bar when unifying with the western association at the end of 1990.

29. For a documentation see Diemut Maier, "Die Überprüfung von Richtern und Staatsanwälten in der ehemaligen DDR," *Zeitschrift für Rechtspolitik* 24 (1991), 171–179; a full account of the purge among civil servants from GDR times by the government agencies of united Germany is given by Hans-Ulrich Derlien, "German Unification and Bureaucratic Transformation," *International Political Science Review* 14 (1993), 319–334.

30. In Berlin there were 370 applicants, of whom 37 judges and 9 prosecutors were reappointed; a few got another chance to reapply in the neighboring state of Brandenburg (press release of the Senator of Justice 1992).

East German states 55 percent of the former judges and 45 percent of the prosecutors regained their positions. Considering the criteria of reappointment, it is no wonder that chances were better for young lawyers who were less likely to have been involved in politically sensitive cases. After reappointment these officials had to undergo a four-year probationary period working beside West German colleagues, some of whom temporarily filled the gaps in courts and in prosecutor's offices and others of whom were newly appointed lawyers. Most of the latter, just graduated from law school in West Germany, saw opportunities for promotion in their judicial career which they might have had their "old country" of West Germany.

A few of the former GDR judges were put before criminal courts in purification procedures after the unification. But while in some of the early cases of Stalinist show trials in the 1950s it was easy to prove "abuse of law," the younger generation of GDR lawyers in the 1970s and 1980s had usually done nothing more (or less) than sometimes to apply valid communist law very harshly. They especially prosecuted public political criticism and attempts to leave the country illegally, usually on the basis of secret service information. More than 100,000 who had been sentenced for such offenses under GDR justice were rehabilitated after the unification.

As the denazification process in the aftermath of World War II had left a trauma especially among younger Germans, criminal investigations against communist prosecutors and judges were taken up by a special staff of government crime prosecutors in Berlin.[31] Lustration as well as the continuing casework of ordinary courts in East Germany had to follow West German procedure after October 3, 1993, the day of the unification. But even though such systematic judicial legitimation of totalitarian surveillance is generally regarded as abuse of the law, it was not easy to assign individual responsibility to judges who had simply contributed to the general pattern of harsh political control. As in trials against former border guards, verdicts in criminal purification procedures had to meet a standard of excessive abuse and clear violation of human rights. The high court did so in December 1993—three years after the unification—with the result that a few former judges were sentenced and others acquitted.[32] The majority of the pending investigations against GDR jurists had to be terminated.

31. War crimes and genocide of the Nazi regime had been dealt with in two waves: initiated immediately after the Second World War by the allied occupation forces, mass procedures for denazification were rounded up by the early 1950s when Cold War issues became paramount; criminal procedures for war crimes and genocide were taken up again in the 1960s; by 1989 the Central Documentation for National Socialist Crimes at Ludwigsburg had registered 98,042 investigations and 6,486 verdicts for criminal acts under the Nazi regime. More than 10,000 investigations are still pending.

32. The leading decision is BGH 5 StR 76/93 of Dec. 13, 1993.

Implementing the Western style of judicial proceedings in East Germany were still in a formative state in the early 1990s. In order to reach the same level of staffing as in West Germany, the East German states would need 4,500 judges and about 1,000 prosecutors. Even if the GDR judiciary had not been diminished by about two-thirds by the purge following unification, courts would be understaffed by West German standards. Also university law faculties are still rebuilding. Only four of the GDR universities had law faculties, but their staff was largely dismissed after unification. Four new law schools have been founded since the unification, and others are still in the planning stage. Professors as well as assistant lecturers were mostly recruited from Western law schools. The number of graduates is very slowly increasing. Legally trained personnel sought by the judiciary and by administrative agencies, by local governments, as well as other organizations, have to be recruited from Western Germany and then convinced to move to the "Eastern provinces."

It was a little easier to persuade private attorneys to settle in the East. By the end of 1992, the Chamber of Advocates in former East Germany had registered about 4,000 members.[33] Many West German lawyers are actually practicing with East German branch offices or jointly with colleagues in East Germany. However, as they are not permitted to register in two districts simultaneously, we have no official data on their numbers.

Litigation Patterns

In describing legal institutions, comparative legal scholars usually focus on the supply side of the legal system. They describe the system of judicial institutions, the statutes on the legal profession, and legal education. When comparing legal cultures we have to supplement such descriptions with behavioral data about the demand for court services. Litigation indicators reflect differences in the scope of disputes which are treated as judicial problems, rather than as issues that belong in nonjudicial arenas. Whether people frame their problems in judicial terms might be seen as part of the general legal consciousness. We should be careful, however, in assuming that general attitudes and values determine the differences between legal cultures. Our comparative research rather suggests that the attitude patterns of the general public reflect the options, which the legal system offers to them.[34] In this sense, the scope of what people treat as legal issues is determined by the inclusiveness of what the legal system offers.

33. Own estimate of about 800 attorneys in East Berlin on the basis of address listings plus exactly 3,284 in the other Eastern states according to the membership data of the bar (Bundesrechtsanwaltskammer).

34. Blankenburg, *Prozessflut, supra* note 23.

Table 5.5. First-Instance Litigation Rates by Main Areas, West Germany
and East Germany, 1989 (per 100,000 population)

	West Germany		East Germany	
	N	rate	N	rate
Criminal courts (persons sentenced)	691,000	1,150	58,400	356
Societal courts (cases treated)	—	—	18,900	115
Summary debt enforcement	5,500,000	9,400	—[a]	118
Civil courts (adversary general)	1,672,000	2,740	62,000	387
Civil courts (divorce)	159,000	260	49,500	309
Labor courts	367,000	601	15,000	93
Administrative courts	117,000	192	—	—
Social security courts	168,000	275	—	—
Fiscal courts	43,000	70	—	—

[a]Labor law cases in East Germany were handled by civil courts.

Source: Judicial statistics, *Statistics Yearbook* 1989.

Data on who invokes courts and against whom lawsuits are directed are
a key to a behavioral analysis of legal culture. A comparison of West and
East German data before unification show the large scope of what is considered "legal" in West Germany, ranging from the high volume of everyday
crime, a high rate of debt collection, civil and labor lawsuits, to an elaborate
system of judicial complaints against the bureaucracies administering social
insurance programs, tax collection, and many other public policies. Life under
communism in the GDR excluded many of these issues from the courts. Petty
crime was partly treated by nonjudicial "societal courts." Debt collections
did not occur because the economy was not based on money as the essential
exchange commodity; labor dismissals were rare. Courts could not review
the actions of bureaucrats.[35]

Given the antilegal doctrine of Marxism and its practice, the East German
communist state experienced a very low level of litigation and had virtually
no judicial review of administrative agencies. Neither the planned economy
nor the gray market economy resorted to courts to process their business
disputes. As the exchange commodity is political power and social relation-

35. Shortly before the breakdown of the regime, in 1988 a very limited judicial complaint
procedure was introduced; it served a few citizens to stage a protest against permission to leave
the country being withheld, but never attained any significance.

ships, monetary claims, which are so prevalent in Western courts, do not make much sense. Thus the limited role of litigation under socialism and the broader role of law as a regulator in a capitalist economy and a welfare state such as prevails in Western Germany are clear.

However, the Marxist prediction that "law would wither away" with the end of capitalist antagonism did not come true in Eastern Germany. Even though crime rates were low and many everyday petty crimes were handled by lay "courts" and commissions in the GDR (as in other socialist countries), the criminal courts were given the highly visible task of suppressing political opposition and attempts to break the border controls along the wall separating East and West Germany. Lacking the administrative, social, and fiscal courts that in West Germany hear claims of citizens against public authorities, complaints against the state and its political organizations could only be launched by letters of petition in East Germany.

Litigation statistics, however, differ not only between East and West Germany, but also vary among Western countries. We shall present comparative civil litigation rates below. By pointing to such differences we can document why we characterize the litigation pattern of the (West) German legal culture as especially inclusive in comparison to some of its Western neighbors. This is true for both criminal and civil cases; criminal litigation will be examined first.

CRIMINAL JUSTICE
Crime Levels and Punitive Attitudes

Modern crime statistics all over the world show a rise in property crime and a general increase of violence, while other offenses such as indecency or vagrancy have almost disappeared from the records. Clearly these trends mirror changing attitudes toward the threats that people and judicial institutions deem serious enough to be criminalized. Other trends indicate a variety of behavioral changes that are insufficiently characterized by the single label of "crime."

A large volume of crime recorded by the police consists of such frequent offenses as shoplifting, petty theft, and vandalism. Among the offenders are middle-class consumers, who do not draw a strict distinction between legal and illegal consumption. Their crime rate grows with mass consumption and increasing urbanization. Other high-frequency offenses arise from the life style patterns in subcultures of drug users and other poverty groups. They accompany the increasing polarization of a rich society where two-thirds of the population are integrated in the world of work and social security while the remaining third remains marginalized. Another segment of the rise in crime stems from the increased ethnic and cultural heterogeneity of the population of Germany. While the first generation of immigrants from Mediterranean laborers to northern Europe in the 1960s and 1970s was less visible in the police statistics than Germans, the second generation now finds itself more often in trouble with the authorities. In the 1980s waves of migration from Eastern Europe increased the pressure on social stability. As in American urban areas, these social changes are related to real crime growth; they also cause diffuse sentiments of insecurity which in election campaigns are coined in terms of fear of crime.

While this pattern may sound familiar to North Americans, it is never as apparent in Europe as in the United States. No West European country suffers under as high a level of violence,[36] nor does public opinion react as punitively as do the majority of Americans (table 5.6). This can be demonstrated by correlating victimization surveys with attitudinal data. Comparable victim surveys in more than twenty countries place the incidence of victimization among West Germans near the upper end of the West Europeans (ranking second to the Netherlands). However, as much of the overall victimization rate consists of petty crime, it may be a direct consequence of the relative degrees of urbanization of these countries. More valid are rates of serious types of crime such as assault or burglary: on all these West Germany (and the Netherlands) rank highest in Western Europe, but even their rates remain considerably lower than those of the United States.[37]

It is tempting to correlate crime indicators with those of fear of crime and attitudes toward punishment with the punitive practice in different countries. The results, however, depend on whether we choose individual correlation of the respondents in these survey studies or ecological correlations of aggregate data comparing countries (as in table 5.6). The individual data suggest

36. Truly comparable indicators on incidence of crime and the public reaction are scarce. Cross-national police statistics are notoriously unreliable, and their categories cannot be interpreted without intimate knowledge of the way they are assembled. Even such seemingly clear categories as "intentionally afflicted violent death" used by the United Nations reveal such implausible results that we are left with speculations as to what they might mean. Their rank order places West Germany together with France in a middle category among the West European countries (with 3 to 4 violent deaths per 100,000 inhabitants per year), the United States with a rate of 11 among the highest while Japan and the communist countries (among them East Germany at a rate of 1 per 100,000) rank lowest. Cf. *UN Compendium of Social Statistics and Indicators* 1988, IX 34, p. 649 ff.

37. Jan van Dijk et al., *Experience of Crime Across the World* (Deventer: Kluwer, 1990). As other chapters of this book have argued victim surveys provide the best comparative indicator of level of crime, even though they have their shortcomings. They only refer to everyday incidents where individuals (rather than organizations) have been victims of property or violent crime. Very serious victimizations cannot be reliably measured that way; and organizations as victims (which make up about one third of the police statistics) and victimless crimes are excluded.

Table 5.6. Victimization Rates, Fear of Crime, and Attitudes toward Punishment

	Incidence					Attitudes[a]		
	Overall	Assault[b]	Household Burglary	Theft from Cars	Fear of Crime[c]		Preferred Punishment	
						Prison	Community Service
West Germany	21.9%	4.7%	1.4%	5.6%	40%	13%	60%
France	19.4	3.0	3.3	7.5	33	13	53
United States	28.8	10.1	5.1	12.4	38	53	30

[a]Punishment attitudes are measured by relating a fictional case of a recidivist burglar who is caught stealing a color television; would the respondent punish him or her in prison, community service, a fine, or other punishment? Preferred punishment figures represent percentage of all respondents; as not all alternatives are given here, percentages do not total 100.
[b]Includes attempted assault.
[c]"Fear" is measured by the percentage of respondents who have taken security precautions before going outside.

Source: Dijk et al., Experience of Crime Across the World (Deventer: Kluwer, 1990).

that people who run the greatest risk of being victimized (young male city dwellers) show the least fear, while people with low risks (women, especially outside the cities) take the most precautions. Also attitudes toward punishment and victimization risks vary independently of each other, if measured individually. The correlations by country, however, show distinct group patterns: West Germany and its Western neighbors combine moderately high crime rates with a mild attitude toward punishment. Community service or a fine are generally seen as the most appropriate sanction for such semi-serious crimes as household burglary, which the majority of North Americans would like to see punished by a prison sentence. The scant evidence from East German surveys shows that even though personal crime experience was very low in communist times and remained below the West German level in the first two years after unification, people expressed more punitive attitudes and were generally astonished at how mild West German court sentences were.[38]

Furthermore, while election campaign managers might be interested in how well they can exploit fear of crime and the punitiveness of the voters, judges on the Continent are sufficiently independent to remain unswayed by public opinion. Trends in the severity of sentencing are more easily explained by examining attitudes of the legal profession, their interaction with social workers and mental health experts, and the discourse among law professors and criminologists. The growing use of diversion from incarceration and the declining use of prison sentences described below are the result of the relative professional autonomy of the judiciary rather than of political pressure or popular support.

Prosecution of Crime in West Germany

Since the early 1950s, after police as well as courts had recovered from the postwar situation, the recording of crime by the police shows a continuous growth, while the caseload of courts increased hardly at all until 1969, then grew somewhat in the 1970s and thereafter again remained fairly stable (figure 5.4). The number of those sentenced in court fell from about 40 per 100 registered crimes in the 1950s to 14 per 100 in the 1980s. The reasons for the growing gap between police-recorded crime and court caseloads can partly be explained by the changing composition of the crime volume. Property crime increasingly constituted the bulk of all crime. Some categories that rose most sharply, such as car and bicycle theft or vandalism, have obviously low clearance rates, and it is not surprising that few suspects are arrested and forwarded to prosecution. Moreover, statistics on petty crimes such as small

---

38. Cf. Helmut Kury et al., *Opfererfahrungen in Ost- und Westdeutschland* (Wiesbaden: Bundeskriminalamt, 1993).

Millions of crimes

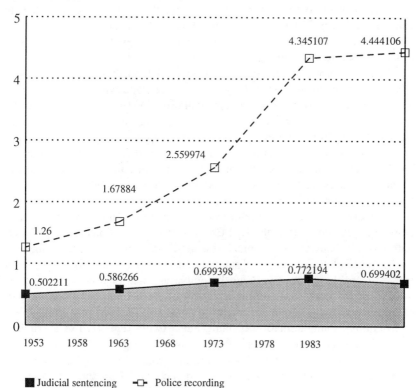

Figure 5.4. Police Recording of Crime Compared to Judicial Sentencing
Source: Günther Kaiser, *Kriminologie* (Karlsruhe: Müller Verlag, 1989).

thefts and minor assaults, which constitute another large proportion of West German crime data, depend both on the propensity of victims to report to the police and on the willingness and the capacity of the police to translate a complaint into an official report. Nevertheless such property crimes have accounted for a greater share in reported crime than ever before. On the other hand, seen over a longer time perspective, misdemeanors such as vagrancy, prostitution, and sexual offenses are less prevalent than at the beginning of the twentieth century.

Other reasons for the growing gap between police statistics and the number of criminal cases in court are the increased discretion of prosecutors to apply their own pretrial sanctions and to dismiss minor cases. A growing share of these cases, which involve fines, are disposed by summary procedures so that fewer defendants in the 1990s have their day in court than in the 1950s. Thus only about half of all criminal offenses which are considered "cleared" by the police in West Germany proceed to a hearing before the criminal courts.

The public prosecution office selects which defendants shall be dismissed, who shall be fined, who shall be given a waiver, and who shall go to trial. These powers derive from a statutory authority. A 1968 amendment to the criminal code "decriminalized" a number of offenses (such as traffic violations, failure to pay radio fees, and not appropriately registering with the population register) by labeling them infractions (*Ordnungswidrigkeiten*) and having offenders fined in an administrative procedure. In 1974 an amendment of the criminal procedural code allowed prosecutors to "conditionally waive" cases "if there is no public interest in prosecution."

The waiver can also be conditioned on making a contribution to a charitable organization such as the Red Cross or the Association for the Rehabilitation of Ex-Convicts. Especially for white-collar crimes, such as embezzlement, fraud, or tax evasion, substantial contributions to charities have been offered in exchange for avoiding the embarrassment of a court hearing on the part of the defendant and the necessity of establishing proof on the part of the prosecutor. The waiver might be considered a kind of a guilty plea, as it requires some admission of fault, but it is not registered as a criminal conviction. Minor cases of shoplifting, failure to pay the fare on public transportation, and similar petty offenses are also treated in this way, although with small contributions. An estimated 10 percent of all those accused of traditional misdemeanors are offered such a conditional waiver, and 80 percent of them accept it.[39]

Another alternative to a public court hearing is a punitive order (Strafbefehl) which may impose a fine or suspend the driver's license (with a prison sentence as a substitute penalty). The prosecutor usually proposes the punitive order without prior negotiation, and a local court judge has to approve it. If accepted by the accused, the matter becomes a mere bureaucratic routine and relieves court calendars of a considerable share of their criminal docket. Fifteen percent of all criminal charges are sanctioned by punitive order, and about 20 percent of the proposed orders are appealed. Especially where prosecutors encounter serious problems of establishing proof, as in economic crime cases—such as violating environmental or labor regulations, embezzlement, fraud, or tax evasion—they prefer such discretionary sanctions. The prosecutor's offer of a conditional waiver as well as the punitive orders have

---

39. Data collected by Erhard Blankenburg on the basis of interviews with prosecutors in Munich, 1986.

been considered a German variant of plea bargaining and are criticized in particular for their frequently use by middle-class offenders.[40]

These practices are quite contrary to the "legality doctrine" defended by law school professors, according to which prosecutors must charge every criminal incident which comes to their knowledge.[41] However, the legislature has increasingly granted prosecutors discretion to drop cases, to require payment of fines without creating a criminal record, and to issue punitive orders that can be administered in summary fashion. The routinization and mass treatment of prosecutorial decisions has spared the criminal courts an avalanche of petty crime cases. These courts are affected by the rise of crime principally by hearing an increasingly selective sample of the more serious cases (see table 5.7).

Prosecution of Political Corruption

One special kind of case which, even though not numerous, but politically very sensitive, concerns investigations of politicians and party organizations. Prosecutors must report cases which involve any members of parliament or politicians in leading government positions to their superiors; these again might report any politically sensitive investigations up the hierarchical line to the Minister of Justice of their respective state (Land).[42] Frequently they receive orders in return as to whether to waive or prosecute. Even though such orders have to "remain within the legal boundaries of discretion" (which means that the lower level prosecutor can ignore the order, if it seems to break the legality principle unlawfully), the prosecutorial hierarchy handles investigations of political corruption with extreme caution. A series of scandals concerning party financing in the 1980s highlighted the precarious dependence of public prosecution on political conditions: government members

---

40. Cf. John Langbein, "Controlling Prosecutorial Discretion in Germany," *University of Chicago Law Review* 41 (1974), 439–467; William Felstiner, "Plea contracts in West Germany," *Law and Society Review* 13 (1979), 309–325. The analogy can be drawn for the conditional waiver; for the punitive order, however, it seems too far-fetched, as the punitive order in most cases is written (by the prosecutor) and countersigned by a judge and can be challenged by a suspect in court. If there is any bargaining, it takes place in written form, mostly without any lawyers involved and usually without any personal contact between the prosecutor and the suspect.

41. The controversy has even spilled over to American law journals; cf. Joachim Herrmann, "The Rule of Compulsory Prosecution and the Scope of Prosecutorial Discretion in Germany," *University of Chicago Law Review* 41 (1974), 468–505; John Langbein, *supra* note 39; Abraham Goldstein and Martin Marcus, "The Myth of Judicial Supervision in Three Inquisitorial Systems: France, Italy and Germany," *Yale Law Journal* 87 (1977), 240–282.

42. Sec. 146 of the Statute on Court Organization to be filled in by guidelines of the state Ministers of Justice.

Table 5.7. Cases Handled by Prosecutors (Estimated for 1989)

No Suspect	Files Opened	Cases Dropped	Summary Procedures	Charged Before Court
2,100,000	2,600,000	650,000	260,000 conditional waivers 390,000 punitive orders without appeal	80,000 punitive orders appealed
				1,150,000 court charges 72,000 speed procedures
% of all files opened:	25	25	25	25

Source: Estimated on the basis of prosecutors' computer tables, provided in 1982–84 by the Northrhine-Westphalian Ministry of Justice, detailed analysis published in Blankenburg, *Prozessflut*, 1989.

in the cabinet of Chancellor Helmut Kohl became vulnerable only because the government and the minister of justice in Northrhine-Westphalia (the state where the capital, Bonn, is located) belonged to the national opposition party (Social Democrats).[43] In the neighboring state of Rhineland-Palatine investigations against Kohl were dropped, and commentators related this to the fact that the minister of justice there belonged to the national government coalition.

Evidently, attempts to use criminal courts to prosecute political corruption have to resist strong counterattacks. Public prosecution can be initiated for such trivial offenses as libel or "breaking judicial confidence" in order to intimidate the media. Searches of media offices and of the homes of journalists have been used repeatedly, but prosecutors have also been successfully attacked by the media in return.[44] Given the increased media competition in the 1990s, such a focus on scandal is likely to increase, with ambitious public prosecutors using publicity to support their investigations. Lacking the investigative competence of French or Italian investigative judges, however, it is unlikely that prosecutors can achieve a similar moral and political standing as they enjoy in these countries.[45]

Federal Prosecutor's Office

For a number of offenses against state and country (such as high treason, threats to parliament, or acts of genocide) the federal prosecutor (Bundesanwalt) at the high court has jurisdiction. He can also take over cases of political importance (such as those concerning endangering national defense or taking part in organizations which have been declared unconstitutional). Depending on the national significance of the case, the charge can be brought to the

43. The judicial handling of the Flick scandal was subject to a parliamentary enquete by the Bundestag in 1986. The Flick case involved a multimillion-mark party financing deal in exchange for a tax exemption of the sale of Flick Industries. In the follow-up some 1,860 investigations against politicians and organizations were initiated by the prosecutor's office at Bonn, 510 of these procedures were dropped because of lack of proof, 519 waived, 119 conditionally waived. Among others two former Ministers of Economic Affairs were punished, the leading manager of the Flick concern was sentenced to a fine of 550,000 mark plus two years of prison on parole. Penalties and conditional waiver payments of the entire scandal reached a total amount of 1,700,000 mark. Cf. our contribution in Arnold Heidenheimer (ed.), *Political Corruption: A Handbook* (New Brunswick, N.J.: Transaction, 1989).

44. The most spectacular such case arose around the arrest of leading journalists of *Der Spiegel* under an alleged suspicion of high treason in 1963, leading to the resignation of then-Minister of Defense F. J. Strauss.

45. Cf. chapter 4 on the wave of scandals that shattered the French republic in 1993–94 initiated by prosecutors and investigative judges (called "the little judge syndrome") with the help of media coverage.

federal high court, a regional appeal court, or special state protection chambers, which have been installed at selected district courts. The federal prosecutor's office may also claim coordinate competence, if investigations have to be coordinated across state boundaries (sec. 200–203 of the guidelines of the penal process).

East Germany

As indicated above, East Germany, like other communist states, consistently reported much lower crime rates than Western countries. While one may question how much information on youth vandalism and similar kinds of undesirable behavior were withheld from the public (and also from the statistics), crime control was much tighter in the East than in the West. The abundance of criminal opportunities which in the West comes with economic affluence and an open society was virtually unimaginable in the face of the social control of the communist state. The Western phenomena of widespread property crimes and violence in public were unknown. Any vandalism, drunkenness, drinking, or fighting that occurred was treated nonjudicially in commissions and neighborhood "social courts." Tied to communist mass organizations, these tribunals exerted a tight preventive control of public behavior. Lower levels of consumption and restrictions on mobility especially deprived young people of delinquent opportunities open to Western youth.[46] However, once the criminal justice system in communist Germany was set into motion, it reacted more harshly than in West Germany. Compared to the selectivity of the West German prosecution, the gap between police incidents and court cases was much smaller in the GDR than in the FRG: 75 percent of suspects were brought to trial.

Included in these figures are those who were prosecuted for political activities such as attempting to leave the country without a permit. There are no exact figures on such political prosecutions; however, one indication is that about 10 percent of all prosecutors in East Germany were in section 1a, the political division. A system of "political guidance" of the judiciary, which was formally tied to a hierarchical inspection of lower court sentencing by the high court of the GDR, saw to it that prosecutors as well as judges acted within the political guidelines set by the politbureau in the capital.[47]

46. Unpublished reports of the Leipzig youth institute of the rise of youth vandalism in the GDR during the 1980s were carefully kept out of the police records; police tactics concentrated on those who ideologically inspired these protest movements.

47. Extensive analyses of the political pressures put on judges, prosecutors, and attorneys in the GDR in Rottleuthner et al. (eds.), *Steuerung der Justiz in der DDR* (Cologne: Bundesanzeiger Verlag, 1994).

The Day in Court

The term *pretrial* used above might be misleading, if it were interpreted to suggest that prosecutors exercised their discretion by threatening a trial in order to pressure defendants to plead guilty or to consent to the proposed penalty. Continental hearings in court are conducted by the bench. The judge initiates most interactions, and the prosecutor presents the evidence which has been available from a file to judges as well as to the defense. As there is no jury in Germany, courtroom interaction remains among professionals. It is usually cooperative rather than adversary. The so-called inquisitorial style allows the judge to prepare on the basis of the evidence in the file, making it unnecessary for the defense to prepare an elaborate inquiry in case there are surprise arguments from the other side.[48]

On the other hand, there is no recognized constitutional right to legal aid for defendants who cannot pay for a lawyer. While every suspect is free to have a paid defense lawyer, in minor cases most suspects appear without representation. Only in district courts (in cases of serious felonies) is an attorney assigned to the defendant. In local courts, the prosecutor may apply for the assignment of a defense counsel, if special circumstances such as a potential penalty of more than five years in jail demand it, or if the defendant has already been detained more than three months.

These very restrictive rights to a defense lawyer for the bulk of cases in local courts are mitigated by a right to appeal. A local court's criminal verdict can be appealed by either the prosecutor and or the defense, which leads to a trial de novo. At the next level, the district court, a decision can only be appealed on legal grounds to the high court. The philosophy behind this architecture of defense and appeal rights is that the criminal court is an arena of professionals. While a single judge in local courts may have to be checked by his superiors, a district court bench will include sufficient professional scrutiny to render another trial superfluous. In the nonadversarial tradition of German courts, prosecutors and defense attorneys are expected to present "objective facts and arguments of law," not just one-sided statements for their respective party. Together with the bench, they are part of a common enterprise "to do justice."

Sentencing

In spite of the ups (and, occasionally, downs) of the crime statistics, the long-term trends of sentencing of criminal courts show remarkable stability. Relative to the population, the rate of those sentenced by court in West Germany

---

48. Cf. John Merryman, *The Civil Law Tradition* (Stanford, Calif.: Stanford University Press, 1969).

continues a stable line from the Kaiserreich and throughout the Weimar Republic. The rate declined only during the world wars and immediately thereafter, not because there was less crime, but because the courts of justice were not working at full capacity.

In the GDR the level of crime was considerably lower, but the East German prison population until the mid-80s is estimated to have been at least twice that of West Germany's jails.[49] This is due to the fact that prosecutors in the GDR were less selective than their West German colleagues and the sentencing was harsher. An estimated 50 percent of all suspects were sent to prison, ten percent of them for political crime (including attempts to leave the country without permission).[50] One remarkable consequence was that it provided an opportunity to sell off prisoners to West Germany for sizable amounts of money. The communist leaders also occasionally tried to gain popular support by announcing mass amnesties. Capital punishment was in use until around 1980. In 1987 it was formally abolished, first by decree and then by legislative enactment. Ironically, the timing of this humanitarian act was aimed at improving the diplomatic climate for the first state visit of the head of state, Erich Honecker, to West Germany; it thereby demonstrated another political use of the judiciary.

However, if we ignore such somber times of repression and the use of courts of justice in wartime, the historical trend shows a continuity of use of milder sentences (figure 5.5).

Two trends overlap in the long term. Those who want to describe the history of criminal law as "progress toward humanization" point to the replacement of capital punishment by prison sentences and to the replacement of prison time by fines. These developments began during the Weimar Republic and continued after World War II in the Federal Republic. Those who wish to stress the overall increase of social control look at the rising volume of criminal cases; although adults increasingly pay fines, imposing fines added to the total volume of criminal control rather than simply abolished incarceration. Relating sentencing figures to the size of the population shows that the rate of those in prison decreased slowly. Since the 1950s an increasing number of prison sentences are suspended and the individual placed on parole. As social workers take over functions in the shadow of law enforcement by implementing parole as well as alternative sanctions, the social con-

49. The yearly publication of the number of prisoners at the end of the year went up and down due to changes of penal policy as well as due to regular amnesty releases before Christmas. Cf. Günther Kaiser, *Strafvollzug im europäischen Vergleich* (Darmstadt: 1983).

50. Estimates based on prison statistics are higher; here I take a conservative estimate based on the caseload of section 1a of the prosecutor's service, which in the mid-1980s was about 10% according to internal statistics.

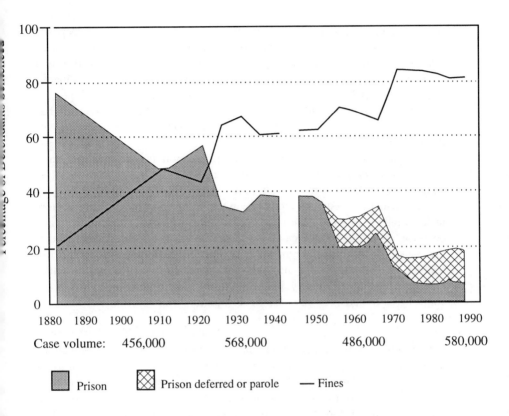

Case volume: 456,000   568,000   486,000   580,000

Prison   Prison deferred or parole   — Fines

Source: Günther Kaiser, *Kriminologie* (Karlsruhe, Müller Verlag, 1989), p. 518.

Figure 5.5. Sentencing in the German Reich and Federal Republic of Germany, 1882–1986

trol imposed by the criminal justice system becomes more finely tuned. If one adds the increased volume of pretrial sanctions (which by definition are not included in the sentencing statistics), the criminal justice system has widened its net and has knit it more densely.

For juveniles, softer forms of control are in use. Up to the age of eighteen (and, upon prosecutorial request, up to twenty-one), prosecutors and courts have discretion over an array of alternative measures and diversion programs. All sanctions are supposed to be considered for their educational effect; fines may not be imposed. Prosecutors may dismiss petty cases (especially for first offenders) after warning the juvenile. They may dismiss a case if the offender offers restitution to the victim, or they might refer the offender to one of several diversion programs. If formally charged, however, a juvenile must be brought before a juvenile judge for a hearing. The judge then again considers restitution or diversion. As the availability of diversion options depends largely on local arrangements with social work institutions, there are substantial differences in the treatment of juveniles. In Hamburg, Berlin, and Bremen between 83 percent and 90 percent of all juvenile suspects are placed in diversion; in Bavaria and other less urban states, only about 55 percent are sent to these programs. However, in all regions, the use of diversion has increased between 1981 and 1991 from 44 percent to 62 percent of all indictable offenses.[51]

It might seem as if the extensive use of diversion and prosecutorial sanctions represents a trend toward decriminalization. In fact, however, it is equally plausible to argue that it shows an increase in control over petty crime. Greater efficiency by the police in recording crimes and by prosecutors in handling cases allows the courts to take in more cases. Procedures have been routinized, and many cases are terminated at the pretrial stage, so that the workload of the courts remains fairly stable. For adult offenders this has resulted in fines for most offenses. For juveniles a welfare state pattern emerges. Linking the heavy hand of police and prosecution to the ''soft control'' of social work has meant ever tighter social control.

Prosecution of Political Extremists

Rather petty offenses hide behind what the police statistics label ''violations of the public order.'' Most of them are simple trespassing, resistance to an arrest, unlicensed demonstrations, or begging. Their share has been decreasing to 5 percent (thirty years ago it was about 15 percent) of all indictable offenses. Maintaining order falls in the competence of local authorities, which increasingly react to infractions without invoking criminal law.

On the other hand, criminal law sanctions have repeatedly been used to stigmatize either communists or rightists. So far neither the radical right-wing nor left-wing parties had any chance to win sizable representation in parliaments. Except for local strongholds they usually fail to reach the necessary minimum of 5 percent of the vote. Outside of the established institutions, however, they have repeatedly caused panic, either by aggressively campaigning or by outrightly engaging in terrorism. Racist propaganda, especially anti-Semitism, is meticulously prosecuted, usually accompanied by official demonstrations of disgust. Bomb attacks on immigrants in the early 1990s were followed by massive counterdemonstrations, often leaving the police in the middle between vandalizing skinheads and peace demonstrators. In the 1970s and 1980s the most aggressive demonstrations have been led by leftist groups, which have their strongholds in big cities and university

---

51. Wolfgang Heinz and Renate Storz, *Die Diversion im Jugendstrafverfahren in der Bundesrepublik Deutschland* (Bonn: Bundesministerium der Justiz, 1992).

towns. Being excluded from the range of established political parties, they tend to form subculture organizations, which can on occasion be mobilized for demonstrative actions. Police action and criminal sanctions usually follow instantly.

Thus, criminal prosecution has been given a permanent task of guarding the borderline of the accepted political spectrum. It became most pronounced in the 1970s when leftist action groups (in the beginning emerging from student activists like Baader and Meinhof) turned to terrorist assaults, bank robberies, kidnapping, and politically motivated murder. The reaction of established institutions ranged from screening and job exclusion of anybody who had been noticed in public support of leftist activism, to massive police actions and criminal sanctions against the hard core of leftists who actively violated the law.[52] When in the course of the 1970s it became clear that the broad marginalization of all those who demonstrated some sympathetic support for the radical leftist opposition escalated conflicts more than it stopped them, the states with Social Democratic governments terminated job screening and discrimination. The more conservative states with Christian Democratic governments followed suit without, however, giving up their law-and-order rhetoric.

Concern for law and order, thus, does play a role in polarizing the political parties in the FRG. In contrast to the United States, it emphasizes the limits of acceptable political activism more than violent crime in general. The most spectacular judiciary action evolved around the lawsuits against terrorists within the Baader-Meinhof Gang and its follow-up organization, the Red Army Faction (RAF). Most of the members of the former student protest group around Baader, Meinhof, and their cohorts were arrested for staging robbery, kidnapping, and murder in 1972, their trial in court started in 1975, ended with the suicide of Meinhof in 1976 and with life prison sentences for a number of others in 1977 (which they terminated by committing collective suicide in the high security prison). Throughout the proceedings, the defense used the courtroom publicity for political propaganda. The prosecution, on the other hand, accused defense attorneys of illegal collaboration with the accused (which was hard to prove, but never completely denied). As a result,

52. Cf. the polemic by a leftist attorney and activist in Sebastian Cobler, *Law, Order and Politics in Germany* (Berlin: Rotbuch, 1976). So-called *Berufsverbote*, officially pertaining only to civil service jobs, but effective also with many big companies. The amount of secret service surveillance, euphemistically called "constitutional protection service," in this period was staggering, but nevertheless highly arbitrary. According to the statistics of the state Ministers of the Interior almost 1.5 million job applicants in the public services were screened between 1972 and 1980, of these only 16,371 (1.1%) led to relevant information on extremist activities, of these 1,078 led to refusal of a public service job.

court rules and legislative amendments were adopted which permanently restrict defense rights in German courts. The prosecution took five years from the initial arrest to the final sentence; it was seen as a political show trial by prosecutors as well as sympathizers. In response to the many violent demonstrations which accompanied it, partly organized from within the prisons, the government constructed high security prisons, adopted restrictive defense rulings, and had parliament pass a number of substantive law changes which allowed police and prosecutors to step over "sufficient cause" rules and privacy protection when investigating persons accused of taking part in illicit organizations. The most notorious substantive law change of the antiterrorist legislation was the introduction of art. 129a StGB, which threatened with stiff sentences any activity which is designed to lead to terrorist organization. The vague formulation of criminalizing mere intent, together with the empowerment of (secret) police surveillance without probable cause, has led to many protests by defense lawyers and law professors. Some of the provisions of substantive law criminalizing mere "propagation of anti-constitutional action" (art. 88a StGB) which were introduced during the antiterrorist panic of the 1970s were repealed again in 1981.

CIVIL LITIGATION

The Volume of Civil Litigation

Civil litigation has been described as a "market" because the parties initiate and direct the proceedings.[53] One might assume that among countries under similar social and economic conditions, such as those compared in this volume, the generation of social conflicts and thus the demand for litigation should be comparably high. High litigation rates, however, do not indicate an abundance of disputes, nor a special density of legal regulation. Disputes may take place in other forums than courts, and regulation may use other forms than law. Litigation frequency, adversariness of court action, and density of legal regulation should be treated as three aspects of the "legalness" of legal culture which can vary independently of one another.[54]

The volume of civil litigation in Germany is very high by Continental standards (table 5.8); if we include summary debt enforcement it would be high even by American standards. Comparing social and economic factors in Germany and the United States to those in France or even Japan, we would not expect such radical differences of the conflict level. We have to look for intermediate factors transforming social conflicts to legal disputes in more or less limited ways. In the literature of legal reforms this is discussed as a

53. Donald Black, "Mobilization of Law," *Journal of Legal Studies* 2 (1973), 175.

54. Japan, a country with a high density of regulations, has the lowest litigation rate by all standards of comparison and a rather nonadversarial style of proceedings.

Table 5.8. Civil Litigation (per 100,000 inhabitants)

	Civil Procedures[a]	First-Instance Adversarial	Appeal de Novo
West Germany (1989)	9,400	3,561	251
France (1982)	3,640	1,950	250
Japan (1986)	—[b]	500	15
England/Wales (1982)	5,300	1,200	16
United States (1989)			
Minnesota	—[b]	4,781	
Massachusetts	—[b]	9,500	

[a]Includes summary debt enforcement.
[b]No such procedure exists.

Sources: Germany: Blankenburg, *Prozessflut.* If German rates for procedures in administrative and labor courts were added, the adversary rate would increase by another 1,350 per 100,000 population, and the appeal rate would rise accordingly. France: Wollschläger, in *Prozessflut,* p. 104. Japan: Data include civil, administrative, and domestic cases for 1986, according to *Statistical Handbook 1988,* p. 145; 1986 data for summary procedures and family courts kindly provided by the Supreme Court of Japan. England/Wales: Procedures are not closely comparable. Data are roughly comparable to continental procedure. Cf. Lord Chancellor's Judicial Statistics, 1982, table 7.1, which reports 2,301,364 civil proceedings in county courts, of which 2,048,586 were money complaints, and 181,853 divorce petitions filed (table 4.1) and 164,396 writs issued by the Queen's Bench of the high court (table 3.1). High court appeals and court of appeals in the civil division totaled 8,156 (table 1.1). Indicators per 50 million inhabitants. In the United States, aggregate data are misleading, as the variance from state to state is very large; among states with unified U.S. court systems, Massachusetts is highest with a rate of 8.695 per 100,000 population, and Minnesota is lowest with 4.781; cf. *State Court Statistics* 1989, p. 9; for comparison add an estimated average of 10% for civil cases in federal courts.

problem of the access to justice. Rather than focusing only on demand factors of levels of societal conflict, it looks at the supply side of the legal market and discusses the institutions which determine the scope of conflicts which are channeled to judicial forums.

Legal Aid

According to some theories of modernization the welfare state has led to an increased "colonization of life by law"; this does not, however, necessarily imply an increased judicialization.[55] On the contrary, the implementation of welfare rights in the most developed Scandinavian welfare states and in the Netherlands rely largely on informal proceedings. Tenants' rights, employment protection, and consumer complaints are typically dealt with by institutions which divert the bulk of the cases away from courts. Only after such

55. Jürgen Habermas, *Theorie des kommunikativen Handelns* (Frankfurt: Suhrkamp, 1981).

informal alternatives have been exhausted can a complainant initiate a formal court proceeding. Legal services for the poor appeared late in the growth of the welfare state in most countries on the European continent. While Scandinavian countries, West Germany, and the Netherlands rank highest in the world in welfare expenditures, on the Continent only the Netherlands and Sweden have built up an infrastructure of legal aid institutions which could be compared to that in Great Britain and the Commonwealth. On the other hand, the British in 1990 spent four times more per person on legal aid than the Germans, and since then the British legal aid budget increased dramatically (even though the standards of applicability were restricted)[56] while the German budgets actually showed a slight decrease. France made an attempt to introduce a more generous legal aid scheme in 1991, but its implementation has so far failed to have much impact.

One possible explanation for the national differences may be found in the role which lawyers play in common-law courts as compared to the civil law tradition. Legal scholars like to emphasize that the adversarial procedure of common law countries puts full responsibility for investigation and argumentation in court on the lawyers representing their clients. There is some truth to this argument. In civil law countries like Germany, the judge actively investigates the facts and legal arguments for both sides. Many judges in Continental courts do not see their role as waiting for lawyers to present a case and listening passively to arguments from both sides. Rather, judges see themselves as the main actor in court who works on the basis of an extensive file prepared for the case and who in court compensates for the weaknesses in argumentation of an unexperienced party by asking questions and searching for evidence on the bench's own initiative. Indeed, as described in chapter 4 on France, it can occasionally be advantageous for a private party in some courts on the Continent not to be represented by a lawyer because that may spur the judge to compensate for an overly clever lawyer on the other side.

Nevertheless, representation in court takes only a fraction of lawyers' time, and it does not exhaust what legal aid should provide. Most clients need advice and assistance before they consider court action. Studies of lawyers at work demonstrate that out-of-court efforts to avoid litigation are as important as assistance in preparing litigation.[57] In the Continental tradition,

56. Erhard Blankenburg, *Civic Justice Quarterly*, 1995. France traditionally grants waivers only for court and lawyer fees related to litigative action. It introduced a more generous scheme by legislation of July 10, 1991, which left the implementation largely in the hands of local bar associations. This might be the reason why the scheme so far was used much less than expected. Cf. Rainer Wasilewski, *Streitverluitung durch Rechtsamsälte* (Cologne: Bundesanzeiger, 1990).

57. For a historical overview, cf. ''Private insurance and the historical waves of legal aid'' in *The Windsor Yearbook of Access to Justice* 14 (1993), 185–201.

however, legal aid was originally designed as a waiver of court and lawyer fees for the poor (Armenrecht) and has been broadened very hesitantly to also include advice and assistance. West Germany enacted a modest legal advice scheme (Beratungshilfegesetz) only in 1981. Compared to other civil law countries with a developed welfare state like the Netherlands or Sweden, the German scheme is very restrictive; compared to Latin countries like France it is quite generous. The comparison to the British legal aid scheme makes it evident that its effectiveness rests on the infrastructure of diverse legal aid bureaus, including consultation bureaus staffed by legally trained consultants who are not admitted to the bar (which in Germany would be illegal).

East Germans, who had been accustomed to having a comprehensive, court-managed consultation service under communism, saw this terminated after unification under the West German statute which grants a monopoly of legal advice and assistance to registered attorneys. Although the need for legal information and advice increased after unification, and even though many people in the East met the poverty standards to be eligible for legal aid, up to 1993 the scheme was used less there than in the former West Germany. The small number of attorneys practicing in the East and their lack of interest in an impoverished clientele prevented the use of even the modest legal aid scheme that the statutes offer.

Table 5.9 compares legal aid expenditures for Germany, France, and England/Wales. Of special interest is the fraction of legal aid spent on first-hand legal advice and assistance. Germany spends little on pretrial advice, and advice in criminal cases is precluded entirely. While the British grant every suspect in a criminal case a right to legal aid, German law allows for a duty solicitor only in very serious criminal cases. Only 10 percent of the German subsidies go to criminal defense lawyers, while in the United Kingdom they receive 60 percent of the legal aid budget. The German legal aid scheme does, however, subsidize divorce cases, which account for 90 percent of the German civil legal aid. Legal aid entitlements are rarely used for legal needs of the welfare population—such as landlord-tenant law, social and labor law, and alien law.

For those who criticize legal aid for allegedly increasing the caseload of courts, it must be amazing that the Germans with their restrictive legal aid scheme nevertheless have to handle much more litigation than the Dutch. In civil litigation German courts attract plaintiffs from the middle classes and especially from repeat players. For plaintiffs who can foresee that they have a good case with winning chances, West German courts are a low-cost facility; in every instance they are quick and efficient so that there is no reason for legally experienced parties to try to avoid them.

Table 5.9. Government Funds Spent on Legal Aid in West Germany
and England/Wales, 1989 (European currency units per head
of population per year)

	West Germany	France (1993)	England/Wales
Change in budget, 1990	−10%	+114%	+220%
Legal advice and assistance	0.19	no data	1.80
Criminal legal aid	0.43	1.5	4.17
Civil (and administrative) legal aid	3.48	0.80	9.54
Total	4.10	2.30	15.51
Citizens' Advice Bureaux	n/a	n/a	1.24

Source: Own budget analysis, gross expenditures, not taking account of revenues. At the time 1 ECU equaled one U.S. dollar. Data for West Germany taken from Northrhine-Westphalia budget, including duty solicitors. France: Ministry of Justice, *Summary of Application of law 91-650 of 10 July 1991.* England/Wales: Legal Aid Board annual reports and Lord Chancellor's budget on duty solicitors. Citizens' Advice Bureaux annual report, 1990.

The generally high litigation rates pose an obvious risk for Germans. Middle-class households therefore very often buy insurance to cover the costs of lawyers and court fees. About 60 percent of car owners are insured for legal costs, about half are insured for legal risks related to car ownership, and the remainder also cover other private legal risks. This flow of money which middle-class insured clients provide for lawyers stands in stark contrast to the low revenue which they can expect from legal aid for the poor. Among the European companies offering legal aid insurance, the Germans are by far the biggest customers, accounting for 70 percent of the industry's total revenue; their revenue in Germany 1989 amounted to 23.5 ecu per capita (thus higher than the sum of all legal aid subsidies) compared to 1.7 ecu in France and 1.1 ecu in the United Kingdom. Table 5.10 relates these figures to the income of practicing attorneys.

It is obvious that in Germany the combination of legal cost insurance with a lawyers' monopoly on rendering services forms a perfect symbiosis—insured cases guarantee a substantial part of attorneys' income. In the neighboring countries (such as France), legal insurance provides in-house legal services first, and it allows for outside attorneys only after they have been consulted. In most cases the insurance agents settle their cases out of court. Thus, they advertise their service as a means to prevent litigation with the argument that the majority of their cases are arbitrated and settled out of court. The German insurance schemes have been under heavy attack for causing much of Germany's litigation explosion throughout the 1970s and 1980s. However, research has shown by a series of control group comparisons that

Table 5.10. Money from Insurance/Legal Aid Subsidy
to Attorneys, West Germany, 1989

From insurance	850 million ECU
Rate per practicing attorney	22,000 ECU
From legal aid	147 million ECU
Rate per practicing attorney	7,660 ECU

Source: Own money flow analysis based on data given by *L'assurance de défense en Europe* 20 (1991); at the time 1 ECU equaled one U.S. dollar.

Germans who hold a legal cost insurance do not litigate significantly more nor are they more risk-inclined.[58] The empirical data show that the purported moral dilemma—posed by legal insurance producing the very behavior that people are insuring against—does not occur. Much to the surprise of legal economists, litigation-proneness of private households turns out to be more price inelastic than had been expected. Only repeat players with many legal risks (such as taxi companies) can calculate their legal costs rationally. People in private disputes try to avoid lawyers and litigation, but if they become involved, they are not deterred by the costs.

Types of Cases, Party Constellations, and Persistence in Litigation

Of course, insiders rarely share our evaluation that German courts might be too efficient to give plaintiffs an incentive to consider alternative dispute institutions. German attorneys—like those in other countries—complain about the high costs and the length of proceedings. Their illustrative evidence, however, usually refers to cases which go through several appeals. Parties have a right to a trial de novo except in small claims and a few other special cases. Indeed, of all the cases that have gone all the way to a judgment in a proceeding, every third in local courts and every other one in district courts is appealed. Appealing for a de novo proceeding means that the costs and the length of the litigation are more than doubled. Even though the loser at each level has to pay all the costs, it may be worthwhile for some parties to play for time.

Complaints about such tactical use of courts tend to overlook the fact that summary procedures, default judgments, and early settlements terminate most

58. Erhard Blankenburg, "Legal Insurance, Litigant Decisions and the Rising Caseloads of Courts," *Law and Society Review* 16 (1981/82), 601–624. A repeat study by Wolfgang Jagodzinski et al., *Rechtsschutzversicherung und Rechtsverfolgung* (Cologne: Bundesanzeiger, 1994) shows likewise that the insured clients are slightly more likely to litigate in some special fields like traffic tort and tenant complaints against landlords. This study also refutes a general inclination of insured parties litigating carelessly.

cases in civil courts within a few weeks. Moreover, some cases are filed only to end in negotiated out-of-court settlement or forced default judgment. In such cases early exit usually achieves the plaintiff's goal, and the courts fulfill purely an enforcement function. In other cases, the parties might have some interests in common when seeking a settlement (such as reducing the costs and the duration of the procedure or settling for a compromise). Continental courts typically allow for settlements to be negotiated in court so that parties receive an enforceable legal order without having to litigate to an adjudicated decision.

There are, of course, parties who litigate through the highest possible appeal in order to get a decision by a federal high court. Such test cases might be initiated by interest groups, companies, and other repeat players. While the number of such cases is small, they are the true clients of the court system who look for a decision that will alter case law.

The courts are most frequently used for monetary claims which are not seriously contested (figure 5.6).

- As the court files of debt collection cases show, two-thirds of defendants do not show up in court, in which case the plaintiff's claim is accepted by default. Plaintiffs use the courts in such cases to get a legal order which permits debt enforcement by a court official although such a request for execution is not always filed.
- A sizable portion of the caseload concerns tort claims after a traffic accident. About half (52 percent) of such claims are filed by attorneys in order to threaten litigation while bargaining out of court. About half of the plaintiffs opt out of the proceedings by not paying any court fees. However, once a court case begins, settlement is unlikely, and 35 percent of the decisions in first-instance courts are appealed.[59]
- The most adversarial of all civil cases involve disputes about construction contracts. There is a proverb: "If you build a house, consult a lawyer first." Eighty percent of the construction cases go to the evidentiary stage, with half of them consulting expert witnesses. Eventually 40 percent of the parties settle, but 40 percent let the court decide, with a high likelihood (40 percent) that court decision will be appealed.
- Many civil court cases regulate the termination of a social relationship: divorce is the classic example of this type of case. An estimated two-thirds of the parties agree on their terms of separation out of court (especially when custody and child support are not in dispute), but they

59. This is in stark contrast to the practice of litigants in the neighboring Netherlands, cf. my analysis in "The Infrastructure of Avoiding Civil Litigation," *Law and Society Review 1994* 28, no. 4 (1994), 789–808. Compare also the avoidance of traffic tort litigation in Japan in chapter 6.

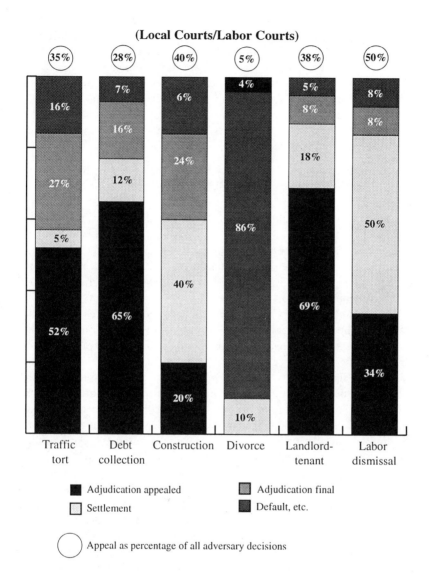

(Local Courts/Labor Courts)

| 35% | 28% | 40% | 5% | 38% | 50% |

| | Traffic tort | Debt collection | Construction | Divorce | Landlord-tenant | Labor dismissal |

- ■ Adjudication appealed
- □ Settlement
- ▨ Adjudication final
- ▨ Default, etc.

◯ Appeal as percentage of all adversary decisions

Source: Author's computer computation of court file statistics from Northrhine-Westphalia 1982–84.

Figure 5.6. Appeal Rates by Type of Case

need to obtain a legally valid decree. The courts here function largely as notaries. Appeal is highly unlikely. Post-decree proceedings about child support and custody, however, are quite common.

• Quite a different set of motivations leads to landlord-tenant disputes. They are predominantly initiated by landlords as a means of collecting rent by threatening an eviction order. They are frequently terminated by *non prosequi* because the tenants pay at least part of their debt just before an eviction order is issued.

Finally in our comparison of case disposal patterns, employment dismissals present the clearest example of mediating rather than adjudicating.[60] Labor courts rarely prevent dismissals, but many dismissed workers can receive compensation by challenging the terms of the dismissal. Bargaining in court and settling with the help of the judge (and eventually the full bench) are the rule. Our data show a 34 percent rate of early case terminations, which might indicate an out-of-court settlement, and 50 percent settlement rate in court. The few cases (16 percent) which go to trial have a high likelihood (50 percent) of being appealed.

The pattern of handling cases in civil and labor courts refutes the common stereotype of litigation as adversarial conflicts that involve a zero-sum game where the outcome is uncertain. In most cases the outcome is predictable for both parties; the plaintiff needs an executable judgment rather than a decision over disputed facts. Moreover, many cases do not primarily involve an adversarial confrontation with the court imposing a decision. Rather, they involve settlements with the court often playing a facilitative role. Shifting back and forth between their adjudicative and mediatory roles, judges often actively use the threat of their decision as an element in the negotiations about a possible settlement (figure 5.7).

A rough estimate of all civil cases in local courts would place about two-thirds in the ''enforcement'' category; the remainder may be characterized as often involving both mediation and adjudication. Notary functions are typically found in divorce cases when both parties act in agreement but nevertheless need to go through a court procedure. District courts handle more cases needing adjudication than do local courts; the more adversariness of their disputes can also be seen from the fact that half of the decisions are appealed against an average of ''only'' one-third of the decisions of local courts.

Except for family law, most cases involve individuals on one side and an organization on the other. The low costs and efficient services of the courts provide many repeat players a routine way of doing business. For instance,

---

60. Labor cases come under the jurisdiction of labor courts. I include their discussion here as they are illustrative of the mediating court function.

Outcome		
	unpredictable	predictable
Interests zero–sum	adjudicaton	enforcement
common	mediation	notarial

Figure 5.7. Functions of Court Litigation

they permit many kinds of businesses to deliver goods and perform services with only the promise of payment by a credit card because they know that they can routinely enforce these arrangements via a court action if they need to do so.

Procedural law in civil law gives the judge much more discretion to direct the proceeding and to evaluate the evidence. Discovery, which in the United States involves elaborate preparations by the lawyers, more often occurs on the Continent at the request of the judge than by demand of the opposing party. Moreover, as there is no sharp distinction between the trial and pretrial phase of litigation, Continental procedure is characterized by the discretion of the judge to shift back and forth between the roles of conciliator and adjudicator. At each stage in a civil proceeding there is the possibility of a nonadjudicative termination either by default or by formal court settlement. Out-of-court settlements are enforceable, if certified by the court.[61]

Conclusion

The West German machinery of civil litigation is efficient, but this may have undesirable social effects. Speedy at every level and allowing easy access to appeal, it is routinely used for everyday disputes such as the enforcement of debts and disputes about contracts or accident liability. Its structure makes it attractive for repeat players. Many middle-class litigants also find access easy because they possess insurance that pays for legal costs. However, the principle that losers pay all costs and the lack of a legal aid infrastructure make the courts rather inaccessible for the occasional small-claim litigant. Public interest groups for consumer protection or environmental liability slowly get used to using test cases to effect legal change. In the tradition of German *civil* law, courts are not political in a partisan way; legal reformers are expected to lobby in the legislative arena, not in court.

61. Cf. Erhard Blankenburg et al., "Phenomena of Legalization: Observations in a German Labour Court," in *European Yearbook on Sociology of Law* (The Hague: Nijhoff, 1980), 33–66.

Nevertheless, substantive civil law has moved away from the principle of complete freedom of contract by compensating for social inequalities in the context of the welfare state. Consumer protection and tenants' protection have improved. Family law has moved away from the fault principle in divorce and toward individualization of rights of women and children. Product and environmental liability have been extended, but German civil law courts have not taken the lead in any of these developments. The federal high court is accustomed to developing sophisticated jurisprudence, once a statutory breakthrough has been adopted in the legislative arena. Germany has a weak infrastructure for mobilizing the courts for innovative lawmaking by litigation.

SPECIALIZED COURT SYSTEMS

Labor Courts

The idea that law should be separated from partisan politics, which is most pronounced in the perception of German civil lawyers, dates back to the positivistic school of jurisprudence at the turn of the twentieth century. It may have been one of the historical forces contributing to the establishment of labor courts separate from the ordinary civil law courts. The main reason for this development, however, lies in the collective bargaining power of the trade unions. Industrywide, strongly centralized, and facing little competition, unions assumed public responsibilities in the framework of industrial democracy.[62] Works councils at the factory level, co-determination in the corporate management of coal and steel industries, and labor-employer coordination of labor market and social policies form the background of present-day German corporatism. In many respects these institutions have made the ideas of an "economic constitution," which stood at the beginnings of the installation of labor courts in 1928, come true.[63]

62. Industrial collective bargaining in the FRG is industrywide and regionally organized, with the regions largely coinciding with the federal states. Public service unions bargain separately for the federal, the state, and the community levels. The strategy, however, is always well coordinated in the national headquarters of the trade unions and employers' organizations. Cf. Wolfgang Streeck, *Industrial Relations in West Germany* (London: Heinemann, 1984). During the Kaiserreich and the Weimar Republic ideological cleavages brought about competition among communist, socialist, and catholic trade unions. Bargaining, however, took place industrywide with privileges for union members (like closed shops) being excluded. During the 1950s in the Federal Republic, ideological splits became less significant, so that in most industries only one uniform trade union prevailed. Cf. Klaus Beyme, *Challenge to Power: Trade Unions and Industrial Relations in Capitalist Countries* (London: Sage, 1980).

63. Cf. Hugo Sinzheimer's concept of the "Wirtschaftsverfassung." It is worth noting that Otto Kahn Freund who in 1971–74 later became an ardent defender of the voluntarist tradition of British labor law had been a member of the same group of Frankfurt lawyers as Sinzheimer; both had to emigrate after the Nazis took over.

Compared to the administrative corporatism of the Scandinavian welfare states, which includes the regulation of individual labor disputes in tripartite bodies, German labor relations remains tied to judicial controls. Labor courts play a role in collective labor disputes when they decide on the legality of strikes or when they are invoked in disputes about the jurisdictional competence of works councils. They also carry a heavy caseload of individual disputes; two-thirds of their cases arise from allegations of unfair dismissals and reductions in work force. Caseloads therefore go up and down with the economy; for example, in 1991 and 1992—while the courts were still in a process of organizational restructuring after the unification—the labor courts in eastern Germany faced a wave of a several hundred thousand dismissal cases, which could be handled only by quickly importing West German labor court judges for temporary service in the East.

An administrative procedure applies to mass dismissals: an employer who wants to lay off more than twenty workers must first negotiate with the labor (and unemployment) administration about the conditions and procedures for doing so; nevertheless, he may still face individual complaints before the labor court by those dismissed.

Employment is the subject of two bodies of law: contract law for individual employment contracts and labor law for collective agreements. Hence, courts must consider both statutory law as well as collective agreements. Company rules might be added as a third source of law, but they invariably are part of the collective agreement. Thus there are three parties to both labor law and labor disputes according to the German way of framing them: the state, labor unions, and employers. This tripartite character of labor law also finds its expression on the bench. After a first court session held by a single judge in an attempt to find a settlement solution, the proceedings go before a bench composed of a professional judge representing the state, one representative of the employers' side, and one of labor.[64] At the appeal level, there are three professional judges. Rather than reproducing the antagonistic relations of the disputes, this arrangement incorporates the judges' more intimate knowledge of industrial relations and often helps them formulate acceptable solutions.

64. The tripartite composition of the bench can also be found at the Prud'hommes in France (see chapter 4) as well as in Industrial Tribunals in the United Kingdom (see chapter 3). They also put procedural emphasis on settlements. The British dismissal proceedings do this institutionally by separating the Arbitration and Conciliation Service (ACAS); industrial tribunals cannot be invoked without having exhausted ACAS attempts to settle. For an empirical comparison of their procedures, cf. Erhard Blankenburg and Ralf Rogowski, "German Labour Courts and the British Industrial Tribunal System: A Socio-legal Comparison of Degrees of Judicialisation," *Journal of Law and Society* 13 (1986), 67–92. It demonstrates the much higher propensity of Germans to bring their complaints to tribunals: in 1984 about 6% of the dismissed did so, as compared to 1% of the British.

Administrative, Social, and Fiscal Courts

As Maine described the evolution of law in the nineteenth century as moving "from status to contract,"[65] we might describe the law in modern welfare states as moving from contract to regulation. Private individuals, as well as organizations, increasingly must enter legal relationships with public agencies. The largest growth of litigation has occurred where citizens and organizations invoke tribunals versus the state. While in contractual relationships parties have a choice of invoking the law or adjusting their operations by renegotiating the contract, regulatory agencies are usually bound by their own legal rules. This implies that most of their decisions are subject to review by internal complaint procedures, as well as by external judicial bodies. It results in a legalistic theory of public law, according to which state bureaucracies can only act in a legal mode (however discretionary their actual decision-making and implementation policy may be). If citizens or affected organizations want to complain, it seems to leave them no choice but to initiate a formal proceeding.

German administrative courts have developed this legalistic understanding of "public law action" (Verwaltungsakt) to perfection. Even where political bodies engage in planning and entrepreneurship, their decisions are constrained by substantive criteria as well as procedural rules. Especially when urban planning and construction permits are at stake, conflicts often arise between all those involved, whether actively or passively. To resolve such disputes, the administrative agencies have to follow a set of procedures permitting anybody concerned to participate. In any major development project, these requirements become so complex that faults and omissions seem unavoidable. This seems to give opponents a safe chance to use internal complaint procedures and subsequent litigation to ask for legal redress. Even if they eventually lose on substantive grounds, they can win time by pushing their complaint through at least two, and often three levels of administrative courts. In 1993, when urgent investment in the eastern parts of Germany was considered necessary, parliament passed a statute which allowed regional authorities to short cut many of the planning prerequisites on projects that were declared national priorities.[66]

Criticisms of the judicialization resulting from the legalistic binding of public authority has emphasized the political costs of strict legal constraints. Policymaking becomes an art of shifting issues from the decision-making arena to that of implementation, and from implementation to that of judicial review. The main effect of such judicialization, however, is anticipatory. It forces administrative agencies to consider the possibility of legal challenges.

65. Henry Sumner Maine, *Ancient Law* (1861).
66. Statute on facilitating investment and regulating housing estates 1993.

The most powerful opponents of the developments are often satisfied by being able to participate in earlier rounds of the planning process, as the result of using complaint procedures or striking deals after using court procedures as mere threat.

In those cases filed before an administrative court, a private citizen or organization invokes the court against a public agency. Communications between the two parties are highly formalized. The decision of the public agency must first be challenged by an internal complaint, which may be decided by the immediately superior level in the hierarchy. Increasingly agencies have created formalized internal complaint procedures in order to reduce the caseload of court proceedings. Only after all internal procedures have been exhausted may a complainant take the dispute to court.

In spite of the attempts to deal with administrative complaints internally, the caseload of administrative courts rose considerably during the 1970s and 1980s. Cases about zoning and construction permits and complaints against police measures and tariffs have shown slow but steady growth. The average chances for success for claimants is not high (only about 15 percent). If, however, timing is the issue, both those who ask for a quick, preliminary injunction as well as those who want to delay projects by a drawn-out procedure are well advised to use the courts.

Other kinds of cases have come flooding into these courts. Examples are disputes involving the rights of aliens, denial of admission to universities, and claims to conscientious objection against military service. These are sometimes indicative of pressures that have built up around public services and duties, as many people lodge complaints in order to force a policy change on the agency. In some cases protest movements (like the boycott against the general population census in the early 1980s) organized voluminous litigation which clogged court calendars until a leading case before the high court or constitutional court provided a precedent by which they could be decided. While such litigation waves have proved to be an effective instrument to change public policies, they sometimes backfire, as in recent developments in immigration law, where litigation led to regulations which were adverse to the interests of those invoking the courts.

The caseloads of fiscal and social insurance courts show less spectacular ups and downs. They are both dominated by experts. The decision making of social insurance courts is heavily influenced by the expert testimony of medical doctors. Tax accountants often initiate litigation in fiscal courts in order to strike an out-of-court deal; alternatively, if they go all the way into appeal, they use the litigation to obtain a new precedent.

In spite of their rather arcane subject matter, administrative, social insurance, and fiscal courts provide for lay participation on the bench in first instance as well as at appeal and on the federal high courts. Altogether they involve an astounding 80,000 volunteers in part-time court participation who are nominated by political parties or interest organizations. Often they are retired persons who have some professional experience in the field.[67] However, professional judges overwhelmingly state that the contribution of lay judges in the process of decision making is insignificant.[68] Their participation may once have been intended to serve as a democratic check on the tendency of professional judges to be in the pocket of the administrative agencies they are supposed to control, but under current conditions they do not make much difference.

Constitutional Courts

In 1950, when the institutions of the Federal Republic were formed on the basis of the postwar constitution, the constitutional court came to the German legal system as a late realization of a liberal nineteenth-century dream. Already the constitutional assembly of the reform movement in 1848 (called the "professors' parliament" at the Paulskirche) had discussed the American Supreme Court experience and proposed a similar body for judicial control of the legislation. Switzerland adopted a similar institution at that time, but in the restorative period of the German Reich during the second half of the nineteenth century, none of the liberal proposals could be realized. In the Continental law tradition, legal decisions had been understood as remaining in a body of law separate from politics; they were to be decided by the high courts of the specialized branches of the judiciary. Only Austria installed a constitutional court as early as 1919 in recognition of Hans Kelsen's argument that all statutory law has to be grounded on basic principles of law which constitute the "legality of law."[69] Germany's western neighbors Belgium and the Netherlands remained in the French tradition of institutionally separating law and politics; they did not even follow when in 1958 France established a constitutional council with limited jurisdiction aver the constitutionality of legislation before promulgation (see chapter 4).

Most other constitutional courts in Europe came after the Second World War as an import from American legal traditions.[70] The German federal con-

67. Cf. David Clark, "The Selection and Accountability of Judges in West Germany," *Southern California Law Review* 61 (1988), 1830.

68. See survey of judges by Ekkehard Klausa, *Ehrenamtliche Richter* (Frankfurt: Athenäum, 1972).

69. Hans Kelsen, *Die Verfassungsgesetze der Republik Österreich*, vol. 5 (Vienna, 1922). Kelsen was a member of the Austrian Constitutional Commission which proposed the court and from 1920 to 1928 was one of its first constitutional judges.

70. Cf. R. T. Cole, "Three Constitutional Courts: A Comparison," in D. Apter and H. Eckstein (eds.), *Comparative Politics* (New York: Free Press, 1968).

stitutional court in the course of its first forty-four years has profoundly changed the perception of law and politics as being two separate arenas of decision making. It forms an instrument for judicial review accessible to anyone who sees a statute conflicting with a provision of the constitution. Constitutional courts are also formed by the states, where they decide on issues of the diverse state constitutions. Usually consisting of a bench of professional judges plus some nonjudicial referees, they only occasionally meet.

The formal role of the federal constitutional court as an actor on the legislative stage is due to its authority to check the constitutionality of any federal or state statute on request of at least one-third of the members of the national parliament or any of the federal or state governments. This kind of challenge allows political conflicts in parliament, as well as in the federal system of governments, to be raised in constitutional court. The number of such cases however, is small. Between 1950 and 1991 the court handled only 112 such challenges.

Most constitutional challenges arise via other routes. One is the raising of a constitutional question by one of the other courts. If it has a doubt about the constitutionality of a statute, any German court may address the constitutional court while holding in abeyance its own decision. By 1991, the constitutional court had heard 2,612 such cases. In a formal sense the court declared a statute unconstitutional in less than 5 percent of these cases. In fact, however, it has a much larger anticipatory effect. No major legislative project proceeds without prior "informative consultation" by government departments, as well as opposition parties with a judge or their collaborators at the constitutional court. In particular the constitutional division at the Federal Ministry of Justice (which has the formal responsibility of checking each legislative project of the government bureaucracy on its constitutional merits) maintains frequent contacts with the court. In addition, the practice of staff members of the court shuttling between positions on the court and in the department facilitates such communications.

However, the most important political issues have not been brought before the court by either high government officials or other courts. Rather, the most controversial issues have been the result of a simple complaint procedure which is open to anyone affected by German law. In its entire history (up to 1991), more than 80,000 citizen complaints have been initiated, of which 64,000 met the formal jurisdictional requirements of the court. Only a small fraction of these, however, passed the initial case selection screening, which is formally decided by a committee of three judges in each of the two divisions of the court; the real work of sifting out those which merit a full treatment is performed by the court's professional staff. These staff persons are usually temporarily assigned from a lower court and represent the specialized knowledge and perspective of their respective branch of courts which at the same time is a field of law and of politics relating to one of the departments of government or parliamentary committee. Whatever passes the initial case selection will be judged on its merits by a panel of three constitutional justices. The success rate for this kind of case is only a few percent, but it occasionally rises when a leading decision suddenly makes a number of parallel complaints acceptable. For example, in 1990 the success rate reached the 20 percent mark as several hundred complaints against refusing political asylum were granted. A very small number of cases, 3 percent on the average, is heard by the full bench of eight justices of one of the divisions.

Several decisions of the constitutional court have shaped the political fate of the Federal Republic. It appears as if a skilled lawyer can transform any issue of governmental policy into a constitutional question. Many single issue groups have done so, as have political parties, state governments (for example, Bavaria against the rest of the Republic). In 1993 the federal government even filed a complaint against itself. This occurred when the foreign minister sought a preliminary injunction against the cabinet's decision to contribute troops to a United Nations force; his action was an attempt to break a political impasse about how involved German troops might become in active combat. Many of the most controversial cases have resulted from the constitutional assembly's intention in 1949 to place some powerful prerogatives firmly in the Constitutional Court. These included defining the limits of any aggressive military action by a German army, actions preserving national unity despite the division of Germany into East and West regimes, crucial issues of foreign policy, such as forming a German army, entering defense alliances (which was a cornerstone of Konrad Adenauer's Western policy in 1955), and signing a treaty between the two German states (which opened the way to Willi Brandt's Eastern policy in 1971).

The court usually justifies its decisions with extensive opinions, which it uses for formulating detailed guidelines on how constitutional criteria could be satisfied. In a number of instances it has challenged both federal and state governments to elaborate their legislation with further rulemaking.[71] By giving very detailed *obiter dictas* as to the conditions under which the implementation of a statute might be constitutional, it has effectively developed authority as a super-legislature. Examples are numerous: in 1972 it ruled on the criteria which had to be satisfied in order to maintain a professors' majority in university administration; in 1978 it set down precise rules to accept conscientious objection; in 1983 it declared the law on the census unconstitutional and stated which conditions a new law would have to meet. The

71. Cf. Donald Kommers, *Constitutional Jurisprudence of the Federal Republic of Germany* (Durham, N.C.: Duke University Press, 1990).

court also has repeatedly ruled on party finance practices and on abortion. In 1984 it decided that donations to political parties up to DM100,000 would be constitutionally permissible but that the names of donors would have to be published, if the amount exceeded fewer marks. In 1993 it declared medical abortions constitutional only under the condition that the woman be given a pro-life consultation; it also ruled that coverage by health insurances might be limited. In all of these decisions went along with an assumed political majority but at the same time formulated a detailed guideline for future policymaking.

There is some controversy among observers in how far the tendency of the court conforms to the policy of changing political majorities. Looking at the tendency of constitutional jurisprudence to follow political shifts, there is clearly some opportunism as to staying within the assumed limits of acceptability in the political arena. However, as the composition of the court follows the parliamentary majorities (with some time lag), it has the effect of slowing change and reinforcing the restraints of all-party compromises inherent in German federalism. Considering the tendency of governments to anticipatorily comply with what the constitutional court might say, the impact of its jurisprudence on the political process is, however, much stronger informally than was ever formally foreseen.

European Courts
With the all-encompassing system of courts and appeals within Germany, one might expect that Germans would need to invoke European courts less frequently than the English or the French. After all, for countries without constitutional courts, the European Court on Human Rights at Strasbourg (where membership includes non-EEC members such as Austria, Switzerland, as well as some of the East European democracies) is in many fields the only judicial review to challenge national legislation. As a consequence, the European Court on Human Rights has had a decisive impact in changing the legal cultures of the Netherlands and the United Kingdom by serving a function similar to German constitutional courts. In Germany the Strasbourg court has functioned as a super-appeal court after all appeals and even the constitutional court process have been exhausted.

Nevertheless, the appeal-mindedness of the German system of courts also draws complaints into the European courts. This is true for both the Human Rights court at Strasbourg and the European Community Court (which principally decides economic issues arising from the European Community treaty). At the European Community Court at Luxembourg, German companies lead the list of complainants with grievances ranging from objections against agricultural and fishing regulations to disputes over competition, antidumping regulations, and subsidy measures.[72] It might be plausible to explain this relatively frequent appearance to their economic weight in the European economy, but such an explanation does not account for French complainants constituting only half and the United Kingdom's only one-third the number of German complaints. The German tendency toward litigation may rather be seen as consistent with their propensity to use any appeal that is provided by the legal system and consistent with the overall features of the German legal culture described.

Conclusion

Like Americans, Germans often blame their compatriots for being overly litigious. The pattern of court mobilization, however, is different in the two countries. Most German plaintiffs in civil courts are repeat players: certain types of business and other organizations routinely invoke courts for debt enforcement, housing administration, or insurance claim regulation; likewise, they use criminal prosecution to fight shoplifting and small theft. Also, administrative agencies rely on court decisions to enforce their policies: special courts treat claims against social insurances, agencies of public administration, or the internal revenue service. Each of these court systems offers the possibility for a trial de novo and an appeal before a federal high court. Together with the federal constitutional court, these courts form potent actors in the political arena.

The principal complaint in German legal culture is excess of regulation rather than excess of adversariness. The volume of litigation is large, but most of the caseload is handled efficiently and reliably. What is lamented is the proliferation of courts and the extravagant use of appeals. If a party wants to carry litigation further, it is difficult to put an end to it. And with the variety of specialized courts, all of them working reliably, the justice system tends to overproduce rather than underperform.

Such criticism also applies to the impact of law on public institutions. Judicial review of administrative decisions makes effective policymaking more complicated. Often the reaction of administrators to judicial review is more defensive rulemaking and more compliance to the letter of the law. The unintended result then is more red tape and stifling limits to public policies. Complaints about the political costs of judicial review especially apply to the interventions of the diverse high courts and the constitutional court, which claim areas of regulation that—according to the critics—might better be left to politics and to other social institutions.

72. Cf. Christopher Harding, "Who Goes to Court in Europe?" *European Law Review* 17 (1992), 105–125.

The extensive involvement of courts in political questions stands in contrast to the idea of the judiciary being independent of politics. Within the judiciary, the civil law divisions and the professional self-image of the judges and attorneys working with them form the stronghold of autonomy. A self-understanding of aloofness from partisan politics can even be observed among prosecutors and judges in criminal courts—they see their role as guardians of law and order, which includes the criminalization of extremist political activities. Only among judges of the various special courts do we find a more openly politicized self-understanding: considering their recruitment from and their routine relationship with the agencies which they control, a judicial symbiosis of social security courts, fiscal courts, and administrative courts is inevitable. The lay participation on the bench of these courts as well as the labor courts can be seen as an institutional safeguard against too much co-optation of the judicial guardians by the guarded agencies, but in the judgment of the professionals they do not exert major substantive influence. Constitutional courts form the other end of a continuum between professional autonomy and political interference; the highly visible political role of constitutional justices is administered by a small elite of career judges and professors rather than attorneys or professional politicians. For the large body of German judges, professional autonomy is institutionalized by granting judges life tenured positions. Even though there are lay referees on the bench of many courts, the judiciary regards its role as that of a professional barrier against political interference rather than as a body which could be democratically controlled itself. Despite their political influence, courts carefully protect their reputation as professional "guardians of the law." Rather than seeking democratic legitimation, they treasure the separation of law from politics.

Contrasting itself to the political abuse of courts by the Nazis, as well as by the communist regime, the official self-image of the judiciary in the Federal Republic emphasizes the principle of autonomy of law as a concomitant of democracy. The legal profession is given public responsibility to maintain the autonomy of law, which in turn legitimizes state control over uniform legal education as well as the strict career management by the departments of justice in the states of the Federal Republic. Considering such administrative control, the rhetoric about the autonomy of the legal profession seems somewhat overdone. For most lawyers, legal training leads to their becoming "organization" men and women, working in the machinery of justice, in governmental agencies or corporate administration.

Attorneys account for less than half the legal profession. While not exerting much influence on the legal profession as a whole, they enjoy a monopoly of representation and advice which has kept the scope of their services within rather traditional boundaries. Attorneys are seen as serving an objective ideal of justice, rather than the one-sided interests of their clients. This corresponds to the Continental ideal of procedure which rests more on a judicial prerogative of finding ''true'' justice, rather than on an adversarial idea of parties fighting for their rights.

In the official rhetoric, of course, the principles of law and democracy tend to be merged. In reality, however, they do not always strike a balance. After several periods in German history when politics manipulated law, the scales have turned to the language of law dominating the discourse of politics.

6

Courts and Law in Japan

JOSEPH SANDERS

The making of Japan's contemporary legal order is . . . the story of the sometimes destructive but always creative interaction between new, imposed legal institutions from the West and the habits and values of Japan's past.[1]

This chapter turns away from the West toward a non-European society. We have not, however, left behind Western legal influence. The beginning of Japan's modern era is generally associated with the Meiji Restoration in 1868. During the middle of the nineteenth century, Britain, France, Russia, Holland, and the United States put increasing pressure on Japan to open itself to trade. In the fifteen years following the arrival of Commodore Perry's fleet in 1853 and 1854, the Western powers slowly extracted concessions from the Japanese and, in the process, dramatically undermined the authority of the Shogun, who during much of this period was seen to be acting against the will of the Emperor. In the late 1860s a combination of internal and external pressures brought an end to the 250-year Tokugawa Era. The supporters of the coup that overthrew the Shogun claimed to have restored the responsibility for governing the country to the Emperor (Meiji). The Meiji Restoration also marks the beginning of the modern Japanese legal order.[2] During the subsequent half century the Japanese borrowed many things Western, not the least of which was Western law.

Prior to contact with the West the role of law in Japanese society was limited. The Japanese did not define law as an all-inclusive corpus of principles or use judicial discourse to discuss social or political values.[3] In the tradition of Chinese juristic thought, from which the Japanese had borrowed

1. John O. Haley, *Authority Without Power: Law and the Japanese Paradox* (New York: Oxford University Press, 1991), p. 67.

2. W. G. Beasley, *The Rise of Modern Japan* (New York: St. Martin's Press, 1990), pp. 21–53.

3. Haley, supra note 1, p. 63.

heavily in earlier times, law was largely public law: a matter of administrative rules and procedures.[4] The adjudicatory and judicial institutions of a private law order were undeveloped. More important, the Tokugawa bureaucracy (Bakufu) governed less by formal legal prescription than by "resort to a complex variety of consensual or contractual means of social control."[5]

During the first decades following the Meiji Restoration Japan replaced the legal and political structures of a feudal society with structures adopted from the West. These included a constitution that created a bicameral Diet, land and tax reform, a modern army and navy, and recruitment of civil servants on the basis of achievements in a Western-style education system and formal tests rather than on the basis of hereditary Samurai status.[6]

Most important for the present discussion were a set of fundamental changes in law and legal organization that created the modern Japanese judiciary. Under the Meiji Constitution of 1889 the emperor was sovereign and the courts, like the other branches of government, were not fully independent. The judiciary was part of the Ministry of Justice, which controlled court budgets and the selection, promotion, transfer, and dismissal of judges. Moreover, the judiciary was limited to hearing private lawsuits. Administrative cases were assigned to separate administrative courts that were, in fact, quasi-judicial administrative agencies staffed by retired government officials.[7] Because the emperor was supreme and because the Diet exercised power in his name, an unconstitutional law was by definition impossible.

Although it was not an independent branch of government, the judiciary was professionalized during this period. The constitution created a Supreme Court, government judges replaced courts operated by feudal lords, and the judiciary was given a measure of independence from politics. Judgeships were civil service career jobs, for which judges were recruited through a national examination and after passing entered an eighteen-month apprenticeship.[8] Being a judge became a high status occupation.

Along with a new constitution came a wide variety of new codes. In 1882 Japan adopted a criminal code that was modeled after the French code. A code of civil procedure, prepared by German and French advisors, was adopted in 1890. Work on a commercial code began in 1881, and a German-based code was implemented in 1899. A civil code, also with German roots, was adopted in 1898.[9] It would be a mistake to conclude that the adoption

4. Beasley, supra note 2, p. 91.

5. Haley, supra note 1, p. 64.

6. Beasley, supra note 2, pp. 56–70, 76–80.

7. Percy R. Luney, Jr., "The Judiciary: Its Organization and Status in the Parliamentary System," *Law and Contemporary Problems* 53 (1990), 137–138.

8. Luney, supra note 7, p. 139.

9. Beasley, supra note 2, pp. 92–93; Haley, supra note 1, p. 70.

of these codes worked a sudden wholesale change in Japanese law. From the early 1880s to the turn of the century traditional institutional practices were replaced gradually with parts of the codes under consideration. In many instances the new institutions, processes, and norms of the codes had counterparts in Tokugawa law. When the Western codes conflicted with traditional practices, efforts were made to make the codes conform to established practices.[10]

Little of this was accomplished without controversy. The civil code, especially those parts dealing with culturally sensitive areas of family and property, was objected to on the grounds that it was too Western, and, as a consequence, its adoption was delayed for several years.[11] Nevertheless, the end result of the adoption process was to reproduce in Japan a body of criminal, civil, and procedural law that was as similar to Western codes as Western legal systems are to each other.[12]

Although Japanese legal codes are largely of Western origin, this does not mean the Japanese legal system is thoroughly westernized. The Japanese legal system, like any legal system, can be thought of as having three components: substantive rules of law, a legal structure (the procedures and institutions that apply the law), and a legal consciousness (the values and assumptions about the origin, nature, and function of law in society). The substantive law, embodied in Japanese legal codes, shares many similarities with the legal rules of the West. But as Galanter notes, "Legal cultures, like languages, can absorb huge amounts of foreign material while preserving a distinctive structure and flavor."[13] The Japanese have developed a set of procedures and institutions—a legal structure—that differs in important ways from that found in the West. These structures reflect a legal consciousness that varies from Western, especially American, culture in some fundamental ways. Because the Japanese share Western substantive law but not all of the other aspects of Western legal systems, the law is a particularly useful window into the ways Japanese society resembles and differs from the United States and European societies.

This chapter is divided into four main sections. The first part discusses the organization of the Japanese bench and bar, including the scope of constitutional review by Japanese courts. The second part explores the Japanese criminal justice system and the methods the Japanese use to maintain order.

10. Haley, supra note 1, pp. 70–71.

11. Ibid., p. 76.

12. Konrad Zweigert and Hein Kötz, *Introduction to Comparative Law*, 2d ed. (Oxford: Clarendon Press, 1987).

13. Marc Galanter, "Predators and Parasites: Lawyer-Bashing and Civil Justice," *Georgia Law Review* 28 (1994), 633, 680.

The third part focuses on civil litigation, paying special attention to automobile accidents and environmental pollution cases as examples of how the Japanese resolve ordinary disputes. The fourth part turns from private litigation to public law and examines interactions between state institutions and corporate actors, especially business corporations, to examine how laws and courts are used by corporate actors and those who wish to challenge the state. Each of these parts will indicate how the Japanese legal structures shape the application of the substantive law and how the legal structure reflects and at the same time reinforces Japanese cultural values and assumptions.

The Organization of the Bench and Bar

The operation of Japanese legal system is shaped by the organization of its lawyers and courts. Both are in relatively short supply: in 1990 for all of Japan there were approximately 2,800 judges, 2,000 prosecutors, and 14,000 practicing attorneys. This translates into 2.3 judges, 1.7 prosecutors, and 11.4 lawyers per 100,000 persons.[14] Not only are there relatively few courts and prosecutors, but the legal system is also highly centralized, with strong control from the top. These two facts fundamentally influence the way courts are used to resolve disputes in Japan.

THE BAR

The legal profession in Japan was created after the Meiji Restoration. Because historically law was viewed as a technique of state control, the government did not intend to develop a strong private bar that could represent citizens in disputes with one another and with the state. Instead, the primary objective was to produce judges, prosecutors, and upper-level state bureaucrats.[15] Most private lawyers were relegated to the role of defending the accused in criminal proceedings. Everyday activities such as divorce or real estate transactions routinely proceeded without the assistance of counsel. After World War II the Practicing Attorneys Act was revised to put practicing lawyers on equal footing with prosecutors and judges. Since then, members of all three groups follow a similar career path.

It is perhaps harder to become a lawyer (*bengoshi*) in Japan than in any other developed capitalist country. Lawyers (as well as prosecutors and judges) go through a three-step process.[16] The first step is a degree from a

14. Shozo Ota and Kahei Rokumoto, "Issues of the Lawyer Population: Japan," *Case Western Reserve Journal of International Law* 25 (1993), 315.

15. Ota and Rokumoto, supra note 14, p. 316.

16. The following materials are taken largely from Melissa J. Krasnow, "The Education and Development of Legal Professionals in Japan," *Journal of the Legal Profession* 18 (1993), 93.

law department of a Japanese university. In Japan, as in most European countries, law is an undergraduate major. Individuals typically take three semesters of general courses and five semesters of specialized courses in public
administration and social sciences as well as law. Legal education revolves
around the six basic codes of Japanese law: the constitution, the civil code,
the penal code, the commercial code, the code of civil procedure, and the
code of criminal procedure. The classroom experience is quite different from
that of American law schools. Students attend lectures on abstract theories
about interpretation and structure of the codes. Students acquire a general
knowledge of the codes and legal reasoning, but little practical knowledge
about the legal system.

Law is a popular undergraduate program in Japan; in 1990 there were
38,000 law majors.[17] Admission to the most prestigious Japanese university
law departments is very competitive. The prestige of a law department is
based in small part on the success of its students in the next step, the National
Bar Examination. A degree from a law department is not a prerequisite to
sitting for the examination, but almost everyone takes this path.

Between 23,000 and 29,000 individuals sit for the three-part National Bar
Examination each year.[18] Four hundred and fifty to five hundred pass. In
1989, of 23,202 who took the examination, 506 passed, a success rate of 2.2
percent.[19] One can retake the examination, and repeated tries are typical. A
Ministry of Justice study found that successful candidates usually take the
examination six times or more and that the average age of those who pass
is twenty-eight.[20] Those who fail, along with law graduates who do not take
the examination, take jobs in the bureaucracy, in private enterprise, or as
quasi lawyers in law-related professions. Law graduates (people with undergraduate majors in law) predominate in the civil service. This is especially
the case in the upper echelons of the bureaucracy. Since World War II more
than half of the elite administrators have been law graduates.[21] Clearly, the
role of legally trained people is much wider than the number of practicing
lawyers would suggest.

Success in running this gauntlet leads to admission into the Legal Training
and Research Institute, an agency of the Supreme Court of Japan. The course
of study lasts two years. The instructors are legal professionals: judges, prosecutors, and bengoshi. During an initial training term students study trial

17. Ota and Rokumoto, supra note 14, p. 318.
18. See Krasnow, supra note 16, for a full description of the examination.
19. Ibid., p. 94.
20. Ota and Rokumoto, supra note 14, p. 318.
21. B. C. Koh, *Japan's Administrative Elite* (Berkeley: University of California Press, 1989),
p. 245.

management and pre-trial procedures, practice drafting legal documents, and attend seminars in topics such as accounting, banking, and forensic medicine. Most of the time at the institute is spent as an apprentice to district courts, prosecutors' offices, and bengoshi throughout Japan. The final few months are spent at the institute, where moot court exercises play an important role. After completion of the course of study students take a Final Qualifying Examination which nearly everyone passes.[22] This bifurcated training—abstract theory at the university and practical instruction after graduation—more nearly resembles legal education in Germany and France than in the United States or Britain.

Upon passing the Final Qualifying Examination legal apprentices enter one of the three branches of the Japanese legal profession. Approximately seventy graduates are appointed as assistant criminal or civil judges, fifty are appointed as public prosecutors, and the rest become bengoshi. Traditionally, more prestige attached to the first two careers, but the substantially greater salaries available to lawyers has made this option much more attractive.[23]

Japan produces approximately 350 new lawyers each year, fewer than Harvard Law School alone. In 1990 in Japan there were 14,433 lawyers. Each year the United States produces nearly three times as many new lawyers; the total number of American lawyers is near 700,000.[24] The differences are not quite as dramatic when Japan is compared to European countries. The United Kingdom has approximately 60,000 solicitors and barristers, and France has but 31,000 avocats. Still, the percentage of lawyers in Japan is remarkably small. In 1987 in the United States there was one attorney for every 350 inhabitants. In the United Kingdom the figure was 1 in 900, in West Germany, 1 in 1,300, and in France, approximately 1 in 1,800. In Japan the ratio of bengoshi to inhabitants was 1 in 9,200.[25] In many areas of the country the ratio is much worse because lawyers are concentrated in the large cities. According to a 1980 survey, nearly half of all lawyers were practicing in the Tokyo area, and two-thirds were practicing in the three largest cities of Tokyo, Osaka, and Nagoya. In contrast, the ratio of lawyers to inhabitants in smaller prefectures was approximately 1 in 50,000.[26]

Legal practice is very much an individual enterprise. The average bengoshi is a solo practitioner with a general civil practice. Lawyers who are not in solo practice are in firms that more nearly resemble European firms in their size. Firms of more than ten attorneys are rare, and the largest Tokyo offices

22. Krasnow, supra note 16, p. 95.
23. Ibid., p. 95.
24. Lawrence Friedman, *Total Justice* (New York: Russell Sage, 1985), p. 8.
25. Hiroshi Oda, *Japanese Law* (London: Butterworths, 1992), p. 102, appendix 2.
26. Ota and Rokumoto, supra note 14, p. 321.

have no more than forty attorneys. This pattern is very similar to that found in Germany, and far different from the large law firms found in the United States and, increasingly, in England and France.[27] Average net income for all bengoshi in 1988 was ¥7,030,000.[28]

Given the relative dearth of bengoshi in Japan, it is not surprising that there are many other people who do lawyerlike work. The general public think of the bengoshi as litigation specialists, people to turn to only when a dispute has become so serious that litigation is the only practical alternative. For less serious matters there are a wide variety of quasi lawyers, including tax attorneys, patent attorneys, judicial scriveners (who handle real estate and incorporation matters), public accountants, administrative scriveners (who draw up documents to be submitted to an administrative office), notaries, and law graduates who work in corporate legal sections. Tax attorneys, patent attorneys, judicial scriveners, and law graduates who work in corporate legal sections number more than 78,000, or five times the number of bengoshi.[29] While these quasi lawyers handle many tasks performed by lawyers in other societies, some question whether they are an adequate substitute.[30] Even if they are, the total number of lawyers and paralegals is far fewer per capita than in the United States. When a Japanese citizen decides to resort to law in Japan there are fewer people to whom one may turn for professional assistance.

THE BENCH

As in France and other civil-law countries, the route to judgeship in Japan routinely requires completion of a specialized program, and most people enter the field with the intention of spending their entire working lives as judges.[31] Appointment as an assistant judge is made by the Cabinet from a list of candidates nominated by the Supreme Court. Immediately after appointment, the new judges return to the Legal Training and Research Institute for two training courses and then are assigned to district courts in large cities where they work under the guidance of full judges as members of three-judge panels. After two years, the assistant judge returns to the institute for a course on administrative and delinquency cases. Three more years of practical experience end with another course at the institute, on the management of trials in a single-judge court. At this point an authorized assistant judge may manage trials and render decisions without

27. See chapter 5.
28. Krasnow, supra note 16, p. 96.
29. Ota and Rokumoto, supra note 14, pp. 323–327.
30. Ibid.
31. See chapter 4.

supervision. A fifth course, taken after nine years of experience, provides more training in court management. After ten years of experience an assistant judge may be promoted to a full judgeship. Per Article 80 of the Japanese constitution, the appointment is for a ten-year term, with a possibility of reappointment. Reappointment is a near certainty, and removal during the ten-year period can only be by way of impeachment.[32] The beginning wage is ¥280,000 per month, and salary cannot be reduced during a judge's tenure. Assistant judges move into a new court system that was established after World War II.

The Allies imposed a new constitution on the Japanese following their victory in the war.[33] Not surprisingly, in many ways the 1947 constitution follows an American model.[34] One fundamental similarity is the separation of powers among the branches of government. As in the United States, the new Japanese constitution gives exclusive jurisdiction over all legal disputes to the Supreme Court and inferior courts created by law. In addition, it confers upon the courts the power to review the constitutionality of any law, order, or regulation.[35]

The Court Organization Law of 1947 established the inferior courts and their jurisdiction. The inferior courts include summary courts, family courts, district courts, and appellate courts. Unlike France and Germany, Japan has not created a set of specialized tribunals such as the German labor courts, finance courts, social courts, and administrative courts.[36] On the other hand, the large district courts such as those in Tokyo and Osaka have divisions specializing in areas like bankruptcy, intellectual property, and administrative cases and some agencies such as the Fair Trade Commission operate quasi-judicial panels to resolve disputes. The rulings of the commissions can be appealed to the regular courts.[37]

32. Krasnow, supra note 16, p. 96.

33. The text of the constitution is reproduced in Hiroshi Itoh, *The Japanese Supreme Court: Constitutional Policies* (New York: Markus Wiener Publishing, 1989), pp. 283–295. For one view of this process see Kyoko Inoue, *MacArthur's Japanese Constitution: A Linguistic and Cultural Study of Its Making* (Chicago: University of Chicago Press, 1991).

34. In many ways, however, it does not. The Japanese retained a parliamentary form of government. Moreover, the Americans in charge of overseeing the redrafting of Japanese codes so that they would conform to the new constitution resisted recasting Japanese law into an Anglo-American common-law mold. As one official noted, "there is democracy in Switzerland, as well as in Iowa" (quoted in Haley, supra note 1, p. 106). Japan has remained a civil-law country.

35. Luney, supra note 7, p. 135. Rajendra Ramlogan, "The Human Rights Revolution in Japan: A Story of New Wine in Old Skins?" *Emory International Law Review* 8 (1994), 147.

36. Oda, supra note 25, p. 67.

37. Ibid., pp. 67, 69.

At the bottom of the Japanese court hierarchy are summary courts, which have jurisdiction over civil cases involving claims not exceeding ¥900,000 and minor crimes punishable by fines and prison terms of up to fifteen days. There are more than 450 summary courts and nearly 800 summary court judges.[38] In urban areas, more than one judge may be assigned to each court. In 1983, approximately 60 percent of cases in the civil docket were filed in Summary Courts.[39] The summary court judge may enter fines up to ¥200,000 and order a debtor to pay creditors without a trial.[40] Rulings can be appealed to higher courts. Summary court judges are not always career judges (judges who have passed the National Bar Examination and gone to the Legal Training and Research Institute). Many were once clerks in a court or public prosecutor's office.

The creators of the summary court had in mind a tribunal similar to American small claims courts, a forum easily accessible to ordinary citizens which could dispose of cases relatively quickly. However, small claims by private citizens constitute only a small part of the courts' docket. As in many American small claims courts, a large part of the docket is taken up by creditors suing individual debtors for defaulting on loans.[41]

Family courts are located next to district courts. The courts are divided into a juvenile division and a family division. There are approximately 200 judges, 150 assistant judges, and 1,500 probation officers working in these courts.[42] The juvenile division is similar to the American juvenile court; it handles offenses of defendants under the age of twenty, including a large number of juvenile traffic offenses. The family division, which handles legal disputes arising out of family relationships, processed 340,000 cases in 1990.[43] Both divisions proceed informally. Juvenile cases and family affairs adjudications are conducted *in camera*. The judge and two conciliators attempt to resolve family disputes, and there is a formal proceeding before the judge only when conciliation fails. Married people may commence a divorce action in district court only after the conclusion of conciliation efforts in the family court.[44]

The district court is the trial court of general jurisdiction. It also hears appeals from civil cases tried in the summary courts. There are 50 district courts, one court for each of Japan's prefectures. The 242 branch offices of

38. Ibid., p. 75.

39. Takaaki Hattori and Dan F. Henderson, *Civil Procedure in Japan* (New York: Matthew Bender, 1985), pp. 3–8.

40. Luney, supra note 7, p. 143. In 1994 the exchange rate was approximately 100–105 yen to the dollar.

41. Oda, supra note 25, p. 76.

42. Ibid., p. 73.

43. Ibid., p. 74.

44. Luney, supra note 7, p. 144.

the court employ approximately 900 judges and 460 assistant judges. Usually cases are decided by a single judge, but a three-judge panel may sit in important cases and must sit when the court is hearing certain criminal cases or is exercising its appellate jurisdiction. There are no dissenting opinions; even when an outcome is based on a two-to-one vote all three judges sign the opinion.

The middle-level appellate courts are called the high courts. The eight high courts are located in major Japanese cities, and each has territorial jurisdiction over part of Japan. The high courts hear appeals from the family courts, the district courts, and summary court criminal cases. They also have original jurisdiction over a number of matters including election disputes and petitions for habeas corpus. The Tokyo High Court has a special status because it has original jurisdiction to review the decisions of such agencies as the Fair Trade Commission. Most appeals are heard by a three-judge panel.

The Supreme Court is at the top of the judicial hierarchy. The court is located in Tokyo and is comprised of fifteen judges, who must be forty years of age or older, appointed by the Cabinet. Appointments are subject to recall at the first general election after a judge's appointment, when the voters are asked if a judge should be recalled. A justice is dismissed from the court if a majority vote for a recall. This process is repeated every ten years the judge is on the bench. No judge has ever been removed through this process.[45] Traditionally five of the judges have come from the ranks of the practicing bar, five have been lower court judges, and five have been bureaucrats, prosecutors, or law professors. In 1994 the first woman was appointed to the Supreme Court.[46]

The court is divided into three Petit Benches of five judges each. Almost all appeals are heard by a Petit Bench. However, appeals that concern constitutional questions or where the court may establish a new judicial precedent are heard by the Grand Bench of all fifteen judges. Most of the court's work is on appeal from the high courts or, occasionally, directly from summary, district, or family courts. Grounds for appeal to the Supreme Court in criminal cases are limited to the unconstitutionality of the appellate court's judgment or a deviation from precedent. In civil matters appeal is limited to alleged errors in the interpretation of the constitution and breaches of law that substantially affect the decision below.[47] The Court's caseload is substantial, in

45. From 1948 through 1989 no judge ever got more than a 16% negative vote. J. Mark Ramseyer, "The Puzzling (In)dependence of Courts: A Comparative Approach," *Journal of Legal Studies* 23 (1994), 724.

46. In 1994 women accounted for 7% of judges, 6% of lawyers, and 3% of prosecutors; Jocelyn Ford, "Women Lawyers Call Supreme Court Appointment Tokenism," Japanese Economic Newswire, Jan. 25, 1994.

47. Oda, supra note 25, pp. 70–71.

part because there are no formal gatekeeping devices such as the United States Supreme Court's writ of certiorari to control the docket. In 1990 the Japanese Supreme Court accepted more than 3,000 civil and administrative cases and nearly 2,000 criminal cases. However, a great majority of the cases receive a pro forma review before being dismissed.[48] Reversal of lower court judgments is a rare event. Oda reports that in 1987 only two of 1,450 criminal appeals resulted in the Supreme Court quashing the lower court judgment. In 1990, 26 of 2,000 appealed civil case judgments were reversed.[49]

JUDICIAL CAREERS

Under the Meiji Constitution the Ministry of Justice controlled court budgets and the selection, promotion, transfer, and dismissal of judges. As part of the 1947 constitution's effort to create an independent and co-equal judicial branch, many of these powers were moved to the Supreme Court. During the court term the justices meet weekly in a judicial conference to conduct administrative business.[50] The day-to-day operation of administrative functions resides in a 750-person General Secretariat. The secretariat is headed by the general secretary, who attends the judicial conference. The general secretary and the heads of the bureaus in the secretariat are themselves judges. Appointment to the secretariat is widely sought after. The general secretary is almost always eventually promoted to the Supreme Court.[51] One of the most important functions of the secretariat is the selection, promotion, and transfer of inferior court judges.[52] All judges are moved around throughout their careers, usually three times during each ten-year appointment, spending one-third of their time, respectively, in small, medium, and large courts.[53] Approximately 50 percent of each judicial cohort leaves the bench before reaching retirement, most for private practice. The remainder have a good chance of being promoted to chief judge of a court.

The decision to surrender a judgeship is, in part, a response to promotion patterns as some judges come to realize that they will not rise to elite positions within the judiciary. Judges who are on a track to high judicial position are more likely to be appointed to the general secretariat or to be "loaned" to the Justice Ministry for a limited term to defend the government in civil cases or to staff the civil legislation bureau.[54]

48. Ibid., p. 71. Itoh, supra note 33, p. 33.
49. Oda, supra note 25, p. 71.
50. Itoh, supra note 33, p. 251.
51. Oda, supra note 25, p. 72.
52. Ibid., p. 71.
53. Setsuo Miyazawa, "Administrative Control of Japanese Judges," *Kobe University Law Review* 25 (1991), 46.
54. Oda, supra note 25, p. 97.

It is frequently said that the general secretariat uses its appointment power to control the content of judicial opinions. Miyazawa observes, "Japanese judges appear to need tremendous courage to decide a case in the way that is likely to displease the general secretariat. This applies especially well to decisions that challenge Supreme Court precedents."[55] The Liberal Democratic Party, because of its long-standing control of the Diet and thus its control over appointments to the Supreme Court, has been able to exert considerable influence on the judiciary and to limit the scope of judicial independence. Inferior court judges who decided controversial cases contrary to Liberal Democratic Party preferences have run the risk of being assigned to obscure rural branch offices. It will be interesting to see whether the end of Liberal Democratic Party domination of the government will lead to a more independent judiciary.[56]

JUDICIAL REVIEW

The 1947 constitution confers upon the courts the power to review the constitutionality of any law, order, or regulation. This power is invested in all the courts, not a special constitutional court. The courts, however, are very circumspect in the use of this power. The reluctance of lower court judges to rule that a law or an administrative decision is unconstitutional may be explained in part by fear of adverse career consequences. This is far from the only reason for judicial restraint, however. The 1947 constitution imposed judicial independence and the power of judicial review on a legal system patterned after Germany and France where the judiciary is historically subordinate to the other branches of government. Judicial deference to governmental decisions has continued throughout the postwar era, not only on the part of lower courts but also on the part of the Supreme Court. Several doctrines and rules of interpretation facilitate deference.

Shortly after the end of the American occupation in 1952 the Supreme Court held that, absent a case or controversy, it did not have the power to issue constitutional rulings, thus eliminating any possibility that the court might develop into a constitutional court such as exists in France.[57] The Supreme Court also refuses to hear cases that become moot. As discussed in the section on corporate actors and public law, the court has developed additional procedural devices that limit the ability of litigants to challenge laws and administrative rulings. Even when a litigant does have standing to liti-

55. Miyazawa, supra note 53, p. 52.

56. Ramseyer, supra note 45, pp. 725–726. Ramseyer argues that among democracies, judicial independence from political control should be greatest where the likelihood of continued electoral government is high and the likelihood of a party's continued victory is low (p. 722).

57. Itoh, supra note 33, p. 38.

gate, the Supreme Court is unlikely to agree with the plaintiff that a statute or regulation is unconstitutional. Itoh argues that the rules of judicial restraint set forth by Justice Brandeis in *Ashwander v. T.V.A.* "have formed the *modus operandi* of the Japanese Supreme Court."[58] Among Brandeis' rules are that a court should, if possible, dispose of a case on nonconstitutional grounds and that wherever possible statutes should be construed so as to avoid a constitutional issue.

When compelled to rule on the constitutionality of a statute or agency rule, the Supreme Court has almost always found the provision to be constitutional. Until 1985 the court had found only three laws to be unconstitutional.[59] In 1964 it struck down a provision of the Pharmaceutical Code that allowed a prefectural governor the power to deny a license to open a new drug store if the site would be too close to existing stores because this would lead to the dispensing of substandard drugs due to excessive competition. In 1973 it struck down a provision in the criminal code that provided for heavier penalties for patricide than other forms of manslaughter.[60]

Sometimes the Diet or a ministry has avoided the threat that a statute or the application of a statute will be ruled unconstitutional by changing the law during litigation. For example, a textbook author sued when his book was rejected by the Ministry of Education for "describing the Second World War in excessively negative terms." The ministry told the author to omit the phrase "reckless war" and to change the phrase "invasion of China" to "advancement to Asia." The district court found that the textbook screening statute was constitutional but that this particular decision violated the right to freedom of education guaranteed in the constitution. The appellate court agreed, but the Supreme Court reversed and remanded on procedural grounds. Upon remand the appellate court again held the ministry action to be unconstitutional, but before the case could return to the Supreme Court the ministry substantially altered its guidelines for textbook screening.[61]

Far more often than not, however, the Supreme Court has affirmed the constitutionality of statutes and administrative rulings. For example, the Supreme Court has held constitutional statutes restricting door-to-door campaigning before the notice of an election, and a general prohibition against government employees' involvement in political activities.[62] Not infrequently, the court has found a provision to be constitutional after a lower court has ruled otherwise.

58. 297 U.S. 288 (1936). Itoh, supra note 33, p. 37.

59. Oda, supra note 25, p. 67. Several times since 1985 the court has ruled against legislative apportionment plans on "one person-one vote" grounds. Id., p. 123.

60. Itoh, supra note 33, pp. 186, 195.

61. Oda, supra note 25, p. 126.

62. Ibid., pp. 121, 119.

By and large, the court has applied a balancing test when assessing constitutionality. For example, in justifying the ban on political activities of government employees, the court said, "Although freedom of expression is limited by this ban, interests which are gained by it (it preserves the political neutrality of public employees and the peoples' trust in unbiased administrative action) are far more important than interests lost by this ban. This ban is not disproportionate."[63] The use of a balancing test has been criticized because it can justify almost any government measure that benefits a majority of citizens.[64] Some have argued that the courts should adopt the United States Supreme Court's approach and focus on interpreting the text of the constitution and protecting specific human rights. However, the Japanese approach to constitutional texts is not unique. For example, Beatty reports a similar approach on the part of the Canadian Supreme Court.[65]

The substantial deference the courts have given to legislative and administrative rulings has severely limited the role of courts and litigation in shaping Japanese laws and regulations. It is one of many ways in which Japanese procedures and legal structures are unlike those in the United States, leading to a very different role for the courts. A similar pattern emerges in the area of criminal law.

The Japanese Criminal Justice System

The Japanese criminal justice system is somewhat distinct from the system in other industrial societies and substantially differs from that found in the United States. The major variations do not involve the substantive rules of law. The Japanese criminal codes list the same offenses as do criminal codes in other industrial societies. The Japanese constitution provides a set of formal due process protections to the accused. Likewise, the relative seriousness of offenses is similar.

The formal legal institutions of the Japanese criminal justice system—the police, the prosecutor's office, the courts, and corrections—are much the same as elsewhere. However, they operate quite unlike those in the United States. Most important, at every stage the authorities enjoy substantial discretion as to how to proceed with a case and autonomy from political influence. These differences in operation result, in part, from a different legal

63. *Japan v. Osawa* (The Sarufutsu Case), 28 Keishu 393 (Sup. Ct., G.B., Nov. 6, 1974). Quoted in Taisuke Kamata, "Adjudication and the Governing Process: Political Questions and Legislative Discretion," *Law and Contemporary Problems* 53 (1990), 197–198.

64. Oda, supra note 25, p. 119.

65. David Beatty, "Protecting Constitutional Rights in Japan and Canada," *American Journal of Comparative Law* 41 (1993), 535.

consciousness. The values and assumptions about the proper way for the state to respond to criminal behavior reflect a fundamental perspective about the relationship of people to the society around them. In the United States people tend to be perceived as individuals whose identity and sense of self stand apart from the community, while in Japan a person's identity is, in substantial part, defined by the context of social relationships.[66]

This section begins with a brief comparison of Japanese and Western crime rates. Next, we review Japanese criminal codes. We then turn to the operation of the Japanese criminal justice system, and, in conclusion, we relate this to Japanese legal cultural values.

CRIME RATES IN JAPAN

Japan enjoys the lowest crime rate of any developed nation.[67] The rate of violent crime (homicide, rape, robbery, and assault) is dramatically lower. Moreover, American rates have been rising and Japanese, dropping for the

66. V. Lee Hamilton and Joseph Sanders, *Everyday Justice: Responsibility and the Individual in Japan and the United States* (New Haven: Yale University Press, 1992), p. 19. For discussions of the "individual actor" orientation in the United States see Frank Johnson, "The Western Concept of Self," in A. J. Marsella, G. DeVos, and F. L. K. Hsu (eds.), *Culture and Self: Asian and Western Perspectives* (New York: Tavistock, 1985); Ian MacNeil, "Bureaucracy, Liberalism, and Community—American Style," *Northwestern University Law Review* 79 (1985), 900–948; Michael Sandel, *Liberalism and the Limits of Justice* (Cambridge: Cambridge University Press, 1982). For discussions of the "contextual actor" orientation in Japan see Hiroshi Azuma, "Secondary Control as a Heterogeneous Category," *American Psychologist* 39 (1984), 97; George DeVos, "Dimensions of the Self in Japanese Culture," in Marsella, DeVos, and Hsu (eds.), *Culture and Self*; Takeo Doi, *The Anatomy of Self* (New York: Kodansha); Esyun Hamaguchi, "A Contextual Model of the Japanese: Toward a Methodological Innovation in Japanese Studies," *Journal of Japanese Studies* 11 (1985), 289; Y. Murakami "Ie Society as a Pattern of Civilization: Response to Criticism," *Journal of Japanese Studies* 11 (1985), 401; Robert J. Smith, *Japanese Society: Tradition, Self, and the Social Order* (Cambridge: Cambridge University Press, 1983); John R. Weisz, Fred M. Rothbaum, and Thomas C. Blackburn, "Standing Out and Standing In: The Psychology of Control in America and Japan," *American Psychologist* 39 (1984), 955.

67. Comparing crime rates across societies is difficult; see Ted Westermann and James Burfeind, *Crime and Justice in Two Societies: Japan and the United States* (Pacific Grove, Calif.: Brooks/Cole Publishing, 1991); Wilson Huang and Charles Wellford, "Assessing Indicators of Crime Among International Crime Data Series," *Criminal Justice Policy Review* 3 (1989), 28–47; Dane Archer and Rosemary Gartner, *Violence and Crime in Cross-National Perspective* (New Haven: Yale University Press, 1984). Underreporting is a significant potential problem with comparisons because the level of underreporting is often unknown. However, with respect to Japanese-American comparisons, underreporting is generally thought to be greater in the United States and, therefore, official statistics probably underestimate the actual difference in crime rates in the two societies; Archer and Gartner, ibid.; Westermann and Burfeind, p. 30.

Table 6.1. Homicides, Rapes, and Robberies Known to the Police
and Crime Rate for Five Countries (1987)

	Crimes Known to the Police	Crime Rate (per 100,000)
Japan	5,375	4.4
West Germany	36,913	60.5
Britain	37,385	74.8
France	56,090	101.5
United States	653,822	271.2

Source: A. Didrick Castberg, *Japanese Criminal Justice* (New York: Praeger, 1990), p. 12.

past quarter of a century. In 1960 the American violent crime rate was less than twice the Japanese rate. By the late 1980s the rate in Japan was 22 per 100,000, while the rate in the United States was more than 630 per 100,000, a twenty-eight-fold difference.[68] Even in comparison to other Western countries, Japan enjoys low rates of violent crime. Table 6.1 reports the combined crime rate for homicide, rape, and robbery in Britain, France, Japan, the United States, and West Germany in 1987.

With respect to nonviolent crimes official statistics indicate smaller, but still substantial differences. The larceny (theft and motor vehicle theft) rate in Japan in 1987 was 1,130 per 100,000. In the United States it was 4,863 per 100,000, which was roughly similar to the rates in Britain (5,797), France (3,693), and West Germany (4,456).[69]

The Japanese larceny rate (one-fourth that found in the United States) would seem very low were it not dwarfed by the differences in violent crime. The impact on Japanese life is readily apparent. As Castberg notes:

Anyone who has spent any time in Japan cannot but be struck by the lack of apparent crime and by the general feeling of safety that this engenders. Shop owners routinely leave merchandise on stands outside their shops unattended, thousands of bicycles are left daily at train and subway stations unsecured or locked only by a flimsy handlebar lock, and stores rarely have anti-shoplifting detection devices, although the larger department stores have store detectives. Unescorted women can

68. Westermann and Burfeind, supra note 67, p. 31.

69. A. Didrick Castberg, *Japanese Criminal Justice* (New York: Praeger, 1990), p. 12. Problems of underreporting increase as we move from more serious to less serious crimes, and one should probably put very little faith in the differences in larceny rates among Western societies.

use buses or subways at any time without fear, although they may have to fend off inebriated businessmen on their way home from the normal drinking bout after work. People can walk the streets at any time of day or night with little fear of crime.[70]

How did the Japanese criminal justices system, which has maintained a remarkably low level of crime, come into existence and how does it operate today?

CRIMINAL CODES SINCE THE MEIJI RESTORATION

Like other aspects of contemporary Japanese law, the penal codes are a complex admixture of Japanese, Chinese, continental, and American influences. After the Meiji Restoration the Japanese initially turned to Chinese law and in 1870 and 1873 adopted criminal codes that emulated earlier Ming statutes. From their inception these early codes were seen as temporary, and over the next decade the Japanese turned more and more to Western codes. At least part of the impetus for moving in this direction was provided by the Western powers who objected to some parts of the early codes, most specifically to the provisions permitting the use of torture to extract confessions.[71]

In 1880 the Japanese adopted a code based largely on French law. This code and a companion code of criminal procedure (1890) remained in place until 1907, when they were replaced with a new code drafted along German lines.[72] The 1907 code still forms the core of Japanese criminal law.[73] The code and an accompanying 1927 code of criminal procedure followed a continental (especially French) model in several important respects. The police and prosecutors conducted an initial investigation, and then a "preliminary judge" conducted a second investigation that included questioning the accused. The results of this preliminary investigation were placed in a file and the trial consisted primarily of a confirmation of the earlier findings based on reviewing this written record and questioning the defendant.[74]

Finally, at the end of the Second World War the Allied Occupation Force imposed a number of new constitutional provisions and a new code of crim-

---

70. Ibid., p. 9.

71. Paul Heng-Chao Ch'eń, *The Formation of the Early Meiji Legal Order* (Oxford: Oxford University Press, 1981), 67–68. For a discussion of Japanese criminal law prior to the Meiji Restoration see Castberg, supra note 69, p. 2; Shigemitsu Dando, *Japanese Criminal Procedure*, B. J. George, trans. (South Hackensack, N.J.: Fred B. Rothman, 1965), p. 12.

72. Haley, supra note 1, p. 70.

73. Castberg, supra note 69, p. 3.

74. Daniel Foote, "The Benevolent Paternalism of Japanese Criminal Justice," *California Law Review* 80 (1992), 330.

inal procedure designed to protect the rights of the accused.[75] The American-led effort directed Japanese criminal law away from its inquisitorial style and toward the adversarial style typical of Anglo-American criminal law. The trial was the centerpiece of the new criminal procedures. The new code abolished the preliminary judge's questioning of the accused. It also established rules against the use of hearsay evidence. Another important reform restricted the role of confessions in Japanese criminal law. Included were a constitutional privilege against self-incrimination, a right to refuse to answer questions, a duty to tell the accused of this right, and prohibitions against the admission of coerced confessions at trial.[76] In spite of these provisions Japanese criminal law continues to reflect its French and German roots, albeit with a number of unique Japanese features.

THE STRUCTURE OF THE CRIMINAL JUSTICE SYSTEM

In Japan, as elsewhere, the criminal justice system is exactly that: a system. The components interact to produce a set of outcomes for reported crimes. This section discusses the operation of the core institutions in the justice system: police, prosecutors, courts, and corrections.

The Police

Japanese police are held in relatively high repute. Surveys of occupational prestige rank policemen in the middle range, typically just ahead of office workers.[77] Corruption is apparently rare, public confidence is high, and the police are self-assured about their own worth and the importance of their role in society.[78]

A large number of police have a rural background, yet more and more officers have a college education. Applicants must pass an examination and then attend police school. During the Meiji period the police were highly centralized. Following World War II, the police system was decentralized and more than 1,600 independent municipal police forces were created. Police oversight was vested in politically neutral public-safety commissions. In 1954

---

75. Castberg, supra note 69, p. 4; Kenzo Takayanagi, "A Century of Innovation: The Development of Japanese Law, 1868–1961," in Arthur von Mehren (ed.), *Law in Japan: The Legal Order in a Changing Society* (Cambridge: Harvard University Press, 1963), 23; Atsushi Nagashima, "The Accused and Society: The Administration of Criminal Justice in Japan," in von Mehren (ed.), *Law in Japan.*

76. Foote, supra note 74, p. 331; Richard Appleton, "Reforms in Japanese Criminal Procedure under Allied Occupation," *Washington Law Review* 24 (1949), 401.

77. Walter Ames, *Police and Community in Japan* (Berkeley: University of California Press, 1981), p. 156.

78. David Bayley, *Forces of Order: Policing in Modern Japan* (Berkeley: University of California Press, 1991), p. 4.

the Police Law was altered to create a more centralized structure. The current system is based on prefectural police units linked together by and under the supervision of the National Police Agency. Public safety commissions supervise police at the prefectural and national level. Commission members are appointed by prefectural governors and, in the case of the national commission, by the prime minister with the consent of the Diet. In practice the commissions have been very deferential to the police, and the police are relatively free from effective formal checks on their operations.[79]

In per capita terms the Japanese police force is quite small. In 1988 there was one officer per 555 citizens, while in the United States there was one officer per 354.[80] However, the police are in many ways in much closer contact with individuals and the community than are American police, primarily because of the existence of fixed police posts (kōban) that are staffed twenty-four hours a day.[81] There are more than six thousand kōban located in urban areas, including nearly one thousand in the Tokyo area alone. Policing in Japan is kōban policing. Nearly 80 percent of all Japanese police officers in urban areas work from a station. This method of policing is so central to the Japanese situation that police officers are addressed by the public as Omawari-san, "Mr. Walkabout."[82]

From the kōban the police acquire an intimate knowledge of the surrounding neighborhood, which averages about one-fifth of a square mile. The closeness is based in part on a twice-yearly visit to every small business and residential unit in the district. During the visit the police gather basic demographic information about the people in each residence and the employees at each place of business. They also ask about whether the resident owns a car, whether there is especially valuable property they should be aware of, whether the resident has observed any suspicious activity, whether any neighbors have been troublesome, and whether the quality of municipal services has been satisfactory.[83] Two important goals of these visits are to collect information for criminal investigations and to maintain surveillance of gangsters, ex-convicts, and others. Far from seeing this as an unwanted intrusion, many Japanese citizens complain if the survey is not done regularly.[84] Bayley notes, "Japanese police officers penetrate the community more extensively

79. Ames, supra note 77, pp. 162–164, 11, 13.

80. Foote, supra note 74, n. 95.

81. In rural areas similar posts are called chūzaisho. The chūzaisho is a residential post, staffed around the clock by an officer who lives with his family in adjoining quarters; Bayley, supra note 78, p. 11.

82. Ibid., pp. 12, 31.

83. Ibid., p. 79.

84. Ames, supra note 77, p. 39.

than American police officers, but they do so in a more routine, less formal fashion."[85]

Bayley also observes that the boundary between police and citizen is more permeable. The police have many nonemergency contacts with citizens, and citizens assume more policelike functions. The first part of this equation is possible because police have time for non–crime-related activities. While the Japanese police force is small when measured per capita, it is relatively large when measured per crime. There is one officer for every 7.2 reported crimes in Japan. The comparable statistic for the United States is one officer per 19.6 crimes.[86] Japan's low crime rate provides its police officers with the luxury of a wider range of contacts with citizens. In some prefectures the police have set up general counseling offices to assist people with a host of personal problems.[87]

The second part of the equation is possible because the Japanese citizenry is well organized to assist with crime prevention functions. Every neighborhood has a Crime Prevention Association. The associations do many of the things that neighborhood watch groups do in the United States, but they undertake additional activities more characteristic of the Guardian Angels, as well. They allow their homes or offices to serve as "contact points" where people may solicit help or obtain information, they sell improved locks and window latches, they contribute money to police stations for the purchase of crime-prevention vans, they maintain surveillance over troublemakers and gangsters, and they organize their own street patrols. Bayley estimates "that several hundred thousand people are actively involved as leaders of crime-prevention associations in Japan or hosts for contact points."[88]

The apprehension of criminal suspects is at the core of policing. The moral authority of the Japanese police and the lack of a sharp boundary between citizens and police permit officers to intrude into suspects' lives in ways that believers in the primacy of individual rights often find objectionable. The extent of police intrusions are reflected in arrest practices, searches and seizures, and confessions.

Perhaps the most remarkable thing about arrests in Japan is their infrequency. In the United States an arrest marks the beginning of the criminal process, the point at which the police can legitimately use the power of the state against the will of the individual. In 1987, 78 percent of all those suspected of serious crimes in Japan were examined and prosecuted without

85. Bayley, supra note 78, p. 80.
86. Foote, supra note 74, n. 95.
87. Bayley, supra note 78, p. 82.
88. Id. at 83, p. 89.

arrest.[89] These individuals have no legal duty to assist the police or prosecutor; nevertheless, cooperation is widespread, partly owing to police "persuasion." Persuasion is condoned by the courts and is justified by the argument that an arrest is a very stigmatizing event to be avoided whenever possible. If interrogation and prosecution on an "at-home basis" were made more difficult, the argument goes, the result would be more stigmatizing arrests.[90]

The postwar reforms put new limits on searches and seizures. Article Thirty-five of the Constitution parallels the language of the Fourth Amendment to the United States Constitution.[91] Nevertheless, the police often engage in warrantless searches that would appear to be without "adequate cause" as required by the Constitution.[92] Japanese courts have been reluctant to invalidate searches. For example, the Supreme Court held in the Sakai case that an officer who unzipped a bowling-ball bag against the wishes of two suspects had not conducted a search, but rather had merely taken a "measure incident to the stopping and questioning" of the suspects.[93] Judicial unwillingness to second-guess police decisions produces a system in which the various organizations in the justice system feel they are working toward a common goal. As Bayley notes, contrary to many officers in the United States, Japanese police do not talk about being "handcuffed" by the courts.[94]

Confessions remain at the center of the Japanese criminal justice system. Police devote significant effort to extracting confessions from suspects and are successful in over 85 percent of all cases.[95] The high confession rate is attributable in part to lengthy period of time authorities are given to question suspects. The police may detain a person for forty-eight hours on their own before the case is turned over to a prosecutor. The prosecutor then has an additional twenty-four hours to apply for a detention order. A judge can authorize another ten days of detention, at the end of which he or she can order ten more days. Thus, an arrested criminal suspect can be detained for a total of twenty-three days before a decision to prosecute must be made.[96]

89. Setsuo Miyazawa, *Policing in Japan: A Study on Making Crime*, Frank Bennett, trans. (Albany: State University of New York Press, 1992), p. 16.

90. Foote, supra note 74, pp. 344–345.

91. Ibid., p. 333.

92. Bayley, supra note 78, p. 37.

93. Foote, supra note 74, pp. 333–334.

94. Bayley, supra note 78, p. 5.

95. Castberg, supra note 69, p. 44.

96. Foote notes that the clock does not begin to run on even this lengthy period of interrogation until an arrest is made; Foote, supra note 74, p. 346. Steinhoff notes that this detention

Judges rarely refuse investigative detention requests.[97] Many people are held beyond the initial forty-eight hours, although most are held less than ten days. During this period there is no bail (bail is available after charges have been filed). As Bayley notes, "a key purpose of precharge detention is to induce confession."[98] Therefore, interrogation is an ongoing activity during this period. Suspects have the right to remain silent and must be advised of this right when they are detained, but they cannot refuse to be questioned, and access to a defense lawyer is at the discretion of the police and prosecutors.[99]

This system is open to potential abuse by the police.[100] Although reports of physical abuse are rare, psychological pressure to confess is substantial and includes the use of techniques such as isolation, lack of privacy, and interrupted sleep.[101] In recent years a number of convictions have been overturned because confessions were held to be untrustworthy.[102] There is no systematic data on the number of false confessions resulting in convictions.

While police intrusiveness invades personal autonomy, it assists the police in connecting suspects to a very large proportion of crimes. Clearance rates measure the number of offenses known to the police that are "cleared" either by arrest or prosecution. In the United States in the mid-1980s the clearance rate for major offenses was approximately 20 percent. Similar figures for the United Kingdom, West Germany, and France were 35 percent, 47 percent, and 40 percent, respectively. In Japan the rate was over 64 percent.[103] The relatively high clearance rate is evidence that Japanese police are doing better than police in other developed countries in suppressing crime.

In the United States clearance rates are usually "clearance by arrest" rates. In Japan, because so many individuals are prosecuted without ever being arrested, the clearance-by-arrest rate is similar to those in the United States. However, a more appropriate rate for Japan, used above, is clearance by submission for prosecution. One way to make comparisons across countries is to ask for what proportion of known offenses is a suspect found, and what proportion of suspects are prosecuted? Bayley estimates that for Japan the

---

period may be extended by rearresting a suspect on a new charge and thereby restarting the detention clock for an additional 10 days; Patricia Steinhoff, "Pursuing the Japanese Police," *Law and Society Review* 27 (1993), 827, 840.

97. Foote, supra note 74, p. 336.

98. Bayley, supra note 78, p. 145.

99. Ibid., p. 146.

100. Chalmers Johnson, *Conspiracy at Matsukawa* (Berkeley: University of California Press, 1972).

101. Bayley, supra note 78, p. 148.

102. Miyazawa, supra note 89, pp. 3–4.

103. Castberg, supra note 69, p. 11.

relevant figures are 60 percent and 65 percent. In the United States the figures are 20 percent and 50 percent. Multiplying these two percentages in each country leads to the conclusion that the Japanese prosecute a suspect for 39 percent of known crimes. In the United States a suspect is prosecuted for 10 percent of known crimes.[104]

If the Japanese police arrange for the prosecution of many suspects that they do not arrest, it is also true that they divert from formal prosecution many suspects who could be prosecuted. Forty percent of adult penal code cases are closed by the police through a process called *bizai shobun* (disposition of trivial crimes).[105] "Trivial" crimes are those so designated by the public prosecutor's office and include simple assault, theft, fraud, embezzlement, and gambling. When the police release a person in this way they are required take certain steps: they must admonish the suspect not to offend in the future; they have the offender sign an apology and promise to obey the law in the future; they are to ask the suspect's family or employer to keep an eye on the suspect; and they must make the suspect provide restitution and take other steps to assist the victim.[106] Foote notes that by using bizai shobun and by recommending to prosecutors that they deal leniently with suspects who have "shown sincere repentance," the police give considerable weight to rehabilitation goals.

Prosecutors and the Courts

Most new prosecutors pass the National Bar Examination and then complete a course of study at the Legal Training and Research Institute. Prosecutors may also be appointed from the ranks of judges, university law faculty members, and bengoshi. The prosecutors are organized in a centralized system that parallels the court structure: a Supreme Court public prosecutor's office, a high court office, and a district court office. The Japanese offices are staffed by civil servants who spend their career as prosecutors. The Prosecutor General is the head of the prosecutors' office division within the Justice Ministry. Like judges, prosecutors rotate from location to location in order to minimize the opportunity of corruption. Unlike judges, prosecutors cannot refuse transfers.

At least every three years the Public Prosecutors Suitability Inquiry Board reviews each prosecutor's record, and an unfavorable review may lead to dismissal. After eight years new Class II prosecutors are promoted to the rank of Class I prosecutor. Unless there is an unfavorable review by the Suitability Board, a prosecutor cannot be removed or suspended from office

104. Bayley, supra note 78, pp. 138–139.
105. Haley, supra note 1, p. 126.
106. Foote, supra note 74, p. 343.

except by mandatory retirement.[107] Like the police, Japan's prosecutors are a professional force that is insulated from the political arena and, therefore, from some degree of political accountability.

Prosecutors sometimes take an active role in the investigation of cases and, like the police, frequently question the accused. The suspect must be told that he or she can refuse to appear and refuse to answer questions, but many do not and there is no right to have an attorney present. If there has been no confession, the questioning will very likely be designed to extract one. More frequently the purpose of the questioning is to fill in gaps in the prosecutor's case. Because there is no formal plea bargaining, at trial the prosecutor must present a complete case against the defendant. Both the police and the prosecutors are prohibited from promising the suspect any reduction in charge or in sentence in exchange for a confession. A third objective of questioning is to allow the prosecutor to assess the character of the defendant.[108] This is similar to the wide-ranging examination typical of French interrogations. As in France, prosecutors explore the suspect's motive, family background, and other circumstances.

The prosecutor must select a course of action based on the strength of the state's case and assessment of the defendant. The available alternatives are: transfer the case to other courts or another prosecutor's office, dismiss for lack of evidence, suspend prosecution, prosecute in a summary proceeding, or prosecute in an ordinary trial proceeding.[109] Japanese prosecutors, like prosecutors in the United States, drop a large number of the cases presented to them. However, the patterns of dismissal are not the same. Between one-third and one-half of American felony arrests are rejected during the screening process or after the case has been filed, and problems with evidence or witnesses account for a majority of these rejections.[110] In Japan a large number of cases are transferred, for example juvenile criminal cases are transferred to family court. In 1987 41 percent of the criminal code cases referred to the prosecutor's office were transferred, but only 4 percent of the offenses were dropped for lack of evidence or other weaknesses in the state's case.[111]

By far the largest group of cases not brought to trial or transferred are those in which the prosecutor recommends a suspension of prosecution. In these cases there is usually strong evidence of guilt, but the prosecutor determines justice would be better served by avoiding a trial. The code of criminal procedure expressly sets forth the factors the prosecutor should con-

107. Krasnow, supra note 16, p. 97.
108. Ibid., p. 58.
109. Haley, supra note 1, p. 126.
110. Westermann and Burfeind, supra note 67, p. 109.
111. Haley, supra note 1, p. 127.

sider in arriving at this decision, including the offender's situation, the gravity of the offense, and whether the offender has apologized and made restitution to the victim.[112] Within these guidelines, the prosecutor enjoys wide discretion in choosing in which cases prosecution should be suspended.[113] In 1987, 23 percent of the prosecutor's criminal caseload was disposed of in this way.[114] This pattern of prosecutorial discretion to apply pre-trial sanctions and dismiss some cases finds a parallel in the discretion afforded German prosecutors, who may waive prosecution with the stipulation that the accused make a contribution to a charitable organization.

Cases that are neither transferred, dismissed, nor suspended are brought to trial. While the prosecutor must always present sufficient evidence to convict the defendant, most tried cases are processed in uncontested summary proceedings using only documentary evidence.[115] The defendant does not need to appear, and generally the court can impose only a maximum fine of ¥500,000.[116] Ninety-nine percent of all trials of motor vehicle offenses are disposed of in summary proceedings, as are one-quarter of trials involving criminal code offenses. Although there is no exact parallel to summary trials in the United States, there are rough counterparts in some European jurisdictions as in Germany's penal order.[117]

Formal trial proceedings must be used for serious offenses that may result in prison terms like rape, robbery, homicide, and extortion. This is true even when the defendant does not contest the charge. Formal trials occurred in 7 percent of 1987 criminal code offenses.[118] A Japanese trial differs in several important ways from a criminal trial in the United States. The greatest difference is that the trial unfolds as a series of separate hearings occurring over time. Hearings may last from less than an hour to a full day and are separated by intervals of two to eight weeks.[119] Very complex cases may take a long time to complete; however, uncontested criminal cases are often completed quickly.

112. Castberg, supra note 69, pp. 60–62.

113. B. J. George, "Discretionary Authority of Public Prosecutors in Japan," *Law in Japan* 17 (1984), 42.

114. Haley, supra note 1, p. 127.

115. Ibid., p. 128.

116. Nobuyoshi Araki, "The Flow of Criminal Cases in the Japanese Criminal Justice System," *Crime and Delinquency* 31 (1985), 619; Haley, supra note 1, p. 128. In 1991 the criminal code and the code of criminal procedure were revised to raise maximum fines from ¥200,000 to ¥500,000, personal correspondence from Professor Masaki Abe to Herbert Jacob, Sept. 12, 1994.

117. William Felstiner, "Plea Contracts in West Germany," *Law and Society Review* 13 (1979), 309.

118. Haley, supra note 1, p. 127.

119. Castberg, supra note 69, p. 90.

Uncontested trials may not have witnesses. The judge reviews the written and documentary evidence and sometimes requires additional evidence. In contested cases the judge adopts the posture of a neutral adjudicator and fact-finder. Similar to the situation in continental systems, the judge plays a more active role in the trial, establishing the order of witnesses and often initiating the questioning.

There are two additional aspects of Japanese trials that should be mentioned. First, there are no juries. In 1923 Japan passed a law providing for right to trial by jury in criminal cases. However, during World War II the law was suspended and has never been reinstated.[120] In the absence of a jury there is less concern with the admissibility of evidence. Second, there is not a separate sentencing hearing subsequent to the determination of guilt. The single trial contains evidence of guilt and innocence and also evidence of aggravation and mitigation that may influence the judge's sentence. Sometimes the defense attorney may even admit the guilt of the defendant in closing argument and plead for leniency.[121]

The judge renders a decision in writing, and the conviction rate is over 99 percent. Like the police and prosecutors, the judge enjoys considerable discretion in sentencing. In extenuating circumstances, minimum sentences can be reduced by half and all sentences of up to three years can be suspended. By combining these two features the judge can and does give a suspended sentence in most cases.[122] Sentences are suspended for nearly 60 percent of adults convicted of penal code offenses, and the great majority of these people are not placed under any formal supervision. By way of comparison, between 30 and 35 percent of those convicted of a felony in the United States are placed on probation.[123] But for the fact that they have gone through a trial and conviction, those given a suspended sentence are in a position similar to that of people whose prosecution was suspended. However, someone who commits an offense after having their sentence suspended

120. Richard Lempert, "A Jury for Japan?" *American Journal of Comparative Law* 40 (1992) 37; Castberg, supra note 69, p. 3; Haruo Abe, "The Accused and Society: Therapeutic and Preventive aspects of Criminal Justice in Japan," in von Mehren (ed.), *Law in Japan*, p. 326.

121. Castberg, supra note 69, p. 92.

122. Foote, supra note 74, p. 351.

123. Westermann and Burfeind, supra note 67, p. 118. Even within specific categories of offenses there is some tendency for Japanese judges to use suspended sentences more often than American judges use probation. Nineteen percent of those convicted of homicide are given a suspended sentence in Japan. In the state felony courts of the United States 4% of those convicted of homicide are given probation. Similar differences exist for those convicted of rape (Japan, 35%; United States, 10%) and assault (Japan, 52%; United States, 26%). Only in the case of robbery are the rates similar (Japan, 13%; United States, 12%); Ibid., p. 120.

is incarcerated. Altogether, fewer than 5 percent of criminal suspects serve any time in prisons, a pattern similar to that in Germany.[124]

For those who are sent to jail, the prison terms are relatively short. The majority of those convicted of a penal code offense receive sentences of two years or less. Less than one percent receive sentences of ten years or more. Even in the case of homicide convictions, the average sentence is well under ten years.[125]

Corrections

The number of people under the supervision of the Japanese corrections system reflects the low crime rate. In 1987, 53,000 people were placed in prison, on probation, or on parole. The similar figure for the United States, a society with approximately twice as many citizens, was just over 1.8 million.[126] Slightly more than 29,000 people were admitted to prison. The average daily prison population was somewhat over 55,000, reflecting the short sentences served by most prisoners, compared to over 585,000 in the United States.[127]

Rehabilitation is a central objective of Japanese corrections. Almost all inmates work a forty-hour week in a wide variety of occupations. Work serves the dual goals of providing the prisoners with an employable skill and strengthening "their will to work, sense of self help, and spirit of cooperation through working together in well-regulated circumstances."[128]

While work is an important part of the rehabilitation effort, psychological or therapeutic counseling plays a very minor role. One important exception that is quite revealing is the use of Naikan therapy. In Naikan the person undergoes a week of all-day meditation, the central focus of which is the person's guilt at failure to fulfill obligations, especially obligations to parents and other authorities.[129] The goal is to become more *sunao*—that is, more obedient, prone to accept others, dependent, not self-centered, honest, and free from antagonisms.[130]

124. Foote, supra note 74, p. 355. See figure 5.4.

125. Ibid., pp. 354–355.

126. Westermann and Burfeind, supra note 67, p. 136.

127. Castberg, supra note 69, p. 109. Department of Justice, Bureau of Justice Statistics, Prisoners in 1992. By 1992 the United States inmate population had risen to more than 880,000.

128. *Corrections Institutions in Japan* 1982 (Corrections Bureau. Tokyo: Ministry of Justice, 1982).

129. T. Murase, "Naikan Therapy," in T. S. Lebra and W. P. Lebra (eds.), *Japanese Culture and Behavior* (Honolulu: University of Hawaii Press, 1974), pp. 431–442.

130. T. Murase, "Sunao: A Central Value in Japanese Psychotherapy," in A. J. Marsella and G. M. White (eds.), *Cultural Conceptions of Mental Health and Therapy* (Dordrecht, Netherlands: D. Reidel, 1982), pp. 317–329.

Parole from prison is at the discretion of the prison superintendent and the parole board. The most unique feature of probation or parole in Japan is the extensive use of volunteers. There are fewer than 1,000 professional probation officers in Japan, and their caseload averages 150 individuals. However, they are assisted by nearly 50,000 volunteers. The caseload of the average volunteer is one or two people. The voluntary probation officer visits an inmate's home at the beginning of incarceration and works to improve the environment to which the prisoner will return. The officer also works to arrange employment and housing for inmates without family. After the inmate is released the officer visits him and his family regularly during the term of parole. Voluntary probation officers also serve on crime prevention associations and thus assist in the detection of new crimes.[131]

THE CRIMINAL JUSTICE SYSTEM AND CULTURAL VALUES

Three central tasks of a criminal justice system are to prevent and suppress crime, to protect individuals from the capricious exercise of state power, and to reintegrate offenders into society.[132] Several commentators have argued that the American criminal justice system can be defined as a struggle for primacy between the first and second tasks, between what Herbert Packer calls a crime control model and a due process model.[133] These two models pay little attention to the rehabilitation and reintegration of offenders into society. In response to Packer, John Griffiths proposed what he called a family model that has at its center a desire to rehabilitate and reintegrate offenders, much as a parent might wish to rehabilitate a child who had done wrong.[134] John Braithwaite notes that the family model uses the offender's sense of shame as part of the sanctioning process. The shaming is reintegrative, not disintegrative. "Reintegrative shaming means that expressions of community disapproval, which may range from mild rebuke to degradation ceremonies, are followed by gestures of reacceptance into the community of law abiding citizens."[135]

An important aspect of the system in the United States is that the institutions (the police, the prosecutor, the courts, and corrections) tend to focus on different goals and respond to their own imperatives.[136] The police and

131. Foote, supra note 74, pp. 358–359.

132. Miyazawa, supra note 89, p. 100.

133. Herbert Packer, *The Limits of the Criminal Sanction* (Stanford, Calif.: Stanford University Press, 1968), pp. 159–160.

134. John Griffiths, "Ideology in Criminal Procedure or a Third 'Model' of the Criminal Process," *Yale Law Journal* 79 (1970), 359.

135. John Braithwaite, *Crime, Shame and Reintegration* (Cambridge: Cambridge University Press, 1989), p. 55.

136. Foote, supra note 74, p. 325. See chapter 2.

the courts have often seen themselves to be on opposite sides of the crime control–due process dichotomy.[137] Crime control frequently dominates police practices and outlooks. In this regard the police have an uncertain ally in the prosecutor's office. However, the prosecutors have often felt caught between the police and the due process concerns of the courts. Rehabilitation perspectives have been left almost entirely to corrections programs.[138] The consequence of this serial apportionment of objectives to different parts of the criminal justice system in the United States has been a fair degree of inter-organizational hostility. Police speak of being "handcuffed" by the courts, who in turn complain about police excesses. Judges, police, and prosecutors unite to criticize parole and probation decisions that they feel are too solicitous of the welfare of the offender.

The Japanese system differs in two fundamental respects. First, as Daniel Foote argues persuasively, to a much greater extent than in the United States and even more than in European countries, the family model, or "benevolent paternalism," as he calls it, best describes the Japanese criminal justice system.[139] The structure of the system is premised on the reintegration of offenders into society. Second, and equally important, this perspective dominates every part of the justice system. Inter-organizational conflicts are substantially muted.

The confession is at the center of the Japanese criminal justice system, much more than in England, France, Germany, or the United States. Its importance can hardly be overestimated. As Haley notes, "Confession, repentance, and absolution provide the underlying theme of the Japanese criminal process. At every stage from initial police investigation through formal proceedings, an individual suspected of criminal conduct gains by confessing, apologizing, and throwing himself upon the mercies of the authorities."[140]

The high confession rate in Japan is in certain ways similar to the high rate of guilty pleas in the United States, where it is estimated that between 80 and 90 percent of defendants plead to some charge.[141] Both confessions and plea bargaining provide a practical alternative to the adversarial trial of criminal cases. Both help to solve the problem of delay and insufficient ca-

137. L. Paul Sutton, "The Fourth Amendment in Action: An Empirical View of the Search Warrant Process," *Criminal Law Bulletin* 22 (1986), 405.

138. Norval Morris and Michael Tonry, *Between Prison and Probation: Intermediate Punishments in a Rational Sentencing System* (New York: Oxford University Press, 1990), p. 46.

139. Foote, supra note 74.

140. John O. Haley, "Sheathing the Sword of Justice in Japan: An Essay on Law Without Sanctions," *Journal of Japanese Studies* 8 (1982), 269.

141. Milton Heumann, *Plea Bargaining: The Experiences of Prosecutors, Judges and Defense Lawyers* (Chicago: University of Chicago Press, 1978).

pacity in the criminal justice system.[142] However, it would be a mistake to view confessions and guilty pleas as interchangeable. Many, perhaps most guilty pleas in the United States are rather rote transactions involving an offer and acceptance without any real bargaining. Even when there is a more explicit negotiation, plea bargaining, as Bayley notes, "is a cost benefit transaction; it is a mutually advantageous trade between the offender and the system. It involves no acknowledgement of moral guilt on the part of the offender. Indeed, it obscures guilt because the suspect is confessing to something less than what was done. The law connives with the offender in misrepresenting the nature of the offense."[143] Indeed, the process of plea bargaining in American criminal courts takes place largely outside the presence of the defendant.[144]

By definition a confession intimately involves the accused. It is an admission of a particular act of wrongdoing; and the quality of the confession is measured by its sincerity and by its completeness. As Haley notes, it is wrong to "focus on the evidentiary importance of confessions to the exclusion of their rehabilitative effect."[145] Confessions are a central component of benevolent paternalism, designed "to teach, to humble, to extract contrition and repentance" from the accused as a first step toward rehabilitation.[146] Moreover, the confession is an admission of wrongdoing that is not explicitly part of a bargain. Indeed, plea bargaining is not permitted in Japan, and the police and prosecutors cannot make promises in return for guilty pleas, although many defendants know that they should confess in order to minimize their punishment. In theory an individual cannot be convicted solely on the basis of a confession. There must be other evidence, although this evidence may be acquired through the process of interrogating the suspect.[147] Miyazawa argues that the Japanese police work on the assumption that the suspect will confess and the confession will match the physical evidence.[148] Like the police, prosecutors also question suspects. As Foote notes, "the authorities regard close one-on-one questioning as their most important tool for leading suspects to accept full moral responsibility for their misdeeds and for setting them on the road to rehabilitation."[149] Concern with family model values is

142. Haley, supra note 1, p. 123.

143. Bayley, supra note 78, p. 147.

144. Douglas Maynard, *Inside Plea Bargaining: The Language of Negotiation* (New York: Plenum, 1984), p. 29.

145. Haley, supra note 1, p. 132.

146. Bayley, supra note 78, p. 149.

147. Ibid., p. 147.

148. Miyazawa, supra note 89, p. 235.

149. Foote, supra note 74, p. 346.

not restricted to confessions. Bizai shobun, closure of minor offenses, is a process of diverting offenders from the criminal process and actively working to reintegrate them into the community.

The centrality of the benevolent paternalism is also reflected in court practices. As Foote notes, "such factors as family relationships, working habits, assurances from sureties and employers, and types of friends play an important role in determining whether sentences are suspended. The attitude of the defendant at trial also carries great weight: a sincere confession evidencing acceptance of moral responsibility and the sincere desire to reform is crucially important."[150] Finally, the corrections system, with its short sentences, emphasis on work and job skills training, Naikan therapy, and substantial post-release efforts at reintegrating the offender, also exhibits a commitment to the family model.

The Japanese justice system's focus on a family model reflects larger societal values. Table 6.2 shows the average evaluations of rationales for imprisonment by a sample of Detroit and Yokohama residents. People were asked to use a five-point scale to rate whether each rationale was a good or bad reason for imprisonment, one being "a very good reason" and five being "a very bad reason." The rehabilitation of offenders, specific deterrence, and labeling are more preferred by Yokohama residents than Detroiters. On the other hand, Detroiters prefer retribution, incapacitation, and general deterrence.[151]

When asked what should happen to people who commit minor acts of wrongdoing, Japanese respondents frequently call for a sanction that restores relationships, e.g., apology and financial restitution. Restorative sanctions are a central component of the Japanese conception of self as a contextual actor whose identity is, in substantial part, embedded in and defined by a community of social relationships. In contrast, American responses reflect a view of wrongdoing as being committed by individual actors and a view of sanctions that isolates wrongdoers from society.[152]

The very low crime rate in Japan makes the Japanese criminal justice system seem attractive to people in other societies. It is important to realize, however, how grounded the system is in Japanese social structure and culture. Informal, integrative systems work in a strongly knit community of social relationships, but they are less successful in the absence of this type

150. Ibid., p. 352.

151. V. Lee Hamilton and Joseph Sanders, "Punishment and the Individual in the United States and Japan," *Law and Society Review* 22 (1988), 319.

152. Hamilton and Sanders, supra note 66; and Joseph Sanders and V. Lee Hamilton, "Legal Cultures and Punishment Repertoires in Japan, Russia, and the United States," *Law and Society Review* 26 (1992), 117.

Table 6.2. Average Agreement with Reasons for Imprisonment by American and Japanese Respondents

	Mean Ratings	
	Detroit	Yokohama
	$N = 294$	$N = 600$
Sending the criminal to prison . . .	2.03	2.47
Retribution		
Incapacitation makes the criminal suffer for his crime.		
removes the criminal from society and keeps him from committing another crime while in prison.	1.56	2.13
General deterrence shows other possible criminals what will happen to them if they commit the crime.	1.91	2.33
Just desserts provides justice for the victim of the crime.	2.67	2.43
Specific deterrence shows the criminal what happens to people who commit crimes and teaches him a lesson.	2.35	1.66
Rehabilitation reforms or reeducates the criminal while he is imprisoned.	2.62	1.54
Labeling shows that society thinks the crime was wrong.	2.05	1.67

1 = Very good reason for imprisonment; 5 = Very bad reason. In the multiple analysis of variance, the overall F statistic $(7,886) = 56.1$; $p < .0001$. All individual choices also differ significantly, with $p < .01$.

Source: V. Lee Hamilton and Joseph Sanders, Everyday Justice: Responsibility and the Individual in Japan and the United States (New Haven: Yale University Press, 1992).

of community. Germany shares with Japan a low incarceration rate but does not share a commitment to rehabilitation as the centerpiece of its criminal justice system. In the United States, the lack of a sense of community stands as a substantial impediment to the implementation of a rehabilitative model.[153]

CONCLUSION

The Japanese crime rate is the envy of the developed world, and at least part of the credit must go to a criminal justice system that is remarkably efficient at clearing crimes and is able to employ a family model of criminal process that successfully reintegrates many offenders back into society. However, this system exists within a larger context of Japanese social organization and values and much of its success is contingent on this underlying structure. The relatively professional and apolitical status of prosecutors and criminal court judges shields them from local pressures to treat some offenders harshly and also mutes calls for greater due process protections against the power of the state. In addition, benevolent paternalism may be much less viable in societies such as the United States and England where crime has become highly politicized and where the fear of crime is a component of daily life. In the next part of the chapter we shall examine the interrelationship of substantive rules, legal structures and legal consciousness within the context of civil disputes.

Resolving Civil Disputes

Private civil disputes arise in every society. Individuals suffer injuries to themselves and their property at the hands of fellow citizens, contracts are breached, doctors commit malpractice, streams are polluted, employees are fired unfairly, companies sell defective goods, automobiles run into people, reputations are ruined by libelous statements, and so forth. Every society with a legal order provides civil remedies for many of these wrongs. However, the nature of the remedies varies from one society to another. The structure of the legal response to civil disputes, like its response to crime, tells us a good deal about the role of law in a society and about society's assumptions concerning the relationship between people and the role of the individual in society.

During the first half century following the Meiji Restoration the Japanese had adopted a large body of Western law. By the end of World War I some in Japan had come to the conclusion that wholesale adoption of Western law,

153. See Anthony Platt, *The Child Savers: The Invention of Delinquency* (Chicago: University of Chicago Press, 1969).

especially Western private law now threatened traditional values. Their concern was not with substantive law, but with process. As Haley summarizes, "The courts could prevent unconstrained exercise of legal rights and harmonize new legal doctrines with traditional practices, but only in the context of litigation, a process that was itself subversive to the traditional moral order."[154]

One of the first products of this renewed concern was the Ad Hoc Commission for the Study of Legal Institutions. In 1922 the commission recommended the creation of a new conciliation-based family court because "The existing system in which family disputes are resolved by means of formal trials fails to maintain the beautiful customs of old."[155] Although the Diet did not enact the commission's family court proposal, the recommendation did establish a blueprint for how to handle outbreaks of disputes. Between the wars, when the government observed a growth in litigation, it passed a conciliation law. Conciliation was voluntary under such early statutes as the original Land Lease and House Lease Conciliation Law, and claimants or defendants could demand a trial. As time passed conciliation became more coercive; the judge could order mandatory conciliation, and the conciliator's recommended settlement could be made binding on the parties. The conciliation statutes maintained Western substantive law while replacing adjudicative procedures with Japanese alternatives.[156] Informal procedures in the United States have sometimes been criticized as indirect ways of benefiting the more powerful party in a dispute.[157] Apparently this was not the case with respect to many of the interwar conciliation statutes. The statutes authorizing conciliation in ordinary commercial and debtor-creditor situations were frequently criticized as being pro-debtor, and the result of the Farm Tenancy Conciliation Law was a significant reduction in rent, to the benefit of tenants.[158]

The post–World War II reorganization of the judiciary and its newfound independence from the executive could have lead to the increased use of adjudication to settle disputes. This has not occurred, however. Rather, the prewar policy of replacing adjudicative procedures with conciliation has continued. The most instructive recent examples are provided by Upham's dis-

154. Haley, supra note 1, p. 85.

155. Ibid., p. 86.

156. John O. Haley, "The Politics of Informal Justice: The Japanese Experience, 1922–1942," in Richard Abel (ed.), The Politics of Informal Justice, vol. 2 (New York: Academic Press, 1982), p. 136.

157. Jerold S. Auerbach, Justice Without Law? Resolving Disputes Without Lawyers (New York: Oxford University Press, 1983).

158. Haley, supra note 1, p. 93.

cussion of disputes concerning water and air pollution and Tanase's insightful article on the resolution of dispute arising out of automobile accidents.[159]

ENVIRONMENTAL POLLUTION

Air and water pollution created one of the most serious postwar problems faced by the Japanese government. Japan's recovery from the war was built on a foundation of rapid industrial growth. Inevitably the goal of rapid economic development came in conflict with the ideal of a clean and safe environment. Pollution problems first surfaced in the mid-1950s. Not until the mid-1960s, however, did they dominate the national political agenda, culminating in a body of new legislation in 1970 that made Japan a leader in pollution control. The history of the fight against pollution reveals how citizens can use the courts to receive redress, but also how regimes can discourage litigation as a method of dispute resolution.

Japanese pollution disputes are forever linked with Minamata, a small city in a fishing and agricultural region in the far south of Japan. The town was the home of the Chisso Corporation, which made chemical fertilizers and, later, plastics. In the early fifties birds and cats in the area began to act strangely, which local fishermen called the "disease of the dancing cats." Within a year or so the humans also began to exhibit symptoms, including trembling, numbness in limbs, and vision and speech problems. Eventually many victims became bedridden, and 40 percent died.[160] Initially some thought the disease was the result of hygienic deficiencies, and victims felt a sense of shame for their illness. However, by 1956 it was discovered that the probable cause of the illness was the consumption of local fish. By 1958 it was clear to the victims that the source of the illness was pollution by the Chisso Corporation. Victims formed a mutual assistance society to negotiate with Chisso, and their claim strengthened when researchers discovered in 1959 that the illness was the result of people eating fish poisoned with mercury.[161] The victims and the local fishermen's union sought compensation and were rebuffed by Chisso, who claimed the cause of their disease was "scientifically ambiguous." The fishermen's response was to storm the factory and take the plant manager hostage overnight. Finally Chisso agreed to

159. Frank Upham, *Law and Social Change in Postwar Japan* (Cambridge: Harvard University Press, 1987). Takao Tanase, "The Management of Disputes: Automobile Accident Compensation in Japan," *Law and Society Review* 24 (1990), 651.

160. The following account of the Minamata pollution case is from Upham, supra note 159, pp. 30–50. Death statistics at p. 31.

161. See S. Kitamura, Y. Hirano, Y. Noguchi, T. Kojima, T. Kakita, and H. Kuwaki, "The Epidemiologic Survey of Minamata Disease (No. 2)," *Journal of Kumamoto Medical Society* 33 (Suppl. 3) (1959), 569.

mediation and settled with the local union but offered no compensation to the victims or unions in adjacent communities. A sit-in at the factory gates followed and the mediation committee recommended a ¥74 million ($200,000) payment to the victims collectively.[162] When the victims refused, the mayor and other officials in the town threatened to dissolve the committee, leaving them with nothing. Faced with this threat, the mutual assistance society settled for very small sums of money: ¥300,000 ($830) per person for deaths, ¥100,000 ($280) annual payment for the disabled, and ¥20,000 ($55) for funeral expenses. More important, the company included a clause in the agreement saying this was a full settlement of present and future claims.

After the 1959 agreement there was a hiatus in the Minamata dispute for several years, and had there been no other pollution problems it might have stood as an example of informal dispute settlement accomplished without the use of the courts or litigation. Chisso continued to deny that there was clear proof that mercury caused the problem and found a powerful ally in the government, which actively covered up existing evidence that Chisso's effluents poisoned the fish and thwarted further research into the problem. Most telling, perhaps, was the government's decision to remove the question of the cause of Minamata disease from the Ministry of Health and Welfare and give it to the Ministry of International Trade and Industry (MITI).

The effort to evade the issue began to unravel when, in 1964, another strange disease of unknown cause arose in Niigata Prefecture. The symptoms were similar to Minamata disease, and the victims' diet consisted of fish from a local river. Not surprisingly, upstream a factory owned by Shōwa Denkō used the same process Chisso used in Minamata. A new study by the Niigata University Medical School was again suppressed by MITI and government funding for the research was halted. This time, however, the report was made public and the victims, with the help of leftist lawyers, sued Shōwa Denkō in 1967. Within two years suits followed in the Yokkaichi air pollution case, the Tōyama cadmium poisoning case, and the Minamata case. Collectively these became known as the Big Four pollution cases.

Upham notes that many of the victims at Minamata were reluctant to join in a lawsuit against Chisso. Doing so brought attention to the fact that one was sick and might threaten the economic well being of an organization that paid 45 percent of the Minamata city taxes. Eventually the victim group split into three factions: one group brought suit, one entered into direct negotiation with Chisso, and a third agreed again to mediation organized by the Ministry of Health and Welfare. The mediation group reached a new agreement with

162. The dollar amount reflects the exchange rate at the time of the payments.

Chisso in 1970, providing for maximum awards of ¥2 million ($5,500) and annuities of ¥50,000 ($140) per person.

Those who did sue in the Minamata case and the other pollution cases were called selfish for pursuing their own ends ahead of the good of the community and other victims. When the litigation began, few thought the plaintiffs stood much of a chance. As the cases progressed, however, victory became possible. The trial courts substantially liberalized the standard of proof for negligence. An opinion in the Yokkaichi case emphasized the high degree of care required in selecting an industrial site and declared that the defendant had a duty to use the best available technology regardless of economic feasibility. Such rules cause a negligence rule to approximate strict liability rules, where proof of a lack of care is unnecessary. The courts also relaxed the proof of causation by allowing the plaintiffs to prevail without showing a "precise medical cause" of their injury.[163] Eventually, the Minamata plaintiffs who pursued a litigation strategy received up to nine times the 1970 mediation awards, with the largest individual awards approaching ¥18 million ($60,000).[164]

Surprisingly, the court award was a starting point for still further negotiations. The plaintiffs demanded and received a promise that all victims, including those who had not been a party to the suit, would receive equal treatment. Equally important, the president of Chisso knelt before the victims and apologized. Later the Chisso Corporation issued the following public apology.

> Chisso deeply apologizes to those patients and their families already in great poverty, who experienced further suffering from contracting Minamata disease, who suffered as a result of Chisso's attitudes, and who experienced various types of humiliation and, as a result, suffered from discrimination by local society.
>
> Furthermore, Chisso deeply apologizes to all of society . . . for its regrettable attitude of evading its responsibility and for delaying a solution, as this caused much inconvenience to society.[165]

Eventually, some Chisso executives were convicted of manslaughter.

It was not only Chisso and its victims, however, who lost a good deal in the pollution controversy. The government lost as well. Upham argues that

---

163. American tort law has also relaxed proof of causation for plaintiffs in similar circumstances. See Michael Dore, "A Commentary on the Use of Epidemiological Evidence in Demonstrating Cause-in-Fact," *Harvard Environmental Law Review* 7 (1983), 429; Stephen Fienberg (ed.), *The Evolving Role of Statistical Assessments as Evidence in the Courts* (New York: Springer Verlag, 1989).

164. Upham, supra note 159, pp. 44, 47.

165. Ibid., p. 48.

the threat to the government was significant. First, of course, was the lack of faith and trust that inevitably followed disclosure of the government's role in the cover-up. Even more important, according to Upham, was the fact that the Big Four cases "challenged the . . . self-image of the Japanese as preferring harmony to conflict. In addition to exposing underlying social conflict, the pollution experience had also demonstrated that rights assertion and litigation could be valuable tools in achieving social justice."[166]

The pollution suits had a direct effect on the political agenda in Japan. They threatened to undermine the mediation and conciliation based approaches to disputing that had been developed before and after World War II and that had been attempted in the 1959 and 1970 Minamata mediation agreements. As Upham notes, "the very posing of fundamental social questions as legal issues meant that . . . informal, closed, particularistic decision-making process . . . would be subject to public and judicial scrutiny, if not actual judicial usurpation." To avoid this the government took three actions. First, it passed a series of strict pollution control statutes; second, it established a polluter-financed scheme to compensate certain pollution victims; and, third, it created a new system to identify and mediate pollution disputes.[167]

Pollution control was in some ways the easiest goal to achieve. Within a decade Japan had moved from being one of the most polluted developed countries to having a relatively clean environment. Much of this was done with legal devices once again borrowed from the West, this time ideas from environmental statutes in the United States.[168] This was an essential first step to diffuse citizens' movements.

In 1967, the Fundamental Act for Environmental Pollution Prevention was enacted. The government's continuing ambivalence concerning the environment was reflected in a "harmony" clause, to the effect that environmental protection efforts should be harmonized with the promotion of industrial development.[169] Pollution problems increased over the next several years, and the act was strengthened in 1970. The harmony clause was removed and both the national and local governments were given the power to establish environmental quality standards, control emissions, and regulate industrial land use.

The Compensation Act for Environmental Pollution-Related Health Injury, enacted in 1973, distinguishes two types of disease: specific diseases traceable

166. Ibid., p. 54.
167. Ibid., pp. 55, 18–19.
168. Ibid., p. 59.
169. Shiro Kawashima, "A Survey of Environmental Law and Policy in Japan," *North Carolina Journal of International Law and Commercial Regulation* 230 (1995), 242.

to a specific cause, such as the Minamata disease, and nonspecific diseases that may be caused or exacerbated by water or air pollution. Included in this latter category are asthma and emphysema. An individual living within a designated Class I area (including Tokyo Metropolitan Districts, Chiba-City, Kawasaki, and Amagasaki) for a specified period of time and who was certified by a local board as suffering from a compensable disease, was eligible for reimbursement for medical expenses paid for by polluters in proportion of their contribution to overall pollution.[170] The plan was generous in terms of both benefits and eligibility requirements.

By the mid-1980s this part of the statute was coming under increasing attack, primarily for two reasons. First, a claimant must live in a geographical area defined as a high pollution area. Two people living across the street from one another and suffering from the same ailment may be treated differently if the high pollution area boundary runs down the middle of the street. Second, the funding formula used to generate revenues for the program focused primarily on sulfur dioxide emissions, the type of air pollution generated by heavy industry. It did not give much weight to nitrogen pollutants, which are associated with automobile emissions. As industrial pollution was brought under control, these became a primary source of air pollution in cities such as Tokyo. In 1988 the parts of the compensation statute dealing with nonspecific injuries were repealed.[171] In 1993 a new statute, the Fundamental Act for the Environment, replaced the Environmental Pollution Prevention Act and merged it with the Natural Environment Preservation Act.[172]

The various pollution acts introduced environmental impact assessment procedures that allow citizens to participate in planning for developments that may have adverse effects on the environment. A detailed set of guidelines govern how the assessment will be conducted. Typical of such Japanese regulatory guidelines, their violation does not create a private cause of action to compel their enforcement. However, as Upham notes, the guidelines are important. Local opposition to a project because it violates the guidelines can delay or cancel it.

The centerpiece of the government's legal response to the pollution crisis is the Law for the Resolution of Pollution Disputes. This law creates a three-tiered system to identify, investigate, and resolve disputes. At the local level, complaint counselors consult with residents, investigate reports of pollution, and advise people as to steps they might take following a pollution incident.

170. Ibid., p. 258.
171. Ibid.
172. Ibid., p. 248.

Pollution review boards at the prefect level are designed to settle complaints that have become disputes. The members of the board tend to be law professors, retired judges, and attorneys. They can mediate, conciliate, and arbitrate disputes between private parties and between citizens and the government. At the national level, the Central Pollution Dispute Coordination Committee also can mediate, conciliate, and arbitrate disputes, either at the request of a complainant or on its own initiative. In addition, it has wide ranging fact-finding powers.

The dispute law attempts to investigate and resolve disputes while they are still small and is similar to mediation systems in other areas.

> The stated purpose was to provide relief to pollution victims that would be cheaper, faster, and more effective than litigation, but the drafter's goals were clearly more ambitious than simple dispute processing. Third-party intervention, in particular governmental intervention, was also touted as consistent with Japanese tradition and responsive to the Japanese preference for informal, noncontentious modes of conflict resolution.[173]

The statute has had the desired effect. Throughout the 1970s complaint counselors processed hundreds of thousands of complaints, and the mediation system handled hundreds of disputes.[174] By the 1980s environmental litigation was greatly reduced, and plaintiffs usually lost as the litigation has moved from questions of public health to the more ambiguous agenda of quality-of-life issues. Much of what a claimant might wish to achieve could be achieved through the mechanisms established under the dispute law, the compensation law, and environmental impact hearings. The Supreme Court also helped to minimize the benefits to bring suits and by denying them the right to injunctive relief against the government.[175] It remains to be seen if the 1993 Fundamental Act for the Environment, along with proposed changes in Japanese civil procedure laws, will cause the courts to become more open to litigation in the future.[176]

RESOLVING AUTOMOBILE ACCIDENT DISPUTES

The substantive law governing Japanese automobile accidents is not very different from that in the United States. It is a comparative fault-based system

---

173. Upham, supra note 159, p. 57.

174. Ibid., p. 65.

175. In the Osaka Airport case the Court refused to allow private plaintiffs to sue to enjoin late-night flights; Ibid., 64. Kawashima, supra note 169, p. 263.

176. Kawashima, supra note 169, p. 270.

with third party insurance.[177] Furthermore, in Japan as in the United States, attorneys are willing to represent plaintiffs on a contingency fee basis, removing economic barriers to litigation.[178] However, in practice the system operates very differently.

As automobiles became widespread in Japan in the 1960s the litigation rate began to climb. In 1971 more than 12,000 personal injury cases were filed. This, however, was the high-water mark. The state had already begun to intervene to reduce the adjudication of automobile accident disputes and again it succeeded. In 1981 there were only 3,600 cases.[179] And unlike some prewar efforts, this time the results were not achieved through the crude mechanism of refusing access to trial but rather by constructing a set of incentives that make litigation relatively unattractive. According to Tanase, the arrangement contains three key elements: it increases the capability of individuals to prosecute their own case, it simplifies the law, and it provides alternative forums for disputes that remain unresolved.

Free legal consultation encourages individual initiative. In 1988 nearly one million consultations were provided by insurance companies, police offices, local government consultation centers, and private consultation centers operated by the insurance industry, the bar association, and others. Tanase estimates that on average there are nearly two free consultations per acci-

---

177. In comparative fault systems, the negligence of each party to the dispute is assessed and damages are awarded based on the comparative negligence of the parties. Thus, if only the plaintiff were injured and he or she suffered $1,000 in damages, and if it were determined that the plaintiff was 30% responsible for the accident while the defendant was 70% responsible, then the plaintiff would be awarded $700. In third-party insurance schemes, each driver insures against the possibility that his or her negligence will cause injury and that the injured party will sue for damages. For discussions of Japanese tort law see Ichiro Kato, "The Treatment of Motor-Vehicle Accidents: The Impact of Technological Change on Legal Relations," in von Mehren (ed.), *Law in Japan*; Seimei Hayashida, "The Necessity for the Rational Basis of Duty-Risk Analysis in Japanese Tort Law: A Comparative Study," *Utah Law Review* (1981), 65; Akio Morishima and Malcolm Smith, "Accident Compensation Schemes in Japan: A Window on the Operation of Law in a Society," *University of British Columbia Law Review* 20 (1986), 491; Susumo Hirano, "Drafts of the Japanese Strict Product Liability Code: Shall Japanese Manufacturers Also Become the Insurers of their Products," *Cornell International Law Journal* 25 (1992), 643; Akio Morishima, "The Japanese Scene and the Present Product Liability Proposal," 15 *University of Hawaii Law Review* 717 (1993); Yutaka Tejima, "Tort and Compensation in Japan: Medical Malpractice and Adverse Effects from Pharmaceuticals," 15 *University of Hawaii Law Review* 728 (1993); Shigeaki Tanaka, "Justice, Accidents and Compensation," 15 *University of Hawaii Law Review* 736 (1993); Robert B. Leflar, "Personal Injury Compensation Systems in Japan: Values Advanced and Values Undermined," 15 *University of Hawaii Law Review* 742 (1993).

178. Tanase, supra note 159, p. 659.

179. Ibid., p. 659.

dent.[180] The consultations cover a wide range of issues involving both substantive law and the details of how to proceed with a case. Many disputants return to consultation to gather new information as their negotiations progress.

The substantial majority of consultations are provided by insurance companies or the government and reflect the provider's bias against formal legal action. Most advice is given by nonlawyers who can have no economic stake in a decision to litigate. Most important for the litigation rate, perhaps, is the fact that most counselors tell the disputant that there is relatively little to be gained by suing. In Japan, unlike the situation in most societies, damages are substantially standardized and the facts of an accident are rarely in dispute.

There are nationwide standards for the assessment of damages. Out-of-pocket expenses are covered by basic insurance that all drivers are required to purchase. The damages must be proven with formal documents such as past tax returns and medical receipts. The damages are assessed by an independent organization, not the insurance company that sold the policy, removing the company's incentive to press for a low award. Once out-of-pocket expenses have been determined, pain and suffering damages are calculated by a standard formula. Moreover, the system strongly favors the injured person, so much so that Tanase argues that in practice it operates more like a no-fault system. Injured parties are very likely to receive compensation.[181]

The standardized compensation scheme could not maintain itself, however, if the courts allowed those who sued to receive sums that were substantially greater than are available under insurance payment formulas. In Japan, as elsewhere, settlement practices must occur in the shadow of the law.[182] A central cog in the standardization machine is the courts' agreement to standardize awards at trial. This has occurred throughout the country.[183] Similar injuries result in similar awards at trial.

180. Ibid., p. 662.

181. Ibid., p. 690. Many drivers carry optional insurance in addition to the basic compulsory policy. Close governmental supervision of the industry (restraining incentives to take advantage of "weak" claimants) along with a desire to keep payments under the optional policies in line with payments under compulsory policies keep these payments relatively standardized as well. However, because optional insurance is intended to cover total liability there is more room for discretion in the amount of pain and suffering damages; Ibid., pp. 670–672.

182. Robert Mnookin and Lewis Kornhauser, "Bargaining in the Shadow of Law: The Case of Divorce," 88 *Yale Law Journal* (1979), 950–997.

183. Tanase, supra note 159, p. 672. Direct judicial supervision of damages is possible because in Japan, as in most European countries, there is no right to jury trial in civil cases. See Lempert, supra note 120, for a discussion of the pros and cons of a civil jury system for Japan.

The remaining element of uncertainty that could upset standardization attempts is a disagreement about the facts of the accident. If the parties are able to cast into doubt the circumstances of the collision they may dispute the issue of fault. The Japanese solution to indeterminacy involves two steps. First, to a degree that would be found startling in the United States, the police report of the accident is given great weight. All accidents involving personal or property damages are to be reported to the authorities, and policemen specializing in traffic accidents are routinely dispatched to the scene. They conduct an investigation, record the testimony of the people involved, and report their findings. These findings are rarely challenged in court. In a sense there is relatively little to challenge, for the police at the scene "adjust differences in factual assertions of the parties and hammer out a consensual story as to what happened to which the parties agree and formally endorse by signing."[184] Thus, the facts of the accident are themselves subject to a conciliation process that occurs at the scene of the accident.

The second step in standardizing the facts is to use rough categories in assigning comparative fault to the parties. In most jurisdictions in the United States, the jury must determine the exact percentage of responsibility attributable to each party in a lawsuit, and the amount of damages each might collect turns on these percentage allocations. A precise determination of these percentages in each case would inevitably cause the damages to remain uncertain. The Japanese solution to this problem is to permit only a few categories of comparative negligence (for example, plantiff = 70 percent; defendant, 30 percent) using only the facts that appear in the police accident report.[185]

Finally, in the rare instance where claims are not accommodated administratively, extrajudicial mechanisms, including court-annexed mediation and the traffic accident dispute resolution center, provide mediation outside the official court system. These alternatives offer quicker and cheaper resolution of disputes than does formal adjudication.[186]

These procedural and institutional arrangements may profitably be compared with those of other societies. In every society with a complex legal system, the resolution of automobile accidents is overwhelmingly an out-of-court process. Litigation always involves costs (monetary and otherwise) to both parties, and these costs create a bargaining space where parties may find it mutually beneficial to settle a claim.[187] The Japanese situation is not fun-

184. Tanase, supra note 159, p. 674.

185. Ibid., p. 691.

186. Ibid., pp. 675–676.

187. Richard Lempert and Joseph Sanders, *An Invitation to Law and Social Science* (Philadelphia: University of Pennsylvania Press, 1986), pp. 137–160.

damentally different. However, in the United States and other Western societies a substantial degree of uncertainty surrounds legal outcomes, especially in cases involving serious injuries. In this regard the Japanese system produces much more predictability than the American system and even European systems. For example, compare the Japanese system of standardized damage payments with the uncertainty surrounding this issue in Britain. Genn reports that one of the greatest difficulties encountered in assessing claims is evaluating damages. Eighty-nine percent of the solicitors she interviewed in her study of tort settlement practices agreed with the statement, "It is difficult to predict how much a judge will award to a successful plaintiff," and 75 percent said it was difficult to estimate general damages. As one solicitor commented, "one never actually knows what is going to happen. One may get the ungenerous judge."[188] In the United States, where the cases are tried before a jury, the range of uncertainty as to damages is even greater.[189] Uncertainty concerning liability is higher in both England and the United States than it is in Japan.

The uncertainty surrounding the value of a claim provides an opportunity for some to exploit this indeterminacy by threatening to go to trial in order to obtain the best possible outcome. By removing most of the indeterminacy of legal outcomes, the Japanese system makes it easier to calculate the value of a claim, eliminates some of the pure bargaining that is typical in other systems, and, as a result, removes a good deal of the incentive to employ counsel.

To summarize, the Japanese have maintained a body of substantive civil law similar to that in the West, but they have replaced Western procedures with a set of institutional arrangements and procedures that offer few incentives to litigate. What does this legal structure tell us about Japanese legal consciousness?

LEGAL STRUCTURE AND LEGAL CONSCIOUSNESS

The Japanese civil justice system offers another window into Japanese society, albeit one that has often been misunderstood. Some have argued that the civil justice legal structure reflects a set of cultural values which dictate that one should forego redress of injury in the name of the common good. Indeed, the interwar conciliation statutes were sometimes justified by an appeal to the cultural value of harmony. It was said that the statutes ensured

---

188. Hazel Genn, *Hard Bargaining: Out of Court Settlement in Personal Injury Actions* (Oxford: Clarendon Press, 1987), pp. 75, 98.

189. H. Laurence Ross, *Settled Out of Court: The Social Process of Insurance Claims Adjustments* (Chicago: Aldine Publishing, 1970); Gerald Williams, *Legal Negotiation and Settlement* (St. Paul, Minn.: West Publishing, 1983), pp. 5–7.

that social disputes would be resolved according to Japanese morals, and at the center of "moral" resolution was an emphasis on harmony that made a demand for recognition of one's rights itself an unworthy act. As we can see from the pollution cases, this belief has remained a central part of Japanese ideology. It is reflected in "a tendency to regard lawsuits as a kind of vice."[190] For example, in a 1976 survey more than 1,000 respondents in the Tokyo area were asked whether it was preferable to sue, use court-appointed mediation, or work out disputes through private discussion. Only 8 percent thought it was better to sue, 43 percent favored mediation, and 41 percent thought it best to settle privately (8 percent did not know or had no answer).[191]

These beliefs have created what Haley has called the "myth" of the reluctant litigant.[192] The myth, in its most extreme form, suggests that a Japanese disputant not only would prefer to settle disputes in some forum other than formal adjudication but also would altruistically forego or compromise an entitlement or a benefit to avoid formal litigation. The Minamata case indicates there is some truth to the myth, in the sense that many prefer an alternative to formal litigation when it is available.

Use of the courts has not grown enormously during the post–World War II period. In fact, the per-capita rate of cases filed for formal trial proceedings was higher during the 1920s than at any time during the post–World War II period.[193] Since 1945 the Japanese civil litigation rate has risen slightly, from fewer than one case per thousand to approximately three cases per thousand in 1993. By way of comparison, the civil litigation rate in Arizona, a typical American state, stood at approximately sixty-four per thousand in 1992.[194] However, one does not have to adopt a theory of universal, individual, altruistic self-denial to explain this fact.

When given the opportunity, many Japanese will behave in a legalistic fashion. As Upham notes when discussing the one-sided terms of settlement of the 1959 Minamata mediation, "One searches in vain for the paternalism, communal sense of responsibility, and preference for legal ambiguity that

190. Haley, supra note 1, pp. 92–93, and 96, quoting Justice Tsuyoshi Mano's dissenting opinion in *Suzuki v. Ishigaki,* 10 Minshū 1355, 1361 (Sup. Ct., G.B., Oct 31, 1956).

191. Setsuo Miyazawa, "Taking Kawashima Seriously: A Review of Japanese Research on Japanese Legal Consciousness and Disputing Behavior," *Law and Society Review* 21 (1987), 226.

192. John O. Haley, "The Myth of the Reluctant Litigant," *Journal of Japanese Studies* 4 (1978), 359.

193. Haley, supra note 1, p. 98.

194. Christian Wollschlüger, "Civil Litigation in Japan, Sweden, and the USA Since the 19th Century: Japanese Legal Culture in the Light of Historical Judicial Statistics," paper presented at the annual meeting of the Research Committee on Sociology of Law, International Sociological Association, Tokyo, August 1995, pp. 3, 9.

stereotypes about Japanese law would lead one to expect."[195] The Big Four pollution cases also indicate that a substantial number of claimants will litigate when other alternatives are unavailable or inferior to litigation.

The causes of low rates of litigation are to be found elsewhere. The courts remain congested, imposing substantial delays on those who choose to litigate. More important, confronted with a legal structure such as exists in the automobile accident area and now exist in the pollution dispute area, a disputant's failure to litigate is an economically rational choice.[196] For a person injured in an automobile accident in Japan the rational thing to do is to settle the case, and in most cases it is to the victim's advantage to settle without the benefit of private counsel.[197] In pollution cases, mediation structures and statutory compensation schemes provide a surer route to recovery than litigation.

From a sociological perspective, however, the pollution control statutes of the 1970s and the automobile accident compensation system tell us a good deal about Japanese legal consciousness. Like the criminal justice system, they are among a large number of other legal structures that minimize formal litigation. Rosch reports how the Japanese Civil Liberties Bureau was, over time, transformed from an organization created to enforce individual rights into an organization that mediates disputes between private parties.[198] Two formal alternatives to "ordinary litigation"—pre-commencement compromise (*wakai*) and civil conciliation (*minji chotei*)—comprise a significant part of the caseload of the summary courts. Reminiscent of interwar policy, when confronted with rising litigation in various areas the government has passed statutes designed to deflect disputes from the formal tort system. The pollution statutes are the most noteworthy example, but similar statutes have been enacted to deal with drugs, vaccines, and other products.[199] The general pat-

195. Upham, supra note 159, p. 33.

196. Nobutoshi Yamanouchi and Samuel J. Cohen, "Understanding the Incidence of Litigation in Japan: A Structural Analysis," *International Lawyer* 25 (1991), 443.

197. Mark Ramseyer and Minoru Nakazato, "The Rational Litigant: Settlement Amounts and Verdict Rates in Japan," *Journal of Legal Studies* 18 (1989), 263.

198. Joel Rosch, "Institutionalizing Mediation: The Evolution of the Civil Liberties Bureau in Japan," *Law and Society Review* 24 (1987), 461–498.

199. Morishima and Smith, supra note 177. Tejima, supra note 177, at 730. There has been no legislation with respect to an area that comprises a large part of the American tort litigation docket, medical malpractice cases. Presumably this is due to the fact that claims per capita are very low: one-sixtieth of that in the United States. Leflar, supra note 177, at 745–746. See Patricia Danzon, "The 'Crisis' in Medical Malpractice: A Comparison of Trends in the United States, Canada, the United Kingdom, and Australia," *Law, Medicine & Health Care* 18 (1990), 48, 50; Gary Schwartz, "Product Liability and Medical Malpractice in Comparative Context," in Peter Huber and Robert Litan (eds.), *The Liability Maze: The Impact of Liability Law on Safety and Innovation* (Washington, D.C.: Brookings Institution, 1991), p. 62.

tern is the same: Events generate a substantial number of suits, and the government responds with a statutory scheme that rejects the judicial system as an appropriate institution for allocating loss, deprives the legal profession of a central role, and "significantly reduces the role of individuals as an instrument of law enforcement or law reform through the enforcement, reinforcement, or assertion of individual rights."[200]

The last point is key. This unwillingness to allow individual actors to be the primary agency of law enforcement once again reflects a societal perception of persons as contextual actors whose identity is defined by social relationships, not as individual actors whose identity is separate from the community.[201]

This perception is due in part to the distribution of social relationships. Both within specific types of relationships and across different relationships, ties between actors in Japan are more complex and more enduring than those of Americans. Perhaps most important, the employment relationship in Japan is denser and more enduring than is typical in the United States.[202] For example, the pattern of after-hours association among white collar workers in larger firms, called *tsukiai*, "involves some four or five hours of socializing with other employees every day after work. The group may go to a bar or two, then to a restaurant, and finally to a coffee shop or another bar. . . . It is because of tsukiai that salaried husbands and fathers are sometimes referred to as 'week-end guests.' "[203]

These aspects of industrial organization produce an employment relationship that is more like family relationships than is typical in the United States. Perhaps the most telling anecdotes on this point come from American workers who find themselves working in plants in the United States operated by Japanese using Japanese management practices. Smith cites comments by workers in the Auburn Steel Company in Auburn, New York. According to many workers, the place has "a family atmosphere" and "it feels like family."[204]

We should be careful not to overstate the difference. As Atsumi points out, it would be a misconception to think that *tsukiai* makes co-workers into close personal friends; theirs is still an employment relationship.[205] Feeling

200. Morishima and Smith, supra note 177, pp. 532–533. Hideo Tanaka and Akio Takeuchi, "The Role of Private Persons in the Enforcement of Law: A Comparative Study of Japanese and American Law," *Law in Japan* 7 (1974), 34.

201. Hamilton and Sanders, supra note 66.

202. Ibid., pp. 26–31.

203. Smith, supra note 66, p. 65.

204. Ibid., p. 61.

205. Reiko Atsumi, "Tsukiai—obligatory personal relationships of Japanese white-collar company employees," *Human Organization* 38 (1979), ch. 1, 63–70.

like family is not the same thing as being family. Nevertheless, given the fundamental importance of the employment relationship in all industrial societies, the fact that the Japanese employee is embedded in a relationship that is more complex and more enduring than that of his American counterpart may be thought of as tilting the entire corpus of potential societal relationships in this direction. To the degree that cultural values are shaped by the modal type of social relationships, Japanese should be more likely to view themselves and others as contextual rather than individualized actors and their legal consciousness should reflect this perception. Indeed, many writers have contrasted the American tendency toward litigation and formal adjudication, asserting the rights of the individual, with the Japanese tendency toward compromise and conciliation, asserting the harmony of the group.[206]

Historically, one way the legal consciousness has reflected this perception is by leaving most "law" in the hands of local communities. As Smith notes with respect to Tokugawa society: "By and large the system did allocate to representatives of groups both complete authority and total responsibility for the performance and conduct of group members, based squarely on the principles of vicarious liability and collective responsibility. . . . Domain [i.e., national] law was never intended to deal with civil disputes in the village, which was expected to see to it that its residents behaved according to local custom and were properly cared for if in need."[207] This type of social control structure is compatible with a contextual actor conception; people are governed by the specific rules of the relationship and not a set of general legal rules. Similarly, throughout the interwar period the movement toward mandatory conciliation was justified as a way to ensure that outcomes would reflect the morality of the specific circumstances surrounding a dispute, not the formal legal rights of the parties. For example, the government report accompanying the Land Lease and House Lease statute stated, "Conciliation means resolution [of disputes] not by adjudication of the rights between the parties but rather in terms of their own morality and their particular circumstances."[208]

The postwar solutions to pollution injuries and automobile accidents are a part of this long tradition. They, too, are an effort to avoid the routine legal assertion of individual, universal legal rights and are perceived by many in Japan as a reflection of Japanese cultural values. As Ramseyer notes, "Jap-

---

206. Takeyoshi Kawashima, "Dispute Resolution in Contemporary Japan," in von Mehren (ed.), *Law in Japan*; Miyazawa, supra note 191; Rosch, supra note 198, pp. 461–498; Hiroshi Wagatsuma and Arthur Rossett, "The Implications of Apology: Law and Culture in Japan and the United States," *Law and Society Review* 20 (1986), 461–498.

207. Smith, supra note 66, p. 38.

208. Haley, supra note 156, p. 137.

anese barbers, taxi-drivers, and bureaucrats still lose no time in telling American law professors that the Japanese, being Japanese, think suing is un-Japanese.''[209] By restricting the ability and the incentive of individuals to litigate, the Japanese legal structure reinforces cultural norms about the relationship of people and society.

The postwar pollution controversies reveal the limits of this set of arrangements. At the beginning of the Minamata controversy, the traditional mechanisms of resolving disputes in a consensual manner clearly broke down. Even more important, so did the social contract between the government and the citizenry. The government failed in its essential obligation to provide citizens with social stability and a safe environment within which to live. This breakdown could not be remedied by consensual institutions. In the Tokugawa era such occasions led to peasant uprisings that were sometimes quite violent.[210] Echoing this earlier era, the pollution cases also led to widespread collective action and mass demonstrations. Litigation is a very useful companion to such actions, and those who litigated the Big Four cases often worked closely with others engaged in mass protest and direct negotiation with defendants.

The court rulings in the pollution cases reflect these extraordinary circumstances. The judiciary recognized that these were not simply private disputes. Perhaps most revealing was the criminal trial of the leader of the direct-negotiation faction of the Minamata victims, Teruo Kawamoto. He was indicted in 1972 on five counts of assault and battery. Because Kawamoto admitted to the acts with which he was charged, the trial court found him guilty, although it allowed him to turn the trial into a trial of the government's complicity in years of cover-up. On appeal the Tokyo High Court went even further, going beyond the facts surrounding the assault charges to write in a wide-ranging opinion recounting the years of negligence and worse on the part of Chisso and the government and the victims' widespread suffering and loss of dignity. The ruling compared the government's vigorous prosecution of people harmed by the pollution with its lenience toward Chisso. The concluding part of the opinion inquired into the nature of justice and cited the Anglo-American maxim that when necessary a good judge will base a decision on equity rather than the strict dictates of the common law. In the end the court concluded that the defendant's behavior was a minor infraction when compared to the government's misconduct and that the government's indictment was unjust.[211]

209. Mark Ramseyer, ''Reluctant Litigant Revisited: Rationality and Disputes in Japan,'' *Journal of Japanese Studies* 14 (1988), 112.

210. Robert Bellah, *Tokugawa Religion: The Values of Pre-Industrial Japan* (Boston: Beacon Press, 1970).

211. Upham, supra note 159, pp. 48–52.

The Japanese Supreme Court was not willing to affirm on the ground that there had been prosecutorial abuse in this case. It did, however, uphold the Tokyo High Court opinion, reviewed the history of the Minamata case, and concluded, "Considering all these factors, it cannot be said that the failure to reverse the High Court would be manifestly unjust."[212]

In the pollution cases the courts played the invaluable role of an institution one could turn to when ordinary governmental institutions fail. This role was played by the Star Chamber in England before that court was corrupted by Henry VIII, and by the United States Supreme Court on occasion, perhaps most notably in *Brown v. Board of Education* when it struck down the legal structures that maintained a segregated South. In Japan, as in other societies, mediative structures cannot work without a substantial degree of trust and good faith on the part of the parties. When these break down, litigation provides a valuable alternative.

The pollution cases reveal a second point about the success of governmental efforts to restrict the use of formal litigation. Such suppression is most successful when there are effective alternatives. In the Big Four cases, the plaintiffs were presented with an unsatisfactory set of alternatives. The Minamata victims who litigated received awards many times larger than the victims who mediated. Only when nonlitigation alternatives offer results equal to or better than litigation will efforts to suppress litigation meet with substantial success. It is not an accident that after the enactment of the pollution Dispute Law, pollution litigation dropped dramatically.

Automobile accident cases never created a crisis for the government, but in another way they pose an even greater threat to a legal system that desires to reduce the role of individuals as an instrument of law enforcement or law reform through the assertion of individual rights. As Tanase notes, automobile accidents pose a special problem for the Japanese legal system because there are often sizable damages and the disputes they generate are nearly always between strangers.

It appears to be a general phenomenon of dispute resolution that social relationships that involve multiple connections and are enduring, such as those found in a family, are more likely to produce settlement styles that search for compromise and consider a wide range of issues relevant to the parties' relationship as well as to their specific dispute.[213] This tendency can

212. Quoted in ibid., p. 53.
213. Stewart Macaulay, "Non-contractual relations in business: A preliminary study," *American Sociological Review* 28 (1963), 55–67; Sheldon Ekland-Olson, "Relational Disturbance and Social Control: A Microstructural Paradigm," in Donald Black (ed.), *Toward a General Theory of Social Control* (New York: Academic Press, 1984); Lempert and Sanders, supra note 187.

be found in Japan, as well as in other cultures. A 1977 study by the Kyoto University Faculty of Law asking people about their willingness to turn to law for a remedy found that, "When a problem involves a continuing social relationship, the trouble is most likely to be ignored and a court is least likely to be used."[214] Likewise, a study by Wada indicated that concern for maintaining the relationship prevented neighborhood and family disputes from escalating to actual negotiation and then mediation or adjudication.[215] When strangers dispute, this restraining factor is absent.

Moreover, when there is no ongoing contextual relationship between the parties to a dispute, there are no specific criteria by which to judge a case. Individual plaintiff-defendant pairs are indistinguishable from each other except by the factors unique to a particular accident. Under these circumstances, the formal litigation of automobile accident cases threatens to generate a body of universal rules to be applied to all similar cases. It will, over time, tend to create a "rights-bearing" individual actor.

From this perspective, the detailed attention the Japanese have given to the extrajudicial resolution of automobile accident injuries is not surprising. Deflecting automobile accident cases from formal adjudication the Japanese legal system maintains consistency between Japanese legal structure and the culture that defines people in terms of sets of interwoven contextual relationships, not as rights-bearing autonomous individuals. It is this reciprocal interaction of structure and culture that creates stable societies and stable legal orders.

Corporate Actors and Public Law in Japan

Much public law involves government efforts to regulate and control corporate behavior. Indeed, the growth of public law is in many ways a reaction to the spread of influence of public actors, especially the modern business corporation. The regulatory effort is usually delegated to various administrative agencies located within governmental departments. In the United States, Cabinet-level departments like the Treasury, Commerce, and Justice contain various administrative agencies assigned the task of overseeing specific industries or activities. The Securities and Exchange Commission regulates stock markets; the Environmental Protection Agency administers the Clean Air Act, the Clean Water Act, and other environmental laws; the Federal Trade Commission and the Antitrust Division of the Justice Department en-

214. Miyazawa, supra note 191, p. 227.
215. Yasuhiro Wada, Nichijo no naka no Funso Shori [Dispute resolution in everyday life], Pts. 1,2, 24:2, 25:1 Tokyo Toritsu Daigaku Hogakakai Zasshi [Tokyo Metropolitan University Journal of Law and Politics] (1983–1984), 1.

force antitrust laws; and the Occupational Safety and Health Administration oversees workplace safety. Likewise, in Japan there are a large number of regulatory agencies located within various ministries. The clean-up of the Japanese environment following the Big Four pollution cases occurred under the direction of the Environment Agency, and the Fair Trade Commission oversees antitrust violations.[216]

A central legal issue with respect to public law regulation of corporate actors is whether parties may use the courts to contest or enforce public law directives. This is really two separate questions. First, to what degree do the government and regulated corporate groups use the courts resolve their disputes? For example, do regulated groups sue to challenge regulations? Second, do third parties use the courts to contest or enforce public law directives? For example, can private citizens sue a corporation for violating antitrust laws, or can an employee sue a corporation for discriminatory employment practices? In the United States the answer to both questions is yes, while in Japan the answer is a qualified no. The next two sections illustrate these conclusions.

ORGANIZATION-STATE RELATIONSHIPS

Japanese industry's relationship to the Ministry of International Trade and Industry (MITI) provides a valuable illustration of the structure of government-industry disputing. The primary task of MITI, one of the most important ministries in Japan, is overseeing industrial policy. MITI was created in 1949 and was substantially restructured in 1952 at the end of the Allied occupation and again in 1973.[217] Because many believe that MITI has played a central role in Japan's postwar prosperity, much has been written about this agency and its relationship with the private business sector.[218] A side benefit of these investigations is a detailed view of the role of the law and the courts in the regulation of the Japanese economy.

MITI is organized into vertical and horizontal bureaus. The vertical units such as the Machinery and Information Industries Bureau deal with problems

216. Upham, supra note 159, p. 56; Chalmers Johnson, *MITI and the Japanese Miracle: The Growth of Industrial Policy, 1925–1975* (Stanford, Calif.: Stanford University Press, 1982), p. 77; Julian Gresser, Koichiro Fujikura, and Akio Morishima, *Environmental Law in Japan* (Cambridge: MIT Press, 1981).

217. Johnson, supra note 216, pp. 192, 221, 296.

218. Ibid.; Richard Samuels, *The Business of the Japanese State: Energy Markets in Comparative and Historical Perspective* (Ithaca, N.Y.: Cornell University Press, 1987); David Friedman, *The Misunderstood Miracle: Industrial Development and Political Change in Japan* (Ithaca, N.Y.: Cornell University Press, 1988); Daniel Okimoto, *Between MITI and the Market: Japanese Industrial Policy for High Technology* (Stanford, Calif.: Stanford University Press, 1989).

in particular industries, while the horizontal units such as the International Trade Policy Bureau and the Industrial Policy Bureau handle issues cutting across many areas of commerce. Interdivisional councils help to integrate divisions.[219]

MITI is staffed by graduates from Japan's leading universities, as a civil service career is much sought after in Japan, as in France. Unlike the United States, where many of the most competent young officials leave for jobs in the private sector by their thirties, Japanese civil servants stay in their jobs until their fifties. Among the various ministries, MITI and the Ministry of Finance get the best students, in part because of the availability of a second career in private industry when they retire from the civil service. This practice is so widespread it has the name *amakudari*, literally, "descending from heaven."[220]

MITI's wide ranging authority derives from a number of general statutes such as the Foreign Exchange and Foreign Trade Control Law, which gives MITI responsibility for international economic policy, narrower statutes such as the Petroleum Industries Law, which directs MITI to promote the petroleum industry, the Depressed Industries Law, which authorizes MITI to assist industries experiencing a downturn in business, and the Large-Scale Retail Stores Law, which protects smaller retailers.[221]

MITI's core activity is administrative guidance—advice or direction by government officials carried out voluntarily by the recipient.[222] Guidance may occur in many areas, including minimizing the environmental impact of new factories, channeling funds to certain industries, promoting industrial research, and managing price and output controls for depressed industries.[223] Many activities facilitate industry initiatives. Other efforts at administrative guidance meet with opposition because they are perceived to favor some businesses over others or because they restrict a firm's action.

Historically, MITI has met the greatest opposition when it has attempted to consolidate production in troubled industries. Therefore, this is a particu-

219. Okimoto, supra note 218, pp. 115, 117. For an outline of the internal organization of the Ministry following the 1973 restructuring see Johnson, supra note 216, p. 336.

220. Upham, supra note 159, p. 167.

221. Ibid., p. 169; Frank Upham, "Privitizing Regulation: The Implementation of the Large-Scale Retail Stores Law," in Gary D. Allinson and Yasunori Sone (eds.), *Political Dynamics in Contemporary Japan* (Ithaca, N.Y.: Cornell University Press, 1993), p. 264.

222. Haley, supra note 1, p. 160; Mitsuo Matsushita, *International Trade and Competition Law in Japan* (Oxford: Oxford University Press, 1993), pp. 59–61.

223. Matsushita defines three types of administrative guidance: promotional, designed to promote business activities; regulatory, designed to control the conduct of enterprises and persons; and adjudicatory, designed to assist enterprises to settle disputes among themselves; Matsushita, supra note 222, pp. 61–63.

larly useful arena in which to examine how the Japanese deal with conflict in government-business relationships. Of particular interest are MITI's efforts to respond to the oil shocks of the 1970s occasioned by the creation of the OPEC oil cartel.[224] Following the OPEC price increases MITI was especially concerned that industries in the middle of their production cycles would be squeezed by increasing input costs on the one hand and declining demand on the other. This led to the passage of the Structurally Depressed Industries Laws.[225] The laws designated industries including chemical fibers, chemical fertilizers, aluminum smelting, and petrochemicals. Before capacity reductions could occur, the relevant ministry (frequently MITI) had to designate the industry as structurally depressed and consult with various groups. The ministry could then formulate a Basic Structural Adjustment Plan that would create guidelines for capacity reduction agreements. If the Fair Trade Commission approved the guidelines, joint activity under the plan was exempted from antitrust laws. Frequently the plans involved the creation of joint operations wherein twenty or so businesses in an industry would form four or five separate arrangements to coordinate production planning, marketing, and distribution of their products.[226]

Upham reviews a particularly complex restructuring in the petrochemical industry that was overseen by MITI. The restructuring was occasioned by a nearly 850 percent increase in the cost of naphtha, the Japanese petrochemical industry's basic feedstock. This problem was exacerbated by the fact that MITI policies had artificially raised the domestic price of naphtha in order to subsidize the petroleum industry. The MITI-affiliated Agency of. Natural Resources and Energy had limited the right to import naphtha to domestic oil companies and allowed them to charge above–world market prices. Faced with rising costs, the petrochemical industry threatened to register to import naphtha directly and in this threat was supported by another branch of MITI, the Basic Industries Bureau. Thus the restructuring involved conflicts not only

224. MITI's first efforts to consolidate industry occurred in the 1960s. At that time MITI attempted to consolidate the machine industry and the automobile industry. These initiatives were vigorously and successfully opposed by the private sector; Friedman, supra note 218, pp. 202–205. On the other hand, MITI's efforts to control output in the steel industry met with greater success; Upham, supra note 159, p. 177.

225. The Law of Special Measures for Stabilization of Depressed Industries was enacted in 1978. By its terms the Stabilization law required the Diet to re-examine the situation in five years, and in 1983 the Diet passed the Special Measures for the Structural Improvement of Specific Industries Act; Michael Young, "Structural Adjustment of Mature Industries in Japan: Legal Institutions, Industry Associations and Bargaining," in Stephen Wilks and Maurice Wright (eds.), The Promotion and Regulation of Industry in Japan (London: Macmillan Academic, 1991), p. 137.

226. Young, supra note 225, p. 139.

between firms in the petrochemical industry, but also between the petrochemical and the petroleum industry and between branches of MITI.[227]

MITI began the process in the typical way, by asking a statutory advisory body, commonly known as a *shingikai*, to suggest solutions.[228] MITI's objective was twofold, to reduce naphtha prices and to restructure the petrochemical industry. The result of the first round of deliberations was a victory for the Agency of Natural Resources and Energy and the petroleum industry, for while the shingikai recommended that the petrochemical industry should have access to low-cost feedstock, it offered no plan to achieve this. As a result, an important member of the shingikai who represented petrochemical interests publicly spoke out against the report, and the industry renewed its threat to register to import naphtha directly. In all of this the petrochemical industry had the support of the Basic Industries Bureau. Threatened with the loss of control over naphtha imports, the petroleum industry and the Agency of Natural Resources and Energy relented. The new agreement left the agency formally in charge of imports, but the petrochemical industry was assured access to naphtha at import prices.

Next, MITI worked on restructuring the industry by eliminating excess capacity and by creating three or four joint investment, purchasing, marketing, and research arrangements. Again, initial efforts met with limited success, in part because of mutual suspicion within the industry. MITI attempted to break this logjam by appointing a Petrochemical Industry System Subcommittee consisting of presidents of the leading firms and a neutral facilitator. When this still failed to produce an agreement, MITI sent the subcommittee members on a trip purportedly to study structural reform in Europe. The primary purpose, however, was to create stronger personal relationships and a greater sense of trust among the company presidents. The strategy worked, for within two weeks following the trip firms began to announce the closing of existing plants and the postponement of planned expansions. Within two months the subcommittee published a new restructuring plan that included specific details as to how capacity reduction would be achieved.[229]

Typical of Japanese administrative guidance, MITI's efforts to restructure the petrochemical industry was accomplished without specific enforceable

227. Upham, supra note 159, p. 193.

228. A *shingikai* is a deliberative council created and staffed by the ministry and comprised of representatives of various interest groups including industry, labor, academe, and consumer groups, but dominated by the ministry and the industry; Upham, supra note 159, p. 168; Johnson, supra note 216, p. 47; Ehyd Harari, "Resolving and Managing Policy Conflicts: Advisory Bodies," in S. N. Eisenstadt and Eyal Ben-Ari (eds.), *Japanese Models of Conflict Resolution* (London: Kegan Paul International, 1990), p. 139. Upham, supra note 159, p. 193.

229. Upham, supra note 159, p. 196. For another example see Young, supra note 225, pp. 147–155.

legal directives. In fact, the Depressed Industry Laws provide no mechanisms by which agencies can compel firms to follow an agreed-upon plan. Given the lack of such directives, the decision to follow administrative guidance is "voluntary" in the sense that the agency cannot use the courts to compel compliance.[230] In developed societies most regulation is done informally. What is unique in Japan is that there is almost nothing else. According to Haley, "In Japan informal enforcement is not *a* process of governing, but has become *the* process of governing.[231]

This does not mean that MITI or other agencies are powerless. Benefits, including attractive financing arrangements, are often used to induce compliance.[232] On very few occasions administrative guidance has led to litigation. Perhaps the best known lawsuit occurred in the oil cartel cases. In the early 1970s, in response to the first oil shock, MITI helped to arrange an oil cartel in the petroleum industry. The arrangement was challenged on antitrust grounds by the Fair Trade Commission. The firms' unsuccessful defense against criminal charges of price-fixing was that they were following MITI's guidance.[233] The lawsuits were as much an attempt by the Fair Trade Commission to assert its jurisdiction vis-à-vis MITI as they were an example of a ministry using the courts to compel a firm to do something it had refused to do previously.

The potential for future conflict of this type was eliminated under the Depressed Industries Laws which, as noted earlier, provide for Fair Trade Commission approval before a restructuring plan goes into effect. Upham notes that the practical effect of this provision is to make the commission another bureau of MITI whose task is to evaluate the competitive effect of plans. For example, the commission objected to MITI's original proposed 1983 reorganization of the petrochemical industry because it consolidated the sales of some products into only three joint sales companies. At the commission's insistence, the final plan included four companies.[234]

One reason litigation is so rare is individual firms that refuse to go along with arrangements agreed to by a ministry and an industry may face threats of collateral sanctions rather than litigation. In the mid-1960s, for example, Sumitomo Metals, an important member of the Sumitomo *keiretsu* (a group of interrelated companies), refused to follow MITI's guidance with respect

230. Young, supra note 225. Michael Young, "Judicial Review of Administrative Guidance: Governmentally Encouraged Consensual Dispute Resolution in Japan," *Columbia Law Review* 84 (1984), 934.

231. Haley, supra note 1, p. 163.

232. Young, supra note 230, p. 934.

233. Upham, supra note 159, p. 185.

234. Ibid., p. 197.

to a production cartel designed to restrict steel output during a time of slack demand. Sumitomo thought that MITI had unfairly favored two other firms, Yawata and Fuji (both part of the prewar nationalized steel industry). Sumitomo's mistrust of its rivals and MITI may have resulted in part from the fact that Sumitomo had refused to hire former bureaucrats as a matter of principle and felt that MITI favored firms that had. Soon after these events Sumitomo changed its policy and hired a MITI vice-minister. Within a decade the ex-civil servant had become president of the company.[235]

MITI's did not threaten to sue Sumitomo to compel compliance; rather, the ministry threatened to use its power under the Foreign Exchange and Foreign Control Law to limit the amount of coking coal Sumitomo would be allowed to import. Sumitomo was forced back to the bargaining table and agreed to abide by 1965 quotas in return for MITI's promise to reconsider allocations in 1966.[236] Overt threats of this sort were unusual during the 1960s, when MITI was at the height of its powers, and even then were thought to be a sign of failure. Within a few months of forcing Sumitomo to comply, the bureaucrat responsible for MITI's decisions retired, saying he had "decided that he had exhausted his usefulness."[237] Today, MITI's role is even less directive and more facilitative—the ministry reigns, but it does not rule.[238]

In addition to it being very rare for a ministry to sue to enforce compliance with its orders, it is rare for a firm or any other group to sue the government claiming that a ministry's directives exceed its authority. The reluctance of regulated firms to challenge ministry guidance in court is explained in part by the fact that many have an ongoing and complex relationship with various government ministries.[239] Courts tend to resolve immediate disputes, not broader conflicts. A court will declare a winner and a loser based on legal rights, rather than devise a compromise solution. As a consequence, parties who litigate their disputes may come to define their relationship as a matter of narrow legal rights and duties rather than a relationship of mutual trust, to the long-term disadvantage of both parties.[240] Moreover, in situations such as these the firm may fear that the ministry will retaliate in the future. Parties in this situation turn to litigation only as a last resort. The deterrent effect is reflected in Young's observation that legal challenges to administrative gui-

235. Ibid., p. 18; Young, supra note 230, p. 950 n. 103.

236. Upham, supra note 159, pp. 178–181.

237. Young, supra note 230, p. 950 n. 103.

238. Okimoto, supra note 218, p. 144. Young, supra note 225, p. 163.

239. Macaulay, supra note 213; Thomas Palay, "Comparative Institutional Economics: The Governance of Rail Freight Contracting," *Journal of Legal Studies* 13 (1984), 265–287.

240. Lempert and Sanders, supra note 187, ch. 7.

dance have almost never involved "a suit against a ministry with which the regulated party was likely to have future regulatory contact of any dimension."[241]

As we saw in the discussion of civil disputes, even when a firm or third party is prepared to litigate, Japanese law has historically made it difficult to obtain judicial review of administrative decisions. The drafters of the Meiji Constitution (1889) followed the European continental model of a strict separation of powers.[242] Direct judicial review of public law directives was thought to be unwise. The constitution called for a special Court of Administrative Litigation to hear suits challenging the legality of measures taken by administrative authorities. When this court had jurisdiction the constitution prohibited courts of general jurisdiction from hearing claims.[243] The only alternative for private litigants was a tort action, seeking damages for injuries caused by certain governmental actions.

The post–World War II constitution abolished the Administrative Court and created a single, unified judiciary along the American model. The National Compensation Law provided for damage awards paid by the state when one was injured due to the negligent or intentional conduct of a public authority or due to a "defect" in the operation of public facilities such as bridges.[244] The Administrative Litigation Special Measures Law and its successor, the Administrative Case Litigation Law (1962), established several categories of suits that could challenge administrative rulings. However, for a number of reasons judicial review is seriously limited.

Japanese courts have shown great deference toward the two elected branches of government. Administrative agencies are given wide discretion in their enabling legislation.[245] The Foreign Exchange and Foreign Trade Control Law, for example, gives MITI the power to regulate imports "for the purpose of sound development of foreign trade and the national economy." Reasons for controlling the importation of a product include "stability of the currency," "safeguarding the balance of international payments," and "rehabilitation and expansion of the national economy."[246] As in most developed legal systems, discretionary administrative decisions are beyond direct legal challenge, absent a clear abuse of discretion. In Japan, lawsuits are

241. Young, supra note 230, p. 951.

242. See the discussion of the French doctrine of separation of powers in chapter 4.

243. John O. Haley, "Japanese Administrative Law: An Introduction," in John Haley (ed.), *Law and Society in Contemporary Japan: American Perspectives* (Dubuque, Iowa: Kendall/Hunt Publishing, 1988), p. 37.

244. Haley, supra note 243, p. 40.

245. Beatty, supra note 65, p. 538.

246. Upham, supra note 159, p. 170.

made even more difficult by the administrative acts doctrine that permits review only when the agency has made a "disposition." By and large, informal decisions are not reviewable, because most of what MITI and other agencies do is informal and a matter of "guidance," not a legal "disposition," and therefore is not reviewable.[247]

With respect to third-party litigants, the "disposition" restriction means that they must show that the administrative action had a concrete effect on a legally protected interest. A mere "factual" interest will not suffice. For example, in *Federation of Housewives v. Fair Trade Commission* a consumer group brought suit against the commission because of its approval of labeling standards for the fruit juice industry, claiming that the Fair Labeling Law required a greater disclosure of ingredients. The court concluded the consumer group had not suffered a direct legal injury and could not challenge the standard in court.[248] In legal terminology, they did not have standing to sue.

Even when a party has standing to sue, the right to sue is sometimes devalued by the fact that the Japanese code of civil procedure does not provide for mandatory class actions, a procedure that can compel the joining of all affected plaintiffs in a single lawsuit. As a consequence, victims of environmental and antitrust violations, each of whom has suffered a real but minor harm, may not find it profitable to litigate. For example, the total damages demanded in two private antitrust suits in response to the MITI-led 1970s oil cartel was less than $20,000. Ramseyer reports that from the time of the enactment of the antitrust law in 1947 through the early 1980s private parties had filed seven antitrust damage suits. Two were settled, and the other five resulted in a finding for the defendant.[249] These barriers to effective litigation are in addition to the roadblocks which confront all Japanese litigants because of the relative lack of judicial capacity and the limited supply of lawyers. Judicial oversight of administrative discretion is nearly nonexistent.

Although firms do not use the courts to oppose ministry directives, this does not mean that they simply bow to agency wishes. Frequently, parts of an industry simply will not comply with MITI's wishes. A second alternative is a resort to the political process. Regulated organizations may enlist the support of public opinion, industrial associations, other ministries, and politicians in their effort to have a ministry alter its directive.[250] This is what the

247. Haley, supra note 243, p. 42.

248. Upham, supra note 159, pp. 171, 172. Matsushita, supra note 222, p. 111.

249. Mark Ramseyer, "The Costs of the Consensual Myth: Antitrust Enforcement and Institutional Barriers to Litigation in Japan," *Yale Law Journal* 94 (1985), 604–645, 631.

250. Young, supra note 230, p. 951.

petrochemical industry did to persuade the Agency of Natural Resources and Energy to allow it direct access to naphtha at world prices. Many firms and industries have used these alternatives successfully to thwart ministry efforts.

By citing examples where MITI has failed to get its way in its efforts to guide an industry, some have argued that Japan is not the strong, interventionist state it is sometimes thought to be. For example, Friedman examines MITI's failed efforts to cartelize the machine tool industry and reviews other occasions in the automobile and banking industries where firms successfully resisted MITI's guidance.[251] Most would agree that over time MITI's powers have lessened.[252] However, an analysis that focuses solely on the relative strength of MITI and the industries under its jurisdiction misses the main point about the role of administrative guidance in Japanese society. Okimoto notes, "Casting government-business relations in Manichaean terms and raising the question of which of the two is stronger misses the subtlety and complexity of the relationship. . . . Their relationship is not adversarial or a tug-of-war. . . . Without industry's willing cooperation, the Japanese state would not be nearly as powerful or effective. Instead of labeling Japan a 'strong' state, therefore, perhaps it would be more accurate to call it a 'societal,' 'relational,' or 'network' state, one whose strength is derived from the convergence of public and private interest and the extensive network of ties binding the two sectors together."[253]

Maintaining and strengthening this network is, perhaps, the MITI bureaucrat's primary task. At an individual level it is not unusual for MITI deputy directors to spend more than half their time with industry association officials, directors of research and development in large corporations, and individuals in other private-sector organizations. As with the practice of tsukiai, the result is a blurring of the line between professional and personal ties. At an organizational level, the ties consist of many formal and informal policy networks. MITI and other ministries create formal networks in the form of public corporations that serve various functions, including making development investments, building social infrastructure, advancing particular industries, promoting trade and investment, carrying out industrial research, and organizing national projects. There are more than one hundred such organizations, and more than twenty-five are under MITI's jurisdiction. There are also private policy networks numbering in the thousands, as well as many informal ties between business leaders and government officials.[254]

What many of MITI's most noted administrative guidance failures share is inadequate consultation and an absence of mutual trust among the par-

251. Friedman supra note 218.
252. Okimoto, supra note 218, 144.
253. Ibid., p. 145.
254. Ibid., pp. 157, 153–154.

ties.[255] As a consequence it was impossible to arrive at a consensus about the appropriate course of action. However, the most notable achievement of the system of administrative guidance is not any particular ministerial victory over a recalcitrant industry. Rather it is the climate of consensual government-business relations engendered by Japanese industrial policy.[256] As Okimoto observes, "Thanks in part to the inter-penetration of public and private domains and to MITI's ability to reconcile private interests with the public good, government-business relations in Japan are informal, close, cooperative, flexible, reciprocal, non-litigious, and long-term in orientation." Comparatively, most business-government relations in the United States, "can be characterized as formal, distant, rigid, suspicious, legalistic, narrow, and short-term oriented."[257]

EMPLOYER-EMPLOYEE RELATIONSHIPS

The Japanese employer-employee relationship has received even more attention in the West than has the government-employer relationship. Japanese management style is frequently studied, and many management practices have been introduced into the workplace in the United States.[258]

As discussed in the section on civil disputes, the employment relationship in Japan typically is denser and more enduring than it is in the United States.[259] Lifetime employment for permanent employees in larger firms ties workers to employers more completely than would otherwise be the case. Wages and promotion are based more on seniority and less on performance.[260] Practices like tsukiai create networks of relationships that blur the distinction between professional colleague and personal friend. At work Japanese employees are more likely to participate in such group activities as quality circles that build group solidarity. Individuals tend to rotate through a number of jobs and enjoy generalist careers.[261] If American workers' careers are usually within an occupation that cuts across firms, Japanese workers' careers are within a firm and cut across occupations.[262]

255. Young, supra note 230, p. 946.

256. Okimoto, supra note 218, p. 231.

257. Ibid., p. 158.

258. W. G. Ouchi, *Theory Z* (New York: Avon, 1981). Marleen A. O'Connor, "A Socio-Economic Approach to the Japanese Corporate Governance Structure" *Washington and Lee Law Review* 50 (1993), 1529.

259. Hamilton and Sanders, supra note 66, pp. 26–31.

260. Richard Wokutch, *Worker Protection, Japanese Style* (Ithaca, N.Y.: ILR Press, 1992), pp. 39–40.

261. David I. Levine, *Reinventing the Workplace: How Business and Employees Can Both Win* (Washington, D.C.: Brookings Institution, 1995), p. 117.

262. James Lincoln and K. McBride, "Japanese industrial organization in comparative perspective" *Annual Review of Sociology* 13 (1987), 297.

The result is a firm that has some familylike characteristics. Relationships are partly contractual, but they are also a matter of kinship. Hsu has called this relationship a "kin-tract," which he defines as a "fixed and unalterable hierarchical arrangement voluntarily entered into among a group of human beings who follow a common code of behavior under a common ideology for a set of common objectives."[263] The sense of a shared code of behavior, ideology, and objectives is developed from the beginning of the employment relationship. For example, Rohlen reports his experience going through the orientation procedure of a Japanese bank. Groups of new employees stay together in a special dormitory for several days. The orientation goes well beyond covering necessary technical information and builds bonds among co-workers as they live together, engage in group exercises, and learn songs. Orientation also involves "spiritual education," for example, in the form of a day spent working at menial tasks without pay for people in the local community. When trainees return from this exercise they discuss what is the meaning of work. "Some had had such an interesting and pleasant time that it had not occurred to them to think of their tasks as work. When this was noticed, it was generally observed that enjoyment of work has less to do with the kind of work performed than with the attitude the person has toward it. . . . Because it must assign rather dull and methodical tasks to many, management finds this lesson of obvious value."[264]

Once inside the company, workers progress according to their seniority; mentors also help them advance. Quality circles incorporate workers into production and safety decisions. Middle-level managers are given considerable decision-making authority through the *ringi* process, whereby they not only draft proposals but also see that the proposals work their way through the firm's hierarchy until approved by top management.[265] Such programs build commitment to the organization and place responsibility for decisions within hierarchical groups, not individuals.[266] These arrangements create an environment of welfare corporatism.[267] The results are measurable. In a recent comparative study of the workplace in Japan and the United States,

263. Francis Hsu, *Iemoto: The Heart of Japan* (New York: Wiley, 1975), p. 62.

264. Thomas Rohlen, *For Harmony and Strength: Japanese White-Collar Organization in Anthropological Perspective* (Berkeley: University of California Press, 1974), pp. 204–205.

265. J. P. Allston, *The American Samurai: Blending American and Japanese Managerial Practices* (New York: DeGruyter, 1986).

266. Ronald Brown, "The Faces of Japanese Labor Relations in Japan and the U.S. and the Emerging Legal Issues under U.S. Labor Law," *Syracuse Journal of International Law and Commerce* 15 (1989), 235.

267. James Lincoln and Arne Kalleberg, *Culture, Control, and Commitment: A Study of Work Organization and Work Attitudes in the United States and Japan* (Cambridge: Cambridge University Press, 1990), pp. 248–250.

Lincoln and Kalleberg found that Japanese workers apparently have more frequent relations with supervisors, on and off the job, and they are more likely to form close friendships with co-workers and to see them after work.[268] For many Japanese workers the firm is not simply their place of employment, but a community with which they identify.[269] This environment leads to predictable ways in which the Japanese resolve disputes between employer and employee and to a reduced role for courts in resolving conflict. Two examples—union-management relations and complaints of gender discrimination—demonstrate how the Japanese manage employee-employer disputes.

Union-Management Disputes

Most Japanese labor relations law has been enacted since World War II and borrows heavily from American law. Again, however, the substantive provisions of the law have been modified by procedural rules, the social organization of employee-employer relations, and the Japanese legal consciousness.

The most important fact about Japanese unions is that most are enterprise unions, which organize workers in a specific enterprise without regard to craft.[270] Unions typically cover both blue-collar and white-collar full-time employees. Officers come from the ranks of the workers in the enterprise and usually maintain their employee status while in office (although they are paid by the union). Because the top executives of a firm are usually promoted from within, management directors are frequently former officials of the firm's union.[271] Such a relationship provides management with a special insight into the union point of view while constraining union officers in much the same way that amakudari constrains MITI bureaucrats.

In the United States, on the other hand, most unions are either craft unions (the Carpenter Union), or industrial unions that organize workers in an entire industry (the United Mine Workers). Some industrial unions in the United States have become general unions that organize workers without regard to

268. Lincoln and Kalleberg, supra note 267, p. 114; James Lincoln and Arne Kalleberg, "Work Organization and Workforce Commitment: A Study of Plants and Employees in the U.S. and Japan," *American Sociological Review* 50 (1985), 738–760.

269. Ronald Dore, *British Factory-Japanese Factory: The Origins of National Diversity in Industrial Relations* (Berkeley: University of California Press, 1973); Taishiro Shirai, "A Theory of Enterprise Unionism," in Taishiro Shirai (ed.), *Contemporary Industrial Relations in Japan,* (Madison: University of Wisconsin Press, 1983), pp. 117–143.

270. Kazuo Sugeno (Leo Kanowitz, trans.) *Japanese Labor Law* (Seattle: University of Washington Press, 1992); Eyal Ben-Ari, "Ritual Strikes, Ceremonial Slowdowns: Some Thoughts on the Management of Conflict in Large Japanese Enterprises," in Eisenstadt and Ben-Ari (eds.), *Japanese Models of Conflict Resolution*, p. 98.

271. Shirai, supra note 269, pp. 119, 139.

their occupation, industry, or enterprise (the Teamsters). Enterprise unions are rare elsewhere as well. For example, most German unions are organized on an industry-wide basis.

Enterprise unions are the organizational form most likely to maintain an environment in which workers and management think of the firm as a community, not just a job. This is reflected in the typical collective bargaining agreement. With the exception of provisions on wages and hours, Japanese collective agreements contain few substantive provisions. Unlike American labor contracts, which list specific management practices about which an employee can grieve, Japanese contracts provide for consultations prior to a number of management decisions. Matsuda sets forth the following reason for the popularity of consultation clauses rather than grievance clauses that are typical of American labor agreements.

> Grievance procedures are not popular in Japan; they are seldom used because employees are extremely reluctant to confront their foremen or supervisors individually even with union representatives present. A consultation clause, by making proper consultation before every personnel change an employer's contractual duty, may prevent the employee concerned from ever having to confront the employer, at least on his or her own initiative. From the employer's standpoint, too, preventing grievances by making use of the consultation system is desirable. Under the procedure, it is expected that when the employer proposes any personnel change, the union will find out from the individual concerned whether he or she has any complaint about the change and will try to persuade the member to obey the order in the future, if and when the union determines that the personnel change is reasonable. A prior consultation system, therefore, is a device with the same goal as a grievance procedure, and yet it enables a foreman to maintain good personal relations with his subordinate workers.[272]

Consultation is not limited to employee discipline and personnel changes. Other topics appropriate for joint consultations include plans for future investment or plant locations, introduction of new technology, work schedules, transfers, training, industrial safety, and environmental problems. Compared to their American counterparts, Japanese unions engage in more joint consultation with management.[273]

272. Yasuhiko Matsuda, ''Conflict Resolution in Japanese Industrial Relations,'' in Taishiro Shirai (ed), *Contemporary Industrial Relations in Japan* (Madison: University of Wisconsin Press, 1983), p. 190.

273. Shirai, supra note 269, p. 120. In this regard Japanese unions are similar to works councils (*Betriebsräte*) in Germany.

Not surprisingly, relatively few days are lost to strikes. In the United States between 1975 and 1988, an average of 172 workdays per 1,000 workers were lost because of industrial disputes. In Japan the average was 25 workdays.[274] Rather than waiting for negotiations to become deadlocked before striking, Japanese unions frequently undertake a short strike early in a dispute to demonstrate they disagree with an employer.[275]

Not only are strikes less disruptive, but fewer disputes are taken to third parties for resolution. In the United States the National Labor Relations Board is authorized to hear, among other things, claims of unfair labor practices. The equivalent institution in Japan is the Labor Commission. There is one Central Labor Commission for the nation as a whole and a local commission for each prefecture. The commissions have a tripartite structure, with an equal number of people representing employers, employees, and the public. Disputes brought to the Labor Commissions may be handled by conciliation, mediation, or arbitration. The number of cases brought to the commission has varied from 500 to 1,500 per year, 95 percent of which are handled by conciliation.[276] By way of comparison, in the United States between 30,000 and 45,000 cases are annually filed with the NLRB.[277]

As in other areas of life, the Japanese are less likely to use the judicial process to resolve their labor disputes than are Americans. And again the reason for this difference is found not in the substantive labor law but in the structure of employee-employer relations and in the Japanese legal consciousness.

Employment Discrimination

The familylike environment of the Japanese workplace is purchased at a price, which comes in several forms. More so than in most societies, Japan

274. Wokutch, supra note 260, p. 43. The rate in both countries has been declining. In 1988 the American rate was 38 workdays per 1,000 workers. In Japan in the same year the rate had fallen to less than 3; Id.

275. Matsuda, supra note 272, p. 195, Ben-Ari, supra note, p. 104.

276. Sugeno, supra note 270, pp. 595–596, 612.

277. William Gould, *Japan's Reshaping of American Labor Law* (Cambridge: MIT Press, 1984), p. 48; Sugeno, supra note 270, pp. 610–611. In Japan, unlike the United States, disputants can, if they wish, take their case directly to district courts, bypassing the Labor Commission; Gould, p. 45. Therefore, the number of cases heard by the Commissions underrepresents the level of disputing before third parties. However, apparently very few unfair labor practice cases are brought in the district court; Matsuda, supra note 272, p. 187. On the other hand, each year employees file between 1,000 and 1,500 suits against their employers because they have been discharged or because of a dispute over wages; Matsuda, supra note 272, p. 191. If we were to include all of these claims with claims before the Labor Commissions the total would still be a fraction of total cases brought to the NLRB each year.

operates a dual-structure economy. The major Japanese companies are able to offer employees a guarantee of long-term employment because they subcontract much of their work to independent contractors and subsidiaries. During an economic downturns the firm protects its permanent employees by bringing work back into the firm and reducing reliance on subcontractors.[278] Equally important, most companies use many part-time employees who can be laid off when necessary.

The loyalty created by a system of lifetime employment and of wages closely tied to seniority comes at the expense of people who wish to enter and leave the work force at various points in life—a disproportionate number of which are women.[279] When young women first enter the labor market they are on a rough par with male counterparts. However, they are frequently given relatively dead-end jobs on the assumption that they will quit when they marry. As Upham notes, it has been very difficult for a woman "to be hired for management track positions. Thus, promotion to supervisory positions—for example, high-level clerical positions—has long been possible, but becoming a member of the managerial elite has not."[280] If women leave their job for marriage or child rearing they lose their status as permanent employees. If they return later they will be relegated to the status of "temporary" workers with lower wages, few fringe benefits, and no job protection guarantees. As women have re-entered the work force in growing numbers after raising a family, this system has produced growing wage differentials. Thus the structure of Japanese workplace, combined with a set of cultural values that locate the woman as homemaker, results in substantial gender inequality.[281]

Employment discrimination is one area of employer-employee disputing where we might expect a plaintiff to turn to the courts for redress. By definition the plaintiff has not been brought fully into the set of familylike relationships that create a community of interests. Moreover, the plaintiff may have very little to lose in terms of future relationships. For example, in the late 1970s the Iron and Steel Federation decided that it had to cease using different wage scales for men and women. Rather than equalizing wages, the solution was to transfer all women who had been promoted into positions of responsibility and to cease hiring women who had graduated from four-year

278. Okimoto, supra note 218, p. 130.

279. For a general discussion of women in the workplace see Mary C. Brinton, *Women and the Economic Miracle* (Berkeley: University of California Press, 1993).

280. Upham, supra note 159, p. 127.

281. Ibid., pp. 124–128. Upham reports the following statement by Ohtsuki Bunpei, the president of the Japan Federation of Employers Associations: "[An equal number of male and female executives] would deprive men of jobs and cause social unrest. By nature, women are better suited for raising children and domestic responsibilities" (quoted in Ibid., p. 128).

universities. Seven women employees brought suit.[282] Thus in employment discrimination disputes, like automobile accident claims, a resort to litigation may not be deterred by a concern for existing relationships, nor, apparently, by a spirit of compromise from the other side. Not surprisingly, over the past thirty years women have used the courts in their efforts to combat discrimination. If there is an area of Japanese life where people have made sustained use of the courts to achieve social change it is in the area of employment discrimination.

Prior to 1986 and the enactment of the Equal Employment Opportunity Act (EEOA), plaintiffs' actions were constrained by the dearth of statutory authority making job discrimination illegal. Plaintiffs were forced to rely on general provisions of the civil code and the Labor Standards Act. Nevertheless, the courts declared most overt acts of wage discrimination to be illegal. Typically the government's response was to pass a statute that it hoped would allow it to regain control of the issue by removing it from the courts and providing alternative methods of dispute resolution.

The debates surrounding the adoption of the EEOA echoed the debates surrounding the adoption of Western legal codes almost a century earlier. Opponents argued that the legislation was being forced on Japan by foreign interests, and that the premises of the proposed legislation were contrary to Japanese cultural values.[283] The individualism underlying the legislation would, over time, replace an environment of cooperation and friendship that is at the core of a communal society with the competition and hostility that is typical of an individualistic culture.[284]

The law that emerged was cast from the same mold that created the environmental law. The new law prohibited discriminatory practices in a number of areas, including retirement and layoff policy, fringe benefits, and basic on-the-job training. However, in the areas of recruitment, hiring, placement, and promotion the law required only that the employer make his or her best effort to avoid discrimination between male and female workers. Most significant, the law contains no sanctions for violations; instead, it creates an informal dispute resolution procedure.[285] Complaints can be heard by an em-

---

282. Ibid., p. 139.

283. In 1980 Japan had signed the United Nations-sponsored Convention on the Elimination of All Forms of Discrimination Against Women, committing the government to providing equal employment for women by 1985; Upham, supra note 159, p. 148. The opponents' argument was based in part on the fact that survey data revealed most Japanese women were satisfied with their existing job situation. In Japan, as in the United States, women generally report greater job satisfaction than men; Lincoln and Kalleberg, supra note 267, p. 153.

284. Upham, supra note 159, p. 151.

285. Ibid., p. 153; Masahiro Kuwahara, "The Equal Employment Opportunity Act," Doing Business in Japan (Aentaro Kitagawa, ed.) 6 (1992), Sec. 4.01–03.

ployee-employer grievance resolution committee, by the regional director of the Women's and Young Worker's Bureau (part of the Ministry of Labor), or, if both parties consent, by the local Equal Opportunity Conciliation Committee (appointed by the Minister of Labor). The powers of the regional director and the Conciliation Committee are restricted to offering administrative guidance and requesting voluntary compliance on the part of the employer.[286] The statute creates no judicially enforceable rights.

Will this law have any impact on the employment situation of women? Ultimately, in this area as elsewhere the efficacy of the law will depend on the bureaucracy. The act empowers the Ministry of Labor to draft guidelines that employers should follow to secure equal treatment and opportunity for women.[287] The guidelines are to be based on a consideration of labor conditions of women workers as well as women's attitudes and perceptions about their employment situation.[288] The statute envisions a gradual approach whereby the Labor Ministry would revise its guidelines as progress is made toward achieving gender equality in employment.

The first round of guidelines were promulgated in 1986. They specify that employers must not set up classifications that eliminate women from consideration in recruiting and hiring. The directives set forth examples of inappropriate practices: job classifications that exclude female applicants; job categories that determine future treatment such as type of work, promotions, and salary and that exclude female applicants; requiring female applicants to be single when no such requirement exists for male applicants. Unacceptable promotion practices include the failure to give female workers an opportunity to advance to management positions or promoting them to lower-level management positions and no higher.[289]

These and similar provisions ban expressly discriminatory policies and have had an immediate effect in reducing overt, explicit discrimination against women employees. The proportion of companies that offered equal starting wages for women and men graduates rose from 36 percent in 1980 to 79 percent in 1987.[290] Help-wanted ads no longer contained gender-specific language. Fewer companies maintained gender-specific hiring categories. Seventy percent of recent college graduates were recruited to positions open to "either male or female," compared to 32 percent the year before. Many

286. Kuwahara, supra note 285, Sec 4.04.

287. Upham, supra note 159, p. 156.

288. Loraine Parkinson, "Japan's Equal Employment Opportunity Law: An Alternative Approach to Social Change," *Columbia Law Review* 89 (1989), 610 n. 16.

289. Ibid., pp. 610–613, provides a complete list of the practices the Ministry of Labor considers to be contrary to its guidelines.

290. Alice Lam, "Equal Employment Opportunities for Japanese Women: Changing Company Practice," in Janet Hunter, ed., *Japanese Women Working* (New York: Routledge, 1993).

firms shifted to a two-track structure for women. Some women could choose a management-trainee track similar to that enjoyed by males. In the past women were relegated to a standard track with little or no opportunity for promotion. The gap between starting salaries for men and women narrowed; in 1986 the starting salary of recent female university graduates was 97 percent of the starting salary of male counterparts. Companies began to review employment rules with respect to company benefits and employment training.[291] Some firms are making modest efforts to allow women to compromise between work and family.[292] One analysis found a significant, albeit weak relationship between the passage of the law and the annual increase in the number of new female four-year college graduates between 1953 and 1990.[293] In 1993 two hundred thousand women were in management positions, an increase of 20,000 over the previous year.[294]

Nevertheless, there are many reasons to remain skeptical about the long-term impact of the statute. The lack of enforcement mechanisms has allowed many firms to drag their feet. Sixty percent of the firms that were offered administrative guidance during the first two years of the law had not rectified their inadequacies by mid-1988.[295] Even with full compliance, employers enjoy wide discretion in the application of facially neutral hiring and promotion policies. As explicit discrimination decreases, some firms are adopting informal ways to maintain the status quo through promotion and hiring policies.[296] For example, some firms recruit men and women on different dates and finish their male interviews before beginning interviews with women. Such a practice is not discriminatory as defined by the Ministry of Labor because women have not been "excluded" from the recruitment process.[297] Moreover, the gradual approach of the statute and the administrative guidance

291. Parkinson, supra note 288, pp. 645–650. These changes are reflected in modest aggregate gains for women. In 1991 women filled 3.6% of middle-management positions in large firms. A decade before, the figure was 2.3%; Takashi Kashima, "Women Find Not-So-Equal Employment Opportunities," *Nikkei Weekly*, Apr. 23, 1993, 21.

292. Alice Lam, *Women and Japanese Management: Discrimination and Reform* (London: Routledge, 1992), p. 182.

293. Kathleen Canning and William Lazonick, "Equal Opportunity and the 'Managerial Woman' in Japan," *Industrial Relations* 33 (1994), 59.

294. Kiyoko Kamio Knapp, "Still Office Flowers: Japanese Women Betrayed by the Equal Employment Law," *Harvard Women's Law Journal* 18 (1995), 94.

295. Mary Saso, *Women in the Japanese Workplace* (London: Hilary Shipman, 1990), p. 108.

296. Upham, supra note 159, p. 143; Michael Bennett, "Gender-Based Employment Discrimination in Japan and the United States," *Loyola of Los Angeles International and Comparative Law Journal* 15 (1992), 149.

297. Lam, supra note 292, p. 211.

directives offer little to long-time female employees who are trapped in dead-end "temporary" positions. This is reflected in all women's average earnings, which hover between 50 and 55 percent of men's.[298]

Some changes may even have a negative effect on the long-term prospects for workplace equality. As Saso notes, with respect to the two-track system, "Although the employers argue that the two-track system is not discriminatory in the eyes of the law, most women are having to make an irreversible choice early in their careers to join the slow track because of their anxiety that transfers may upset the stability of their future family."[299] Lam observes, "Compared to men, relatively few women are in the 'managerial career track.'"[300] One survey indicates that the number of women who say that "a permanent career" is their preferred form of employment declined during the 1980s.[301]

There is even some indication that the Japanese recession of the early 1990s has restricted employment opportunities for female university graduates. Japanese university students typically receive job offers in the fall of their senior year. In 1993 the Ministry of Labor reported that 66 percent of women versus 85 percent of men who were to graduate in the spring of 1994 had found jobs.[302]

In the face of these trends, women continue to turn to the courts to seek redress for what they believe are discriminatory policies. Successful suits have been brought by female workers at the Social Insurance Medical Fee Payment Fund and at Hitachi in 1992 and at a publishing firm in 1993. The courts continue to push the Labor Ministry toward the reduction of gender discrimination in the workplace. As Upham notes, however, here as elsewhere the primary engine for change is the government and the bureaucracy, not the courts; politics, not law, determines the course of events.[303]

In sum, the public law that regulates corporate actors exhibits many of the same attributes as other parts of Japanese law. The courts play a very minor role in controlling corporate behavior or government excess. Instead, ministries attempt to achieve compliance through a process of negotiation and consensus building.

CONCLUSION

The role of lawyers, judges, and courts in Japan is much different from its role in the United States. In the criminal law area, the justice system legiti-

298. Saso, supra note 295, p. 11.
299. Ibid., p. 65.
300. Lam, supra note 292, p. 132.
301. Kashima, supra note 291, p. 21.
302. Knapp, supra note 294, pp. 113-115.
303. Upham, supra note 159, p. 218.

mates wide discretion on the part of legal authorities. The system is organized to encourage the offender to confess wrongdoing and then to be reintegrated into the society. From police to prisons, the system is communal in its orientation.

The differences between Japan and the United States are even greater in the civil law area. Formal litigation is rarely used to resolve disputes. As the last two sections have indicated, the government has created a legal system that strongly discourages and even occasionally prohibits private suits to redress grievances. The relative lack of lawyers, court delays, strict standing rules, the unavailability of class actions, and the relative certainty of outcomes all conspire to make litigation an unattractive alternative. However, unlike socialist legal systems in Eastern Europe, the courts are also largely unavailable to the government. If corporations and citizens cannot sue to oppose ministry directives, neither can ministries easily sue to compel obedience to them. Statutes such as the Depressed Industries Laws force ministries to find other avenues to compliance.

In the area of constitutional litigation, Japanese courts are very reluctant to intervene and hold a statute or regulation to be unconstitutional. The legislature, and especially the executive, play a dominant role. The judiciary is equal in name only.

When we compare Japan solely to the United States the differences are truly dramatic. When, however, we compare the Japanese legal system to those of the other nations examined in this volume the differences are much less significant. This is especially true with respect to France and Germany, where legal education is similar to that in Japan, and the judiciary is primarily staffed by professional civil servants who begin their careers immediately after leaving the university.[304] In spite of the American influence through the 1947 constitution, the legal system remains firmly in the civil law tradition and the codes still strongly reflect their French and German roots.

Japanese criminal procedure also looks more like that in Germany and France. In both countries, as in Japan, the trial is basically inquisitorial rather than adversarial. Parallels to France are particularly strong. The French examining magistrate plays a role not dissimilar to the Japanese prosecutor. As in Japan, French critics charge that the judiciary does not do enough to control police excesses. Overall, both systems have strong paternalistic strains.

Civil litigation in Japan also more nearly resembles that on the Continent. Efforts are made to steer parties away from litigation. European countries not represented in this volume are even more similar to the Japanese in this regard. The Dutch, for example, have created a number of nonjudicial forums to settle disputes.

304. Even in England legal training and judicial careers are more similar to Japan than to the United States, especially in the upper level English courts.

The French and Germans also have a strong, highly skilled, professional bureaucracy at the center of the government. Not surprisingly, the power of the bureaucracy is reflected in the limited ability of individuals and enterprises to challenge governmental regulation, although perhaps this is changing as countries become more integrated into the European Union.

From a European perspective Japan appears much less unique. Nevertheless, it is fair to say that Japan does represent the end point on several continua. Litigation rates are very low and the government continues to take active steps to discourage widespread use of courts to settle disputes. The bureaucracy continues to dominate the government and the judiciary continues to show considerable deference to the legislature and executive at a time when European courts are becoming more active. At least part of the explanation for this continuing pattern may be found in a Japanese legal consciousness that equates litigation with conflict and Western individualism. Litigation threatens the normative dominance of consensus.[305]

Ultimately, however, the success of a legal system grounded in compromise and consensus rather than conflict depends upon a set of social arrangements that create and maintain trust. From the police officer in the kōban, to the employee engaged in after-work socializing, to the MITI official keeping constant personal contact with counterparts in industry, to month-long factfinding trips abroad, to the manager who once was an officer in the company union, the Japanese build trust on the foundation of constant, long-term interactions. A legal system that does not rely on the coercive capacity of courts can remain effective only as long as mutual trust makes compromise possible.

Trust does break down, as in the Big Four pollution cases. More recently, some firms have demonstrated an absence of trust and compromise in their continuing employment discrimination against women. Yet the greatest threat to trust in Japan in the 1990s is the seemingly endless round of scandals involving senior government officials.[306] The Recruit scandal epitomizes this type of wrongdoing. The Recruit Company was established in 1960 as an advertising agency with three employees. By the late 1980s it had grown to a conglomerate with over 6,000 employees in twenty-seven separate firms with sales of nearly ¥200 billion.[307] In addition, Recruit contained data-communication and real-estate components. A subsidiary, Recruit Cosmos, was at the heart of the scandal. In 1984 Recruit's founder, Hiromasa Ezoe, offered 1.25 million unlisted Recruit Cosmos shares to seventy-six

305. Upham, supra note 159, p. 207.

306. See Edwin M. Reingold, *Chrysanthemums and Thorns: The Untold Story of Modern Japan* (New York: St. Martin's Press, 1992), p. 238.

307. Albrecht Rothacher, *The Japanese Power Elite* (New York: St. Martin's Press, 1993), p. 109.

persons at the price of ¥1,200. In September 1986 he offered an additional 760,000 shares to an additional group of eighty-three persons for ¥3,000. In October 1986, when the firm went public, the shares rose to ¥5,270 the first day. Some beneficiaries of this deal had received as many as 30,000 shares and turned a quick profit of ¥120 million. Among those who received shares either directly or through aides were Yasuhiro Nakasone, a former prime minister; Shirtaro Abe, the secretary general of the Liberal Democratic Party (LDP); prime minister Noboru Takeshita; and finance minister (and future prime minister) Kiichi Miyazawa.[308] In addition Recruit made large donations to politicians through the purchase of fund-raising party tickets.

Ziemba and Schwartz note that this scandal, like those before and after, is rooted in the Japanese political tradition of government officials giving gifts at weddings, funerals, and other occasions. The stunning expense of the practice explains why government officials are so corruptible. Because of the burden of gift-giving, the average member of the Diet must collect around ¥100 million ($1 million) each year to stay in office. The Liberal Democratic Party spent more than 200 billion in the 1989 election.[309] Money has been a constant need, a constant source of corruption, and an ever-present threat to the legitimacy of the government.[310]

In return for the stock and the contributions, Recruit received many favors. Founder Hiromasa Ezoe was arrested for giving bribes, as was the president of First Finance, a Recruit subsidiary.[311] In addition, some minor governmental officials faced criminal charges. Kunio Takaishi, an official in the Ministry of Education, had appointed Ezoe to various advisory councils. Takashi Kato, an official at the Ministry of Labor, worked to weaken draft legislation that would affect part of Recruit's publishing business. Both men were arrested for taking bribes.[312] Prime Minister Takeshita was forced to

308. Ibid., pp. 109, 114.

309. William T. Ziemba and Sandra L. Schwartz, *Power Japan: How and Why the Japanese Economy Works* (Chicago: Probus Publishing, 1992), p. 276. Since the Recruit scandal there have been scandals involving schemes whereby large clients were protected against stock market losses. There have also been scandals involving bribes from the Kyowa Corporation, a steel fabricator, and Tokyo Sagawa Kyubin, a moving company involved in real estate speculation; Ibid., at 294–299. This latter scandal is still unfolding. By way of comparison, the year-long 1988 presidential election in the United States cost $400 million for all candidates.

310. In November 1994 the Diet passed a series of electoral reform provisions. Among them was legislation restricting the amounts corporations may donate to campaigns and heavier penalties for those who violate campaign financing laws. In addition, the act provides for partial public financing of campaigns. "Japanese Pass Bills on Electoral Reform," *New York Times,* Nov. 3, 1994, A9, col. 1.

311. Ibid., p. 282.

312. Rothacher, supra note 307, p. 116.

resign.[313] However, neither he nor any of the other leaders of the party were indicted, and by November 1991 Kiichi Miyazawa was prime minister.[314] The ability of the leadership to avoid prosecution is in part due to the use of the name stamp as an official's legal signature. The name stamp literally gives a power of attorney to its holder. For example, secretaries handled the Recruit shares for people such as Takeshita and Miyazawa. Because subordinates possess the name stamp of higher officials, the officials are able to deny involvement in wrongdoing. Nevertheless, the recurring scandals eventually led to the defeat of the Liberal Democratic Party in the summer of 1993.[315] In the spring of 1994 prosecutors took an unprecedented step when they charged a sitting member of the Diet on a bribe-taking charge.[316]

Throughout the scandals the courts, in keeping with the role of the judiciary in Japanese society, have been in the background. It does not appear, however, that the prosecutors or the courts have been taking bribes. They have remained a source of legitimate authority in the face of widespread corruption.

Here, as in most legitimacy crises, the courts play an important role. Although Japanese courts are not central to the day-to-day processing of disputes, they are essential when trust is absent. They have been the canary in the coal mine, an early warning system signaling the breakdown of trust.

In the environmental area the government responded with a set of institutions and arrangements that have restored a substantial degree of trust. The EEOA represents a similar attempt. Efforts at political reform have met with less success, but such reform is essential. The continued effectiveness of the Japanese style of conflict resolution is contingent on the ability of these statutes to build and maintain the spirit of trust and community upon which the Japanese legal consciousness rests.

313. His secretary and financial advisor committed suicide; Ziemba and Schwartz, supra note 309, p. 282.

314. Rothacher, supra note 307, p. 118. Miyazawa himself became implicated in subsequent scandals; Ziemba and Schwartz, supra note 309, p. 298.

315. *New York Times,* July 19, 1993, A1, col. 6.

316. Kishiro Nakamura, a former LDP Construction Minister, was accused of receiving a bribe of ¥10 million from Kajima, a civil-engineering company that was part of a construction cartel known as the Saitama Saturday Association. *Economist,* Mar. 19, 1994, p. 76.

7

Conclusion

HERBERT JACOB

This book opened with the assertions that an understanding of law and courts significantly assists our understanding of politics in countries other than the United States and that legal institutions and political arenas engage in a continuing dialogue. It is now time to put these assertions to the test in the light of the preceding chapters. We can begin to do so by asking several counterfactual questions. Would politics in the United States, England, France, Germany, and Japan be significantly different if there were no courts, or if courts operated under substantially different ground rules?

The previous chapters make clear that many political events would have unfolded differently in the absence of law or the courts as we have described them. The then-ruling Socialist Party of France would not be sullied by the AIDS-tainted blood supply scandal that unfolded in French criminal courts. Japan's ruling Liberal Democratic Party would not have fallen without the investigation of corruption by public prosecutors, nor would the government have been tainted by the Minamata and other cases of industrial pollution, had prosecutors and the courts not exposed the government's indifference. In Germany, numerous decisions of the constitutional court (among many others) helped define the character of postwar German politics, while in England the criminal courts have played a central role in the struggle with Northern Irish terrorists. Finally, in the United States, there is little doubt that Supreme Court decisions defined political agendas for entire decades—first, the desegregation decisions, beginning with *Brown v. Board of Education*,[1] and then the abortion policy decisions, beginning with *Roe v. Wade*.[2]

But in much less spectacular ways the law and courts have defined not only the politics but also the social life of each of these countries. Law and courts have provided a cocoon of domestic peace and commercial stability

1. 347 U.S. 483 (1954).
2. 410 U.S. 113 (1973).

so necessary to economic development and personal satisfaction. They are responsible at least in part for widespread acceptance of governance in each of these countries.

The second assertion of this book—that courts reflect political conditions—is also affirmed by the previous chapters. The counterfactual case— what would courts be like if politics were fundamentally different—is illustrated nicely by the contrast drawn by Erhard Blankenburg between law and courts in the former German Democratic Republic under Communist rule and law and courts in the West German Federal Republic. In the GDR, law and courts were clearly subservient to politics; fewer legal remedies existed, even for personal disputes; no one dared to challenge the acts of government officials in a court. The unification of Germany in 1990 involved the wholesale importation of norms and procedures from the West to the East.

The previous chapters provide many illustrations of the complex relationships that exist among law, courts, and politics in the five countries examined. They enable us to draw some broader conclusions.

One result of the interaction of these three spheres is that law and courts act as conservative forces on political life. This is particularly apparent in the staffing of the courts. Although the details of judicial selection vary greatly, the outcome is similar: the men and women selected to judgeships almost always hold safe, sound, middle-of-the-road opinions.

The United States arguably utilizes the most partisan selection processes. Much political maneuvering surrounds the selection of both trial and appellate judges. Many win their office through election; those who are appointed (as in all the federal courts) need the sponsorship of elective office holders and usually must pass inspection by legislators. The result is that judges in the United States often bring to the bench considerable experience from the world of politics. The process also assures that most men and women who come to the bench bring with them views that reflect the general consensus of those holding high political offices; they are firmly committed to the core values of the regime and its strong supporters. Yet the norms of judicial behavior prohibit direct intervention by other government officials in cases brought to court, except if those officials are a party to the case. Those norms stringently forbid informal contacts between judges and party officials, legislators, bureaucrats, and lobbyists.

The process of judicial selection and the norms of judicial conduct produce similar results in the other countries. In England, the selection process is far less political in the partisan sense of the term. The Lord Chancellor (a member of the cabinet) selects judges from lists of barristers (and occasionally solicitors) who have been vetted by bureaucrats working under his supervision. The seasoned lawyers chosen in this way are also strongly committed to regime norms, but, as in the United States, ex parte contacts with the government or others almost never take place. The government cannot *order* a particular result from a court, but the result it prefers often occurs as a consequence of the value commitments of its judges. In France, Germany, and Japan the government does not select judges from seasoned attorneys. Rather it recruits them from university students enrolled in specialized law programs and carefully provides its judicial apprentices training and indoctrination which assure that judges are politically reliable. Initial selection depends on having done well in the training program and its concluding examinations; promotion depends on winning the high regard of judicial superiors. The process is designed to discourage risk taking or the development of novel decisions. Yet as in the United States and England, once judges sit on the bench, government ministries do not direct verdicts in the cases they hear. Judges enjoy autonomy within the environs of the carefully vetted preferences they bring to their position.

Thus each country obtains reliability, moderation, and adherence to regime norms from its judiciary, although the processes by which they obtain those values vary. In these countries the courts are autonomous and yet strongly linked to the values of their regimes. However, important consequences of the differences in the selection procedures remain. Most notably, the procedures used in the United States produce judges who are more likely to render novel decisions, although even in the United States, judges exercise greater self-restraint than legislators and elected executives. The French, German, and Japanese selection procedures produce judges who are more thoroughly trained in the art of judging.

A second point of intersection among law, courts, and politics arises from the decisions that courts render. Both the routine decisions coming from the ordinary disputes that reach courts and the decisions arising out of extraordinary cases affect the political arena in each of these countries. Once again, the processes vary but the results are similar.

Routine dispute processing dominates the judiciary in each of the countries. In each, the courts handle a large number of charges of criminal misconduct and play a central role in helping the regime maintain social order by enforcing the criminal code. This is not generally a matter of sweeping the streets clean of criminals; with the exception of the United States, lengthy incarceration is reserved only for the most serious offenders. However, by convicting offenders and punishing them (albeit without long prison terms), the courts reinforce community norms of conduct and reinforce social order.

In all these countries courts are tugged to a greater or lesser degree on the one hand by the value the regime places on stability and on the other by its desire for legitimacy. Stability often requires prompt and forceful action in criminal cases. That may mean swift arrest, aggressive interrogation, and thorough use of the fruits of that interrogation in the subsequent trial. Yet in all these countries uneasiness about abuse of these powers threatens the legitimacy of court decisions in criminal cases where such abuse has been alleged. In the United States, those countervailing forces have led to the continual testing of the limits of constitutional provisions requiring due process of law, prohibiting unlawful searches and seizures, calling for a speedy trial, and other such guarantees. This has led to repeated clashes in the political arena between law-and-order proponents and defenders of courts whose judges feel bound by such constitutional provisions. In Germany, France, and England, similar cross-pressures exist and have been reinforced by the possibility of appeal to the European Court of Human Rights; this is particularly significant for the English, who do not have a written constitution or a court which hears appeals on such fundamental rights. Only the Japanese courts appear to be relatively docile in these matters; they rarely challenge police practices even though the police are more intrusive and aggressive in their interrogation of defendants in Japan than in other countries.

The social control role of the courts in processing social disputes not involving allegations of criminal behavior is more complex. In all five countries many routine disputes are processed by negotiations of some sort; however, England, France, and Japan have many more disputing venues than the United States. Prototypical are cases arising from automobile accidents. In the United States, lawyers bring more such disputes to ordinary courts than in the other countries, even when both parties expect eventually to negotiate a settlement. In all the countries examined, disputants engage in quite standardized negotiations for claims about property damages from automobile accidents; however, in England, France, and Germany, medical costs, which are the source of much disputing in the United States, are routinely paid by medical insurance schemes. Japan possesses the most elaborate out-of-court procedures for deflecting automobile accident claims from the judiciary, and the few claims that do reach trial produce highly standardized decisions. Such diversion of claims from the courts through structured conciliation and mediation procedures is a general pattern for routine dispute processing in Japan.

In England, France, and Germany many routine disputes go to specialized tribunals which proceed less formally and require the defendant to have less legal assistance than do the regular courts. Thus many landlord-tenant disputes go to specialized housing tribunals in England, and employment disputes go to labor courts in England, Germany and France. Divorces require less formal court action outside the United States. In all of these disputes, the role of courts (whether general courts as in the United States or specialized tribunals in the other countries) is to buttress social control by making decisions according to the norms incorporated in law, which in most instances are themselves the result of prior political struggles in legislatures. Their application by the courts is analogous to the implementation of public policy by administrative bodies. The action by courts is neutral in the sense that only the facts privileged by the law affect the outcome; it is political in the sense that the courts play an important role in the authoritative allocation of values as they engage in the act of maintaining social control.

The courts are also the arena for power struggles between individuals and government agencies. The reach of government is far longer in England, France, and Germany than in the United States. Consequently, there are more disputes of this sort and a more sophisticated set of specialized tribunals for processing them in these other countries. Both France and Germany have highly developed sets of administrative tribunals complete with special sets of judges and layers of trial courts and appellate tribunals for handling complaints about administrative decisions, taxes, and the administration of social welfare programs. England also has such tribunals although they are less fully developed than those in France and Germany. The United States has special tribunals for hearing tax disputes, welfare cases, and other administrative actions, but these tribunals differ across the landscape of its federal structure. In both England and the United States, the path of complaint eventually leads to the general court system, with appeals heard by general appellate courts rather than by the sort of special appeals courts that France and Germany possess. Japan does not have as complex a system of administrative tribunals as France and Germany because it depends much more on informal processes of conciliation and mediation and less on litigation.

The consequences of this structure of appeals by individuals against government are significant. At one extreme, American appellate judges possess a potentially powerful veto over administrative actions in a wide variety of circumstances. They can and do develop legal standards that apply to a wide range of agencies; they actively supervise the administration of public policy in a general way and sometimes become involved in the minutiae of daily administration. In England, appellate judges have the same powers, although they exercise them more cautiously. In France and Germany, challenges to administrative decisions are scattered among many specialized tribunals, and no one set of judges occupies a position from which they can single-handedly alter or block government policy in a wide range of situations, although they also intervene in significant ways in many administrative matters. Administrative agencies in Japan are the most shielded from judicial interference; although courts occasionally intervene, their structure makes them less hospitable to challenges of government authority.

These differences delineate substantially different political roles for courts. In the United States, the courts of general jurisdiction—and particularly their appellate tribunals—have become significant participants in the policymaking and implementation processes. Their contribution does not lie primarily in the substance of the policies—for instance, whether or not to regulate tobacco products—but in the procedures which must be followed to implement such policies. The same judges who decide criminal and civil cases make such decisions in administrative matters. In England, administrative appeals also flow to general appellate judges, but they have been more deferential to administrative decisions than their American counterparts. In France and Germany, administrative judges play an analogous role but each set of courts has a narrower jurisdiction; consequently, no single set of judges possesses the power that American judges enjoy even though within their specific areas of competence, they may become active overseers of administrative actions. Finally, in Japan judges play a much more subordinate role in controlling the administrative process. Their occasional intervention does not match the more substantial role of their counterparts in the United States, England, France, or Germany.

The differences are multiplied by the role that courts play in reviewing the constitutionality of legislation. This kind of judicial review scarcely exists in England; what the English call judicial review is the review of administrative actions. Once again, the United States is the outlier in the extraordinary power that its ordinary courts exercise in reviewing the constitutionality of legislation; France and Germany occupy intermediate positions, and the Japanese courts are least active. In the United States, the same judges who hear routine criminal and civil trials or who adjudicate such appeals also decide constitutional issues. Thus ordinary judges interpret the meaning of constitutional provisions and play a significant role in setting the agenda for other branches of government. Constitutional challenges also occur in France and Germany, but ordinary judges sitting in ordinary courts do not exercise those powers. Constitutional review is reserved for special courts whose judges are selected by a much more openly political process than are ordinary judges; in both countries, some judges on the constitutional courts have substantial experience in the political arena. Moreover, the procedure by which constitutional review occurs differs in both. While the German constitutional court hears challenges from individuals, it also may review the constitutionality of *proposed* legislation. In France, constitutional review operates entirely through the mechanism of examining proposed legislation on the request of specified high officials or of a segment of the National Assembly; however, after the National Assembly has adopted a proposal, it is no longer subject to constitutional review. Finally, in Japan, the Supreme Court possesses the power of constitutional review but has rarely exercised it. More than the French and German constitutional courts, Japan's highest court is staffed by career judges who have been trained to defer to government and parliamentary decisions.

The accumulation of the power to hear ordinary cases, review administrative actions, and review the constitutionality of legislation makes ordinary judges in the United States far more powerful political figures than elsewhere. The power that is concentrated in the ordinary judge in the United States is divided among several different sets of judges in the other countries. The ordinary judge in the United States also has the most political background and the most substantial political connections. What distinguishes judges on constitutional courts in France, Germany, and Japan from those sitting on ordinary courts and specialized tribunals is that the judges on the constitutional tribunals generally not only have more judicial experience but also possess more political experience and connections. Thus we see both variation in the degree of political power judges hold and constancy in the attempt by regimes to assure themselves that courts—while structurally autonomous—do not take entirely independent political directions. The selection of judges constrains the courts. That does not mean that they do not occasionally irritate and upset the chief executive or the dominant parliamentary coalition. Such actions, however, are exceptional; ordinarily, judges defer to decisions from elected officials because for the most part those who might issue continual challenges are not chosen for constitutional court judgeships.

The law's and courts' role in policymaking and social control also depends on the propensity of complainants to use law and the courts. As we have seen, wide variations exist among these countries both in their actual litigation rates and in perceptions of litigiousness. The propensity to litigate is important because courts in these countries hear only those cases that complainants bring to them. The disputes and conflicts that complainants refrain from litigating cannot provide a basis for court intervention in the political arena.

Both institutional structure and the perceptions about the law affect the flow of disputes to the courts. Differences in institutional structures consist not only of the organization of the courts and alternative disputing forums but also of the infrastructure surrounding courts. On both dimensions, the five countries we have examined display considerable differences.

Each of the five countries has a different constellation of disputing forums. Germany has perhaps the most dense set of formal tribunals with its large number of specialized courts and, as Blankenburg indicates, the exceptionally large number of German judges. The French have a somewhat smaller variety of courts; England and the United States follow in that order. Japan has the smallest number.

However, counting the variety of courts that exist and their number is by itself misleading. We must add to that the assortment of other disputing forums which result in legally binding results. In many instances, those forums are private and informal, such as those established within business enterprises; others have been organized by the state for the explicit purpose of diverting disputes from the courts. Sanders describes one such instance: after the Minamata cases had made their way through the courts, multi-tiered conciliation and mediation structures were established to handle disputes concerning injuries arising from industrial pollution. Japan is particularly rich in such formally established mediation devices, in addition to a dense thicket of informal procedures which divert disputes from their courts.

Second, we need to take into account the ease or difficulty with which disputants can bring their complaint to a court or to alternative official tribunals—a complex issue. Ease of litigation depends in part on the need for and availability of legal assistance in pursuing cases. As we have seen, the United States has the largest contingent of lawyers, but the other countries have other professionals who perform many legal services, and most United States lawyers spend relatively little time in court (especially in comparison with English barristers). Moreover, lawyers are almost required for litigation in the United States. In personal injury suits and a few other kinds of cases, complainants have little difficulty in obtaining lawyers because contingent fees motivate lawyers to take on the plaintiff's case; in criminal cases, lawyers paid out of the public purse are always available if defendants cannot afford their own. In other kinds of cases, however, obtaining a lawyer may be quite expensive, keeping some complainants out of the courts. Finally, in the United States, the jurisdictional rules that allow cases to come into a court are not particularly rigorous. The problem in the United States is not getting *into* court; the problem is getting *out* with a decision.

Each of these characteristics is somewhat different in the four other countries. Under England's bifurcated legal profession, clients select a solicitor, who, in turn, chooses a barrister if one is needed. Advice, particularly on such matters as on how to deal with the bureaucracy, is often available from Citizens' Advice Bureaux, and initial contacts with solicitors are often paid by legal aid. There is, however, no contingent fee, and the rule that the loser of a case must pay the legal costs of the winner makes court action much riskier for a complainant than in the United States. In France, the possibility of piggybacking civil suits onto criminal cases not only expedites the civil proceedings but also makes it much less costly to initiate them. On the other hand, the potential awards are likely to be smaller than in the United States, in part because they are influenced by judges who sit with the jury rather than being determined by juries alone. Germany is distinguished by its large number of tribunals, which have a reputation for efficient service, and by exceptionally accessible assistance from lawyers as a result of widespread use of insurance policies that pay for legal assistance in civil disputes. In Japan, by contrast, there are very few lawyers and considerable barriers to initiating litigation; however, there are many sources for advice about the handling of disputes.

All of these institutional characteristics together account for the institutional accessibility of the courts to disputes. We can roughly array these five countries on a continuum with the United States and Germany at the high end of accessibility, France and England in the middle (although also toward the high end), and Japan some considerable distance away at the low end.

In addition, perceptions about law and litigation inform any analysis of what brings disputes to courts.[3] Even within the English-speaking world, we cannot disentangle law from variations in connotation. In England, for example, law continues to be very closely and specifically linked with issues traditionally considered in the courts, such as punishing criminals, owning and inheriting property and proscribing libel and slander. However, in the United States law is associated with a much broader range of issues and activities, reflecting in significant part the founding of the country as a "a government of laws, and not of men."[4] In studying the legislative process in the United States, Americans regularly speak of a "bill becoming law"; that is, law emerges directly out of a political process, and when Americans think of law they associate its creation with the legislature. Furthermore, in the United States public policy is largely established by passing laws. On the other hand, in England the term *law* is associated with a much more narrow range of governmental activity. The Government can often establish policies without the passage of an Act of Parliament. Thus, much public policy for which the Government is accountable to Parliament is not based on statutes, and for many policy areas, even if a policy is based on Acts of Parliament, those statutes do not loom in the public mind as "laws." Thus, the degree to which law may be seen as integral to the policy process varies even in the English-speaking world.

The difficulties multiply when going beyond the English language. We translate as *law* the French *la loi* and *la droit,* the German *Gesetz* and *Recht,*[5] and the Japanese *Ho* and *Horitsu,* even though the connotations in the original language differ significantly from the connotations of the English word. In part, differences in French and German usages stem from the distinction between common law and civil law systems (see chapter 1). Within the civil law tradition, law is a set of general guiding principles that can be applied to specific situations in a deductive, "scientific" fashion by persons with

3. The following four paragraphs are based on a draft by Herbert M. Kritzer.

4. John Adams, *Original Draft of the Massachusetts Constitution,* 1799, cited in John Bartlett, *Familiar Quotations,* 13th ed. (Boston: Little, Brown, 1955), p. 368.

5. For a discussion of some of the connotations of these words in German, see Erhard Blankenburg, "Empirisch Messbare Dimensionen von Rechtsgefühl, Rechtsbewusstsein und Vertrauen in Recht," *Recht und Verhalten* (Baden-Baden: Nomos Verlagsgesellschaft, 1994), pp. 83–109.

appropriate training, whereas within the common law tradition, law is rules established to deal with specific situations. Thus, the connotations of the French and German words we translate as "law" are closely tied to the civil law images of the law as involving broad, general principles.

A final dimension of notions about law is its perceived breadth. Law may be perceived as central to both public and private relationships or it may be seen as peripheral. Japan represents the extreme version of a legal culture where law remains to a large degree peripheral; that is the consequence of many explicit public choices. In Japan relationships are tied more closely to ideas of community and various types of everyday interdependencies than to formal, legally established relationships. Sanders illustrates this in his discussion of both the employment relationship and in the relationship between government and industry. The United States and Germany stand at the other end of the spectrum, where many people are likely to think of a large number of their relationships in terms defined by law. When relationships are thought of in legal terms, people are more likely to be conscious of law and see law as extending into a wide variety of settings. The role of "rights" becomes much more central to legal discourse, which in turn leads to what political and legal scholars have referred to as "rights consciousness."[6]

Considerable variations may exist about these perceptions among different participants in legal processes. In the United States, some disputants in divorce proceedings think about their problems in legalistic ways, but many do not. Some think about their "right" to have custody of their children while others focus on their continuing relationship with them.[7] Lawyers think more legalistically than nonlawyers. Even in the United States, where legalistic thinking is presumed to be widespread, it is also greeted with considerable antagonism, as witnessed by the large number of jokes that belittle lawyers and their work. Few systematic studies based on reliable survey research exist on these issues in any country; almost no truly comparative data exist over an array of countries.

Even if we must rely on impressionistic evidence, the resulting congruence of institutions and perceptions about law suggests considerable differences among the legal processes of the countries examined. In the United States and Germany the configuration of courts and the work structure of the legal profession make courts highly accessible. In addition, law is broadly defined by many disputants and by legal professionals. These factors lead courts in the United States and Germany to entertain more disputes and be more fre-

6. Cf. Stuart Scheingold, *The Politics of Rights* (New Haven: Yale University Press, 1974); Mary Ann Glendon, *Rights Talk* (New York: Free Press, 1991).

7. Herbert Jacob, "The Elusive Shadow of the Law," *Law and Society Review* 26 (1992), pp. 565–590.

quently involved in policymaking and constitutional disputes. France and England are intermediate cases; in a variety of ways, courts are made less accessible than in Germany and the United States and the legal profession is less aggressive in bringing cases to the courts. In addition, law is not conceived quite as broadly by disputants and legal professionals. This does not mean that disputing in England and France is stifled; rather, more disputes go to nonjudicial forums. Consequently, courts play a somewhat more constrained role in the policymaking process and in constitutional disputes but they are not entirely excluded. Finally, in Japan, the most extreme case, courts have been structured to discourage litigation and the legal profession is kept to very small numbers. Law is perceived by disputants and professionals as peripheral to disputes more often in Japan than in the other countries. Thus it is not surprising that the Japanese courts play a far more modest role in policymaking and constitutional interpretation than in the other four countries.

In chapter 1, I also speculated about the consequences of centralization for the ways in which law, courts, and politics intersect. As the preceding discussion suggests, simple correlations between centralization of government structure and judicial "power" are likely to be misleading. However, the United States and Germany, the two most decentralized governments among the five examined here, are also the two with the most accessible courts, with more widely held perceptions of law as relevant to policymaking and, consequently, more active and powerful judiciaries. In the more centralized states among the five—France, England, and Japan—judiciaries are less accessible, conceptions of law are more shriveled, and courts assert themselves less in policymaking and constitutional review. As I argued in chapter 1, strong central governments use a variety of strategies to defeat competitors; those who control the executive or legislative branches of strongly centralized states have little desire to encourage meddling by courts whose judges must enjoy some degree of autonomy in order to retain their legitimacy. This rationale is most clearly expressed in France, where courts were explicitly stripped of their potential power during the French Revolution in order to keep them from interfering with the sovereign power of the National Assembly. Likewise, in England, the long tradition of Parliamentary supremacy keeps the judiciary in a subordinate political role. The same result is more subtly achieved in Japan, where the judiciary is kept under tight control by the agency that controls the careers of judges.

Although there are many significant differences in the manner in which law, courts, and politics intersect in the five countries studied here, there are also strong indications that these differences are slowly being submerged by the rising tide of international trade and supranational legal institutions. This is most apparent among the three European nations, all of which are members of the European Union and subject to its courts. Disputes over a wide array of commercial transactions and regulations may be brought to the European Court of Justice, which has become an important instrument for creating common commercial rules and norms throughout the Union's member nations.[8] The European Court for Human Rights in Strasbourg, France, plays a similar role for disputes about fundamental political and civil rights for citizens of those nations. Thus the English are in the process of acquiring constitutional rights, even though they do not have a written constitution; French courts are beginning to decide their own cases on the basis of decisions emanating from EU courts; Germans find that they have an additional level of appeal beyond their own high courts. In addition, burgeoning international trade beyond the boundaries of the European Union requires agreement on terms of trade among parties from several countries; such trade also familiarizes many legal professionals with practices from other countries. One important cause for such convergence may be found in the growing phenomenon of legal professionals doing business in a variety of countries. Large American law firms have established branch offices in many commercial centers in Europe (and to a lesser degree, Japan).

The impact of the internationalization of law and judicial processes remains unclear. We have seen that in the past common roots spawned quite distinctive practices. For instance, the French civil code tradition developed distinctively in Germany, just as the English common law tradition evolved in a uniquely American way in the United States. The way in which the Japanese adapted both Continental and American legal traditions is even more striking; legal structures that look like those in Europe and the United States in fact operate in an emphatically Japanese manner. However, the internationalization of law seems to be a different phenomenon; it does not import law and institutions but imposes a continuing pressure to conform to common substantive norms and judicial procedures. It is likely to alter the legal processes and the links with their political arenas in all of these countries, but the details will become clear only with the passage of time.

8. J. H. H. Weiler, "A Quiet Revolution: The European Court of Justice and Its Interlocutors," *Comparative Political Studies* 26 (1994), pp. 510–534; Karen J. Alter and Sophie Meunier-Aitsahalia, "Judicial Politics in the European Community," *Comparative Political Studies* 26 (1994), pp. 535–561.

Index